The Sino-Soviet Conflict

1956–1961

By Donald S. Zagoria

"Not a moment too soon comes this superbly researched, refreshingly sensible and—given the gobbledegook raw material—surprisingly readable analysis . . . Mr. Zagoria is a sure guide through the murky corners of Communist theology. He not only translates it well but provides one of the finest explanations of how to read the Reds and how it is that we know so much about the many things they try to hide."—*Max Frankel*
New York Times

". . . carefully and lucidly unfolds, stage by stage and with orderly elegance, the most complicated and fascinating political drama of modern times . . . explains, better than I have seen it explained anywhere, how to read between the lines of Communist pronouncements, not because this is clever or smart, but because they are deliberately so constructed that they can only be read between the lines."—*Edward Crankshaw*
The Observer

484 pages. $8.50

Order from your bookstore, or
PRINCETON UNIVERSITY PRESS
Princeton, New Jersey

0710585
102806

VOLUME 349

SEPTEMBER 1963

THE ANNALS

of The American Academy *of* Political
and Social Science

THORSTEN SELLIN, *Editor*

MARVIN E. WOLFGANG, *Assistant Editor*

COMMUNIST CHINA AND THE SOVIET BLOC

Special Editor of this Volume

DONALD S. ZAGORIA
Research Fellow
Research Institute on
Communist Affairs
Assistant Professor of Government
Columbia University

PHILADELPHIA
1963

Issued bimonthly by The American Academy of Political and Social Science at Prince and Lemon Sts., Lancaster, Pennsylvania.

Editorial and Business Office, 3937 Chestnut Street, Philadelphia 4, Pennsylvania.

CONTENTS

BOOK DEPARTMENT
PAGE

INTERNATIONAL RELATIONS

BEATON, LEONARD, and JOHN MADDOX. *The Spread of Nuclear Weapons.* Edgar S. Furniss, Jr., Mershon Professor of Political Science, Ohio State University .. 183

BELL, CORAL. *Negotiation from Strength.* John Robinson Beal, Bureau Chief, Time, Incorporated, Ottawa 182

BEMIS, SAMUEL FLAGG. *American Foreign Policy and the Blessings of Liberty and Other Essays.* Robert H. Ferrell, Indiana University 185

BLUM, ROBERT (Ed.). *Cultural Affairs and Foreign Relations.* Frederick C. Mosher, Professor of Political Science, University of California, Berkeley 184

CLAUDE, INIS L. *Power and International Relations.* A. F. K. Organski, Professor of Political Science, Brooklyn College, City University of New York 189

DALLIN, ALEXANDER. *The Soviet Union at the United Nations.* Quincy Wright, Visiting Professor, Columbia University 188

LUARD, EVAN. *Britain and China.* Herrymon Maurer, Consultant in Cultural Anthropology, Bureau of Research in Psychiatry and Neurology, State of New Jersey 187

MODELSKI, GEORGE (Ed.). *SEATO.* Paul W. van der Veur, Senior Research Fellow, Australian National University 186

Personnel for the New Diplomacy. Halford L. Hoskins, Senior Specialist in International Relations, Legislative Reference Service, Library of Congress 183

PLETCHER, DAVID M. *The Awkward Years.* Wilfred E. Binkley, Professor of Political Science, Ohio Northern University 186

AMERICAN GOVERNMENT AND HISTORY

DRAPER, THEODORE. *Castro's Revolution.* Dana G. Munro, William Stewart Tod Professor of History, Emeritus, Princeton University 197

FRANKLIN, BENJAMIN. *The Papers of Benjamin Franklin,* Vol. 6: *April 1, 1755 through September 30, 1756.* Edited by Leonard W. Labaree, in association with Ralph L. Ketcham, and assisted by Helen C. Boatfield and Helene H. Fineman. Viola F. Barnes, Professor of History, Emeritus, Mount Holyoke College 195

FRANKLIN, JOHN HOPE. *The Emancipation Proclamation.* Henry H. Simms, Professor of History, Ohio State University 194

HAVARD, WILLIAM C., and LOREN P. BETH. *The Politics of Mis-Representation.* Franklin L. Burdette, Professor and Director, Bureau of Governmental Research, University of Maryland 192

KELLAWAY, WILLIAM. *The New England Company, 1649–1776.* Frank J. Klingberg, Professor of History, Emeritus, University of California, Los Angeles 196

KRAUS, SIDNEY (Ed.). *The Great Debates.* J. H. Leek, University of Oklahoma 190

MASON, ALPHEUS THOMAS. *The Supreme Court.* Henry M. Holland, Jr., Associate Professor of Government, State University College, Geneseo, New York .. 191

MORRISON, JOSEPH L. *Josephus Daniels Says. . . .* Arthur S. Link, Princeton University 193

NOGGLE, BURL. *Teapot Dome.* Roland Young, Professor of Political Science, Northwestern University 192

SMITH, PAGE. *John Adams,* Vol. 1: *1735–1784;* Vol. 2: *1784–1826.* George Osborn, Professor of Social Science, University of Florida 194

EUROPEAN GOVERNMENT AND HISTORY

BOWEN, JAMES. *Soviet Education.* Ivor Kraft, United States Department of Health, Education, and Welfare 205

ASIA AND AFRICA

ECONOMICS AND LABOR

SOCIOLOGY AND ANTHROPOLOGY

The articles appearing in THE ANNALS are indexed in the *Reader's Guide to Periodical Literature*.

Lewis M. Stevens

1898–1963

Lewis M. Stevens, a member of the Board of Directors and General Counsel of this Academy, died in a Philadelphia hospital 15 July 1963, in his sixty-sixth year.

Mr. Stevens was born in Meriden, Connecticut, and graduated from Princeton University and the Harvard Law School. In 1926 he became a partner in the law firm of Stradley, Ronon, Stevens, and Young, where he maintained an affiliation until his death. He was also active in political and civic affairs, serving as a member and Secretary of the Philadelphia Charter Commission, chairman of the Finance Committee of the City Council, chairman of Pennsylvania Volunteers for Stevenson, co-founder of the Greater Philadelphia Movement, and Secretary of Highways of Pennsylvania. He was a director or chairman of the Samuel S. Fels Fund, the Associated Hospital Service, the World Affairs Council, the Presbyterian Hospital, Lincoln University, the West Philadelphia Corporation, and the Whyte-Williams Foundation. He served a term as Moderator of the Presbyterian Church in Philadelphia. He was a soldier in World War I and a civilian leader of several war activities in World War II.

Mr. Stevens served with distinction as an officer of this Academy and was most diligent in his attention to Academy affairs.

FOREWORD

Not the least significant consequence of the Sino-Soviet conflict has been the growing dialogue between Sinologists and Soviet specialists in the West. The numerous articles which have already been written on Sino-Soviet relations and the various conferences of Russian and Chinese specialists now being planned are indicative of this dialogue.

The purpose of the present volume is twofold. These articles provide some of the background necessary to understanding the Sino-Soviet conflict and to viewing the over-all relationship between Russia and Communist China in a wide variety of historical, political, economic, ideological, and cultural perspective. Equally important, however, these articles have been assembled with the idea that they might collectively represent a modest, initial step toward a comparative study of Russian and Chinese communism.

Some of these articles are controversial and inevitably so. If they serve no other purpose, they may at least encourage others to address themselves to the same insistent problems. No attempt has been made, nor has it been thought desirable, to reconcile or to eliminate differences of view and emphasis which appear throughout. In part, these differences reflect different disciplinary approaches.

Ideally, it would have been desirable to have at least some of these articles co-authored by one Russian and one Chinese expert interested in a similar question. Such collaboration will undoubtedly be necessary in the future. It was not attempted here only because of stringent time considerations.

The comparative study of Russian and Chinese communism will not only require much greater collaboration between Russian and Chinese specialists, but it will also require the training of students capable of using both languages and of applying the tools of a particular discipline to problems which transcend national boundaries. We shall require comparative studies of the Russian and Chinese Communist elites, decision-making processes, foreign policies, development strategies, conceptions of Marxism-Leninism, and so on.

Moreover, comparative studies of Russian and Chinese communism are but one, albeit critical, part of much broader field of comparative communism in which even the most basic work yet remains to be done. The shattering of the monolithic unity of the Communist world and the rise of pluralism and polycentrism thus represent a challenge not only to Western policy-makers but to scholars as well.

DONALD S. ZAGORIA

Donald S. Zagoria, Ph.D., New York City, New York, is Research Fellow at the Research Institute of Communist Affairs and Assistant Professor of Government, Columbia University. He was an analyst of Communist bloc affairs for the United States government, 1951–1961, and a member of the Social Science Department of the Rand Corporation, 1961–1963. He has lectured on various aspects of Sino-Soviet relations at University of California in Los Angeles, University of Michigan, and Southern Methodist University. He is author of the Sino-Soviet Conflict (Princeton: Princeton University Press, 1962), which has been translated and published in German and Japanese. He is a frequent contributor of articles to scholarly and general journals. Among his recent articles, two related to the subject of the present volume are "The Sino-Soviet Conflict and the West," which appeared in Foreign Affairs in October 1962, and an essay on the differences in Soviet and Chinese paths to socialism which appeared in The Future of Communist Society, edited by Walter Laqueur and Leopold Labedz (New York: Praeger Paperbacks, 1962).

The Chinese and the Russians*

By Klaus Mehnert

Abstract: The Russians have been and still are Europeans, not less so than other peoples who—like the Spaniards—have lived part of their history under foreign domination—in Russia's case, this was Tatar domination. Hence, the Russians differ from the Chinese as much as other Europeans do. This fact is illustrated by comparison of the Chinese and the Russians with regard to their intellectual, spiritual, and emotional aspects. In some respects, the Russians are even remoter from the Chinese than other European peoples because they have been molded by a particularly emotional form of Christianity which is very far removed from the matter-of-factness of Confucianism. In the field of social organization, the two main peculiarities of China—the power of the clan over its members and the formation of the ruling elite by examinations—have no counterpart in Russia. In turn, the slavelike position of the Russian peasant and the power of the hereditary nobility around the czar were unknown in China. The explanation for the victory of communism in the two vastly different countries is, thus, not to be found in a particular predisposition of the Chinese and the Russians to communism but in peculiar historical circumstances, forces, and personalities which operated in each country, largely as a result of the Western impact which hit both these huge, proud, gifted, and economically backward nations.

Klaus Mehnert, Ph.D., is Professor of Political Science, Institute of Technology, Aachen, Germany. He has traveled extensively in the Soviet Union and in China, including Communist China. He is editor of four reviews dealing with East European and Soviet problems. He is a regular commentator on world affairs for two German radio networks and one television network. He is author of a number of books, including, in English, Youth in Soviet Russia (1933), The Russians in Hawaii, 1804–1819 (1939), Stalin versus Marx (1954), Soviet Man and His World (1961), and Peking and Moscow (1963).

* This article is an extract of the introductory part of the English edition, to be published in autumn 1963 in New York and London under the title of *Peking and Moscow,* of the author's latest book, treating of relations between the two Communist powers up to the end of the Sino-Soviet Conference at Moscow in July 1963.

THE question of whether one can speak of "the" Chinese, "the" Russians, "the" Soviet people, "the" Americans has been the subject of thorough and often heated discussion. The late Felix M. Keesing, the New Zealand anthropologist, summarized his findings in two theses: [1] first, in the case of each nation, it is possible to prove the existence of a certain national character which distinguishes it from other nations; second, this national character is a variable, not a constant, quantity. In other words: The Chinese differ from the Russians. And the Chinese of today are different from the Chinese of the Confucian era; the Soviet Russian is no longer the muzhik of the days of the czars. Therefore, although national minorities, often with sharply distinguishing characteristics, have long existed both in China and in Russia, we may speak of "the Chinese" and "the Russians," for, in both cases, a politically powerful and culturally outstanding race—in China, the Han (that is, the real Chinese); in Russia, the Great Russians—constituted the vital element which characterized the population as a whole.

Is it correct to say that Chinese or Russian communism is the logical crowning of their history, or is it more accurate to regard it as being in complete contradiction to all that is Chinese or Russian? The thesis of communism as the continuation, the culmination, of the history of these two peoples is propagated not only by Communist leaders, by Stalin, Khrushchev, and Mao, but also—although, of course, with different arguments and different prognoses—by some Western observers, Amaury de Riencourt, for example, when he writes: "The triumph of Marxism in China implies to a very great ex-

tent a return to the past," or "Marxism . . . restored China's traditional way of thinking." Riencourt, who is anything but a Communist, has described Chinese communism as "psychologically predetermined." [2] A similarly one-sided view is expressed by an Indian observer: "To substitute the gospel according to Mao for the gospel according to Confucius, conforms to this [that is, traditional Chinese] pattern." [3]

A second thesis, that communism is the complete antithesis of the true nature of China and Russia, is maintained by the Chinese and Russian opponents of communism—Chiang Kai-shek, for instance, and the leaders of the Russian émigrés—and many foreigners who, as businessmen and missionaries, became personally acquainted with the China and Russia of the past and who are convinced that the people whom they came to know and respect as human beings are enduring the Communist regime solely because they are compelled to do so by the most brutal terrorism and are yearning for the day when China will re-emerge "as a free united nation" and they can take part in the "triumph of freedom over slavery throughout the world."[4]

Reality corresponds to neither of these two theses; it is more complicated, and thus more interesting, and still leaves the door open to all kinds of possibilities.

THE MAN

When Aristotle defined man as a *zoon politikon,* a "social animal," he had no idea that in a highly developed culture there already existed a classic example

---

[1] Felix M. Keesing, *Cultural Anthropology* (New York, 1958), pp. 34 ff.

[2] Amaury de Riencourt, *The Soul of China* (New York, 1958), pp. xviii, 216, 250.

[3] Frank Moraes, *Report on Mao's China* (New York, 1953), p. 21.

[4] Chiang Kai-shek, *Soviet Russia in China* (New York, 1957), p. 349.

of this concept unlike anything in the Hellenistic world. If the Occidental has always been inclined to give priority to the individual over society, to freedom over bondage, and to pursue individualism to the point of egoism, hedonism, and solipsism, and liberalism to the point of anarchy, the very opposite is true of the Chinese. The Chinese is conditioned by his surroundings, "situation centered," to use the formula of a Chinese sociologist,[5] to an extent almost beyond our Western comprehension, a fact we must accept if we are to understand him.

Chinese ability of adaptation expresses itself with an ingenuity and naturalness that is rather disarming, especially as it is at the same time both rational and wise. The European, with his inhibitions and his preoccupation with principles, is at a loss to find the right word for it; "matter-of-factness" is perhaps the closest. Why get upset about things we can do nothing about anyway! As long as the storm rages over the countryside, the bamboo bends; when calm returns, it rises up again.

Anyone who has lived even for a short time in China is aware of the versatility and adaptability of its people, qualities which enable them to cope with sudden surprises as well as with external pressures which may have been going on for years. It always seemed to me that they positively enjoyed being confronted with the unexpected. For example, our Chinese servants were never happier than when twelve guests turned up for dinner instead of the expected four. They outdid themselves in imagination and inspiration and bustled about, hurrying to the shops across the street, borrowing from the cook of the family downstairs, changing the menu, and stretching whatever food was on hand with the aid of camouflaging sauces.

[5] Francis L. K. Hsu, *Americans and Chinese* (New York, 1953), p. 10.

Ethical rules and taboos apply mainly to behavior toward the family and its members, also toward members of the same sect, but hardly ever to one's "neighbor." Reformers like Mo-tzu, who preached love toward all men, rather than only toward relatives and friends, were not in the long run successful. Mencius, the great restorer of Confucianism, went so far as to assert that a general love for humanity would have an unfavorable effect on filial piety and public justice: to acknowledge neither king nor father was "to be in the state of a beast." [6] Lao-tzu's teaching, the main theme of which was "nonaction," was, of course, still less designed to promote humanitarian consciousness.

When directed inwardly, however, as a force not only shaping but penetrating human nature, this attitude is bound to have an anti-impulsive, antiemotional effect. The imperturbability with which a Chinese can accept his own misfortunes as well as those of others is more than a mask, assumed as the result of generations of caution and training, to hide otherwise uncontrollable passions. He does not demand of life an opportunity to develop his personality, a demand taken for granted by the Western man. As a result, when this opportunity is denied him, he does not suffer, or at least he suffers less. He finds no difficulty in conforming to his environment.

Language and thought

If we have so far tried to grasp the psyche of the Chinese principally in his relation to his natural environment, we must now mention a powerful historical factor in the formation of his character: his language, both spoken and written.

The Chinese requires thousands of hours—almost his whole life if he is an

[6] Mencius, III/2, Ch. IX/9.

intellectual or professional—just to become—and remain—proficient in reading and writing. On the one hand, this learning process develops to an astonishing degree his memory, his visual powers of absorption for even minute details, and his aesthetic sense; but, on the other hand, it does not encourage the faculty for logical, analytical thought which has become such a firm tradition in the West since Greek and Roman times. And how indeed should it be exercised, when a sentence is created merely by stringing together a series of undeclined words!

An understanding of the reciprocity between language and thought must be regarded as basic to the modern science of linguistics. Races and cultures have evolved their own immutable forms of linguistic expression, and these in turn exert a formative influence on man: he is "very much at the mercy of the particular language which has become the medium of expression of their society." [7]

I myself have a vivid memory of the Chinese aversion to logic and systematism from the days when I was editing a magazine in Shanghai. The manuscripts of Chinese contributors, at least of those who had not had a Western education, consisted simply of a number of facts or thoughts strung together without logical or causal connection, with not even a conclusion drawn from the sum total. A manuscript concerning, say, modern film-making or some recently published books resembled a catalogue. No attempt was made to arrange the films or books according to subject, significance, or political views of the writer, or any other point of view, or to draw any conclusion or lay down any consistent thesis. Mao Tse-tung once described this Chinese peculiarity as an arrangement of "items in A, B, C, D

. . . as if setting up a Chinese drugstore." [8]

Unless he has been Western-trained, the Chinese does not express his opinion by what we would call logical steps but advances it in little thrusts, first from one side, then from the other. His thinking is an "encircling or embracing" process, to quote Lily Abegg. She compares Chinese thinking with arrows which begin by flying around in all directions and only converge on a certain target—the goal or result of the thought —when they sense its nearness. [9] In this process, the Chinese is capable of a degree of concentration which the Occidental, without the Ariadne thread of logical connection, could never attain.

In Hawaii and Shanghai I used to watch my Chinese students writing essays; they sat motionless for a long time beside their Western classmates. These were already busy writing and erasing, but the Chinese would wait till they had completed the composition in their heads and then proceed to write it down at great speed and without further reflection.

Contrast of Russia and China

If we turn our attention to the Russians, we are immediately struck by the contrast between them and the Chinese on the emotional as well as the rational plane. As long as they were permitted to be themselves, the Russians were conditioned more by emotion than by the mind or the will and were inclined to dream rather than to act, to suffer rather than to resist, to an amiable laziness rather than to systematic effort. When their consciousness was awakened, it was often the best among them who suffered from their inability to

[7] Benjamin L. Whorf, quoted by Harry Hoÿer (ed.), *Language in Culture* (Chicago, 1954), p. 92.

[8] *Selected Works of Mao Tse-tung*, Vol. IV (London and New York, 1956), p. 54.

[9] Lily Abegg, *Ostasien denkt anders* (Zurich, 1949), p. 48.

emerge from their deep and passionate discussions onto the road of determined action, and they felt they were "superfluous."

This emotional and impulsive temperament of the Russians exemplifies, among all the people of Europe, the strongest contrast to the rational wisdom of the Chinese, at least of the educated Chinese, to his self-control arising out of his continual state of harmony with his environment. More passionately, more fervently than the West, Russia has proclaimed the message of the priority of the soul over the body, the spiritual over the material, of eternal salvation over worldly profit, and, even in our mass age, its great writers have presented the introvert in his most radical form. At the same time, it has provided a vast reserve of wide-eyed, self-immolating idealism, indeed of the utmost fanaticism, for the cultivation of doctrines of salvation and utopias of a very different kind of origin.

It has often been said that Christian dualism, face to face inexorably with the Absolute, has given rise to a new dynamism and has impelled the European spirit to embark on ever new voyages of search and discovery and active reshaping of the world. It was the dialectic principle which led European thought, blossoming to its first full perfection in ancient Greece, later to take its decisive turn toward the idea of constant and inevitable progress. That the first country to be conquered by this idea in its extreme form of Marxism should have been Russia, a country that had experienced neither the strict discipline of the Roman spirit nor the awakening of the Renaissance and of humanism, and that had been affected by the age of enlightenment on the highest social level only, is in my opinion but a further proof of the power of the common European heritage.

In China, as we have seen, these fundamental conditions were lacking: not only the dialectic principle itself, but causal thought in general, the reasoning of strict logic, the reciprocity of analysis and synthesis, of knowledge and its practical application, are all imports from the West and must be systematically acquired if China is to catch up with the West—including the Soviet Union. Meanwhile, those familiar with the industriousness, the endurance, and the patience of the Chinese know better than to pronounce such a thing as impossible; why, by another token, should not China succeed in a task which scarcely a hundred years ago the Japanese people achieved in a few decades?

THE HERITAGE

The Chinese are no more lacking in technical intelligence than the Russians. In many fields, this intelligence led them thousands of years ago to perform feats which would have been unthinkable in the Europe of that time. To Marco Polo, coming from a part of Europe that was particularly advanced for those days, the China of the thirteenth century seemed a highly developed wonderland. But, between Marco Polo's days and our own, nothing much has been added. Generally speaking, things remained as they were until well into the nineteenth century, and we may assume they would have continued to do so had it not been for the stimulus from the West.

The passion for exact weighing, measuring, counting, and experimenting, without which modern natural science could not exist, is typically occidental. The Chinese showed little inclination to do the same. It did not fit into his *Weltanschauung*, into that ancient Chinese conception of the interrelationship of all things in the cosmos—embracing all mankind and its actions—whose harmony was inviolate even to the educated Confucian. When he tried to explore this cosmos, it was only in order to become a part of it, to act in harmony with it, not to rule it, let alone change it. This can be seen from Confucius' cosmic moral code:

It is through the power of right behavior that heaven and earth work together, that the four seasons harmonize, that the sun and moon shine, that the stars trace their courses, that the rivers flow, that all things flourish, that good and evil are differentiated, that joy and anger find their proper expression, that inferior men obey, that superior men are enlightened, that all things regardless of change are not brought into confusion. If one departs from it, all perishes.[10]

This explains why Chinese philosophy is concerned expressly with problems of daily life; in other words, it is pragmatic. Its interest in metaphysics and in epistemology is slight, and "unfortunately there has been but little development of logic in Chinese philosophy."[11] In essence, then, this philosophy is almost synonymous with ethics. Yet, to call Confucius' teaching utilitarian would be to misunderstand the Master completely. That which benefits not the individual but society is right.

When the occidental—and, in the end, that meant the Christian—observer was confronted with this world of ideas, he was bound to ask, no matter how much he respected its spiritual intensity: Could one speak here of what had long been familiar to him as the most powerful force in his whole existence; was this religion? In Chinese *Weltanschauung,* God and the gods have become dim shadowy forms, and, in their social function, too, they are now almost superfluous. To the Chinese intellectual, they never meant anything; he has no feeling whatsoever for the existential power of religion. The passionate search for a path to God and the world beyond, for redemption and salvation, a search which has never ceased to occupy the finest minds of Russia, in fact of the entire West, is —always allowing for exceptions—unknown to him. As for popular religion, it has no clearly defined limits and no solid structure, other than the Taoist church of the first century A.D., which disintegrated at the beginning of the Tang period. Imperial religious practices were mainly of a ceremonial nature and had little in common with popular religion. The Chinese peasant did not profess to be either a Buddhist or a Taoist; instead, he worshipped gods, spirits, and temples of every imaginable kind and derivation and sought help against demons and the forces of nature wherever he could.

Here we must say something about the renowned tolerance of the Chinese. This is often contrasted with the intolerance practiced in Europe—including Russia, from the schism of the church in 1666 to Stalin's "purges"— and the persecution and branding of dissenters as heretics.

In a work written during the anti-European Boxer rebellion and still showing the effects of the agitation of that time, J. J. M. de Groot has compiled a long list of religious persecutions and religious wars in China.[21] When we examine this more closely, however, we see that the causes of this suppression were mainly political. The ruling class in China restricted its tolerance to such manifestations as did not jeopardize the basic structure of their personal and public life. The accusations which they

[10] Li Gi, *Das Buch der Sitte* (*Li Chi; The Book of Rites*), German edition with commentary by Richard Wilhelm (Dusseldorf-Cologne), p. 205.

[11] Fung Yu-lan, *A History of Chinese Philosophy,* Vol. II (Princeton), p. 571.

[12] Jan Jacob M. de Groot, *Sectarianism and Religious Persecution in China,* Vol. I–II (Amsterdam, 1903–1904).

leveled against their opponents are, therefore, not philosophical in nature but of a social and political kind.

We see, then, that it is not intolerance as such, which exists in Russia as well as in China, that is of interest, but the direction taken by its attacks. In the West it was largely concerned with faith and dogma; in China with state and society.

The Russian antithesis of China

In its spiritual heritage, old Russia, among all the peoples of Europe, is the antithesis of classical China. The Russian people have been conditioned, permeated, and molded by Christianity more forcefully and more exclusively than any other, except perhaps the Spanish. For almost a thousand years —in 988 it became the state religion— Christianity has been the most powerful spiritual force in Russia, for the peasants until well into the twentieth century, for the upper classes as a whole until the time of Peter the Great and even later for the overwhelming majority of them.

Intellectual life in Russia was until the sixteenth century entirely and until the eighteenth century almost entirely identical with the life of the church and was carried on by men of the church. It was not until the eighteenth century that the influence of the secular West became noticeable. But the great writers —Gogol, Dostoyevsky, Leskov, Tolstoy —to whom not only Russia but the whole world was beginning to listen, remained searchers after God. The formation of a separate intellectual stratum of partially atheistic leanings did not take place until the last two or three generations. The fact that some of its leaders—Chernyshevsky, Dobrolyubov, and the professional revolutionary Stalin, to cite but a few—owed their earliest education to theological seminaries is one of the ironies of history.

Russian thought has been—and still is—of an intensely speculative nature; it ponders ultimate and sublime things, roams infinite spaces—one of the reasons why the Russian loves and extols his own country is its vast size—and only reluctantly finds its way to the shaping of concrete reality. Suffering itself appears as a distinctive virtue. The very words for suffering, endurance, patience, "long-suffering (*dolgoterpénie*), had for the Russians a sacred ring.

Passionate sectarian movements have dramatically demonstrated the inclination of the Russian nature for extreme and radical upheavals. At times—the most impressive example being Dostoyevsky—these movements took on the proportions of messianic missionary faith embracing the whole human race. In all of them there existed the anticipation of an everlasting kingdom, a kingdom toward which, so they believed, the whole history of mankind was moving.

Thus, the ground was psychologically prepared for the new doctrine of world salvation, albeit only of this world. Idealistic devotion to utopian ideas, the sacrifice of the present in favor of a better future, were as familiar to the Russian as the demand—so puzzling to Westerners—for "partisanship" (*partiynost*). Indeed, as I found often enough in talking even to non-Communist Russians, they were inclined to regard tolerance and willingness for discussion as weakness, or even as a denial of truth.

But the Christian essence of the Russian people contributed a still further element to Lenin's revolution, an element to which it, like the French Revolution, owes a considerable part of its innate strength and vital impetus: the concept of brotherly love.

To what extent have the spiritual heritage and the historically rooted cultures of both races provided a favorable soil for communism? To what extent are they likely to make it endure? Two conclusions present themselves.

First, old Russia owes almost all its cultural impulses to the one among all the great religions of the world which is most concerned with the Hereafter; it was this that gave metaphysical depth to the innate restlessness of the Russian, endowing him with a dynamic impulse toward the Absolute; it was this that shaped the type of man capable of religious devotion and boundless self-sacrifice, without which communism's secular doctrine of salvation cannot exist either.

These psychological conditions could not be produced by the classical culture of China, with its marked preoccupation with this world, with its emphasis on harmony and beauty as the highest of all values. For this reason, it will not be easy for Mao and his followers to maintain the revolutionary impetus of the early days and to renew it from generation to generation. For the first time in Chinese history, communism subordinates the existence of every individual to an absolute goal. Until now, the Chinese were completely indifferent to the fate of others; those who were not Chinese were barbarians. Dostoyevsky's words, "We are all responsible for one another," would have been unthinkable from the lips of a Chinese. Now he is called upon not only to accept the Communist doctrine of salvation himself and to act upon it, but, at the expense of his own sacrifices, to spread it throughout the world.

Second, however, the very nature of the Christian tradition in Russia was bound to be the chief obstacle in the way of communism's final victory. Between the materialistic view, which sees every event as a process either of natural law or of economics, and the belief in an almighty creator and preserver of the world, there can be no reconcilia-

tion. Even during the last few years I found people in the Soviet Union who said quite openly to me, a foreigner, that they regarded Stalin as the Antichrist.

In China, however, there has never been a religious force with anything like comparable powers of resistance. Philosophical convictions, even of so ancient a tradition as the Confucian, are no substitute; they exist in outstanding individuals but not in the masses. As for popular religion, this was declining long before the advent of communism; in any case, in its variety and typically Chinese polytheism, it would be incapable of offering any prolonged resistance to the totalitarian ersatz religion.

In short, of the two forces at work in world communism—materialism and messianism—the Chinese respond to materialism, but not to one of an intolerant-messianic type, while the Russians respond to messianism, although not necessarily to one which seeks salvation on the materialistic-utilitarian level.

SOCIETY

In any discussion of Red China, the standard question recurs: how could communism triumph in a country in which the family is so strong? The Chinese family system was run on strict hierarchical lines and had the two dominating principles: the older generation always took precedence over the younger—likewise, the older members of each generation had priority over the younger—and the man had priority over the woman. Hence, the younger relative owed obedience to the older one, even when they did not live under the same roof, and the woman owed obedience to the man. But this system also surrounded the life of the individual with human warmth and affection and gave it the outward and inward security which today, in our highly civilized world, shut in by the "walls of loneliness," he often so painfully lacks.

The harshness of the system mainly affected the woman: wedded to a man not of her choosing, often literally bought by his family, living in his family's house as a stranger, separated from her own clan, which was not even allowed to take part in the wedding ceremonies, a servant of her parents-in-law, above all expected to bear sons, virtually without recourse to divorce but at the same time not assured of respect as the sole wife, for the husband, if she gave him no son—and even, if he was a rich man, simply for prestige reasons—was free to take concubines. According to one Chinese sociologist: "The unity of the big family was insured at the expense of the wife." [13]

By far the majority of families, particularly in the country, differed little in size and way of life from those of other peoples at a similar stage of development. Usually they formed a production unit, in farming as well as in handicrafts and trade, and were small, consisting of parents and children, with the grandparents often living with them. Their size has been calculated, after painstaking statistical research, at from four to seven persons, depending on the regions studied.[14]

If, then, certain exaggerated elements have been eliminated from our image of the Chinese family, we must now stress the overwhelming importance—compared to the West—of the larger family unit: the clan (*tsu*). The size of the clans ranged from a few hundred heads to many thousands. Their strength and importance depended on whether their members attained rank and dignity, thus bringing honor and worldly goods to the clan. A rise of this kind was usually followed after a few generations by impoverishment, sometimes decay. There have been many clans, however, which have managed to retain their solidarity, if not their respected position, for hundreds of years. Family and clan embraced a man's life from birth to death and even beyond and were the measure and the core of his existence.

The elite and the state

Another sociological peculiarity of China was that group which the West has become accustomed to call the "gentry."

As an institution, the gentry was the instrument of the absolutist and centralized state as it was founded following the overthrow of the old feudal system in the third century B.C. The vast expanse of the empire and the multifarious dialects, if not languages, were enough to require an army of officials capable of understanding the language of the capital and of reading orders from headquarters. Who else could be considered for this task but the guardians of the old writings and traditions, the graduates from the schools of the "philosophers," headed by and soon consisting exclusively of Confucians, who had always demanded that the rulers be advised by men of wisdom and noble character? Thus, the mastery of all the principal areas of Chinese culture, and above all of Confucianism, to be demonstrated in state examinations, became the real proof of qualification of the official. This system of examination and selection was developed with great consistency.

Reality, of course, was not quite so democratic. Apart from the members of a few despised occupations, anyone was free to apply for admission to the examinations, but the knowledge re-

[13] F. L. K. Hsu, *op. cit.*, p. 131.
[14] C. K. Yang, *A Chinese Family in the Communist Revolution* (Cambridge, Mass., 1959), pp. 7 ff., and Chang Chung-li, *The Chinese Gentry* (Seattle, 1955), pp. 112 ff.

quired for them demanded years of study, which only a minority could afford. This was where the clan could come to the rescue with stipends: it was always worth while to have an active representative of the clan in the regional or, better still, the central administration. But here, too, the outsiders could not compete with the wealth at the disposal of well-established clans, not to mention the possibilities such clans had of furthering the chances of their own people by having relatives in the examination and selection commissions.

Generally speaking, the strength of the upper classes lay not so much in the exercise of administrative and political functions or in material possessions as in their inner solidarity. They lived on the Confucian heritage which, in spite of many reversals, always renewed itself, and the state examinations were enough to ensure that each successive generation could take possession of it unchanged.

In spite of all the dramatic vicissitudes of its history, this elite has survived two thousand years and, next to the family system, has proved to be the second pillar supporting classical China. Conservative and loyal to its Confucian heritage, as an institution it remained firmly united to the state. The usual danger—present in Russia, too—of a potentially explosive tension between power and intellect was thus largely neutralized, and the creation of an anti-government or anarchistic intelligentsia was prevented.

After all this, one might wonder that the monarchy could have so easily and almost without resistance been uprooted by Sun Yat-sen and his revolutionaries. But, in the thousands of years of history which it spanned, had it ever been really deeply rooted in the consciousness and emotions of the people? Of course, the peasant needed his "son of heaven" who —even if he was of foreign race—was the mediator between the cosmos and mankind and thus responsible for the weather. But in that very capacity the emperor was too far above him for any human contact, any emotional tie, to develop.

To serve the emperor: that was the duty of the officials. From them was expected loyalty even to an already declining dynasty—and even, although to a lesser degree, at the fall of foreign dynasties.[15] Emperors came and went, dynasties rose and fell, but fields, family, and clan remained. In their self-sufficient life, the peasants felt no need whatever to wax enthusiastic about distant emperors or other heroes.

One must, therefore, in considering the relationship of the Chinese to freedom, distinguish between two things: In his clan, he was not free; there he was bound up in a network of relationships, subject to countless rules and limitations of his freedom of movement and choice. But, in his relationship to the state, he enjoyed a great deal of freedom. Not even in the days of the First Emperor in the third century B.C., and certainly never since that time, have the Chinese people known a government as severe and totalitarian as that of the Communist state.

If any feeling of positive identity with the state was entirely absent, there was also very little nationalist feeling in traditional China. Inwardly, the clan claimed the loyalty of the individual; outwardly, China did not indulge in constant quarrels with other powers of similar strength. After the conquerors had been absorbed, it could quietly go on developing as the Middle Kingdom, which, with its superior power and culture, looked upon other races as bar-

[15] Frederick W. Mole, "Confucian Eremitism in the Yüan Period," in Arthur F. Wright (ed.), *The Confucian Persuasion* (Stanford, 1960), pp. 229, 238 ff.

barians. Its feeling of cultural superiority—which finally reached the stage of belief in a Chinese cultural monopoly —was so strong that, for centuries, the people endured the rule of foreign dynasties without losing their sense of inner security. It was not until the nineteenth century that, as a result of the challenge of the West, the Chinese became nationalistic in our sense of the word. Until that time, we should speak of a cultural rather than of a political nationalism.

So this people achieved unity principally through a common cultural heritage and not least—bridging all variations in dialect and all outside influences of the times—through a common system of writing.

The different history of Russia

Against this background, the Russia of czarist times moves still closer to the rest of Europe, all the more so as recent experience has taught us that Russia's technological backwardness as compared to the West was to be overcome more quickly than expected. While, in China, the clan, legitimized by the state and a powerful moral factor in the people's life, was able to maintain itself until the clash came with the West; in Russia, as far back as the beginning of recorded history, we find it existing as a real power virtually only among the nobility—internal migrations, which took place from early times and far exceeded anything known to the West, may have contributed considerably to the clan's decay. What remained did not differ essentially from the normal European family before the latter began to shrink to the small family of our day.

All the more pronounced was the integration of the Russian with his class, his social environment; on the lowest level, this amounted for hundreds of years to a total integration. As distinct from China, the mass of the peasants was relegated to this lowest level, and, the longer this continued, the more marked it became. In what they were forced to produce in taxes and labor, they formed the broad base of the Muscovite state. The creation of a new service nobility—since Ivan IV and later by Peter the Great and his successors, in particular Catherine II— would have been impossible without the economic maintenance of this service nobility by land and "souls"—that is, without the peasants who worked for it. The difference which originally existed on the great estates between free peasants and serfs gradually disappeared.

This Russian form of serfdom was far harsher than that of Central and Western Europe, and it came very close to slavery; there were no legal restrictions on the exploitation of the human work force. The peasants broke out in bloody revolts which sometimes lasted for years; that of Stenka Razin in the seventeenth century and of Yemelyan Pugachov in the eighteenth are the best known.

The phenomenon of the Chinese gentry is inconceivable either in Russia or the West. The formation of the typically Russian "intelligentsia" could not take place until the encounter with Western culture had advanced on a wide front, and the scarcely less typical figure of the chinóvnik, the lower- or middle-class official, belongs to more modern times. Czar Alexis and his son Peter the Great were the first to set up a corps of paid professional officials, in which the sons of the nobility—those, that is, who did not choose a military career—were obliged to serve and which, by way of its higher ranks, also enabled the middle classes to enter the nobility.

The Russian service nobility remained far behind the Chinese gentry in intellectual and professional solidarity and, for this reason, could not oppose the ruler. In addition, however, we must take into account—because Russia, unlike China, was never granted long periods of peace—the continuing preponderance of the military element over the civilian; the system of military discipline strengthened the authority of the czar himself as well. For the masses, and for his devout predecessors on the throne, the power of the czar came from God. This sacred quality was bestowed on the grand dukes by chronicles going back to the twelfth century. What is more important for us, however, is that the church, in proclaiming to the devout that obedience to the czar was a divine duty and manifesting this continually in ceremony and prayer, contributed in large measure, if not decisively, toward making the concept of the "little father" a living reality to the people and, so, to rooting it much more firmly and intimately among the masses than was ever possible with the far-off "son of heaven."

Here, then, we have something, in the upper classes as well as in the masses, which in China has scarcely ever existed: a positive and, in its intensely personal character, extremely effective patriotic feeling for state and nation. Historical events contributed considerably to this patriotism by forcing the Russians to maintain themselves in bitter and fluctuating battles, first against the nomads of the steppes, whose influence was much stronger on Russian evolution than on the Chinese, and later against Turks, Swedes, Poles, and Germans. The fact that these enemies were all of other faiths gave a particular flavor to Russian patriotism.

From these traditions, therefore, the Russian people drew a good portion of their national strength: first in maintaining themselves even under foreign domination, then in long defensive struggles against superior enemies, and later as a driving, dynamic, often aggressive force such as could never result from the cyclical historical thinking of the Chinese. In spite of all the savagery of the struggle for power and all the harshness of oppression, this dynamic force created a community extending from the czar to the serf, and, as a result, the Russian people were far better equipped for their clash with the West than were the Chinese.

SUMMARY

In summing up the results of our comparative observations, we clearly see that the preconditions for the Communist seizure and retention of power differ even more radically in the social and political structure of China and Russia than on the intellectual plane. In both countries, a tradition of freedom is lacking; in both, the individual has become accustomed over the years—thousands of years, even—to find his place in the ranks of a society not of his choosing— but, in its extent and nature, this process differed considerably in the czarist empire and classical China. Not only had the Chinese peasant as an individual remained a free man but even the clan, which so largely circumscribed his life, never held him in almost total servitude, as did the serfdom imposed on the Russian peasant and the tyrannical political power of centuries. Furthermore, the ties of the Chinese peasant were of a completely personal nature and so were not felt to be compulsory to the same extent as the Russian obligations which degraded those subjected to them to the status of slaves.

If, finally, we ask ourselves whether the two nations were prepared to a greater or lesser extent for communism, we find a strangely contradictory picture. On the one hand, to classical China this—or any other—ideology emanating from the West remained, due to the nature and traditions of the people, completely strange; in Russia, in its psychological and sociological structure, one can trace conditions and forces which provide points of contact for this ideology and which it could turn to its own use. Yet, on the other hand, in its struggle with Western ideas, this same China was far more deeply and fatefully convulsed, and hence prepared for drastic changes at all levels, than was ever the case with czarist Russia. The penetration by the West, which the Russian people was in the process of assimilating, brought to the Chinese the end of a world—for thousands of years the only world they could imagine.

The Persistence of Tradition in Chinese Foreign Policy

By MARK MANCALL

ABSTRACT: Communications are poor between Communist China and both the Soviet Union and the United States. According to the traditional Chinese world view, the world order was hierarchical, not egalitarian, with the central authority being China; Chinese centrality was a function of civilization and virtue; the world hierarchy was universal; national power was the reflection of national virtue; external society was the extension of internal society. The tribute system and the use of physical and economic power in times of strength and the technique of "divide and rule" in periods of weakness were tactics which enabled China to maintain pre-eminence. China and Russia evaded clash for purposes of commerce. The great and unresolved challenge to the Chinese system came from the Western maritime powers. European imperialism forced China to recognize the existence of an alternative international power materially more powerful than China and broke down the autonomous Sinitic world order. The breakdown of the institutions of the traditional world system after 1842 took place faster than the erosion of the assumptions on which the order was based. Survivals of the tradition in Communist China grow into and reinforce modern nationalism and provide China with a distinct sense of superiority over all foreigners, including Russians. Accommodation between Peking and Moscow, if it comes, will, of necessity, be conscious and contrived.—Ed.

Mark Mancall, Ph.D., Cambridge, Massachusetts, is an Instructor in the History Department and a Research Fellow in East Asian Studies, East Asian Research Center, Harvard University.

tionally, in the world order. Ideologically, this order was an extension of the Confucian hierarchic and inegalitarian social order of China herself. If China was civilized, the rest of the world lived in descending states of barbarism the farther away they were from China's political and cultural frontiers. The barbarians could become civilized by accommodating themselves to China. Accommodation meant the acceptance of various facets of China's culture and the political recognition of China's power. Institutionally, China's centrality found expression in the tribute system, which reached the level of classical development in the Ming (1368–1644) and Ch'ing (1644–1911) dynasties. The validity of this Sinocentric East Asian world order was proved, for both the Chinese and the barbarians, by the fact that even the non-Chinese nomads of Inner Asia and Manchuria, finding themselves in power in China for about half of the last two millenia, used the Chinese tradition in international relations.

Although it is not possible in the context of this article to detail the entire nature of the complex Confucian world view, it is possible to isolate certain separate but closely related traditional Chinese assumptions concerning the nature of the world order. These assumptions differ significantly from Western assumptions, yesterday and today. Traditionally, these assumptions were accepted by those who participated in the tribute system, to a greater or lesser degree depending on the extent to which the non-Chinese participants had absorbed Chinese culture. Thus, the Koreans consciously accepted and acted on these assumptions right down to the end of the nineteenth century, while the Dutch, outside of East Asia, paid lip service to them in the seventeenth century in order to obtain the benefits of trade with China. Britain, in the nine-

teenth century, refused to accept these assumptions as the basis for intercourse with China and insisted on free trade and free access to the Chinese market. War resulted.

TRADITIONAL CHINESE ASSUMPTIONS

The traditional Chinese conception of the world order may be summarized, in abbreviated and somewhat oversimplified form, within the framework of the following five assumptions:

(1) The traditional world order is hierarchical, not egalitarian. The concept of the legal equality or the sovereignty of the individual political units in the world order did not exist. All political units arranged themselves hierarchically. There was a central recognized authority. Traditionally, that central authority was China. China's authority was institutionalized in the tribute system. All forms of international intercourse, including political, cultural, and economic relations, took place within the framework of the tribute system.[3] This system was valuable for both the tributary (tribute-payer) and the tribute-receiver. The presentation of tribute enabled the tributary to trade with China through the exchange of tribute for gifts at the court and through the legalization of controlled trade along the frontiers. Politically, the tributary often received validation for his political power in his own environment from the Chinese emperor, in the form of patents of office and investiture. This was a valuable technique for the establishment of legitimacy by local native rulers.

China, the tribute-receiver, also benefited from the system in a variety of

---

[3] On the tribute system, see John K. Fairbank and Ssu-yü Teng, *Ch'ing Administration: Three Studies,* Harvard-Yenching Institute Studies XIX (Cambridge, Mass., 1960), pp. 107–246.

ways. The surrounding tributary barbarians recognized that, to participate in the benefits of China's civilization, they had to recognize the existence of China's power and, consequently, the inviolability of China's frontiers. When, in the course of the dynastic cycle, China was weak, the system would break down. China, at the same time, was also able to trade with the barbarians for items necessary to her economy without admitting her dependence for these items on trade with the barbarians. For instance, the Central Asian nomads were "permitted" to present horses in tribute and to trade horses for Chinese products at frontier markets as a gracious boon granted by the emperor. China, needing horses for her armies, actually though not theoretically depended on the nomads for this important item. In this way, the myth of China's self-sufficiency was preserved. In 1793 the Ch'ien-lung emperor could issue an edict to the King of England in which he insisted that, among other things, ". . . The Celestial Empire, ruling all within the four seas, simply concentrates on carrying out the affairs of Government properly, and does not value rare and precious things . . . we have never valued ingenious articles, nor do we have the slightest need of your Country's manufactures." [4]

(2) China's centrality in the world order was a function of her civilization and virtue, particularly the virtue of China's ruler. The world order was as much an ethical as a political phenomenon. Harmony on the international scene, as on the domestic, was the product of the emperor's virtue. If he committed unvirtuous acts, the rivers would flood, the mountains shake, the

people revolt. By extension, the world order would crumble while the barbarians invaded China's frontier. The "Mandate of Heaven" extended to international society through China's primacy in the tribute system.

(3) The world hierarchy was universal. There were no other hierarchies and no other sources of power on the international scene. Because of the absence of alternative powers, no concept of the "balance of power" ever developed.[5] *All* units within the system were subservient to China, and those political units which were geographically too distant to participate simply lived in a kind of limbo or international political vacuum. In modern parlance, one might say that all states were satellites of China. Within the satellites, a great deal of "self-determination" existed, but opposition to China was considered rebellion against the established order and the valid tradition, to be dealt with accordingly.

(4) National power was the reflection of national virtue. Power was, therefore, by definition more "moral" than in the West, because it derived from the possession of virtue. Consequently, there was no conflict between "right" and "might." To the traditional Chinese political thinker, "might" never made "right"; on the contrary "right made might." Right and might were, in fact, synonymous in China. Hence, the use of might was justified by its very existence, because, without right, there would have been no might in the first place.[6]

---

[4] For a partial translation of Ch'ien-lung's edict to George III, see Ssu-yü Teng and John K. Fairbank, *China's Response to the West* (Cambridge, Mass., 1954), p. 19.

[5] The concept of "balance of power" differs from the traditional Chinese "use the barbarians to control the barbarians" in that the former implies the juxtaposition of equal powers but the latter is a technique relying on the exploitation of the strengths or weaknesses of one power to "control" the other, with China always the superior and guiding third (and only) "power."

[6] This is the "Wang-tao" concept of power.

(5) International society was the extension of internal society. There were no "nation-states," and concepts such as "international" and "interstate" are inappropriate to describe the situation. Clear boundaries of jurisdiction and power simply did not exist. What boundaries there were were cultural. The Great Wall demarcated the boundary between China's sedentary agricultural bureaucratic Confucian society and the barbarians' nomadic steppe societies. It was never a political or even a jurisdictional boundary. Nor was the ocean a boundary, for Japan, Korea, the Ryukyus, and the Southeast Asian kingdoms came to China across the seas within the framework of the tribute system, and, therefore, China's power, despite her continental orientation, extended culturally and often politically to maritime nations as well.

OPERATIONAL TECHNIQUES

In fact, the principle of hierarchy, which was operative in almost all Asian societies internally, governed relations even among states in situations where China was not a factor. Korea, for instance, often conducted its relations with Japan on a tribute pattern. Ladakh presented tribute to Tibet, and Cambodia might present tribute to a stronger Thailand. The Nguyen rulers of Vietnam might call themselves "emperors" at home, but, in communicating with China, they called themselves "kings," a clear example of the extension of hierarchy.

Furthermore, just as factionalism was condemned at home, so was it condemned abroad as well. Inside China, society was, theoretically, unitary. There was no official recognition of the distinction between state and party, either at court or in the bureaucracy. Where combinations might develop among the barbarians to challenge China's power primacy, it was conscious Chinese policy to "use the barbarians against the barbarians." For instance, a constant theme in Chinese foreign policy from 1858 on has been the use of Russia against the rest of the West, whether it meant the use of British fears of Russian penetration into Asia in the second half of the nineteenth century to obtain British co-operation in the maintenance of the Manchu dynasty in power or the use of the Soviet Union's nuclear umbrella to shield China from "American imperialism" in the middle of the twentieth century.

Traditionally, in other words, political techniques developed for control inside China could be used externally as well. Developments in the mid-nineteenth century provide a good example. The Manchu dynasty was weak in the face of a rising tide of rebellion which swept over South and Central China. It lacked sufficient military power internally to suppress the rebellion on its own. Consequently, relying on orthodox Confucian loyalties, it was able, as the symbol of Confucian orthodoxy and stability, to win or keep the loyalty of such Chinese leaders as Tseng Kuofan and Tso Tsung-t'ang who, though clearly recognizing that the Manchus were outlanders, nevertheless wholeheartedly supported the dynasty as the only alternative to chaos and an unknown future. Chaos and instability were anathema to the imperial Confucianists, and order and stability were highly prized conditions. In the same way, the Manchus were able to convince the British and other Westerners that the dynasty's continued power was the only hope for a stable China which would be open to commercial penetration. Thus, at several points when the West could easily have toppled the dynasty, it hesitated to do so for fear that the consequent instability would damage commerce. In 1860, when the British and French occupied Peking, they carefully refrained from overthrowing the Manchu throne. In 1900, when the Allied army occupied Peking in the wake of the Boxer affair, the West carefully maintained the fiction that what had actually been a war between China and the West had only been a rebellion by the Boxers against the dynasty, which the West had helped to subdue. Without this fiction, the Western powers would, by the logic of their own arguments, have been forced to inflict a disastrous defeat on the dynasty, which would have resulted in its overthrow. In this fashion, China's rulers have often been able to maintain their positions at moments of weakness as well as at moments of strength, both internally and internationally.

Consequently, external stability—like internal stability—was not dependent on a balance of power between rival forces or competing nation-states. At moments of strength, the dynasty could maintain international stability by virtue of its ability to wield great physical and economic power. At moments of weakness, the dynasty could still command the Confucian loyalties of its cultural satellites and could use such techniques as "divide and rule" to maintain its position and the world hierarchy.

Chinese external policy was obviously based on China's assumptions concerning the world order. In other words, its primary objective, its axiomatic policy, was the maintenance of the only conceivable order, the world hierarchy. There were no other primary values to conflict with this, no moral inhibitions to prevent the development of calculated policies, in Professor May's definition. Nor was there any conflict concerning the means to be used to obtain the primary policy objective. Disagreement might take place, as it often did, over the efficiency of one calculated policy or another. But the only inhibitions placed on the development of a wide range of diplomatic—and military —weapons was physical. Consequently, China's policy-makers had a remarkable degree of flexibility in the formulation of immediate policies. China could go to great lengths to maintain her centrality, even to the extent of recognizing the superiority of a barbarian dynasty or ruler, such as the Manchus. In the end, of course, whether or not the barbarian was "Sinicized," he had to rule China, and the East Asian world order, on the basis of China's traditional hierarchical assumptions. It was simply inconceivable for anyone to challenge the superiority of China's ruler, whether that ruler was Chinese or barbarian.

The Sinitic world system faced its greatest challenge with the arrival in East Asia of Western powers who did not accept the assumptions on which the system itself was based. In the face of the Russians, who arrived in East Asia in the middle of the seventeenth century and immediately posed a challenge to the system, the Confucian world order demonstrated a remarkable resilience and capacity for compromise. The vigorous and capable K'ang-hsi emperor of the Manchu dynasty clearly recognized that the Russians had to be dealt with in such a way that the assumptions of the traditional order itself were not challenged. Consequently, a unique system of political and commercial institutions was developed for communications between the Manchu and Russian empires, consciously avoiding questioning basic assumptions. For instance, communications between Petersburg and Peking took place between court officials of secondary or tertiary rank, thus bypassing the issue of the czar's having to address the emperor as a superior. Russian trade caravans to Peking, though consciously recognized by both sides as strictly commercial enterprises devoid of politico-cultural content, could be entered in official Manchu court records as tribute caravans, if necessary. Gifts to court officials, which normally accompanied trade anyway, could be considered tribute even though the Russian caravan masters and merchants were never required to perform the tribute ceremonial of the kowtow. The kowtow was necessary for admission to the emperor's presence on formal court occasions, but a merchant did not necessarily have access to the emperor. This system worked remarkably well from 1728 to about 1858. The Manchu emperors could rest secure in the thought that the hierarchical world order remained unchallenged by the Russians, while the Russians were content with the thought that they had obtained their objective, trade, without having to participate directly in the onerous tribute system. The Manchus could accept the compromise out of fear, reasonable or not, of Russian power to disturb the stability of Central Asia, an area of prime importance to all dynasties in China.

THE CLASH OF SYSTEMS

The great and unresolved challenge to the system came from the Western maritime powers. Although at an earlier date, the Dutch were prepared to be enrolled in the tribute system to gain material advantages, the English, by the middle of the nineteenth century, were not. English pride and theories of international practice prevented any compromise. Profit and progress, commerce and civilization, were part of a European syndrome of self-confident capitalism in the middle of the nineteenth century. When the Canton system failed to satisfy the commercial hopes of the Manchester magnates, London demanded free and uncontrolled access to the Chinese market and the establishment of permanent British representatives at Peking to defend British inter-

ests, on the model of European diplomatic practice. Although opium was the immediate cause of the Opium War, it was in a more profound sense the conflict of two diametrically opposed concepts of the world system—East Asian hierarchy as opposed to European egalitarianism—which resulted in the first serious armed clashes between China and the West.

After 1842 China, now internally weak and externally facing enemies from Europe and America who did not accept the validity of the assumptions on which the East Asian world order rested, saw the breakdown of her traditional system. Former tributary states became European colonies. Foreign representatives were established in Peking on an equal footing with Chinese officials. European diplomatic institutions had to be adopted, and European international law was studied and used to combat the West. In short, European imperialism, which forced China to recognize the existence of an alternative international power that was, in fact, materially more powerful than China, broke down the autonomous Sinitic world order. By 1949 China possessed a complete set of Western diplomatic institutions.[7]

The breakdown of the institutions of the traditional world system after 1842 took place far faster than did the erosion of the assumptions on which the Confucian internal and external social order was based. For instance, during the decades of the "self-strengthening" movement which followed China's humiliation between 1842 and 1860, Western arms were adopted and Western diplomatic institutions were adapted for

[7] Often, however, she used them in a traditionally Chinese fashion. The Chiang-Roosevelt diplomacy of World War II remains a superb example of traditional Chinese diplomatic method. China, from a position of great weakness, was recognized as one of the Great Powers.

China's use. Ambassadors were sent abroad, a prototype of a foreign office—the *Tsung-li yamen*—was established in Peking, and textbooks on Western international law and other subjects were translated into Chinese. But, significantly, all this activity in studying and adopting Western material and diplomatic techniques was justified on the basis of utility: it was all a means of defending China and of preserving Chinese civilization from the West. Furthermore, at the same time that China was forced to deal with the West on the West's terms, Korea remained anchored to China through the traditional tribute system, a fact which created no little confusion and dismay in Western chancelleries.

There are concrete survivals of the tradition in the twentieth century as well. Chiang Kai-shek's New Life Movement in the thirties was a conscious and sincere effort to strengthen the national morale through the Confucian virtues of righteousness, integrity, decorum, and a sense of shame. In the same way, in foreign policy, his government on Taiwan has consistently pursued its objectives on the assumption that there is no conflict between "right" and "might," because the two are synonymous, and that the state should know no moral inhibitions in the pursuit of its goals, even if this means encouraging a third world war—this has, by the way, been actual policy at various times in the last decade, when the Chiang regime has wanted to take precipitous action on the mainland which might result in a third world war and, therefore, in American support for his reconquest of China.

That the Confucian tradition still operates outside of China proper is also evident, for instance, in Vietnam. Ngo Dinh Diem's "Personalist" ideology is the application of Confucianism to modern Vietnam, growing directly out of tradition. The problems the American advisers face in dealing with the officials of Diem's government and army are more than a simple echo of America's wartime experiences in China itself. They belong to the same category precisely because, despite the decades of French colonialist rule, Vietnam still faces the problem of institutional asymmetry in its relations with the West. The Ngo family is, after all, less than a generation removed from the traditional Confucian court at Hue.

Nor need one go too far to find survivals of the tradition in Communist China as well. On a broad and general plane, the Sinocentric world view grows into and reinforces modern nationalism. This provides China in modern times with a distinct sense of superiority over all foreigners, including Russians, which is, in turn, reinforced by sheer size and by the historical record. This may find expression in the discovery that China was historically more progressive than the West. Some Chinese historians, roundly condemned by the Soviets, incidentally, tried to show that capitalism had its beginnings in the Sung dynasty (960–1279). More recently, Chinese historians writing in the pages of *Li-shih yen-chiu* (*Historical Studies*) have been redefining the nature of Chinese feudalism and demonstrating that it was "better" and more progressive than Western feudalism. This form of nationalism, of course, constitutes a real challenge and threat to Marxist historicism.

On another level, the apparent lack of the traditional Western dichotomy between state and party reflects the Chinese tradition as well. Traditionally, there was no institutionalized struggle for power. Even more important, factionalism at court or anywhere in the society was condemned and opposed. The Western concept of the state as an institution which various groups sought to control through legitimate political organizations, which was accepted in nineteenth-century Western Europe, never developed in China. Consequently, the dichotomy between state and party, which is apparently preserved even in the Soviet Union where the party captured the state apparatus, is simply lacking in Chinese thinking today. This reinforces, and is reinforced by, the experience of the Chinese Communist party, which *was* the state in the borderlands in the thirties and forties.

CONTEMPORARY FOREIGN POLICY

On a more immediate and concrete plane, the influence of tradition can be observed on several levels in Chinese Communist foreign policy.

A vivid sense of outrage

Modern Chinese nationalism thrives on a vivid sense of outrage, directed at the Western imperialist powers who contributed pivotly to the erosion of China's tradition and China's integrity. This is particularly true in the field of international relations, where the imperialists established enclaves in Chinese cities and lived under the protection of extraterritoriality; the Communists feel that the imperialists also deprived China of vast territories which were traditionally part of China. The famous map published in 1954 showing the territories taken by the imperialists from China interestingly includes most of the Asian countries which traditionally paid tribute to China, such as Burma, Siam, all of Indo-China, and the like. As preposterous as these claims may be to a Westerner, they do not appear, apparently, preposterous to a Chinese. On the contrary, they feed his modern nationalist sense of outrage.

The tradition of China's primacy

On a less abstract level, the tradition of China's primacy in the originally separate East Asian world and the institutionalized techniques expressive of that primacy are reflected in the techniques of China's Asian diplomacy. Peking's relations with Pakistan, Nepal, Burma, and Cambodia, for instance, are based on the assumption that there is only one power in Asia, China, and that all other states in Asia can exist only in the shadow of China's power and with China's good will. The clear demarcation of frontiers is one of the modern techniques used by Peking to demonstrate the validity of this traditional assumption. Pakistan, Nepal, and Burma have all signed border agreements with Peking. Those agreements, due to the disparity in power between China and her neighbors, obviously depend on China's good will for their validity. Cambodia, though lacking a common frontier with China, has also clearly recognized that she exists at China's sufferance. The political expression of this is Cambodian neutrality. In short, there is a distinct echo of the traditional hierarchical world order in the new international order emerging along China's frontiers today. India, posing as a rival to China in Asia, ignored this development at her peril.

This situation stands in stark contrast to the Western Hemisphere, where another power, the United States, stands in a position of overwhelming power compared to the other states of the "inter-American system." The institutions of the system—the Organization of American States, the concept of collective security, of legal equality between the members of the system—are based on entirely different assumptions from China's in Asia. These assumptions place great restraints on American political maneuverability, so that, as often as not, Latin-American governments exist or come into power despite American displeasure.

Personalized diplomacy

As Professor Robert Scalapino has pointed out, "The influence of tradition is not confined to theory; indeed, it is far more apparent in practice." [8] The immediate techniques of Chinese diplomacy reflect the tradition. Whereas traditional gifts-in-return of precious stones, silks, brocades, and even brides were an inherent part of the tribute system, Peking now makes remarkably extensive use of cultural missions and official visits. This is the "personalized diplomacy" which distinguished traditional Chinese diplomatic practice. Gifts now go, as Scalapino points out, not to courts but to the people. In commemoration of the ratification of the Sino-Burmese boundary treaty in 1961, the Burmese government gave several thousands of tons of rice and salt to people on the Chinese side of the frontier, while Peking distributed 2.4 million meters of printed cloth and 600,000 pieces of porcelain—traditional gifts-in-return—to the inhabitants of the Burmese side of the border.

Furthermore, while the visits of Asian heads of state are reciprocated by high-ranking members of the Chinese leadership, Mao Tse-tung, overwhelmingly the symbol of contemporary China, has steadfastly retained one of the traditional attributes of power in China: inaccessibility. Given present conditions, the context of Chinese power simply could not allow Mao to gallivant around the world as Khrushchev and Kennedy do. Scalapino even suggests that Mao's two visits to Moscow—the only record of his having traveled abroad—were in the nature of visits to his—ideological

[8] Robert A. Scalapino, "Tradition and Transition in the Asian Policy of Communist China," in Edward Szczepanik (ed.), Symposium on Economic and Social Problems of the Far East (Hong Kong, 1962), pp. 262–277, especially pp. 265–266.

—ancestral home. Certainly, at least from a Chinese point of view, they belong to a different genre of journey than Gomułka's or Kádár's visits to Moscow.

VALUES AND HISTORY TODAY

If traditional values and assumptions erode at different speeds than traditional institutions—values, for instance, may erode more rapidly than the institutions they support, leaving a society saddled with institutional anachronisms; assumptions may erode more slowly, embuing newly borrowed institutions with a character quite different from the original—they may also be reinforced by a particular set of historical circumstances. The trend of progressive decay of the power of the centralized Chinese state after the middle of the nineteenth century and its virtual disappearance in the second and third decades of the twentieth was reversed in 1949 and after when, for the first time in one hundred years, China had an efficient centralized state which commanded power and, to a large extent, the loyalty of its people. In such circumstances, it is not unreasonable to suggest that the decay of traditional assumptions may also have been checked and even reversed. The very reaction to those Western values which had contributed to the weakness of China, as the Chinese understand that weakness, may have contributed to or reinforced the validity of the tradition in certain areas. Furthermore, the great Marxist concern with history—the amount of historical research in Communist China is staggering—would also be a contributing factor. The Chinese, even the Chinese Communists, are blessed—or cursed—with a great sense of their own history and tradition and with a commitment to the unity and uniqueness of the Chinese people.

The survival of elements of the tradition into the contemporary scene has not necessarily brought the Chinese Marxist into a sharp schizophrenic conflict with his own tradition as a Chinese. Quite the contrary, it would appear that, in large areas, the tradition may well reinforce certain Marxist-Leninist assumptions, at least as these assumptions have developed out of an amalgam of Chinese Communist revolutionary experience and Marxist-Leninist revolutionary theory. To take but one brief and general example: the unitary nature of the traditional Chinese state together with the traditional existence of an official ideology—Confucianism—which served as the intellectual basis for the state certainly do not conflict with, and in fact reinforce, the Chinese Communist tendency to see no real or apparent dichotomy between the state and the party, a tendency which evolved directly out of Chinese revolutionary experience. Or another: the traditional hierarchic view of the world order together with the traditional respect due elders may well have contributed to the creation of an intellectual disposition to acquiesce to Stalin's approach to bloc organization, enabling Mao, as a Communist, to accept Stalin's leadership despite his own dissatisfactions with Stalin's leadership in China during the revolutionary struggle.

In assessing the extent to which the Sino-Soviet conflict must be viewed in the perspective of Chinese historical tradition, several obvious thoughts must be kept in mind. First, the Sino-Soviet conflict is global. In other words, it does not concern solely bilateral Sino-Soviet relations. Russian behavior in Cuba or Berlin, Chinese behavior in India, the Taiwan Straits, or Zanzibar, are also subject to dispute. Action may derive from, as well as contribute to, the dispute. Second, if Chinese behavior derives today from several sources—Marxism-Leninism, national strategic considerations, Chinese nationalism, tra-

ditional intellectual and political dispositions—Soviet behavior derives no less from a similar complex of sources. Third, both Chinese and Soviet behavior changed through time and will continue to do so. Dynamic change on each side is one of the variables which the other must take into account in formulating not only policy toward the other members of the bloc but global policy as well.

If, therefore, Chinese policy assumptions and actions present a challenge in comprehension to the Soviets, no less do Soviet policy assumptions and actions present a challenge to the Chinese. Khrushchev's concepts of "peaceful coexistence," of the theoretical as well as practical recognition of American power, of a bloc which is certainly not hierarchically ordered—as was Stalin's—of Western egalitarianism in short, all conflict with the assumptions, reinforced by tradition, of the Chinese leaders. Certainly, Khrushchev's efforts to develop, through frequent meetings of Communist leaders, something closer to a form of parliamentarism than a monolithic hierarchy must be anathema to a man whose image of his own position derives from a tradition where the ruler possesses a special "virtue and prestige, which if maintained prolong his rule," and where "face" is necessary to the possession of power and criticism is, by definition, subversive to the entire system.[9]

In short, the years since Stalin's death have seen Soviet and Chinese communism grow further away from each other, in theory as well as in practice. Each is the result of the totality of numerous variable factors, including historical experience, contemporary problems, and a wide range of theoretical

[9] John K. Fairbank, *Communist China and Taiwan in United States Foreign Policy*, The Brien McMahon Lectures, University of Connecticut, November 21, 1960, p. 15.

assumptions. Their mutual problem is that the variable factors for each differ widely in certain areas. It could not have been otherwise. Accommodation, if it comes, will, of necessity, be conscious and contrived. At present, neither Moscow nor Peking can completely escape their historical differences. The Soviet Union developed out of a society with a strong Western orientation—in fact, it is Western—deeply influenced by political and intellectual developments in Western Europe. Communist China, influenced though it may have been by the West, continues to be influenced at the same time by its own Chinese tradition. These differences are much greater, after all, than those bedeviling the Western community or relations between Washington and Moscow today. Much more might be said about the influence of China's historical milieu on its contemporary policies. But the influence must be recognized at the outset and inquiry carried on in depth.

Demons in Paradise: The Chinese Images of Russia

By T. A. HSIA

ABSTRACT: Russia is an object of both hatred and hope for the Chinese. Those who remember Russia's record of aggression regard the Russians as demons, but those who place hopes in the October revolution of 1917 regard Russia as if it were already a paradise. There is reason to believe that Mao's polemics against the "revisionists" meet with greater welcome in Communist China than did his former policy of "leaning to one side." Russian literature should present a more profound picture of Russian life, but, if it has failed to do so in China, it is perhaps because its influence does not equal the strong nationalist or ideological prejudice.

T. A. Hsia, Berkeley, California, is Associate Research Linguist at the University of California, Berkeley. He is author of a monograph, A Terminological Study of the Hsia Fang Movement, published by the Center for Chinese Studies, University of California at Berkeley, and of a number of articles, including "Heroes and Hero-worship in Chinese Communist Fiction" and "Twenty Years After the Yenan Forum," both of which appeared in the China Quarterly (January–March 1963).

THE Chinese names *o-lo-ssu, su-wei-ai, su-o,* and *su-lien* stand, respectively, for Russia, Soviet, Soviet Russia, and Soviet Union. The characters which are combined to make these names convey very little sense if compared with *ying* for England and *mei* for America, which suggest bravery and beauty. Since the Chinese do feel strongly about Russia, she is sometimes known by other names that bear, as it were, the stamp of either approval or disapproval without too much distortion of the sound. An attempt was once made to change the Chinese name for Soviet Union into a pun with a positive connotation. Ko Kung-chen, a well-known journalist, who visited the Soviet Union in 1933—after the resumption of Sino-Soviet diplomatic relations which had been broken off since 1927—and stayed there for two years and a half, invented a new name, *shu-lien,* to replace the familiar *su-lien. Lien* means "union"—an abbreviation of *lien-pang* —but *shu* calls up an image that *su* does not. *Shu,* character number 5,874 in Mathews' Chinese-English Dictionary, conveys: "A multitude. The whole, all, a great number. The people, the masses." Ko was a sympathetic observer in his reports on the life in the Soviet Union under the Second Five-Year Plan and he believed that he had a good reason to adopt a new name to represent Soviet Union "both phonetically and semantically." Although his correspondence was widely read and very influential in winning Chinese admiration for the Russian determination to build a "socialist" state,[1] the term he invented never won the popularity he thought it deserved. The less expressive *su-lien* has remained the standard term.

HATRED AND HOPE

In times much earlier than the leftist-inclined 1930's, the Russians had a name with a very bad connotation. According to Hu Ch'iu-yüan's *An Outline of the History of Russian Aggression Against China,*[2] the Russians were known to be cannibals when they came into contact with the Chinese in the seventeenth century. So they were confused, in the minds of the terrified Chinese, with *lo-sha,* or *Rakshas,* man-eating demons in Buddhist books.[3] As late as 1885, Ts'ao T'ing-chieh, in his report on the miserable conditions of the Chinese living in Eastern Siberia, quoted them as referring to the Russians as *lo-sha,* although Ts'ao himself used *o-jen* to designate the Russian people.[4] Chapter Two of Hu's book bears the title: "Our Country's Border and the Eastward Move of the *Lo-sha,*" but, in general usage today, *lo-sha* refers to the demons only, not to the Russians.

These two terms, *shu-lien* and *lo-sha,* although currently not in use, speak, nevertheless, for two concepts, two Chinese attitudes towards Russia. Russia as a People's Union and Russia as a tribe of demons are images not derived from her name or names but, rather, as a result of China's complicated relations with Russia. One image sees Russia in transition, taking heroic strides towards democracy, socialism, and universal love—Russia as an example for the backward China and as an indication for a happy future to be shared with her "Chinese brethren." The other image resides in the memory

---

[1] Ko Kung-chen, *Ts'ung tung-pei tao shu-lien (From Manchuria to the Soviet Union)* (Shanghai, 1935). Ko's correspondence originally appeared in some of the most widely read periodicals of his time, such as the *Life Weekly,* the *Kuo-wen Weekly,* and so on.

[2] Hu, *O-ti ch'in-hua shih-kang* (Taipei, 1952).

[3] *Ibid.,* p. 32.

[4] *Ibid.,* p. 83.

of Russia's ignoble past, of her bloody sins that added greatly to China's woe and shame. Russia's achievements and aspiration, her record of barbarism, her protestations of friendship, and her treachery are facts hard to reconcile, and, so far, no attempt at reconciliation has been successful. That is why Chinese reaction to Russia can be violent and can often go to the extreme. In whatever other area the Peking regime may try to rewrite history, it can do little to whitewash the reputation of Russia before 1917. The best it can do in its advocacy of a pro-Russian policy is to call attention to the difference between the "People's Russia" and the czarist Russia—for Russia's record before 1917 was something that no Russophile in China can ever defend. It is to be admitted that Hu Ch'iu-yüan's book, published in Taipei, does not avoid a strong "Nationalist" bias. But "national" sentiments are found in such a book as P'eng Ming's *History of Sino-Soviet Friendship,* published in 1957 in Peking.[5] In the first part of the book, there is a quotation from Lenin—from an article he wrote for *Iskra* in 1900 on "The Chinese War"—which seems rather to confirm the image of czarist troops as bloodthirsty Rakshas.[6] Then, in his own words, P'eng writes:

In 1903 the czarist government, under the influence of the extremely reactionary militarists and feudal lords, adopted an even more aggressive policy. In August the czar appointed Admiral Alekseev as Viceroy of the Far East. With his base in Lü-shun (Port Arthur), Alekseev assumed absolute control of administrative, military, and foreign affairs (on Chinese territory) and put himself up as a Super-monarch (over the Chinese government). Meanwhile, the atrocities of the czarist

troops, instead of showing signs of abatement, mounted in incidence.

Thus the relations between China and Russia deteriorated badly—a situation for which even that faction traditionally pro-Russian could find no excuse.[7]

Although P'eng's book has an entirely different intent from Hu's, as its title clearly indicates, it is significant that both "histories" have similar contents when they come to certain periods in Sino-Soviet relations. To a historian in Communist China, therefore, the Soviet Union still carries the "luggage" of czarist Russia. He may try to explain them away, but he cannot ignore Russian "atrocities" even in his work on "Sino-Soviet friendship."

"The whole world watches Soviet Russia: while one group does this with hope; the other with hatred," said Ilya Ehrenburg.[8] Hope and hatred are also found in the Chinese attitudes toward Russia. The new Russophiles that emerged in China after the collapse of Admiral Alekseev's "supermonarchical" government in Manchuria were intellectuals who developed a love for Russian ideals such as were expounded by Tolstoy and Kropotkin or became attracted to Communist ideology after the 1917 revolution in Russia. Of course, hatred can also be generated from ideological reasons—such as, Russians are bad because they are Communists. But it is the countinuing history of Russian "aggression"—or the public image of that history—in spite of some signs of friendship from Russia, that makes it impossible for pro-Russianism to prevail. It weighs on the mind of even those Chinese who have perhaps less difficulty in embracing

5 P'eng Ming, *Chung-su yu-yi shih* (Peking, 1957).

6 *Ibid.,* pp. 29–30.

7 *Ibid.,* p. 32.

8 A quotation by Chou Li-po who interviewed Ehrenburg in 1950. Chou, *Su-lien cha-chi (Random Notes on the Soviet Union)* (Peking, 1953).

Russian communism than in accepting Russia as a true friend.

The contradiction of hope and hatred in the Chinese reaction to Russia is found, on a small scale, in Taiwan today, where a strong anti-Russian position is maintained. But, if one name is honored in Taiwan, it is Sun Yatsen's. And Dr. Sun said in his *Three People's Principles* that mankind had found "a great hope" in the Russian revolution of 1917.[9] Dr. Sun is, indeed, corrected by Chiang Kai-shek in his *Soviet Russia in China,* which demonstrates, rather, that Russia after 1917 has never changed her habits of aggression.[10] So, two opposite points of view, both as regards Russia, are presented in Taiwan—Sun's and Chiang's. But it is only fair to add that Dr. Sun's hopes about the Bolshevik revolution, so stirring to himself and to his followers in the early twenties but so shattered by the cruelty of subsequent events, have become a source of endless embarrassment to the Kuomintang, a heritage which it can hardly destroy for piety's or memory's sake, but a heresy whose circulation it cannot tolerate either.

The vast amount of pro-Russian propaganda put out by the Communist regime over a number of years is perhaps a hindrance to observers who try to get a picture of the "true public opinion" in Communist China, for it has created a false image, if not of Russia, at least of China—but this image has largely diminished, thanks to the recent dispute between the "fraternal parties." By its own declarations, the Chinese Communist party

willingly froze itself into an attitude of "leaning to one side,"[11] at a time when the party and its Chairman, Mao Tse-tung, began to hold the fate of the nation in their hands. The Chinese Communist propaganda machine was once so busily occupied with striking such an awkward attitude that no other attitude was thought to be possible. Only rarely was any voice from Communist China audible to indicate that the Chinese love for Russia was less than perfect. Now that all the cadres of the Chinese Communist party and a great many people under its control are attending sessions to study the lengthy polemics against Comrades Togliatti, Thorez, and so on, they may be puzzling over the meaning of the earlier documents about "internationalism" and "Sino-Soviet friendship," which, as they well remember, they were once compelled to study with no less diligence. The incompatibility between the two series of documents is obvious. In the light of the new party line, the Russian people remain good, as People—including American "people"—are always good. Russia, as a Socialist state, is also good—but she used to be very good under Stalin. What has made her less good is the present Russian leadership, which needs reform. If the Russian leadership refuses to reform, then the consequences can be serious. That much, I think, is what a reader must gather from the latest Communist Chinese polemics. Relations between Communist China and Soviet Russia have indeed entered a new phase. Public reaction in Mainland China to this new development should be a subject of the highest interest.

At the time of writing, I do not have

[9] Sun, "On Nationalism," Lecture IV in *Three People's Principles* (1924).

[10] Chiang, *Su-o tsai chung-kuo* (Taipei, 1956). It should be noted that the name for Russia preferred in Taiwan is either Russia or Soviet Russia, with emphasis on the continuity of Russian history. The name preferred in Communist China is the Soviet Union, with emphasis on discontinuity.

[11] "On People's Democratic Dictatorship" (1949). Mao, *Hsüan-chi* (*Selected Works*) (Peking, 1960), Vol. 4, p. 1477; *Selected Works* (English language; New York, 1962), Vol. 5, p. 415.

much evidence of this reaction. But I should like to point out that, in launching a new policy vis-à-vis Soviet Russia, Mao can expect to rally the support of two groups of Chinese people: those whose image of Russia is always tainted with fear, suspicion, and even hatred, and those others who feel too great an enthusiasm for their angelically bright image of Russia to allow it to be tarnished by "revisionism." The one has too little, while the other has too much, love for Russia. The former may be called "rightists" whose opinion is generally suppressed but who, even by official admission, have never been entirely wiped out or reformed. The latter is the articulate group, whose praise of Soviet Russia used to form the material for pro-Russian propaganda. It is composed of the idealists and the theoretical purists among the Communists, but it also includes those who are not party members who really believe that "the Russian path is our path." They will support Mao in his effort to restore Bolshevik vigor and purity to the world Communist movement in general and to Soviet Russia in particular. The rightists, who, for that matter, do not think, indeed, much differently from Chiang Kai-shek or Hu Ch'iu-yüan, were never happy about the policy of "leaning to one side." Little do they care whether it is Stalin or Khrushchev who rules Russia or whether Russia is czarist or Socialist. To them, Russia is a traditional enemy, a potential enemy, and, at best, a treacherous friend. They will perhaps welcome Mao's new move as a first step, though a belated one, in reaffirming China's independence and dignity—a policy they have been looking forward to since 1949, if not earlier.

The existence of the two groups in Communist China is a thing quickly proven. Their reaction to the latest Chinese Communist polemics is a con-jecture that can be inferred from their earlier utterances.

THE QUESTION OF IMPERIALISM

There were always writers for honest, unabashed, or even vehement nationalism in China before 1949. It was only after 1949 that a balanced outlook of nationalism and internaticnalism was urged as the only correct way of thinking for Communists and good citizens alike. The first leftist writer who had the audacity to ask questions about Sino-Soviet friendship was Hsiao Chün, whose *Village in August* (1935), a novel about guerrillas in Manchuria, had spoken for both patriotism and international communism.[12] Beginning from 1947, after he had been made editor of a newspaper in Harbin under the Chinese Communist control, he published a number of articles which regarded the Russians in Manchuria as scarcely better than the defeated Japanese overlords. His essay on "Imperialism in Various Colors" was actually intended to register a shock that there was such a thing as "red" imperialism. He also published a sketch of a little incident that probably occurred. A Russian old lady and a little Russian girl were having tea in a garden. Three Chinese children were peering in from outside. What they saw was the beautiful garden, beautiful garden furniture, silver tea service, milk and sugar. The lady and the girl, annoyed at their unwelcome appearance and perhaps hungry looks, shouted at them, "Go away! What are you doing there? You go away!" One of the Chinese children threw in a rock as an answer to their rudeness.[13] The sketch

[12] Cf. C. T. Hsia, *A History of Modern Chinese Fiction* (New Haven, 1961), p. 273.

[13] C. T. Hsia, *ibid.,* gives a fine summary of the Hsiao Chün case. See also Liu Shou-sung, *Chung-kuo hsin-wen-hsüeh-shih ch'u-kao (A History of Modern Chinese Litera-*

had for its title a quotation from a Confucian classic: "Courtesy demands reciprocity," a saying which, it may be recalled, also appeared in the *People's Daily's* recent reply to Comrade Thorez.[14]

To a Chinese reader accustomed to the leftist literature of the 1930's, such a little scene as described above should be reasonably expected to have occurred at the mansion belonging to a rich British dowager in Shanghai. Were not the British imperialists? But that the Russians could behave as rudely as the British to the poor Chinese children was a shock to the author. No blood is shed in this little drama, but the fence that separates the luxurious, tea-sipping Russians from the rock-throwing Chinese urchins is a symbol that has perhaps even a deeper meaning today than it did sixteen years ago.

According to Miss Ting Ling, who joined the mob in 1949 to denounce Hsiao Chün, Hsiao enjoyed great popularity in Manchuria. He thought that he had public opinion behind him.[15] Such a support he probably had, if we remember the Chinese sentiments after the Yalta Conference. The fire that kindled the hearts of the marchers in May 1919 who protested against the oppression of China after World War I was displayed again in demonstrations against Russia in February 1946. Russian claims on Outer Mongolia, Port Arthur, Dairen, and the Chinese East-

ern Railway were grim reminders of the czarist aggression; the physical presence of the Russian army in Manchuria revived the memories of the years 1900–1904. Such an impression was not easily removed. So, after 1949 the Communists had an extremely hard task of persuasion to bring the Chinese people over to a pro-Russian attitude.

Anti-Russian feelings were amply represented in a book published in 1950 in both Shanghai and Peking: *Why Lean to One Side?*[16] At the "study sessions" sponsored by the Chinese Communist party, the book tells us, the policy of "leaning to one side" was often a subject of heated debate:

The opinion of a great many people was correct. But there were also a group of people who did not believe that Soviet Union is the Chinese people's good friend. They opposed "leaning to one side." They alleged that Soviet Union was an "aggressor" against China. Some of the arguments they advanced were:

"Outer Mongolia is controlled by Soviet Union."

"Manchuria is a Soviet sphere of influence."

"The 1945 Treaty of Sino-Soviet Friendship and Alliance was an unequal treaty."

"The full contents of the new Sino-Soviet Treaty[17] are not published; there are secret agreements."

"Soviet Union has territorial ambitions on Port Arthur and Dairen."

"If China seeks independence, she should not receive foreign aid. Soviet Union will not give unconditional help to China."[18]

Some of the dissident opinions quoted indicate a deep-rooted chauvinism or willful obstinacy which obviously can hardly be overcome by reasoning:

---

ture: A Preliminary Draft) (Peking, 1956), Vol. 2, pp. 222 ff., and Ti Chia, *Chung-kung tsen-yang tui-tai wen-yi-kung-tso-che* (*How the Chinese Communists Treat the Literary Workers*) (Hong Kong, 1953), pp. 92 ff.

[14] The quotation from the *Li Chi* (*Book of the Rites*) appears in "Whence the Differences? A Reply to Thorez and Other Comrades," *People's Daily,* February 27, 1963, p. 1. An English version is found in *Peking Review,* No. 9 (1963), p. 8.

[15] Ting Ling, *K'ua-tao hsin-ti-shih-tai lai* (*Entering a New Era*) (Peking, 1951), p. 86. The work is a collection of essays.

[16] Hai Fu, *Wai-shen-mo i-pien-tao?* (Shanghai and Peking, 1950).

[17] Referring to the Sino-Soviet Treaty of Friendship, Alliance, and Mutual Assistance of 1950.

[18] Hai Fu, *op. cit.,* pp. 1–2.

"U. S. is of course bad; England, Germany, Italy, Japan, and others, they are all very bad. They all treat China badly and oppress China. Czarist Russia in the past was also an aggressor against China. The Soviet Union is still a foreign country. How could she become so good?" [19]

"You may repeat that Soviet Union is good; but I won't believe. I won't listen to your propaganda." [20]

The important fact about these sessions was that the Communists could not lose a debate so long as they could enforce obedience. Their arguments were not always convincing; for example, "Why should 'independence' be granted to Outer Mongolia but denied to Tibet?" was a question raised, but, it seems to me, not satisfactorily answered. But anti-Russian sentiments were, thereafter, little registered until 1957, the year of the Hundred Flowers movement and the antirightist movement. In that year, for a few months, the view that "the Soviet Union is guilty of aggression against China" was again circulating in the air.[21] In addition to the old scores between the two countries, there arose the problems of the payments of the expenses incurred in the anti-America, aid-Korea war and of the repayment of the loans from the Soviet Union. As a collector of debts, Russia did not look even as generous as the United States.[22] I do not know how such charges of Russian meanness were answered; they were perhaps simply silenced.

THE ISSUE OF REVISIONISM

Nineteen fifty-seven marked also the fortieth anniversary of the Bolshevik revolution. At the Supreme Soviet in Moscow, Mao talked about "revisionism" as a worse enemy than "dogmatism" and hinted at the possible contradiction between "interests" and "ideals" when he said, "Common interests and common ideals have bound us [Communist China and Soviet Russia] in a close tie." [23] But the general theme of the big celebrations held in China was the combination of internationalism with nationalism. The celebrations were meant also as a part of the mass movement to reform the rightists who had to listen to, and also to make, pro-Russian speeches. A typical document that came from the movement contains such a passage:

However, even within our Party, there are Rightists who, starting from bourgeois nationalism, respond to the reactionary views of the bourgeois Rightists (who oppose our policy of "leaning to one side") by setting up patriotism as opposed to internationalism, setting up national interests as opposed to the general interests of international proletarian movement, and blurring the line between the friend and the enemy that our state and our people have in the world. We must persist in proletarian internationalism; we must hold up against surrender to bourgeois nationalism.[24]

The author of the above piece, Hsiung Fu by name, classifies the "nationalists" among the Communists with the "bourgeois rightists." This is apparently not always the case, for nationalism can be viewed in another light. The writer for *Pravda*, who pens the following sentence, thinks that nationalism is, rather, a disease that afflicts the "leftists": "The disorder of Leftist sectarianism nourishes nationalism; it is

[19] *Ibid.*, p. 4.
[20] *Ibid.*, p. 11.
[21] Roderick MacFarquhar, *The Hundred Flowers Campaign and the Chinese Intellectuals* (New York, 1960), p. 163.
[22] *Ibid.*, p. 50.

[23] *People's Daily,* November 7, 1957, pp. 1–2.
[24] Hsiung Fu, "The Light of the October Revolution Shines on the Chinese People's Road to Victory," *People's Daily,* November 10, 1957, p. 7.

also nourished by nationalism."[25] If
nationalism can infiltrate from both
left and right, it must be a serious
threat to the international Communist
movement indeed.

Party member or nonparty member,
whoever in Communist China harbors
national sentiments will probably find
Mao's new line more to his taste than
the earlier one. But the recent Chinese
Communist polemics contain no direct
appeal to nationalism; the appeal is
rather for the purity of Marxism-Leninism, which knows no national boundaries. There is no evidence to indicate
that all Chinese Communists are more
or less inclined to nationalism. To a
large number of them, the important
division of mankind is still between the
two classes: the exploiters and the ex-
ploited. The Bolshevik revolution of
1917 is believed to have ushered in a
society "free from exploitation of man
by man." It is this belief, expressed,
for example, by Mao in his speech at
the Supreme Soviet in 1957, that forms
the basis of the hope for the Soviet
Union. Among the Chinese Communists there must remain a large number whose inspiration is derived from
that primary source—the 1917 revolution—with a disregard of the fluctua-
tions, veers, retreats, and turnabouts
that have occurred since in the policy
of the Soviet Union. They shut their
eyes to the unpleasant facts so that
their hope may not suffer, and they
leap to the facts which seem to support
their hope. It is hard to say how many
of them really care to know, or have
had a chance to know, the significance
of the changes that happened in the
Soviet Union after Stalin's death. An
important feature of the 1957 celebrations was the refusal, on the part of the
Chinese Communists, to recognize the

importance of either Stalinism or de-
Stalinization. A perusal of the more
than sixty articles published for that
occasion[26] does not leave the reader
with the impression that the Soviet
Union was departing from any of the
Leninist doctrines or the Stalinist practices. Through the entire reading, he
feels a great pull toward the sacred
name of Revolution. And the image of
the Bolshevik revolution was preserved
in its pristine freshness.

It can be presumed that those who
have embraced the ideals of the Bolshevik revolution will find the utterances by Togliatti, Thorez, and Khrushchev distasteful. They will probably
agree with Mao that "revisionism" is a
worse enemy than "dogmatism" to the
international Communist movement.

In 1957 the novelist Ai Wu visited
Russia as leader of a Chinese Communist delegation to participate in the
Russian celebrations of the anniversary.
In his reports, there is almost no reference to the many aspects of de-Stalinization which may have alarmed him,
or even pained him, during his stay
in the Soviet Union—de-Stalinization
understood as either obliteration of the
physical relics of the "personality cult"
or the abolition of Stalinist practices.
However, in Georgia he reports that he
saw a huge portrait of Stalin and Mao
standing shoulder by shoulder in a
botanical institute[27] and that the peasants of a kolkhoz, at the entertainment
after dinner, sang songs recalling
Stalin's name.[28] Inasmuch as he does

25 The article appeared in *Pravda,* January
7, 1963; Chinese translation, *People's Daily,*
February 21, 1963, p. 6.

26 The collection is compiled by the Sino-
Soviet Amity Association and entitled, *Chung-
kuo jen-min ch'ing-chu shih-yüeh-ko-ming
ssu-shih-chou-nien chi-nien wen-chi* (*A Collection of Commemorative Articles by Chinese
People in Celebration of the Fortieth Anniversary of the October Revolution*) (Peking,
1958).

27 Ai Wu, *Ou-hsing-chi* (*A Trip to Europe*)
(Tientsin, 1959), p. 53.

28 *Ibid.,* p. 94.

not mention that he was perhaps missing similar portraits and songs in other parts of the Soviet Union, the impression his reports create is that Stalin could still command as much "love" and "reverence" as before his death. He does mention that, at Gori, Stalin's birthplace, a "museum" had been torn down with blocks of cement still scattered about. But, inasmuch as he expressed no emotion at the ruin and there was another "museum" to take its place, the reader will perhaps not notice that anything had gone wrong.[29]

Chou Chieh-fu, another member of the delegation, describes the progress of the Lenin Kolkhoz in Georgia. In 1953, he was told, a cow yielded an annual average of 423 kilograms of milk. In 1957 the output was raised to 1,500 kilograms.[30] The mention of the year 1953 by Chou's Russian—or Georgian—informant was cruel, a point Chou does not comment upon. Compared with the Chinese Communist writings on Russia in the early fifties, up to the time of Stalin's death in 1953, the reports of Ai Wu and Chou Chieh-fu show a remarkable tone of embarrassment. Here is the Soviet Union that they are bound to praise, but it is not the same Soviet Union that they are taught to believe in.

Unlike Ch'ü Ch'iu-po [31] and Ko Kung-chen, who saw Russia in the twenties and thirties respectively—that is, a Russia in a shape not yet quite presentable—the writers of the period between 1949 and 1953 saw no need to modify their praise and made no exception to the perfection that they believed they actually saw. I shall cite a few examples:

Miss Ting Ling visited Russia in 1949 and 1950. Among the things she saw were nurseries and children's homes, which she called "The Children's Paradise." Then she added:

Expressions like "heaven," "paradise," and the "fairyland" are clumsy words to describe the happiness of the children living in the Soviet Union today. Life in paradise is understood to consist in being well fed and leading a leisurely life—but for what good is that? In that paradise there would be no concern about education or the cultivation of talent, so that every one might live for a high ideal and do one's best to develop one's ability. There would be no need for one to endow oneself with noble qualities or to live in the most intelligent and the most rational way. But it is indeed a pity that I have still to pick up a hackneyed expression for the title of my report. Perhaps a better expression is already available in the Soviet Union, since language in the Soviet Union must move ahead with the life there. However, since I do not know Russian, I can only settle for a word that I do not like.[32]

Here is Chou Li-po's reflection on a kolkhoz near Moscow which he visited in 1950:

As far back as 1933, the living standard of the poor peasant in the Soviet Union was already raised to that of the middle peasant. Stalin then said, "This is of course good, but not good enough." "We have to make every member of the kolkhoz live in affluent circumstances."

Stalin's words have long since become a reality. Great Stalin never says anything but he puts it into effect. There is no kolkhoz now but all its members do live in affluent circumstances.

. . . In his famous 1933 speech, Stalin promised the women members of the kolkhoz: "We Bolsheviks will try to en-

[29] Ibid., p. 101.
[30] Chou Chieh-fu, Fang-su san-chi (Random Notes on a Visit to Soviet Union) (Peking, 1959), p. 126.
[31] See Chü Ch'iu-po, Ch'üan-chi (Complete Works) (Peking, 1953), Vol. 1. I have written a study on Ch'ü, whom I called a "tender-hearted Communist."
[32] Ting Ling, Ou-hsing san-chi (Random Notes on a Trip to Europe) (Peking, 1951), p. 136.

able each household in the kolkhoz to own a milch cow." This promise has long since been redeemed, too. Today every collective farmer can feed his children and his family with milk fresh from the cow.[33]

Li Po-ning, who must have been familiar with such reports as are cited above, when he visited the Soviet Union in 1952 assured his reader nevertheless that the reality was even better than he had expected:

> Before we came to the Soviet Union, we had imagined the happiness of the Soviet peasants. But the reality turns out to be even richer, even more beautiful. . . . If we Chinese peasants want to establish such an earthly paradise, we can only follow the path of the Soviet peasants. . . . We have reason to believe that in the not distant future, our rural village will become like this paradise, too! [34]

After Khrushchev's admission of Stalin's tyrannical rule and the failures in the Soviet economy, especially in agriculture, one wonders how the Chinese Communist travelers could find a "paradise" in Russia in those days. Either they were dishonest in their reports or they were overpowered by an image which blinded them to the reality. This image of Russia is important, because, as the above quotation shows, it supposedly serves as a guide to the Chinese peasants on "their road to paradise." The attitude of identifying Russia's present with China's future was a common one. "What the kolkhoz is today," said Chou Li-po, "will our vast rural areas be tomorrow." [35] "What Moscow is today, will be our Peking tomorrow." [36] And the

poet, Hsi Chien, was ecstatic over what he discovered in a kolkhoz in 1951:

> I don't know what to say; but I feel happy.
> These are the things that peasants for ages have desired.
> But this is not a miracle. Right here Is the Tomorrow of our own peasants.[37]

So long as "Russia of today" could be grasped ·in a simple, bright, heavenly image, the Chinese people under the influence of Communist propaganda would find it less difficult to envision their own future. What Khrushchev, the "revisionist," did was to revise that image. Khrushchev, of course, has offered a substitute image, an image not so bright and bold, which, somehow or other, Mao has refused to accept.

THE PROBLEM OF UNDERSTANDING

Next to Communist ideology, Russian literature exerts a great influence in forming a favorable attitude toward Russia. But interpretation of Russian literature is left largely in the hands of ideologists. Lu Hsün's remark in 1932 illustrates eminently how literary appreciation in China, which barely escapes a nationalist bias, is caught again in the Marxist straight jacket.

> For from it [Russian literature] we can see the kindly soul of the oppressed, their sufferings and struggles. Hope blazed up in our hearts when we read the works of the forties and sorrow flooded over our souls when we read those of the sixties. Of course we knew that czarist Russia was invading China, but that literature taught us the important lesson that there are two sorts of men in the world: the exploiters and the exploited.[38]

[33] Chou, op. cit. (note 8), p. 26.

[34] Li Po-ning, Sui chung-kuo-nung-min-tai-piao-t'uan fu-su ts'an-kuan chi (Report on a Tour in the Soviet Union with the Chinese Peasants' Delegation) (Peking, 1953), p. 41.

[35] Chou, op. cit., p. 29.

[36] Ibid., p. 85.

[37] Feng Hsueh-feng and Others, Wo-men fang-wen-liao mo-ssu-k'o (We Visited Moscow) (Peking, 1952), p. 275.

[38] "China's Debt to Russian Literature." Lu Hsün, Ch'üan-chi (Complete Works) (Peking, 1957), Vol. 4, p. 351; Selected Works of Lu Hsün (English language; Peking, 1959), Vol. 3, p. 181.

Obviously the "lesson" was one derived from Communist ideology rather than from Russian literature of the nineteenth century, the meaning of which is too rich to be compressed into a formula.

Ting Ling shows a better appreciation of Russian literature. In spite of her gibberish about "paradise," her mind is not all coarse, as the following quotation will show. Her mistake was that she misplaced her hope.

Russian literature is particularly our favorite. In it do we regularly make discoveries about our own problems, our fate and our people. We love those Cossacks, Belorussians, Ukrainians, and Tartars; we love those guerrilla fighters with bushy beard, those freckled youth, and girls with plaited hair; those old men, cobblers, and coach-drivers. We have feelings about the little huts in the village, the birch woods, the blizzards, and the fine, sunny days.

We can feel, too, the emotions that are hidden inside the woods, by the fireside, around the samovar, or covered under a shawl . . .[39]

One thing that the Chinese have yet to understand is the Russian emotions that are "hidden inside the woods, by the fireside, around the samovar, or covered under a shawl." For Russian emotions, deep and hidden, have no place either for the Chinese "rightists" or the Chinese "leftists" who tend to regard Russia with extreme prejudice. Only an independent soul, like Ting Ling's, can feel that the Russians are not merely "builders of a paradise" or devils incarnate but that they have emotions, too. Since Ting Ling has been made silent in Mainland China, the voice such as she made is ever more rarely heard from the Chinese nowadays.

[39] Ting Ling, *Ou-hsing san-chi,* p. 72.

Sino-Soviet Relations—The Question of Authority

By Benjamin Schwartz

ABSTRACT: Sino-Soviet relations are enormously complex. Many explanations have been attempted—in terms of "hard" factors of national interest as well as in terms of "deep" anthropological, sociological, historical, and economic theories. Regardless of the part these explanations play in appreciating Sino-Soviet relations, no real understanding is possible without reference to Marxism-Leninism. Although much of ideology is now verbal ballast, there still remains a point at which ideology becomes directly related to power—becomes in itself a factor of power. This is in the myth of the Communist party, the assumptions in terms of which the authority of the organization is legitimized. Essentially, the myth involves the ascription to the Communist party—conceived as the total world Communist movement—of all the transcendental and messianic qualities attributed by conventional Marxism to the world proletariat. The infallibility and monolithic unity presupposed in the myth can be maintained only so long as the party speaks with one voice, so long as there is an unquestioned ultimate instance of authority. Both the Chinese and the Soviets have claimed for themselves the full authority conferred by the myth of the Communist party. The re-establishment of precarious solidarity on the basis of some kind of Communist parliamentarianism is not impossible, although it would have to be achieved at the expense of the myth by recognizing that the world proletariat can speak with many voices on the same issue. In the meantime, the "toughness" of China and the "moderation" of the Soviet Union, both subject to change, are less fundamental to the crisis in the Communist world than the question of whether the myth of the Communist party is any longer viable.—Ed.

Benjamin Schwartz, Ph.D., Cambridge, Massachusetts, is Professor of History and Government at Harvard University and a member of the Executive Committee of the East Asian Research Center there. He is coauthor, with Brandt and Fairbank, of A Documentary History of Chinese Communism (1952). He is author of Chinese Communism and Rise of Mao and of other books and articles.

ON the face of it, there seems little cause for wonder that two contiguous super nation-states should develop conflicts of interest. Those worldly philosophers who have always explained Sino-Soviet relations in terms of "hard" factors of national interest are finding little difficulty in enumerating the obvious divergencies of national interest which account for the current rift. It is, of course, true that many of the same worldly philosophers found little difficulty in the past in enumerating the "hard" factors which bound the Soviet Union and Communist China together in seemingly monolithic unity —for example, the common interest in ousting the United States from East Asia; the long common frontier, which has now become a point of conflict; the economic dependence of China on the Soviet Union; and so on.

Now it would, of course, be nonsense to deny that the Soviet Union and Communist China are nation-states in the broadest sense, each with a strong sense of self-identity, or that they are states which think in terms of national interest. One can hardly deny the presence of nationalism in both states. The nationalism of the Communist Chinese leadership is indeed virulent in intensity and its beginning can already be clearly discerned in the Yenan period. I would submit that the Mao Tse-tung of the early 1940's no longer views Chinese nationalism "from the outside" simply as a Leninist manipulator but from the inside as a Chinese nationalist. Indeed, viewed in secular terms, the general evolution of communism may perhaps be described in terms of the gradual victory of the nation-state over Marxism-Leninism. The time may indeed come when the relations between the Soviet Union and Communist China may be adequately described wholly in terms of a national-interest calculus. I would simply urge that the time is not yet and that one should not describe the present in terms of plausible extrapolations of the future. It is not true as of the present that the syndrome of elements which we call communism is *nothing but* the myth of Soviet nationalism or the myth of Chinese nationalism. To the extent that the two states have been bound together, the intensity of their bond had something to do with communism. To the extent that they are drifting apart, the nature of the tension between them can not be understood apart from communism. As a matter of fact, there is ample reason to believe that, at least on the Chinese side, the interest in Communist solidarity has, in the past, been sufficiently powerful to inhibit the assertion of national interests. The nationalist "irredentism" of the Chinese Communists has, in general, been maximalist in nature, yet the regime has, till now, sedulously refrained from reasserting the Chinese claim to Outer Mongolia. In the years immediately after 1949, it accepted without murmur, if not without chagrin, the Soviet special privileges in Manchuria, the Soviet rape of Manchurian industry, and the joint commercial enterprises. Recently, as we know, it has finally been openly hinted that China is no more reconciled to its present "imperialistically" imposed borders with the Soviet Union than it is to the Macmahon line. As the tension between the Soviet Union and Communist China becomes more exacerbated, the inhibitions on the assertion of the regime's conception of its nationalist interest become constantly more enfeebled. All the latent sources of conflict of national interest have, however, been present from the outset. I would, therefore, doubt whether they alone suffice to explain the contents of the pronunciamentos and fulminations which have been passing back and forth between Peking and Moscow.

If the calculators of national interests

find nothing unusual in recent Sino-Soviet relations, there are, on the other hand, those who will settle for nothing less than the "profoundest" explanations of the current Sino-Soviet rift. There is already available a cluster of theories—anthropological, sociological, historical, and economic (economic-development theory)—designed to account particularly for the most recent developments in Sino-Soviet relations.

There are some who feel that the current relations between the Soviet Union and China can be understood only in terms of deep cultural differences which have their roots in the distant past. Now, while wholeheartedly accepting the view that Chinese and Russian cultures are profoundly different from each other—although there are, as we know, sociocultural theories, such as the theory of oriental despotism, which stress their fundamental similarity—and while granting that these differences may have a decisive effect on the future development of both societies, I see no need to invoke these differences in order to explain all aspects of Sino-Soviet relations during the last few years. There is much in the relations of political bodies which may be explained in terms of situational and general human factors—which would, in this case, include the conscious ideas of the protagonists—even where such political bodies are associated with different cultures. The effort to explain China's present international policies and posture in terms of Chinese culture may lead to a stress on precisely those strains in the culture which presumably favored the current development. If there were counter tendencies within this millennial culture, these are not likely to be mentioned. The net result may be not an illumination of the present but a simplification of China's complex and turbulent past.

The problem of the past may itself be divided into two parts, at least as far as the Chinese are concerned. There is the past of the last century, which is by no means coterminous with "Chinese tradition." There can be no doubt whatever that the Chinese Communist movement has been profoundly shaped by the conditions which emerged in China during this period. The extreme nationalism of the Chinese Communists undoubtedly reflects the humiliations of the Chinese state during this period. The strategy developed by Mao Tse-tung cannot be understood apart from the phenomenon of regional militarism which dominates the whole period since 1911. There are many features of the historic situation in China before 1949 which facilitated the creation by the Chinese Communists of their own genuinely independent organization. This is, of course, a fact most immediately relevant to Sino-Soviet relations. Finally, there are many other features of the Chinese scene during the twentieth century which sharply differentiate China from Russia and which have continued to condition the responses of the Chinese leadership. Chinese industrial development was far behind that of Russia in 1917. China is an agrarian society in a much more overwhelming sense than was Russia, and China has had to confront a population problem of fearsome proportions. While all these are aspects of the situation differentiating China from Russia, they are by no means peculiar to "Chinese culture" and are general conditions shared with many "nondeveloped" agrarian societies.

When we turn to that past which can be described without reservation in terms of Chinese culture or Chinese tradition, it is probably quite true that this millennial culture will continue to shape the internal development of China and that many of its aspects may, in the long run, prove more durable than many aspects of Marxism-Leninism. It still profoundly influences the habits of thought and behavior of the Chinese Communist leadership, Mao Tse-tung in particular. The fact that China was, in the past, the center of a unique civilization may lend a certain intensity to its present nationalism not readily found elsewhere. The universalism of Confucianism may have created a disposition favorable to the universalistic claims of Marxism-Leninism. Yet, in the immediate scene, the fact that the positive content of Marxism-Leninism is in many ways entirely different from the positive content of Confucianism may be even more important than their common universalism. In dealing concretely with Sino-Soviet relations, I would urge that there is much that can still be explained in terms of the logic of power relations and with reference to the specificities of the uses of Marxist-Leninist ideology without invoking the whole of Chinese and Russian culture, even though these may be assumed to be pervasively present in both cases.

Another quite different type of "deep" explanation very much favored in the United States is that which explains Sino-Soviet differences in terms of stages of economic development. It is interesting that the Soviet documents have themselves begun to play with this theory. In the letter of the Communist party of the Soviet Union to the Chinese Communist party published in *Pravda* on April 3rd, it is stated that "differing attitudes may arise on issues relating to domestic development and the international Communist movement and on forms and methods of our cooperation. This is possible for the countries in the world socialist system find themselves at different stages in the building of the new society." Peking is, however, not likely to accept this explanation of its own position. It can, after all, point out that the Soviet Un-

ion has in its own development emphasized the "advantages of backwardness" and the notion that the last shall be first. In the West, the notion that Chinese "toughness" is a function of the fact that it is now in the "Stalinist stage of its industrialization process" while Soviet "moderation" is a result of its higher development wins ready assent among that vast host committed to what might be called the ideology of industrialism. Whether the whole conflict between the Soviet Union and China can be understood entirely in terms of the present issue of "hardness" and "moderation" is a question I should like to consider below. Whether, in fact, we really know anything about the supposed "functional" relation between stages of economic development and hardness or moderation of policy is an even more serious question. Soviet policy during the height of Stalinist development in the Soviet Union was isolationist and cautious. While Chinese policy has been consistent vis-à-vis the United States—as has been American policy vis-à-vis Communist China—its policy on other fronts has fluctuated within the limits set by communism. There is no reason to believe that Communist China was in a less "Stalinist" phase of its development when it proclaimed the Bandung doctrine in its relations to the nonaligned world than it is now when it is committed to quite another approach. The economic power of the Soviet Union and the economic weakness of China undoubtedly condition the responses of the two leaderships in some fashion but do not necessarily dictate the particular policies adopted.

THE MYTH OF THE COMMUNIST PARTY

Many of the factors mentioned as well as those unmentioned undoubtedly enter in some way into the enormously complex skein of Sino-Soviet relations. I would nevertheless urge that one can still not understand these relations without reference to the realm known as Marxism-Leninism. It is not a question of seeking the center of gravity in "ideology" as such, for much of the sum total of ideology is by now dead letter and verbal ballast. There is, however, one point at which ideology still becomes directly related to power—becomes in itself a factor of power—that is, in the myth of the Communist party. By the myth of the Communist party, I refer not to the bare doctrine of organization but to the assumptions in terms of which the authority of the organization is legitimized. It is this myth, it seems to me, which remains at present the living heart of Marxism-Leninism. Whether the myth is genuinely believed or whether those whose power is based on it simply believe that its preservation is vital to the survival of their authority makes little difference in terms of practical consequence. The fact remains that the leaders of the Communist party of the Soviet Union and of the Chinese Communist party are not simply interested in those aspects of power involved with "national interests." They are perhaps even more immediately interested in their claims to total authority within the societies which they control. Both are still ardently interested in extending their authority over areas of the world where their national interests in the tangible sense are not immediately involved. Finally, both attempt to assert their authority over Communist parties both within and outside the bloc. To the extent that this authority is not based on the opportunity to exercise direct coercion, it must rest on the myth of the Communist party. Essentially, the myth involves the ascription to the Communist party—conceived of as the total world Communist movement—of all these transcendental and messianic qualities attributed by conventional Marxism to the world proletariat. The proletariat is an international class and its mission is a universal world historic mission. Only the proletariat can achieve socialism and communism. The proletariat is the first class in human history destined to confront the Truth about man and the world without beclouding delusions. "The proletariat cannot abolish itself without the realization of philosophy." Since the Truth is one, it follows that the proletariat is held together by an undivided general will. It is a class held together in iron unity by a kind of pre-established harmony. To these notions, the myth of the Communist party adds the further notion that all of the attributes of the proletariat become incarnate in the Communist party or, rather, in the present leader or leadership of the Communist party, for the fact is that, in tracing the origins of this development, one must begin not with the Communist party but with the person of Lenin. What we have at the outset is Lenin's own burning conviction that he and only he understands the general will of the Russian proletariat. The emergence of the Communist party may be considered a result of the groping effort to embody this personal charisma within an institution or "church."

It must also be added that Lenin—and the Communist party after him—make a kind of truth claim for the proletariat which goes beyond the truth claim of earlier Marxism which stresses the grasp of certain large fundamental truths about the nature of man and the world. In fact, Lenin negates the assumption that the unfolding flux of political events can be simply deduced from the larger framework of Marxist truth. He negates the view that the road ahead is clearly discernible. On the contrary, reality is rich in unforeseen twists and turns, and only the proletariat—or rather its vanguard—can know how to apply the larger universal truths to unforeseen emergent situations. In the words of Stalin, theory provided "the right orientation in any situation" and makes it possible "to understand the inner connection of current events and to foresee their future course." The latter remark would seem to imply that theory applied to action or "party line" projects the future as well as describes the present. Thus, Lenin's "Democratic Dictatorship of the Workers and Peasants" was a theory designed to project the future as well as to describe the present. Yet, when the same Lenin boldly upset his own projection in 1917 on the ground that "life's green tree" had given rise to a new and unanticipated situation, he presumably lost none of his proletarian infallibility, for the fountainhead of the truth was to be sought not so much in the previous theory as in Lenin himself or in the party leadership which succeeded him. The Communist party, thus, has the unique power to proclaim absolute truths concerning the unfolding flux of world events. The truths themselves may change with every shift in circumstance, but their validity is beyond question so long as they are promulgated by the vanguard of the proletariat.

Not only may the truth shift in time, it may also vary in space. It was, of course, Lenin himself who proclaimed the notion of "many paths to socialism," contrary to certain stereotypes. Stalin also paid due respect to this doctrine. It was, indeed, his claim that he had himself discovered the peculiarities and particularities of the Chinese revolution and prescribed the strategy appropriate to that revolution. After World War II, the notion of "people's democracy" was credited to Stalin as an alternate path to socialism appropriate to Eastern Europe. It is true that running counter to this tendency to acknowledge variant paths to social-

ism one finds a strong countertendency to stress the universal relevance of one's own model. After the Tito crisis, the slogan of variant paths to socialism swiftly gave way to the slogan that the model of people's democracy was, in essence, the same as the model of the Soviet Union. The Chinese Communists who have constantly stressed the particularity of their path to socialism incessantly stress the universal applicability of their own model to Asian, African, and Latin-American conditions. However, whether the stress is on variation or on the universal model, the crux of the matter is that it is the exclusive prerogative of the leadership of the world Communist movement to decide these matters. It is not a question of whether variant paths to socialism are possible. It is a question of who promulgates and sanctions these paths. Furthermore, the authority to apply doctrine infallibly in time and space also involves the most awesome power of all —the power to decide which of the accepted "changeless and universal truths of Marxism-Leninism" may be rendered relative or superannuated by a "creative" application of doctrine.

The history of communism has often been compared to the history of the church. Such comparisons may be illuminating so long as one bears in mind the differences in the specific doctrine of given churches. No church which has ever existed has enjoyed the "truth-making" powers of the Communist party. Not only does it promulgate absolute truths concerning the flow of contingent events. It also possesses the power to change apparently unchanging and universal dogmas at will. Looking back from Marx to Hegel, one may say that the party itself embodies the *Weltgeist* as it manifests itself in the course of human history.

The grounds on which the Communist party has claimed proletarian authority have, of course, changed and grown more attenuated over time. Contrary to frequent assertions, Lenin was, on the whole, vitally interested in maintaining a tangible connection with the industrial proletariat. Even today, where the party actually enjoys an industrial proletarian base, as in France and Italy, there is a tendency in the Soviet Union to make much of this fact. It was, however, the Chinese experience, with its absolute divorce of the party from any tangible connection with the industrial proletariat, which led to the Chinese doctrine that the Communist party in itself embodies what might be called the spiritual essence of the proletariat—an essence no longer dependent in any way on the social composition of the party or on any connection with the class. Where the Communist party of the Soviet Union has found it to its advantage, it has also occasionally appropriated this doctrine to its own uses. Whatever the grounds on which this authority is claimed, however, both the Chinese and Russian parties still cling convulsively to the attributes of authority which they derive from the myth of the Communist party. The Chinese party has, under the leadership of Mao, tended to combine this myth with formulas which allow a maximum appeal to populist-nationalist sentiment. Mao Tse-tung may incarnate "proletarian internationalism," but he is also the incarnation of the will of the Chinese people, and, in the image which it projects to the "third world," the Chinese Communist party has in fact tended to stress the high degree of tolerance allowed by "the teachings of Mao Tse-tung" to populist-nationalist sentiment. Nevertheless, the Chinese Communist party has shown no inclination whatever to relinquish the type of transcendental authority which it derives from the myth of the Communist party.

Internal contradiction

If the myth of the Communist party remains the vital core of communism, it is a myth which—to borrow a phrase from the Communists—bears an internal contradiction at its very heart. The infallibility and monolithic unity presupposed in the myth can be maintained only so long as the party speaks with one voice, so long as there is an unquestioned ultimate instance of authority. When the Communist International was formed, Lenin did not plan in any premeditated fashion to impose the authority of the Russian party on the world movement. Yet, his own conviction that there was only one correct proletarian line for, let us say, the German and Italian proletariat, the assurance with which he lectured the Germans on their infantilism and the Italians on their manifold errors, inexorably extended to the world proletariat the type of authority which Lenin had already come to claim for himself vis-à-vis the Russian proletariat. Omniscience was implicit in his whole outlook, and, here again, the institution becomes an extension of the man. In fact, Lenin was able, up to a point, to maintain the unquestioned authority of the Communist party of the Soviet Union within the international Communist world by the sheer power of his spiritual influence. Stalin, who, of course, lacked this charisma, also conspicuously lacked the faith in intangible methods of maintaining authority. The infallible and unquestioned authority of the center was to be maintained where possible by direct administrative and coercive methods. Stalin was probably correct in his assumption that the kind of authority claimed by Moscow could be maintained only by such methods.

It is interesting to note in this connection the dilemmas of Trotsky and other oppositionists during the twenties.

Trotsky was fervently convinced of his own rightness but fervently committed to the party myth. The center of authority in the party had, however, been captured by Stalin, and the tortured question arose as to how one could be right *against the party?* This dilemma was finally resolved by the establishment of the Fourth International, which was, however, unable to challenge Stalin's possession of Leninist authority. Authority flourishes best where it is nourished by power.

Within this context, the assumption by Mao Tse-tung in the early forties of the authority to apply the "universal truths of Marxism-Leninism" to the particular situation of China marks a most important point in the church history of communism. Behind it lie such factors as Mao's achievement of effective control of the Chinese Communist party, the clear emergence of Chinese nationalism within the Chinese Communist movement, and Mao's own *hubris* as the great leader based, no doubt, on the genuine belief that he understood matters in China better than the men in the Kremlin. While the factor of Chinese nationalism is undoubtedly of primary importance, it must nevertheless be noted that Mao's gesture simultaneously—and paradoxically—involved a reaffirmation of the myth of the Communist party. Precisely because Mao was now arrogating to himself a portion of the authority sanctioned by the myth of the Communist party, it was more necessary than ever to reaffirm the bases of this authority. His famous pronouncements—and those of his co-theorist Liu Shao-ch'i—on "thought remolding" do, in fact, forcefully restate the whole myth in Chinese terms.

Mao had, to be sure, claimed only a portion of the World Communist Movement's authority—that is, the authority to apply the universal truths of Marxism-Leninism to China's situation. There

was no challenge to Stalin's ultimate authority in the world Communist movement at large, and presumably Mao's "creative extension" of Marxism-Leninism-Stalinism was in complete harmony with what had gone before. There is little reason to believe, however, that Stalin ever accepted his claim, and all Soviet accounts of the Chinese Communist victory until Stalin's death treat that victory as the result of Mao's successful implementation of Stalin's theories on the nature of the Chinese revolution. Nevertheless, Stalin's unfortunate experience in Yugoslavia may have led to a certain caution in dealing with the Chinese even though both the Yugoslav and Chinese cases actually lent weight to his view that the authority of Moscow was safe only where local parties were directly and tangibly controlled from the center. Certainly, his behavior in Eastern Europe, where he did enjoy tangible control, gives ample evidence that he had not changed his basic approach where he felt that he could safely apply it.

The era of Khrushchev and of the Twentieth Party Congress of the Communist party of the Soviet Union undoubtedly mark a new turning point in the attitude toward the exercise of authority. Just as Khrushchev seems to have truly believed that the fundamental authority of the party could be maintained within the Soviet Union with a reduction of terror, he seems also to have been optimistic about the possibility of maintaining Moscow's authority within the bloc with a minimum of coercive control. After all, Communist parties shared certain fundamental universal doctrines. The reiteration at the Twentieth Congress of the doctrine of varied paths to socialism by no means implied a renunciation of Moscow's authority in sanctioning such paths. Yet the paths which had been independently pursued by China and Yugoslavia—

after 1948—were given a kind of limited ex post facto ratification, probably in the hope that all further elaborations of paths to socialism would be made with due regard for Moscow's authority.

The Chinese, on their side, welcomed the loosening of Moscow's authority, whatever their misgivings regarding the secret speech on Stalin. Like Khrushchev, they probably genuinely believed that the consensus required by the party myth could be maintained even with some dispersion of party authority. The ideological autonomy of the Chinese Communist movement was now openly proclaimed, and, in fact, in 1956–1957 the Chinese proceeded to elaborate a new "creative extension" of Marxism-Leninism in the so-called Hundred Flowers movement. There is no evidence that this movement was ratified by Moscow. On the contrary, whatever meager evidence we have would indicate as decided a lack of enthusiasm about such notions as "non-antagonistic contradictions among social classes" within Socialist society as was later to be manifested toward the whole commune experiment. On the other hand, the East European "liberals" drew considerable aid and comfort from the Hundred Flowers slogan. At the present time, when there is a widespread supposition that Sino-Soviet differences hinge solely on the question of Chinese "hardness" and Soviet "moderation," it is well to remind ourselves that, as recently as 1956–1957, the Chinese were, in Eastern Europe, the symbol of a flexible "creative" approach while Khrushchev was the defender of orthodoxy. If Khrushchev's experience in Eastern Europe during the latter months of 1956 brought him sharp disappointments, his experience with China probably convinced him that China remained a separate, incalculable entity not amenable to Soviet authority either in its domestic or foreign policies.

AUTHORITY

I shall not enter here into a detailed discussion of the substantive issues which have emerged between the Soviet Union and China since 1957. The issues of the "communes," of coexistence, and of policy vis-à-vis the nonaligned world have been quite adequately covered elsewhere—for example, in Mr. Zagoria's book *The Sino-Soviet Conflict*. I shall, rather, focus briefly on the question of authority which is deeply involved with and yet may override the substantive issues. While the substantive issues—particularly the differing postures on the question of coexistence—are real enough, shifts of position on both sides can by no means be precluded, and it is precisely here that overly "profound" explanations of the current substantive issues in terms of culture, history, and sociology may lead us to attribute a fixity to these positions which may not be warranted. There have, in fact, been actual marked oscillations in both the Chinese and Soviet lines toward the nonaligned world, which has so far failed, on the whole, to respond to the expectations of either. The Chinese have not found the emergence of broad revolutionary united fronts under Communist party leadership. In the absence of the desired model, they have, on the one hand, enthusiastically supported revolution everywhere, Communist-led or otherwise, and, on the other, maintained good relations with established "bourgeois" (in their sense) regimes where it has suited their purpose. The Soviets have so far had reason to be disappointed in their expectations that "national democracy" would necessarily provide favorable "objective conditions" for the activities of Communist parties. On the one hand, they have continued to support these regimes. On the other, they have talked more and more insistently about the necessity of supporting and fostering independent Communist parties in these areas.

Cutting through all substantive issues, the crisis of authority has deepened progressively over time. In November 1957, on the occasion of Mao's visit to Moscow, we seem to have a paradoxical situation in which Mao Tse-tung insists on Moscow's central position in the bloc even while Khrushchev disavows the "need for a center which would guide the Communist movement."[1] The reality is much more complex. The late 1956 events in the bloc as well as domestic events in China had, to be sure, strongly reinforced Mao's own realization that the myth of the Communist party requires an ultimate unchallengeable instance of authority. The very context, however, in which Mao announced the fact that "the socialist camp must have a head" actually gives evidence of new pretensions to authority on the part of the Chinese Communist party. It is in his speech in Moscow that Mao assumes the mantle of co-creator of policy for the Communist bloc as a whole. If Moscow was to remain the symbolic center of authority, Moscow should henceforth make bloc policy with the sanction of Peking. On the other hand, Khrushchev's disavowal of Moscow's pretensions to lead the bloc—disavowals which have been repeated over and over in many varying formulas—represent not a real renunciation of Moscow's central authority but rather a continued effort to avoid the appearance of Stalinist domination. It is not that Moscow insists on its own leadership. It is rather that all Communist parties naturally look to Moscow as the historically destined center of authority. If proletarian unity is to be based on the correct Marxist-Lenin-ist line, who is to determine this line? If all watches are to be synchronized, on whose watch shall they be synchronized? Khrushchev modestly abstains from pressing Moscow's authority. Yet the meetings of the various national party congresses at the end of 1962 "naturally" recognized the Soviet position as the "rallying center of all the forces fighting for national independence, peace, democracy and socialism."[2] It is, of course, true that, with the decline of Moscow's authority, "polycentrism" has indeed become an emerging reality. It would be a grievous mistake to suppose, however, that it is a reality in any way welcomed by the Soviet leadership.

It might be asked again, however—why can a basic unity not be achieved within the Communist world on a kind of "federal" basis? The conference of 1957 did actually establish a kind of minimum Communist credo agreed upon by both the Chinese and the Soviets designed to separate Marxist-Leninist goats from all the sheep outside. As we know, however, this credo, which is still accepted by both sides, has not prevented a further deterioration of authority, because both the Chinese and Soviets have ever since claimed for themselves the full authority conferred by the myth of the Communist party. The Soviets have exercised their prerogative to make a "creative" revision of Leninism. To the Chinese, they have violated one of the "universal truths of Marxism-Leninism." In 1958 the Chinese Communists presumed to create their own definition of the prerequisites of the Communist stage of society—a definition which the Soviets could hardly ignore, for they have been busily engaged in fashioning their own definition, and, on this matter, the Russians are

[1] Interview with Henry Shapiro cited in Donald S. Zagoria, *The Sino-Soviet Conflict, 1956–1961,* (Princeton: Princeton University Press, 1962), p. 147.

[2] "Cementing the Unity of the Communist Movement is our International Duty," *World Marxist Review,* February 1963, p. 4.

the more orthodox. The Chinese have presumed to question .the right of the Soviet Union to eject the Albanian party from the fold and have, since 1960, put forth the striking thesis that "no one has the right to demand that all fraternal parties should accept the theses of any one Party." This plea for absolute equality is, however, simultaneously accompanied by the constant assertion that only the Chinese party has correctly interpreted Marxism-Leninism.

It is still not impossible that the Communist world may again re-establish a kind of precarious solidarity on the basis of some kind of Communist parliamentarianism. Such solidarity can be achieved, however, only at the expense of the myth of the Communist party. It will have to be recognized that the "world proletariat" may speak with many voices on the same issue, that, contrary to Chou En-lai's formula at the Twenty-second Congress, the monolithic unanimity of the "world proletariat" can hardly be achieved by consultation. It will finally have to be recognized that sectors of the proletariat which persist in their "wrong" views can no longer be relegated to the limbo of anti-Leninism. A "world proletariat" which behaves in this way is hardly the "world proletariat" which

figures in the party myth. To achieve solidarity on such a basis may indeed be too high a price to pay, for the myth remains of vital importance to both Chinese and Soviets in terms of the authority of the leadership within their own societies.

Viewing the whole development from the outside, it seems to me that the weakening of this central myth of Marxism-Leninism can only be regarded as a most welcome development. It does not necessarily imply the weakening of either Communist China or the Soviet Union as world states, but it does strengthen the hope of the possible emergence of international relations in which the role of absolutist political ideology may be reduced. Whether the United States government can do very much to effect this development is perhaps doubtful, but it can be alert to the emergence of all sorts of new possibilities. In facing these possibilities, it would again be well to bear in mind that the crisis in the Communist world does not merely revolve around China's "toughness" and the Soviet Union's "moderation," both of which are probably subject to change, but around an issue which is probably even more fundamental—the question of whether the myth of the Communist part is any longer viable.

Economic Policy and Political Power in Communist China

By Franz Schurmann

ABSTRACT: Developmental strategy in Communist China is a complex of ideological, political, economic, and social variables. During the fourteen years of the Chinese People's Republic, the leadership has applied two distinct developmental strategies, one for each of the two five-year plan periods. The first strategy, adapted from the Soviet model, aimed at select development of a modern sector with savings largely generated by the remainder of the economy. The political means chosen were centralized planning and direction with strong emphasis on administrative authority. Hardly were the preconditions for carrying out the first strategy present when the leadership began to modify the system, moving gradually toward a new strategy which achieved full form during the Great Leap Forward. This, in many significant respects, reversed earlier policies. Simultaneous development of the entire economy was stressed. Politically, it involved a far-reaching decentralization of authority, with newly created regional and local power wielded by party committees. Socially, it stressed the functions of the party and the working masses, correspondingly squeezing administrators, technicians, and "intellectuals." Over-all disorganization led early in 1961 to radical modification of Great Leap Forward policy toward national economic "balance." There has been a return to rational bureaucratic modes of operation, but much economic decentralization effected late in 1957 remains. Though the economy appears again to be moving, there are indications of political indecision. No new further strategy of development has been announced.

Franz Schurmann, Ph.D., Berkeley, California, is Associate Professor in the Departments of Sociology and History, University of California, Berkeley. He is author of articles and papers on organizational problems in Communist China. At present, he is finishing an over-all study of organization in Communist China, Ideology and Organization in Communist China. He is also engaged in work on a study of industrial management in Communist China, under a grant from the Committee on the Chinese Economy.

IT was almost immediately upon victory in 1949 that the new government of China launched its long-awaited program of economic development, with a central economic strategy more or less based on the Soviet model. All efforts were to be directed toward building up a nexus of heavy industry in a few favored sectors with savings generated largely by the remainder of the economy. Following its Soviet model, the new regime chose the organizational instrument of central economic planning.[1] But carrying out a system of national planning was not simple. For one thing, over-all national planning could not take place until the country had been politically unified. That did not occur until the summer of 1954 when the "large administrative regions" were finally abolished. For another, it required the standardization of economic institutions and practices. This, too, was not an easy task, judging from the experimental introduction of one or another "system of industrial management" during the early 1950's. Planning, moreover, required a nationwide staff of planners, managers, and technicians. It needed a controlled market situation, a smoothly functioning supply and distribution system, and effective state control over the price structure. Though planning was introduced into Manchuria before 1949 and proclaimed for the country as a whole shortly after victory, the fact that perspective details of the First Five-Year Plan were only published in 1955 indicates that only then was the regime confident enough to announce its long-range economic goals.[2]

[1] "Nationwide" state plan annual control figures were first set in 1951. See Li Fu-ch'un's speech to the Eighth Party Congress, *Jen-min shou-ts'e*, 1957, p. 109.

[2] See Choh-ming Li, *Economic Development of Communist China* (Los Angeles and Berkeley: University of California Press, 1951), pp. 5–7.

PLANNING AND POLICY

Concretely speaking, planning in a Soviet-type economy means that the state assigns enterprises a series of current tasks which are formulated in the framework of larger economic goals. Five-year plans are, in theory, the framework within which annual plans are drawn up, which in turn become the basis for the quarterly and monthly plans of the enterprise. The more the state demands that the economy be responsive to its perspective goals, the greater the need for concentration of command power at the top and for comprehensive control over the economy as a whole. The converse of this proposition—namely, the less responsive the economy is both to perspective and current plans, the less concentrated and comprehensive state power—is not in itself necessarily true. However, in the Chinese case, there are grounds for arguing that the shift in economic strategy from longer- to shorter-range goals has been tied in with corresponding shifts in the nature and distribution of political power. Moreover, shifts in economic strategy and political organization are usually tied in with certain social policies, which amount to the state's giving certain social groupings preferential attention over others. Major policy decisions in Soviet-type countries have tended to be of the across-the-board variety—that is, in one manner or another, all major sectors of the society are affected. This gives the decision complex something in the nature of a *gestalt*, in which ideological, political, economic, and social elements are woven together.

If perspective planning requires concentrated and comprehensive political power, then it is not surprising that the First Five-Year Plan was revealed in detail only in 1955. In 1954 the so-called "independent kingdom" which

Kao Kang had allegedly built up in Manchuria was incorporated into the national body politic. The proclamation of a constitution and the formal establishment of a people's republic symbolized the new unification. But it was also around 1954 that the regime had succeeded in building up an effective urban party apparatus, a functioning administrative system, and in filling managerial positions with trained cadres. It might be said, therefore, that only in 1954 had the organizational prerequisites for centralized planning been achieved.

But, even then, the entire economy of a country as backward and economically disunited as China could not be integrated into a single planning system. Thus, the economy was divided into a planned and nonplanned sector. The former consisted of the country's major goods and service industries and the latter of the remainder of the economy. The planned sector was not only granted investment preference but was actively directed by the state. The nonplanned sector was subject to a web of controls, manipulations through what was called "indirect planning,"[3] largely for the purpose of maximizing savings in the interest of the preferred sector. All major economic enterprises came under direct central control, bypassing local authorities. Minor state-owned enterprises were put under regional jurisdiction. Private industry was tolerated for a while but subjected to heavy taxation. The handicraft industry was gradually co-operativized.

The adoption of a Soviet-type economic strategy had its parallels in the regime's political and social policies. Liberation brought about an abrupt change in party organizational policy from one of large-scale recruitment of peasant cadres to one of building up an urban party apparatus based on working-class recruits. More important than simple quantitative recruitment was the improvement in the party's organizational effectiveness. Despite the continuing commitment to a mass-line policy, the regime, during the early 1950's, made its greatest efforts in building up organization at the leadership or "top" level. A new bureaucracy had to be created and staffed with trusted administrators. Revolution brought about the loss of a sizable group of technical and administrative talent which had to be replaced. Thus, it is not surprising that, during this period, the party became top-heavy with cadres nor that party organization was unevenly distributed throughout the country, with its greatest strength and effectiveness in the major cities.[4]

This was, for the most part, a good period for managers. Whatever their doubts as to the loyalty of the remaining managers and technicians, desperate need for their talents forced the regime to keep them on the job wherever possible. Gradually, the regime, again following the Soviet example, increased the scope of managerial authority in the form of the so-called "one-man management system"—the counterpart of the Soviet *edinonachalie*—a policy which gave managers quasi-autocratic powers over industrial operations while protecting them from party interference.[5]

[4] See *Jen-min jih-pao*, February 28, 1956.

[5] Note, for example, the following comment made in favor of the one-man management system: "At the present time, the major problem regarding production administration in many state-owned textile factories is that of the Party committee's monopolization of leadership . . . All sorts of facts prove that the present system of factory manager responsibility under the collective leadership of the Party and the small shop system are no longer suitable for the further development of production. . . ." Tientsin *Ta Kung Pao*, September 17, 1954.

[3] See Li Fu-ch'un's speech to the Eighth Congress, *loc. cit.*

One of the consequences of the admitted need for technical and managerial talent was the filling up of administrative and staff offices. Preliberation China, like other underdeveloped countries, was usually top-heavy on the administrative side—a pattern which persisted well into the 1950's.[6] Management-level personnel was largely drawn from the ranks of the country's "intellectuals"—that is, graduates of higher schools. Despite attempts to create a peasant-workers intelligentsia, most of the country's technicians still appear to consider themselves as members of the "intellectual" class.[7] Skilled workers were also favored during this period. Large numbers of skilled workers were promoted to line leadership positions, sometimes even to posts of factory manager.[8] Skill was rewarded by a complex wage and salary system which allowed for broad gaps between trained

[6] The growth of the "functionary" class can be seen in the following figure for enterprises in the industrial city of Penhsi:

Year	1952	1953	1954	1955	1956
Percentage of workers	71.9	69.5	68.7	68.3	72.3
Percentage of "functionaries"	10.9	11.8	12.4	13.3	10.9
Nonindustrial employees	4.8	7.2	9.1	7.9	8.4
Total	87.6	88.5	90.2	89.5	91.6

Target ratios for "functionaries" and workers were supposed to be 15:100, but actual ratios for the years 1952–1956 were 15.1, 16.9, 18.1, 19.5, 15.0. The reason for the drop in 1956 was the beginning of a campaign to "simplify administrative structures" which ultimately led to the *hsiafang* movement of 1957. See *T'ung-chi kung-tso*, Vol. 7 (1957), p. 30.

[7] On the problem of technicians and intellectuals, see *Red Flag*, No. 8–9 (1962), pp. 42–45.

[8] Large numbers of articles on "the promotion of workers" appeared during the early 1950's. See for example: Shanghai *Chieh-fang jih-pao*, August 15, 1952; *Chung-kuo Ch'ing-nien-pao*, March 29, 1956; *Nan-fang jih-pao*, May 1, 1955; *Kan-su jih-pao*, April 27, 1956.

and untrained personnel.[9] The growing use of piece-rate systems further acted to favor skill and industriousness. In short, this was a period of building up administrative and technical cadres, and the main organizational principle followed was "vertical rule"—that is, strict line command.

But, although many of the preconditions for national planning were present by 1954, the system did not operate very well. The further an enterprise stood from the ideal—a complex industrial enterprise under direct central control (and thus favored with talent) —the less did factory managers understand the workings of the planning system. Moreover, even with experienced managerial personnel, the complexity of the demands made on them in the form of plan targets made it almost impossible to fulfill one target without endangering the others. Even if targets were held fixed for annual plans, the difficulty of "juggling all the balls" created continuing headaches for managers. The fact was that neither were targets held steady nor did external conditions, such as the supply situation and prices, remain constant enough to allow for operation according to plan. To complicate matters even more, factory managers soon came face to face with another source of demand on them, namely, party policy.

Policy, in its everyday manifestation, expressed some urgent demand on the part of the state: combat waste, keep output norms up or down, as the case was, increase output, emphasize this or that assortment of products, train

[9] Minimum and maximum monthly wages in the Anshan Steel Factory, for example, were 34.5 and 110.40 *yüan*, or a spread of 1:3.2. This is somewhat higher than the rate in the Soviet steel industry (1:3) and contrasts with the 1:2 rate curent in the United States steel industry. See *Chûgoku nenkan*, 1958 (Tokyo, 1958), p. 309; Nicolas Spulber, *The Soviet Economy* (New York, 1962), p. 42.

workers, root out counterrevolutionaries, fight corruption, and so on. What made demands of policy particularly ominous for the manager was that they came from the direction of the party committee. While the one-man management system kept the party out of the field of technical production management, it by no means deprived the party of the right to hold management to account in regard to the carrying out of periodic policy. Thus, while the factory manager struggled to satisfy the multiple demands of higher echelons in the ministries, he constantly saw his efforts at co-ordination threatened by the *ad hoc* demands of the party committee. This situation alone acted to create a juxtaposition between party committee and management, but it was not the only factor. The social composition of party and management organization in the enterprise served to exacerbate the situation, for, while management personnel was still largely "intellectual" in its social composition, the party was for the most part of worker origin.[10]

[10] Since factory managers often were unable to achieve over-all fulfillment of plan targets as well as meet periodic policy demands, they took the safest way out, namely, engaging in "blind production," *i.e.,* simply maximizing their output quotas. To correct this, a new procedure was gradually adopted, that of stressing so-called "central tasks" or "key problems." But the sudden switch in emphasis to "central tasks" invariably meant that other production targets were neglected, endangering over-all plan fulfillment. The gradual transfer of decision-making authority to the factory party committees was justified on the grounds that the party committees were better able to resolve "key problems" than management. By the time of the Great Leap Forward, the principle of "politics takes command" had been firmly implanted, which meant that all major production problems were decided on by the party committee. This ultimately led to widespread instances of total disregard of planning. See Ts'ao Ti-ch'iu, "Raise the Leadership Level of State-owned

The conflict between planning and policy in many ways became one between long- and short-term goals. The manager was held to account for the fulfillment of his annual plan, a task which never went smoothly. Whether for monthly, quarterly, or annual plans, the common practice was to speed up production during the last part of the plan period, for it was only then that management had some idea as to where and how they had failed to meet their targets. Often, while management was frantically trying to achieve "all-rounded fulfillment of plan targets," the party secretary appeared with the announcement of a new policy directive from above. It is not surprising, therefore, that acute frustration arose on all sides, a condition expressed in many articles beginning to appear in 1956 which attack shortcomings in the planning system and in industrial management. The manager soon perceived that the state was primarily interested in two main targets, output and profit.[11] Enterprise profits gradually became the major source of state budgetary receipts, and the state insisted on collecting its profit share periodically,

Factory and Mine Cadres in Administering Enterprises," *Szechwan jih-pao,* January 15, 1955; see also Li Hsüeh-feng's report to the VIII Party Congress, *Jen-min shou-ts'e 1957,* p. 111–113; Li Hsüeh-feng, "Regarding Problems of the Mass Line in Relation to Methods of Enterprise Administration," *Red Flag,* August 1, 1958, pp. 12–15; Yang Ying-chieh, "On Unified Planning and Divided Administration," *Chi-hua ching-chi,* Vol. 11 (November 1958), pp. 3–5.

[11] See "Wherein Lies the Split in Opinions," *T'ung-chi kung-tso,* Vol. 24 (1956), pp. 5–8; Yü I-ch'ien, "Can One Substitute 'Profit' for 'Product Value'?" *T'ung-chi kung-tso,* Vol. 5 (1957), p. 16; Sun Yeh-fang, "Speaking about 'Gross Product Value,'" *T'ung-chi kung-tso,* Vol. 13 (1957), pp. 8–14. See also T'ao Sheng-yü, "A Study of Problems Concerning the Collection of Enterprise Premium Funds in State-owned Enterprises," *Ts'ai-cheng,* Vol. 3 (1956), p. 9.

regardless of the performance of the enterprise.[12] The ministries, on the other hand, always paid particular attention, as in the Soviet Union, to making sure that the enterprises had fulfilled their output quotas. However, inasmuch as output was measured in value rather than physical terms—"gross product value," the Chinese equivalent of the Russian *valovaia produktsiia*—the enterprise manager could perform a variety of gyrations and manipulations to come up with an acceptable set of figures and goods for delivery at the time set.[13] That this led to waste, deterioration of quality, uneconomical use of high-priced raw materials, and so forth is hardly news for anyone who has watched the Soviet scene. But the other targets could not entirely be neglected, for there was always policy waiting to insist that this or that norm also be met. But, with all the difficulties, the Chinese industrial economy grew with great strides during this period. Both gross physical output and enterprise profits expanded greatly. The multiple demands made by the state unnerved factory managers, but they produced solid effort.

DECENTRALIZATION

After the intensive efforts made in 1955 to speed up target fulfillment in industry and to collectivize agriculture, the leadership decided to go slow and

consolidate during the years 1956 and 1957. It was in 1956 that a number of articles began to appear citing defects in the planning system and suggesting improvements. These dissatisfactions with the planning system were voiced by Li Fu-ch'un, Kao Kang's successor as chairman of the State Planning Commission, in his report to the Eighth Party Congress. The substance of Li Fu-ch'un's criticisms are familiar to students of the Soviet planning system, but they in fact foreshadowed radical changes which did not reach full fruition until the decentralization of late 1957. Li noted that planning took two forms in China, one "direct," which was applied to major state-owned sectors, and the other "indirect," which was applied to agriculture, the handicraft industry, and private industries and business. He admitted that "plans were handed down too late, and changed too much." Particularly, he stressed the lack of "knowledge of basic-level conditions." "Too much attention has been given to central state-owned industries, and not enough to local industries, agriculture, commerce, educational-cultural work and other sectors," he added. He called for more emphasis on "over-all balance" in the economy. He then went on to criticize the Soviet system of detailed, centralized planning and indicated that the party would press for less detailed planning and more flexibility at lower levels of the economic system, in particular allowing lower echelons greater flexibility in setting their own targets.[14]

Although the spirit of over-all balance was far different from the policy of high speed which was to launch the Great Leap Forward, the decentralization measures of late 1957 in effect carried out in rather extreme fashion the policies proposed by Li Fu-ch'un.

---

[12] In 1958 profits from state-owned enterprises constituted 60 per cent of state budgetary receipts. See T'ao Sheng-yü, Tan Ya-sheng, "Revised Opinions about the Retained Share System of Enterprise Profits," *Ts'ai-cheng*, Vol. 15 (1959), p. 13. Note also Sun Yeh-fang's ironic comment: "Since profit quotas to be remitted upward are fixed, what is called the profit plan is arbitrarily subtracted by the bank when the time comes, regardless of the financial condition of the enterprise." *Op. cit.*, p .10.

[13] See Sun Yeh-fang, *op. cit.*, pp. 9–10.

[14] See Li Fu-ch'un's speech to the Eighth Party Congress, *Jen-min shou-ts'e 1957*, pp. 108–111.

The dominant slogan which emerged from the Eighth Party Congress was the "mass line," which in time was to take on increasingly concrete meaning. There is a consistent pattern in Li Fu-ch'un's description of the faults of the planning system, which may be summed up as "too much at the top, too little at the bottom." The Soviet system of planning, with its detailed targets and controls, was operable only in the most advanced industries. Central state-owned industry was greatly favored over local industries. There was too much control from the top, too little flexibility at the bottom. The solution, in Li Fu-ch'un's words, was "to carry out divided administration."

The policy of emulating the Soviet model had led to impressive gains but, admittedly, at great cost. Because of preferential investment policies, managers of the larger industries, as has been the case in other Soviet-type economies, made liberal use of high-priced capital goods in order to meet their output targets, or, as the Chinese put it, preferred to produce products "with high material and low labor inputs." [15] High prices for industrial, and especially heavy industrial, products brought about large enterprise profits in the bigger industries, which created another source of "inequity." Inasmuch as the premium system was tied to profit, the bigger and centrally operated enterprises were able to earn far greater premiums than the smaller and regional enterprises. [16] A number of articles appeared in 1956 and 1957 urging a revision of the premium system in order to create greater equity, specifically proposals for tying in at least a portion of the total premium fund with the size of the labor force—thus indirectly getting managers to shift toward a policy of greater labor inputs. [17] One of the chief complaints of the time was that the existing system of industrial management made for capital-intensive types of operations in a country with vast, untapped labor resources. "Vertical rule" created other difficulties. Inasmuch as co-ordination between centrally operated enterprises under different jurisdictions was difficult to achieve, there was little collaboration at the local level to assure optimal utilization of local resources and optimal satisfaction of local needs. This situation was to be rectified by the gradual extension of the principle of "dual rule," whereby local governments acquired greater voice in the operation of industrial enterprises located in the territory they administered.

In the discussions on the function of plan targets which appeared in the press during these years, there was general agreement that something had to be done to rectify the tendency of plant managers to aim simply at the "beating the output" plan with its consequences for waste, declining quality, and the like. A number of proposals were made which suggested that the gross-product-value target be scrapped and that profit be made the main plan target. In effect, the state had been operating for the most part anyway with two major plan targets—output and profit—and the intent of these proposals was that the state

[15] See Sun Yeh-fang, *op. cit.*, p. 9, also Yü I-ch'ien, *op. cit.* The same phenomenon exists in other Soviet-type economies; see János Kornai, *Overcentralization in Economic Administration* (London: Oxford University Press, 1959), p. 32.

[16] See T'ao Sheng-yü, *op. cit.*, pp. 9 ff.; Sun Yeh-fang, *op. cit.*, p. 10.

[17] See T'ao Sheng-yü, *op. cit.;* Yang Pang-ch'un, "Collecting the Enterprise Premium Fund according to the Total Number of Employees," *Ts'ai-cheng*, Vol. 6 (1957), pp. 13–14; Wang Ch'i-hsien, "Discussion of a Number of Problems on the Collecting of Enterprise Premium Funds by State-owned Enterprises," *Ts'ai-cheng*, Vol. 8 (1957), pp. 19, 33.

gradually shift its emphasis from output to profit.

Li Fu-ch'un called for decentralization, but it was not until late in 1957 that the leadership acted in the form of a series of far-reaching decentralization measures. Much had happened between the Eighth Party Congress and the fall of 1957. Within China, the relative stability on the political and social scene—paralleling similar policies in the economy—ended abruptly with the launching of the nationwide antirightist campaign. Outside of China, there were the major changes in Soviet economic administration in the direction of apparent decentralization. In general, it appeared to be a period in which the world balance of power had shifted to the Soviet bloc. There can be little doubt that the changed internal and external situations had much to do with the timing and the degree of the decisions which were taken in the fall of 1957. However, the nature of the changes was already foreshadowed in the new line adopted at the Eighth Party Congress. Furthermore, the changes decided on at this time occurred in the context of a general political and social situation which had been developing even before the Eighth Party Congress. The most significant element in this general situation was the steady growth of a regional and local party apparatus that was increasingly asserting itself at the lower levels of the system.

The decentralization measures were formally put through by the State Council on November 18, 1957, but it is clear that the basic decisions were taken during the long sessions of the third plenum (September 20 to October 9, 1957). The main subjects taken up during these sessions were the antirightist movement, problems of economic administration, agriculture, and wages and welfare. Four draft proposals were prepared—on industrial, commercial, and financial management and on wages and welfare.[18] Just prior to the meetings of the third plenum, the Central Committee had issued a number of directives on agriculture which were essentially conservative in tone. Agriculture had always been an issue of series contention among the leadership, and it seems likely that no hard and fast agreement was reached on any radically new turn in agricultural policy, as is evident in the assertion that the organization of the APC's would "not be altered for ten years."[19] However, there was no doubt in anyone's mind that the greatly expanded efforts of the Second Five-Year Plan would require a considerable increase in agricultural output. This was to be achieved by a massive nationwide program of waterworks and irrigation to be carried out by labor mobilization.[20] The draft proposal on wages and welfare was not promulgated, most likely because any explicitly new policy on wages would only create difficulties in the highly fluid situation arising out of the labor-mobilization policy. Thus it was that only the proposals on industrial, commercial, and financial management were put into effect.[21]

The directive on industrial management announced that the bulk of medium- and small-scale industry hitherto under central operation would be transferred to the provincial authorities. Furthermore, those enterprises remaining under central operation were to become subject to dual leadership— that is, that provincial authorities would have a voice in management. Although the center retained control over the allocation of materials and equipment, the provincial authorities acquired new

[18] *Jen-min shou-ts'e 1958*, p. 182.
[19] *Ibid.*, p. 519.
[20] *Ibid.*, pp. 533–534.
[21] *Ibid.*, pp. 491–492, 551–552, 568.

powers to reallocate materials and equipment within their own provinces, on the assumption that the state plan would not be endangered. Provincial authorities were to get a cut of above-target production and, within limits, could also demand above-target production from enterprises under central operation. A profit-sharing system was introduced which gave the provincial authorities 20 per cent of the gross profits of the newly transferred industries. Provincial authorities received far-reaching powers over personnel in state-owned enterprises; hiring, firing, and transfer of personnel, save for a few top-ranking technicians and administrators, came under provincial control. The existing system of plan targets was to be radically modified. Henceforth, all targets were to be classified as "commanding" or "non-commanding," the former being such targets as had absolutely to be fulfilled. The number of commanding targets was reduced to four: (1) major product volume targets, (2) total number of employees, (3) total wage quotas, and (4) profit. Branches, ministries, and provincial authorities could set their own special plan targets. Provincial authorities got the right to reallocate investment quotas set by the State Council. Henceforth the State Council would only hand down annual plans, leaving it to lower echelons to draw up quarterly and monthly plans. Planning procedures were to be reduced to three steps: handing down of control figures, presentation of draft plan, and setting of final plan from above. Profit-sharing indices for enterprises were to be based on three factors: first, according to the outlays current during the First Five-Year Plan for the so-called "four categories" of expenditures —technical-organizational-operational expeditures, new product test expenditures, welfare expenditures, miscellane-

ous; secondly, according to the size of the premium funds; thirdly, a flat cut of 40 per cent of all above-target profits. No further state appropriations were to be made in the annual budgets for the four categories and the premium funds. Retained profit was to be used for enterprise investment and welfare in that order of priority.

The directive on commercial management decreed that henceforth the state would set only four major targets: purchase targets, sales targets, total number of employees, and profit targets. A 5 per cent flexibility was to be allowed either way in regard to purchase and sales targets. However, targets regarding grain, edible oils, and cotton—all major export items—could not be changed. Control over profits was to be gradually "transferred downward" to the provincial level, but not to the enterprise level, for fear that the latter might meet profit targets through illicit means. A profit-sharing scheme between the center and the provinces was to be adopted along the same lines as for industry, namely, at a ratio of 80 per cent to 20 per cent. The state would continue to maintain strict price controls over agricultural products, as well as industrial items subject to central allocation. But prices of other goods could be set at the provincial level in accordance with central directives. Similarly, sales prices for first-class markets and first-class goods would remain under central control but for second-class markets and goods could be set at the provincial level. Annual price conferences would be held "to fix price levels for the whole year."

The directive on financial decentralization was designed to increase the revenues of provincial administrations. In addition to existing sources of revenue, the provincial authorities now could get a share of enterprise profits and a share of tax revenues which formerly went entirely to the central government. If fixed income was not sufficient to meet outlays, an additional cut of enterprise profits would be made available, and, if necessary, special central appropriations. Provincial authorities could retain budget surpluses and apply them to the following year's budgets.

Somewhat over a year later, the regime completed the picture of financial decentralization by announcing that all allocations of working capital, formerly made directly by the state to industrial enterprises, would be transformed into bank loans drawn on local branches of the People's Bank of China, repayable with interest. The loans would be made in accordance with budgetary appropriations determined by the Ministry of Finance.[22]

Before looking at what lay behind the decentralization, we might examine briefly what were some of the consequences of decentralization. By 1959 enterprise profit accounted for 60 per cent of state budgetary receipts, but the size of the retained profit share of state-owned enterprises far exceeded what had been planned for in the budget. In 1958 the planned retained profit share of enterprises was set at something over one billion *yüan;* by the year's end, the actual amount had risen to close to three billion *yüan.* Most of the retained profit was used for "extra-plan capital construction" and for "employees' welfare," to such an extent that it was "squeezing materials needed by many basic construction projects arranged by the state plan, and affecting the materials supply plan of the state." [23] Yang Ying-chieh, deputy

chairman of the State Planning Commission, already late in 1958 attacked some of the extreme advocates of the Great Leap Forward policy and revealed some of the consequences of these policies:[24]

[There are those who think] that the less the state plan governs, the better it is, that the more flexibility that is given the branches and the regions the better it is, that the state plan need not be unified, that the various levels of the plan framework need not coordinate. . . . They think that inasmuch as one wants to get the best out of each area, one must always think of what is best for each area. All one needs is the convenience of each area, and if it harms overall unity a bit, it does not matter. They think that since you have got to give each area flexibility one can allow several plans to exist at the same time. They call this euphemistically 'encouraging the positivism of each area.' Operation according to this kind of thinking has given rise to much confusion which has seriously impeded the planned and proportionate development of the national economy. Some regions, without the permission of the state or higher echelons, on their own decided on major capital construction programs, and to build these projects, made use of materials destined for central state construction projects, sometimes even arbitrarily seizing materials passing through their territory. Investment in capital construction in some areas greatly exceeded figures allowed by the state or higher echelons; if materials were lacking, recourse was not taken to state allocation plans or to contractation methods, with the serious consequence often that one thing would be substituted for another. In some areas and enterprises, commodity plans were constantly changed,

---

[22] *Jen-min jih-pao,* December 23, 1958; see also *Chung-yang ts'ai-cheng fa-kuei hui-pien,* January-June 1959, pp. 81–95.

[23] See T'ao Sheng-yü and Tan Ya-sheng, *op. cit.* Already before 1958 enterprise premium funds had been largely used for collective welfare purposes. See Ch'en An-

huai, "Setting up a Rational and Positivistic Enterprise Premium Fund System," *Ts'ai-cheng,* Vol. 6 (1957), p. 15. Given the collectivist emphasis of the Great Leap Forward period, such expenditures increased greatly at this time.

[24] Yang Ying-chieh, "On Unified Planning and Divided Administration," *Chi-hua ching-chi,* Vol. 11 (November 1958), pp. 3–4.

plans were vaguely drawn up, and if plans could not be fulfilled, they got angry at higher echelons and so on. The result was that nonproductive construction squeezed productive construction, unessential construction squeezed essential construction. Money and materials were wasted, plan fulfillment was uneven, bringing about artificial tightness in commodities and avoidable confusion. These erroneous opinions were quite current late in 1957 and early in 1958.

The general consequences of the Great Leap Forward are well known by now: overproduction, overinvestment, especially in economically unsound projects, shortages, breakdown and cloggings in the transportation system, financial chaos, serious decline in central budgetary revenues, plus all the moral, political, and social consequences of these conditions. Already by late 1958, the regime was alarmed and tried to achieve some kind of nationwide co-ordination through the policy of "all the country is a single chessboard." However, the new developments which had been unleashed late in 1957 and which rested on the basis of a solid earlier history were not to be reversed with simple means. Only the radical shift in policy which was carried out with the ninth plenum in January 1961 was to usher in a new period of "balance." What, therefore, was the thinking and what were the real conditions which launched such a radical new step?

A basic change in economic strategy took place in China around this time, symbolized in the concept of "economic co-operation regions." Since China was too vast a country to be developed with comprehensive national planning and nationwide exchange of goods and supplies, the regions had to be pushed in semiautarchic directions.[25]

Ideas of decentralization and regional economic co-operation were also current in the Soviet Union since 1957, with the formation of the *sovnarkhozy* and later—in 1961—with the setting up of seventeen major economic regions in the Soviet Union.[26] But, whatever the difficulties which central planning generated in the Soviet Union, they were far more serious in a country like China. Not only did even limited "direct planning" not work effectively, but large areas of the country's economy could not be activated in the interests of maximally rapid development. One difference between the Soviet and the Chinese situations was that decentralization in China aimed not only at improving economic co-ordination by reducing central controls but mainly at creating conditions which would activate and speed up economic development at the most basic levels of the economy: agriculture and medium- and small-scale industry. Rapid development of agriculture and regional industry would create not only imbalance that could not be rectified with the distant and cumbersome machinery of the state but would generate constantly changing demand and supply conditions necessitating great flexibility at the lowest possible levels. Furthermore, rapid economic development would create demands for new products in remote areas which could not be supplied on a national scale. Hence, recourse would have to be taken to finding substitute materials within the frame-

[25] See Liu Tsai-hsing, "On Problems in Establishing Complete Industrial Systems in the Economic Co-operation Regions," *Hsin Chien-she*, Vol. 10 (1958), pp. 45–57; Wang Shou-li, "Consideration of the Principles in Outlining Economic Regions within Provinces," *Ching-chi yen-chiu*, Vol. 1 (1958), pp. 18–21. According to this scheme, the country was to be divided into "seven major economic co-operation regions."

[26] See Alec Nove, "The Industrial Planning System: Reforms in Prospect," *Soviet Studies*, Vol. 14 (July 1962), pp. 1 ff.

work of the local economic co-operation region.

But the adoption of this new economic strategy meant a sharp shift of emphasis from things stressed during the First Five-Year Plan to new things. It meant a shift in relative emphasis from large- to medium- and small-scale industry, of relative emphasis from industry in general to agriculture, of relative emphasis from city to village. The principle of "simultaneous development" meant that the hitherto neglected sectors of the economy would experience the same rapid development as those sectors earlier favored with highest priority. Politically, the new strategy meant a relative shift in emphasis from central to provincial administration, a general displacement of decision-making power from the center to lower echelons. If allocation powers over materials and investment were to be transferred downward, so, in general, did the framework of decision-making powers of lower echelons have to be broadened. But here we come face to face with a crucial political fact. The farther one went down the organizational system, the stronger the power of the local party committees. Until 1955 party power was unevenly distributed throughout the country, still largely concentrated in the major urban and economic areas. But, with the great recruitment drives commencing in 1955, the regional party apparatus began to develop rapidly. However, not only did the party bureaucracy develop but also, most of all, basic-level party formations. The more one went along the spectrum from heavy to light industry, from central to regional government, from management to workers, from top to bottom, the greater the power of the party cadres, and the less that of administrators and technicians. The abandonment of the one-man management system had opened the way for increasing party power in the councils of industrial management. But the event that began to see a new "leap forward" in local party power was the antirightist movement of the summer of 1957. Although highly articulate criticism in the major universities set the spark for the antirightist movement, the brunt of the attack was felt by the technical intelligentsia. Rightist intellectuals were attacked throughout the country, and the farther away from Peking, the more likely it was that these rightists were to be found in technical and administrative positions. The final blow came through the great *hsiafang* campaign launched during the latter part of 1957. Although "administrative simplification" had already begun earlier and had led to numerous layoffs of staff and managerial personnel, now offices were often reduced by more than three-quarters of their employees, many, if not most, of whom were "intellectuals." Factory managers were attacked sharply during the winter, spring, and summer of 1958 for conservatism—that is, unwillingness to push the policies of the Great Leap Forward to their extreme.[27] Managers were sent down to the front lines of production, and workers were encouraged "to participate in management." Management, in fact, became the target of almost anything that went wrong.

But there were other changes, all of which became a part of the new *gestalt*. Policy won out over planning, and policy for all practical purposes was maximization of crude physical output and construction. The attack on management—and bureaucracy in general—was paired with an emphasis on mass work; the mass movement became the symbol of the new production effort. In general, a shift took place from individual to collective incentives, from

[27] See, for example, *Jen-min jih-pao*, January 5, 19, 30, 1958 and June 14, 1958.

individual work to collective work. Premiums, rather sizable during this time with greatly increased enterprise profits, were used for collective welfare. Piece-rate systems gave way once again to time wages.[28] The production team, rather than the individually motivated worker, became the center of the production effort.[29] There was even a change in the image of the ideal worker, from the skilled worker who could carry out his assigned task in a complex division of labor, to the "multifaceted worker" (*tomien-shou*) who worked as a member of a team, doing this today and that tomorrow.[30]

Decentralization meant, in effect, another kind of centralization, but at a lower level of the hierarchy. In the factory, the party committees, with their arms reaching out into every corner of the factory and with their powerful contacts with the authorities beyond the factory, monopolized all policy-making powers in their hands.

Thus, while "technical" decisions were decentralized downward to the production floor, "policy" decisions were rigorously centralized. But leadership power in the hands of the party meant that, within a given region, the possibilities for a high degree of co-ordination existed. The party was territorially organized and crossed all sector and branch lines. Thus, where a manager essentially could deal only with his own ministry, the party cadre had a direct pipeline into every organization within the local area. Consider the banking system, for example. Given the ease with which "short-term loans" were floated to satisfy the rapidly growing capital needs of the new projects that were being launched locally, it is not unlikely that a telephone call from a factory party cadre to his comrade in the local branch bank—which controlled all the financial transactions of the enterprise—resulted in rapid granting of the loan.[31] There are strong indications that the strength of the local party apparatus fortified them against criticisms from the central government for defaulting on this or that plan target, withholding critical materials, failing to adhere to their financial and budgetary plans.

If any one political factor can be cited which gave the regime confidence to attempt the decentralization of 1957, with the grave risks that administrative decentralization has always meant in

---

[28] For a discussion of Communist China's wage and incentive systems, see Charles Hoffman, "The Basis of Communist China's Incentive Police," *Asian Survey,* Vol. 3, No. 5 (May 1963), pp. 245–257.

[29] See, for example, *Jen-min jih-pao,* December 17, 1960.

[30] During the Great Leap Forward, there was a general movement away from a type of work organization in which there was considerable specialization within the production team to one where each production team concentrated on producing one product or one item. This is a type of production organization which the Russians have described as "item specialization" (*podetal'naia spetsializatsiia*), in contrast to technological and product specialization; see S. Kamenitser, V. Kontorovich, G. Pishchulin, *Ekonomika, organizatsiia, i planirovanie promyshlennogo predpriiatiia* (Moscow, 1958), pp. 95–98. The effect for the individual worker was a shift in emphasis from "the master of one technique" to the "multifaceted expert." What this meant for production operations during the Great Leap Forward is described in an article entitled "Which is Better, the Master of One Technique or the Multi-faceted Expert," *Jen-min jih-pao,* November 20, 1961.

[31] The journal *Red Flag,* calling for a reform of the banking system, describes the attitude current during the Great Leap Forward: "Among some comrades the erroneous view has arisen that if operations administration in their own enterprises is a bit poor it does not matter. If capital circulation is a bit sluggish, the banks can make loans. If they cannot pay back in time, or delay a few days, it makes no great difference. In any case the bank will always help out financially, because it cannot afford the enterprise stopping production." *Red Flag,* Vol. 6 (1962), p. 12.

Chinese history, it was the power of the regional and local party apparatus. It was a party apparatus that was young in years, not yet inextricably involved with the local bureaucratic system, anxious for power, and still subject to the discipline of a far from routinized organization.

THE AFTERMATH OF DECENTRALIZATION

By the winter of 1960–1961, the internal situation of China became so serious that the leadership decided to call a halt to the Great Leap Forward. Food was in short supply; industries were seriously short of raw materials; trade with the Soviet Union had fallen off sharply. In one sense, the leadership had already started to modify the extreme effects of the Great Leap Forward not long after its inception, as, for example, in the attempt at national co-ordination in the "all the country is a single chessboard" campaign. The communes had been in a process of modification almost since their beginnings. In the fall of 1960, the leadership decided on a far-reaching alteration of the commune system, making the small production brigade the operative unit of planning, production, and accounting. But it was only at the time of the ninth plenum that the leadership decided to strike at the root of the problem: party direction and control of the economy. The hold of party committees and cadres over economic activity at all levels was not easy to break, and the leadership took recourse to a method used before against other groups: a rectification campaign. But the campaign was carried out "in bits and stages" in order not to disturb the structure of control. Party cadres, particularly in the rural regions, were subjected to barrages of criticism which in many areas left the party in a state of bewilderment. There is reason to believe that a serious demoralization problem developed in party ranks, with ominous implications for the country as a whole—given the fact that earlier policy had aimed at concentrating all leadership and control powers in the hands of the party. The erosion of control reached serious proportions in the spring of 1962 and led to a call for greater party unity and authority. By the time of the tenth plenum in September 1962, the leadership was visibly tightening the reins of control again. Since that time, there has been noticeable a slight swing in the pendulum back to more emphasis on the role of the party, on the importance of the collective-farm economy, and a concomitant de-emphasis of many of the "small freedoms" which cropped up during the *détente* of 1961–1962. Nevertheless, the ninth plenum marks a decisive watershed, in which the Great Leap Forward principle of "politics takes command"—that is, party leadership in all things—was abandoned and decision-making powers were returned to other social groups—namely, the managers in industry and the "old peasants" in agriculture. The recent intensification of party *control* has not meant a return to party *leadership*.

The decisions taken at the ninth plenum had serious consequences for industry. With the new policy of concentrating all resources on agriculture, specifically of moving toward a policy of intensive capital investment in agriculture, investment quotas and output targets of most industrial enterprises were sharply cut. Furthermore, even major industries were called upon to reorient their production to the needs of agriculture and the consumer. Hardest hit were the many medium- and small-scale industries which had sprouted up in great numbers during the Great Leap Forward. These industries, which had been the pride of local party cadres, were often simply closed down and their equipment transferred to larger enterprises. Workers were laid off and sent back to their "home villages" in an attempt to ease the burden of sudden unemployment in the cities.[32] More important was the shift in emphasis from quantity to quality. Industries were ordered to lay off excess workers, to improve productivity, to make more efficient use of capital, and to return to a system of planned, rational production.

One of the most important sociological consequences of the new policy was a renewed tolerance for the "expert." Staff work, disdained during the Great Leap Forward, was once again emphasized, and staff positions were once again filled with technicians—that is, "intellectuals." The emphasis on correct management gave new authority to chief engineers, top-level administrators, planners, accountants. The over-all policy of renewed tolerance toward intellectuals in general,[33] manifest in the new "hundred flowers" atmosphere and in the relatively free writing on a variety of "technical" subjects which has been going on in China since the spring of 1961, was a counterpart of the recognition of the vital role of the technician-administrator in getting the economy back on its feet again.

Following the present party line of "balance," the leadership has taken broad measures to undo the chaos of the Great Leap Forward. The whole financial system has been reformed and tightened up, particularly the loose banking structure which had allowed the freewheeling floating of short-term development loans to local industries. Production management has been improved. Local control over allocation has been reduced. But the question arises: To what extent does all this mean recentralization? There is little doubt that factory managers once again enjoy broad powers to direct production operations in their own industries. However, does this mean that tight ministerial direction has been reimposed? That is not at all clear. One of the themes that crops up again and again in the discussions of the last few years has been the emphasis on the "independent operational authority" of the factory managers. To what extent this "independent" authority is real is difficult to judge. However, there is reason for believing that much of the decentralization which was put through late in 1957 remains in effect today, except that it is no longer the party committee, but the managers, who make the crucial decisions, decisions which are increasingly seen as "technical" and not "political." For one thing, there are no signs that many of the significant decentralization measures have actually been repealed. Thus, the profit-sharing system remains in effect, even though the leadership has tightened up the reins and reduced the size of the retained share of the enterprise.[34] But there also are other objective factors that make the reinstitution of centralized planning—therefore, centralized control—difficult. The main performance target during the First Five-Year Plan period was gross product value, as it has been in the Soviet Union. There is no indication that there has been a return to the gross-product-value target. In fact, all the signs are that the major success indicator of the enterprise in China today is enterprise profit.[35] Most of the economic and ad-

[32] See, for example, Kung-jen jih-pao, May 11, 23, 1962.
[33] See Red Flag, No. 8-9 (1962), pp. 42–45; Kung-jen jih-pao, January 11, 1962.

[34] See Sung Hsin-chung, "Our Country's Enterprise Profit Retained Share System." Peking Ta Kung Pao, May 12, 1961.
[35] That the profit target, rather than output targets, is at present the major success in-

ministrative discussions that have been going on during the last two years deal with improved methods of achieving profit targets: cost reduction, raising labor and capital productivity, improving quality, and so on. Inasmuch as the over-all economic strategy of the present period has been to cut production but improve the quality and effective use of output and, at the same time, generate increasing savings for accumulation purposes, it would not make much sense to return to the old pre-1957 target system.

The state still demands that each enterprise produce certain lines of goods given high priority by state planners. However, for the rest, the factory managers appear to enjoy considerable autonomy in determining their own commodity mixes. For one thing, the re-orientation of industry to agriculture has made flexibility in accepting and delivering orders more necessary than before. There has been a great expansion of the contractation system [36] and greater use made of advertising media in order to connect up supply and demand. Flexibility in determining output volume and mixes of course must imply some freedom in obtaining supplies and equipment. How much of the post-1957 flexibility in the program

of national allocation remains is not certain, but, in the absence of highly detailed planning, one might assume that some flexibility remains at the local level. From the recent literature, it appears that the leadership is emphasizing financial controls over enterprise operations rather than going back to a system of detailed production targets. The reform of the banking system, tight controls clamped down on loans, investment quotas, and the constant stress of the profit target testifies to the importance which the regime attaches to the financial mechanisms at its disposal. The return to material incentives has also meant a switch from collective back to individual rewards, but the size of the premium fund remains a function of the above-target profit earned by the enterprise. In fact, the leadership appears to be striving to create conditions which will motivate management to work for all-round achievement of the profit target and financial-accounting targets in general, such as cost reduction. Another indication of the new powers allowed factory managers is the fact that the policy appears to be to make the awarding of premiums a function of over-all enterprise success, leaving the internal distribution of rewards in the hands of the managers.[37]

The impression one gains is that, despite "creeping recentralization" in some respects, the leadership is retaining the format of decentralization but giving it different content. Significantly, it was the 1957 decentralization which

---

dicator for industrial enterprises in China is apparent from a variety of theoretical and concrete articles that have been appearing over the last two years. See, in particular, Ko Chih-ta and Ho Cheng, "The Meaning of and Paths to Socialist Enterprise Profits," *Ching-chi yen-chiu,* Vol. 10 (1962), pp. 42–47, and, in particular, articles dealing with the premium fund system, *e.g.,* in Peking *Ta Kung Pao,* May 14, 1962, and August 22, 1962. What merits serious comparative study is the similarity in Chinese theory and practice regarding industrial profit as a major success indicator to the Liberman proposals in the Soviet Union. See Alec Nove, "The Liberman Proposals," *Survey,* Vol. 47 (April 1963), pp. 112–118.

[36] See *Jen-min jih-pao,* April 2, 1963.

[37] Arguments are now advanced suggesting that premium distribution within an enterprise be made a function of over-all enterprise success and clearly disassociated from the wage fund. This thus increases the incentive effect of the premium fund vis-à-vis management. See Ch'en P'ei-i, "Discussion of a Number of Concrete Problems Concerning the Premium System," Peking *Ta Kung Pao,* August 22, 1962.

established profit as a major production target for enterprises. However, given the dominant economic strategy of the time, high profits were to be gained by maximization of output and turnover. Because this was the "policy" and because the party committees were in a position to make sure that the policy of "much and fast" was being implemented, greatly increased output coupled with obligatory state purchases assured the enterprise of expanded profits. However, the situation has changed drastically now. Maximization of output is no longer stressed, and factory managers must meet their profit quotas through improved management. However, as long as the leadership does not return to a system of production controls, it is doubtful whether it can reinstitute a planning system even of the sort which existed during the First Five-Year Plan. Perspective planning had already lost much of its importance during the Great Leap Forward, and how important annual plans were, under conditions of extreme decentralization, is doubtful. Financial planning and control are becoming increasingly important, but this in itself does not portend the shrinking of the managers' independent operational authority.

There are sociological parallels to the period of the First Five-Year Plan. The renewed emphasis on skills, talents, on competent administrators and technicians, with greatly decreased party interference in production, is reminiscent of a similar policy during the early 1950's. However, at that time, ministerial centralization—vertical rule—was the dominant organizational theme, the effect of which was to circumscribe the manager's autonomy. That does not appear to be the situation at the present time. The Chinese Communists have always looked with suspicion on the development of a "functionary" class with its identity formed to a large

extent by its "intellectual" status. But, since the spring of 1961, the leadership has again created new conditions for this group to develop. In fact, even the remnant bourgeoisie has been given a new lease on life, and refugee reports indicate that they are enjoying their "new freedom" by more prominent spending and consumption. The return of the intellectuals as a significant social group has its parallel in the reassertion of native peasant leadership in the villages. In some ways, certain features of traditional Chinese social structure are beginning to reappear, except, it might be noted, that the "intellectual" of today is a professional and not an amateur, as was his imperial predecessor. The "generalists" of today are the party cadres.

STRATEGIES OF DEVELOPMENT

During the fourteen-year history of the Chinese People's Republic, the Chinese Communists have applied two distinct strategies of development, each coinciding with a five-year plan. The first was more or less based on the Soviet model, but the second, symbolized by the Great Leap Forward, was a distinctly Chinese approach to the problem of development. In neither case was the strategy adopted pursued to its ultimate end. Though the system of centralized planning only started to operate around 1954, already by 1956 it was in the process of serious modification. Similarly, hardly had the Great Leap Forward begun when the leadership was already trying to modify some of its excesses. It can be argued that, given the extremism which so often marks major new policies in both China and the Soviet Union, once such policies are launched, they are not easy to modify. But the extremism may be the result of another element in the situation. New development strategies

TABLE 1—MAJOR VARIABLES IN STRATEGIES OF DEVELOPMENT

	I	II
ECONOMIC VARIABLES		
Economic Sectors		
	modern sector	traditional sector
	large-scale industry	medium- and small-scale industry
	national-level economy	economic co-operation regions
Economic Strategy		
	select development	simultaneous development
	long-term goals	short-term goals
Production		
	output	profit
	capital intensive	labor intensive
POLITICAL VARIABLES		
Economic Administration		
	central planning	regional planning
	centralization	decentralization
	target fulfillment	independent operational authority
Organization of the Command Structure		
	centralized administration	downward transfer of authority
	vertical rule	dual rule
	parallel bureaucracies	co-ordinated committees
	ministerial leadership	party leadership
Institutions		
	central government	local government
	management	party organization
SOCIAL VARIABLES		
Social Strata		
	bureaucrats	masses
	intellectuals	workers
	technicians	semiskilled and unskilled labor
	specialists	generalists
Social Cohesion		
	individual	collectivity
	division of labor	team
Motivation and Incentive		
	individual rewards	collective rewards
	wages	distribution
	piece-rate systems	time wages

are constituted by a complex of decisions which involve political, social, ideological, as well as economic variables. Decision complexes of such magnitude are not easy to launch but, once launched, create a momentum which cannot easily be slowed down and changed.

What have been the major variables in these two strategies of development? A complete answer to this question would require societal analysis at a most general level. But a partial answer can be suggested on the basis of those variables which the Chinese Communist leadership itself has stressed. During the period of the First Five-Year Plan, as we have indicated above, there was a pattern in the concatenation of political, economic, and social policy elements. As dissatisfaction with the workings of the First Five-Year Plan grew, alternatives began to be considered. Following the Chinese Communist mode of "dialectical" thinking, alternatives were often formulated in terms of concept pairs, in which the weighting of one often was construed as having an inverse effect on the other. We may regard these as pairs of variables which played a major part in the drafting of developmental strategy. The list of variables in Table 1 is tentative and incomplete, but the variables indicated have played a major part in developmental strategy.

As a whole, the strategy of the first five-year plan gave priority preference to the first vertical set of variables. We have already dealt briefly with most of the variables indicated, but a few additional comments might be made. The regime was as concerned with maximizing accumulation—savings—as it was with maximizing output, but the burden of accumulation, at least initially, lay on the nonpreferred sectors of the economy. Does the output-accumulation pair of variables constitute a "contradictory duality?" It might be pointed out again that, for many enterprises, the attainment of output targets, during the First Five-Year Plan period, was given priority over accumulation targets, and, conversely, the present period is one of overriding concern with enterprise profit, with a corresponding de-emphasis of output targets. Similarly, one can argue that the regime was as concerned with building up the party organization during the period of the First Five-Year Plan as later. Yet, the picture is not quite so simple as that. Party recruitment slackened during the early 1950's, and it was the regime's policy to build up party strength at top rather than bottom levels, a policy which only started to change in 1955. The one-man management system, moreover, was specifically designed, among other things, to keep the party apparatus out of the actual management of industry.

Starting around 1956, the Chinese Communist leadership began to move in the direction of greater stress on the second set of variables, without clearly diminishing emphasis on the first set. Greater attention was given to medium- and small-scale industry, as evidenced by the full socialization of private enterprise. De-emphasis of central and perspective planning led to greater importance being attached to short-term goals. Party organization expanded with an increase in party power and influence. The Eighth Party Congress called for a greater decision-making power at lower levels of the system. Planners demanded a change in the habits of managers of preferring capital to labor-intensive forms of production.

The Great Leap Forward saw an almost complete change in emphasis from the first to the second set of variables. Major stress was given the problem of economic transformation of the traditional sector, notably agriculture. Capital and labor investment in smaller-scale and regional industries greatly increased. Planning in some ways ceased altogether as all attention was concentrated on the achievement of short-term production goals. Obviously, the regime put major stress on the achievement of output targets—maximizing output at all costs —yet, curiously, the decentralization measures of 1957 did away with the gross-output-value target, so important in Soviet industrial management, and substituted profit as the main "commanding" enterprise target. Decentralization brought about greater regional control, and intensified party leadership. The Great Leap Forward was a period of collective effort, distribution, collective rewards, stress on general rather than specific skills—praise of the multifaceted expert. The Great Leap Forward saw a turning away from individual incentives back to hourly wages.

The shift in policy emphasis to the

second set of variables had the ultimate effect, whether the regime wanted it or not, of adversely affecting the first set. The modern sector suffered through shortages of materials, decline in Soviet imports, and shortages in investment funds. National-level economic co-ordination was imperiled. Capital-intensive forms of production were eschewed in favor of a policy of maximal use of labor. Central planning broke down. Vertical rule, even in the remnant central sector, was threatened by the power of regional governments. Bureaucrats, intellectuals, technicians, specialists—all suffered in the form of denunciations, criticisms, mass movements directed against them. The decline in individual incentives was a major factor in the deterioration of morale in the country's major enterprises.

If the period of consolidation during 1956–1957 was marked by a gradual shift from the first to the second set of variables, the present period is one marked by a move in the opposite direction. But the move back is not of the same order for the three categories of variables we have singled out. Perhaps the most clear-cut move back has been in regard to the social variables. Despite a recent re-emphasis on collective work, the leadership, as a whole, has moved back in regard to each of the variables we have singled out: from masses back to bureaucrats, workers to intellectuals, generalists to specialists, back to rational division of labor, back from collective to individual rewards. But, in regard to the other two categories of variables, economic and political, the picture is not so clear. As a whole, it would appear that the leadership continues to emphasize all of the major economic variables of the second set. Major investment efforts are still being directed toward agriculture and light industry. The policy of fostering regional economic co-operation remains

very much in effect.[38] The slowing down of economic growth in the modern sector must still be seen as a continuation of the policy of simultaneous development of industry and agriculture. In contrast to the Great Leap Forward period, the regime is now giving main emphasis to accumulation goals—for example, stress on profit targets, cost-reduction targets, and so on. Given the serious shortage of capital goods, it is doubtful that there has been any tendency to go back to the wasteful procedures of the First Five-Year Plan period. All in all, therefore, it would appear that the periodic assertion on the part of the leadership that the "three banners" are still being carried aloft has a basis in fact. Though the means to achieve the economic goals of the Great Leap Forward period have changed, and the pace slowed down, the goals themselves remain.

It is in regard to the political variables that the picture is most unclear. That there has been some "creeping recentralization" cannot be doubted, but the question is how much? Has the weakening of regional-level party control meant greater ministerial power, or has control actually passed into the hands of regional bureaucrats? Or, for that matter, one might ask, how much in fact has party control at the regional level diminished? There still is continuing stress on the importance of independent operational authority, which may even, in some cases, extend to price-fixing powers for factory managers.[39] What sort of central planning is now underway for the third five-year plan period? The failure to convene a Ninth Party Congress most likely indicates that the regime has yet to work out a clear-cut political line for the new plan period. In fact, the slackening of party control early in 1961

[38] See Jen-min jih-pao, April 2, 1963.
[39] Ibid.

and the subsequent call for greater party control would indicate that there is a major problem of political indecision. The regime can not bring itself to renounce its cherished principle of basic-level party leadership, but it can neither afford to return to policy of the Great Leap Forward period nor to return to centralized leadership of the First Five-Year Plan period type.

Is China at the moment in a New Economic Policy period? Is there a kind of "creeping revisionism" which the regime has been forced to acquiesce in? Whatever the case, present-day reality in China is different from what one would assume from the unchanged militancy of the ideology. Most of the militant practices of the Great Leap Forward period, notably the "mass movement," have disappeared from the scene. Life has become easier for classes of the population which were the targets of extreme pressure during the Great Leap Forward. The food situation has improved, even in many rural areas. A low-key Hundred Flowers period for the intellectuals seems still to be in progress. And yet the ideological militancy remains. In some ways, this is the first time since the Yenan period that there is a serious gap between ideology and organization. While the ideology still proclaims the importance of mass action, there is a bureaucratic revival in the country.

With a shift from party leadership to control, ideology has become an even more important weapon in maintaining organizational cohesion—this may be one explanation for the continuing ideological militancy. Moreover, since the ideology of the Great Leap Forward is too closely identified with the present leadership of the party, abandonment of the ideology, without a new line to replace the old one, might endanger the continuity of that leadership. The signs indicate serious political indecision in the country.

The regime is, at the moment, pursuing an economic policy of "balance" aimed at creating growing linkages between industry and agriculture and raising living standards. Will such a policy ultimately spell stagnation or growth? That is a question which is difficult to answer, even for China's leadership. But there is a further serious problem. The continuation of a policy of economic and political decentralization, but one no longer under tight party control, creates problems of what the Soviets have called "localism." Localism may be the only way for getting the economy moving again, but it creates major political problems for a command society. As the regime moves to determine the future course of its strategies of development, one may be sure that the noneconomic variables, political and social, will be as important as the purely economic variables.

Centralization versus Decentralization in Mainland China and the Soviet Union

By Dwight H. Perkins

ABSTRACT: In both Communist China and the Soviet Union, one of the major problems facing the leadership is how to ensure that farmers and factory managers act in accordance with the dictates of the central plan. To accomplish this aim, they have at their disposal two types of controls. These are centralized controls, which rely on direct orders to the producing units, and decentralized controls, which either operate through the market mechanism or, as is often the case in China, through the Communist party apparatus. Although both countries rely more heavily on centralized controls than their free-enterprise counterparts, there is a greater tendency in China to experiment with various forms of decentralization. In the agricultural sector, this is the result of the much lower per capita income and the comparative surplus of labor which exist in Mainland China. In industry, it is a result of the relatively greater importance and large number of small-scale industries using disparate and comparatively primitive technology. The Soviet Union, in contrast, has stuck closely to centralized controls even though this has become increasingly difficult as the economy has become more complex.

Dwight H. Perkins, Cambridge, Massachusetts, is an Instructor in Economics at Harvard University. During the past three years, he has been working on a study of price formation in Communist China at Harvard and in Hong Kong under a grant from the Ford Foundation and with guidance from Professor Abram Bergson.

ONE of the major problems facing any nation wishing to guide its economy according to the dictates of a central plan is how to ensure that the farmers and factory managers who ultimately determine what is to be produced act in accordance with that plan. Control of this nature also exists in a free-enterprise economy, but it operates automatically through the market and price mechanism, and those determine what output goals will be are consumers and not planners.

It is often assumed, particularly by the various Communist states, that central planning in a Socialist economy in and of itself necessitates a high degree of centralized control where plan goals are transmitted to individual factories in the form of direct orders to increase output either in physical or value terms. Unlike the free-enterprise plant manager, whose main objective is to maximize profits in any of a wide variety of ways, the Communist manager has very little room for maneuver. Not only is he provided with a list of the major products which he must produce but there are also limits on the number of workers he can hire, the quantities of raw materials which he can use, and many other aspects of his job as well.

THE LANGE-LERNER MODEL

That centralization was not necessary, in theory at least, even in Socialist economies was demonstrated in two separate but similar theoretical models by Oskar Lange and Abba Lerner.[1] They showed how central planners could simulate market conditions and then set prices so as to clear the market just as in free-enterprise economies— even better, they argued, because, in their simulated markets, monopolistic practices could be eliminated. Both Lange and Lerner envisaged economies where consumer sovereignty was the rule—that is, where the wishes of consumers were what determined what was to be produced—but, in China and the Soviet Union, production is determined by the planning authorities largely irrespective of what the consumer desires. Consumer sovereignty, however, can be eliminated from the system without materially reducing the usefulness of decentralized control through the price mechanism. To prevent prices on the consumers' goods market from influencing production and still preserve the role of prices in influencing production, both the Chinese and the Russians have introduced the turnover and profits taxes. These taxes make it possible, in effect, to have two independently determined prices for any one commodity, one for the consumer and the other for the producer.

VALUE TARGETS

It is also assumed by both Lange and Lerner that all heads of enterprises will attempt to maximize the firm's profits not because they themselves will receive those profits but, rather, because it is upon the basis of their success in this area that their performance will be judged. This assumption can also be removed from the model without eliminating decentralized price controls provided that a substitute criterion of success for the plant manager is found which embodies some value concept— for example, gross value of output rather than physical quantities of particular products.[2]

[1] O. Lange, "On the Economic Theory of Socialism," in O. Lange and F. Taylor, *On the Economic Theory of Socialism* (Minneapolis: University of Minnesota Press, 1938), and A. P. Lerner, *The Economics of Control* (New York: Macmillan, 1944).

[2] A. Wakar and J. G. Zielinski, "Socialist Operational Price Systems," *American Economic Review*, Vol. 53, No. 1, Part 1 (March 1963), pp. 109–127.

Prices are not the only means whereby decision-making can be decentralized without the loss of ultimate control in the hands of the central planners. There are also various forms of administrative decentralization which have been tried in both China and the Soviet Union. The commune movement in China, for example, was in part an attempt to create an organization whereby primary control over various small-scale industries and commercial bodies could be decentralized without complete loss of certain central influences, in this case conveyed through the various levels of the party apparatus.

Both the Chinese and Soviet leaderships, therefore, were constantly confronted with a number of choices over which forms of control to use. For a number of reasons which will be discussed below, the Russians have stuck closely to centralized physical controls in all areas of their economy except on the consumers' goods and labor markets, whereas the Chinese have experimented extensively with various forms of decentralization, although centralized controls have usually been predominant in the crucial sectors of heavy industry, state investment, and certain aspects of agricultural production.

ADVANTAGES OF CENTRALIZATION

The reasons for the relatively greater importance of decentralized controls in China are not immediately obvious, particularly given the often-cited advantages for centralized controls in an underdeveloped economy. These arguments usually start by pointing out that the price structure of underdeveloped economies is so distorted and that there are so many potential external economies—projects which in effect benefit the economy as a whole but which are not profitable to the individual entrepreneur—that reliance on control through the price mechanism leads to a serious misallocation of resources. They then proceed to show that centralized controls are relatively easy to apply in an underdeveloped economy for a number of reasons:

(1) The economies of these countries are simpler in structure, and, in particular, there are fewer interdependencies between various sectors.

(2) The number of investment projects which must be co-ordinated is small.

(3) These economies produce only a limited range of goods initially and must import many key inputs so that shortages caused by planning can be offset by merely importing more of the short commodity rather than ceasing production until the item could be produced from domestic sources.

(4) New technology can be borrowed and disseminated quickly through direct orders in early stages, whereas, in later stages, technology must be adapted to the increasingly complex structure of the economy.[3]

Given these conditions, it also follows that, as a country becomes more highly developed, the increasing complexity of the economy makes it more difficult to maintain direct control over all aspects of the economy. In actual practice, however, it has been the comparatively highly developed economy of the Soviet Union which has resisted most moves toward decentralization, whereas the Chinese have been in a continual process of experimentation with indirect controls.

THE CHINESE PROBLEM

This experimentation by the Chinese Communists does not result from the

[3] This is a simplified version of the points made in J. M. Montias, "The Soviet Economic Model and the Underdeveloped Economies," in N. Spulber (ed.), *Study of the Soviet Economy* (Bloomington: Indiana University, 1961), pp. 66–67.

inapplicability of the above-mentioned conditions to China but, rather, from the fact that there are a number of other aspects which must be taken into account. The first of these is that, although the Chinese economy is uncomplex in terms of economic interdependencies and the number of commodities produced, it is quite complex when one takes into account the number of producing units which must be controlled and the diversity of techniques used by these units not only in agriculture but in industry as well. Secondly, the problem of training a sufficient number of people who can first accurately collect the necessary statistics and then turn them over to others who will have enough training to use them effectively is no easy task. Except for the falsification of statistics in 1958 and 1959, most of the problems of data collection faced by the Chinese Communists have been similar in nature to and usually less in degree than those facing other underdeveloped economies with the same problems, such as India.[4] Nevertheless, in spite of this ability of China to collect better data than many other underdeveloped economies, Chinese statistics in many areas have been so inaccurate as to be completely inadequate guides to action. One can even make a case for the fact that highly developed economies are often in a better position to plan than the underdeveloped because they have good statistics and the potential for training highly skilled planners. This certainly, in part at least, explains why the Soviet Union has not been forced to abandon or even fundamentally modify its system of centralized controls. Finally, one cannot ignore the question of incentives,

although there is no simple relationship between incentives and the degree of decentralization. In some cases, constant pressure from the top is the only way of ensuring that a job will be completed. In other cases, overcentralized controls lead to dampening of incentives and perfunctory job performance. The latter situation is particularly likely to exist in agriculture, where the complexity of the problem of control is so great that centralized controls tend to be applied mechanically, with the result that individual peasant farmers put the minimum possible effort into collective activities and transfer their effort and imagination to their private plots and household activities. This transfer of effort is partly due to the fact that the peasant's reward from his private activities is much greater in proportion to the effort invested than from his collective efforts, but, in China at least, it is also due to the inability of centralized directives to take into account many adjustments which might benefit the state while enhancing the individual peasants' incentives.

Rather than continue this discussion in general terms, it is desirable at this point to turn to a more detailed analysis of the methods of control used in the various individual sectors of the economies of Mainland China and the Soviet Union. The analysis will begin with the agricultural sector, because that is where the contrast between conditions prevailing in the two countries is the greatest, and then will proceed to a discussion of the nature of controls in industry.

AGRICULTURAL CONTROLS

The most fundamental difference between the economies of Communist China and the Soviet Union on the eve of each country's first five-year plan lay not so much in the relatively greater industrial development which

---

[4] For a discussion of why 1958–1959 statistics in China are a special case, see C. M. Li, *The Statistical System of Communist China* (Berkeley and Los Angeles: University of California Press, 1962).

had taken place in the latter, although the difference there was substantial, as in the very low level of per capita agricultural output in China compared to that existing in the Soviet Union. The Soviet Union, in one of its poorest grain production years, 1932, produced approximately 0.4 of a ton per capita, whereas China, in a fairly good year, 1957, claims to have produced only about 0.28 of a ton of grain per capita. The figure for the Soviet Union in 1937 was about 0.7 of a ton,[5] two and one-half times that of China in 1957. It should not be implied from this that Chinese farm output was right at the minimum subsistence level. Even at the low levels of output prevailing in 1952, China's per capita output of all crops was from 25 to 30 per cent higher than that of India, and the disparity is even greater if the comparison is confined to grain crops.[6] If one assumes that India was at the minimum subsistence level, then the room for maneuver left to the Chinese Communists was not great, but it did exist.

LABOR TRANSFER

The second major difference between China and the Soviet Union which is relevant to the question of the nature of controls over agricultural production is the disparity between the size of the two countries' populations both in absolute terms and as related to the amount of available cultivable land. In effect, China had such a large popula-

tion on the land that large numbers—in absolute terms—could be transferred to the cities without making any appreciable dent in the number remaining on the farm, but this was not the case in the Soviet Union. This is best illustrated by statistics, which show that, during the process of early industrialization in the Soviet Union between 1926 and 1939, the rural population had to be reduced from 82.1 per cent of the total to 57.2 per cent, whereas, in China, the drop between 1950 and 1956 was only from 88.9 per cent to 85.8 per cent while the absolute level of the rural population actually increased by nearly fifty million.[7] In the Soviet Union, this major shift in population had to be encouraged by considerable efforts on the part of the state, without which the entire industrialization program would have been slowed considerably due to a shortage of labor. On the Chinese mainland, the major problem was the opposite one of how to stop the natural flow of surplus rural labor to the cities, where the expense of feeding and housing them was considerably greater.[8]

The significance of these two differences between Mainland China and the Soviet Union for agricultural organization and control was profound. The major objectives of collectivization in the Soviet Union were, first of all, to ensure that a large portion of agricultural production was marketed so that the increasing urban population could be fed and imports of producers' goods paid for with grain exports as they had

[5] The Chinese statistic is derived from data in *Ten Great Years* (Peking: Foreign Languages Press, 1960), pp. 8, 119. The Soviet statistics are derived from materials in H. Schwartz, *Russia's Soviet Economy* (New York: Prentice-Hall, 1954), p. 358, and W. Eason, "Population and Labor Force," in A. Bergson (ed.), *Soviet Economic Growth* (Evanston: Row, Peterson and Co., 1953), p. 102.

[6] A. Eckstein, *The National Income of Communist China* (Glencoe: The Free Press, 1961), p. 67.

[7] The Chinese figures are from H. and Y. C. Yin, *Economic Statistics of Mainland China (1949–1957)* (Cambridge: Center for East Asian Studies, Harvard University, 1960), p. 6. The Soviet data is from Schwartz, *op. cit.*, p. 32.

[8] S. Ishikawa, *Chugoku Ni Okeru Shihon Chikuseki Kiko (Capital Formation in China)* (Tokyo: Iwanami Bookstore, 1960), pp. 52–54.

been under the czars before the great landed estates of the nobility had been broken up during the course of the 1917 revolution; secondly, to make possible a change in organization which would ensure the freeing of a large portion of the rural work force, mainly through the mechanization of agriculture.[9] An increase in agricultural output itself was undoubtedly considered desirable but of distinctly secondary importance. As a result, the key to Soviet agricultural organization was tight central control, first, to ensure that the necessary agricultural products would be delivered to the state without having to increase substantially the delivery of industrial consumers' goods to rural areas in exchange and, second, to ensure that the adoption of mechanization would be rapid where necessary.

PRIORITY TO PRODUCTION

China, in contrast, had to give first priority in agriculture to increasing production. A marketed surplus was also of importance, because it was this surplus which directly or indirectly provided 75 per cent of all exports and the raw materials for 70 per cent of consumers' goods industrial products as well as food for the urban population and farmers producing industrial crops. This surplus, however, could not be increased without first raising production. That the size of the marketed surplus in China depended on the level of production was dramatically illustrated by the events of the recent period of agricultural crisis which probably began with the fall harvest of 1959 and continued at least until the fall of 1962. This crisis not only necessitated sharp cuts in food rations but also a drop in

exports and the expenditure of valuable foreign exchange on the import of grain from Canada, Australia, and France. In addition, evidence from refugees of very small cotton-cloth, edible-oil, and other rations seems to indicate that much of the consumers' goods industrial sector has been operating at well below 50 per cent of capacity.[10] Thus, the crisis in agriculture necessitated a slowdown throughout the economy, including in the key producers' goods industrial sector. The successful development of the Chinese economy, therefore, depends on the ability of the regime to raise agricultural output. Since the problem of increasing agricultural production is far more complex than increasing the marketed portion of that production, it is natural that the Chinese would have to rely far more heavily on the knowledge and initiative of the peasants and cadres directly involved in production and could attempt to direct their efforts only through indirect means which did not interfere with their incentives or initiative.

The effect which these differences in objectives have had on the choice between centralized and decentralized controls in the two countries, however, can only partly be seen from a comparison of the formal organizational structure of the Russian collectives and the Chinese higher-level producers' cooperatives and communes. The Russian collectives of the 1930's were actually smaller in terms of the number of members than the Chinese although larger in land area and total output. The only major difference in formal organization was the existence of Ma-

[9] Mechanization of agriculture would have been necessary even without any removal of population from the farms due to the great slaughter of livestock which took place during the collectivization drives.

[10] This information is based on a number of refugee interviews made by the author and others. What little available evidence there is suggests that the fall harvest of 1962 was significantly above that of 1960–1961. See, for example, "Pace of Survival: Communist China's Economy Falters On," *Current Scene,* Vol. 2, No. 11 (April 1, 1963), p. 3.

chine Tractor Stations in the Soviet Union. The concentration of large machinery such as tractors in an organization not under the control of the collectives had as one of its major purposes the maintenance of tight central direction over the collective and its output. In spite of what came to be realized as the obvious inefficiency of these stations, which were primarily only interested in mechanically fulfilling quotas for such things as the amount of area plowed, the state maintained them in existence until well after the death of Stalin because of their important control functions.

PROCUREMENT PRICES

The major difference between control in the two countries was not the existence of Machine Tractor Stations in the Soviet Union, however, but the disparity in the ways in which the collective form of organization was imposed and utilized after its imposition. Where Stalin essentially ordered the peasantry to form collectives and backed up the order with force, the Chinese Communists made great efforts to persuade the peasants to join voluntarily. There was, in fact, considerable force and pressure on the Chinese peasant, but it was usually veiled and more subtly applied. Once the collectives were firmly established in Russia, the state imposed severe compulsory delivery quotas for which it gave compensation, but, because the procurement prices were held down while retail prices were rising rapidly, these prices soon came to be very low in real terms, thus turning the compulsory quotas into little more than a direct tax on output.[11] In China, on the other hand, compulsory quotas were also introduced, but the resulting in-

crease in grain deliveries was comparatively small and the farmers or co-operatives were paid at the price prevailing before the introduction of quotas.[12] As in the Soviet Union, quotas were also introduced for certain other crops as well, but the major means of control over these crops was the Chinese government's ability to manipulate their procurement prices and not their quotas. Central planning of agricultural production through the setting of physical targets was also tried in one year—1956—in China, but it proved to be such an obvious failure that it was quickly abandoned.[13] The Chinese, therefore, in principle, continued to rely heavily on decentralized control through the price mechanism to control the agricultural product mix,

[11] F. Holzman, *Soviet Taxation* (Cambridge: Harvard University Press, 1955), pp. 166–167.

[12] Government Affairs Council, "Order Putting Into Effect the Planned Purchase and Supply of Grain," *Hsin-hua yueh-pao*, No. 4 (April 25, 1954), pp. 158–159. That the increase in grain deliveries between 1952–1953 (before compulsory quotas) and 1953–1954 (after quotas) was only 36 per cent can be derived from data in *T'ung-chi kung-tso* data office, "The Basic Situation with Respect to Our Country's Unified Purchase and Sale of Grain," *Hsin-hua pan-yueh-k'an*, No. 22 (November 25, 1957), p. 171, and Wu Shuo, "An Inquiry into the Grain Situation During the Transition Period," *Liang-shih*, No. 1 (January 25, 1957) in *Extracts of China Mainland Magazines*, No. 85, p. 12. Other sources show an increase by 1958–1959 of only 84 per cent over 1952–1953, in contrast to which the Soviet increase in grain deliveries between 1926–1927 and 1952–1953 was nearly 300 per cent (Schwartz, *op. cit.*, p. 362). The period covered by the Chinese statistics is shorter, but the increase in total grain output in the two countries over the periods covered was roughly comparable (43 per cent in the Soviet Union and probably around 30 per cent in the case of China).

[13] "Several Points of View on Setting Up and Reforming Agricultural Producers' Cooperatives Plan Work," *Chi-hua ching-chi*, No. 10 (October 23, 1956), pp. 16–19, and *Jen-min jih-pao* editorial, "Do We Still Want to Plan," *Hsin-hua pan-yueh-k'an*, No. 19 (October 6, 1956), p. 62.

whereas the Soviets relied more on direct compulsory quotas.

CO-OPERATIVES, COMMUNES, AND AFTER

Although the Chinese relied in principle on price controls, these prices ceased to operate effectively after co-operativization because the cadres in charge of the co-operatives were only interested in maximizing output of grain and, to a lesser extent, cotton rather than income or profits. The ineffectiveness of the price mechanism combined with general dissatisfaction with the pace of development in Chinese agriculture did not, however, lead to the imposition of more centralized controls but, if anything, the reverse. The establishment of the communes in 1958 which were usually formed from the amalgamation of approximately twenty to thirty co-operatives did centralize control over many activities, but only at the commune level. The authority of the central government in the direction of basic-level agricultural activities was, in fact, considerably reduced on the belief that the way to maximize output was to give as much initiative as possible to reliable local cadres. As is now well known, the commune experiment has largely failed, partly because of its effect on individual peasant incentives and partly because of the difficulty which cadres had in efficiently planning and directing the production of a unit of over four thousand families. Given these difficulties in operating even a unit of such size, it is not surprising that the Chinese did not seek to solve the crisis in agriculture by moving toward more centralized controls but have, rather, moved back toward greater reliance on price-and-income incentives and controls.

The comparatively heavy reliance on direct controls in Soviet agriculture should not, however, be overempha-sized. The collective-farm markets always had an important influence on many of the crops produced and marketed just as did the free market in China. Furthermore, in recent years, with the shift in emphasis under Khrushchev away from marketing and toward increases in farm output, the Soviet Union has made greater use of prices in controlling the output of collectives, and the Machine Tractor Stations have finally been abandoned. Procurement prices are now set above cost so as to stimulate production.[14] Nevertheless, there has also been a movement toward the consolidation of collectives from the 254,000 which existed in 1950 to one-tenth that number at present, and state farms, where farmers are paid regular wages rather than incomes based on the output of the farm after taxes and quotas have been met, have become increasingly important particularly since 1960. The Soviet moves, therefore, have not really involved a general decentralization of authority so much as an improvement in the efficiency of the existing system.

QUOTAS AND PRICES IN INDUSTRY

In the industrial sectors of the Soviet Union and Communist China, the similarity in the two countries' formal institutional structures is even more pronounced. This is not surprising given the fact that most of the forms of industrial organization used in China were taken directly from the Soviet Union. Translations of Russian textbooks and organizational handbooks were used almost exclusively in the initial years of Communist control in China, and thousands of Soviet technicians were imported to give technical advice. By 1956 Chinese industry had

[14] M. Bornstein, "The Soviet Price System," *American Economic Review*, Vol. 52, No. 1 (March 1962), pp. 84–88.

mostly been socialized, and Soviet-type controls were, thus, predominant in the entire industrial sector.

The essential feature of this system in both countries is that the output of each individual firm is to be determined according to the requirements of annual plans prepared by the central authorities in Peking or Moscow. These plans lay down a number of targets which must be met or surpassed, the most important of which is the output target expressed either in value or physical terms. In addition, there are usually targets for cost reduction, profits, the number of workers who can be hired, the wages which can be paid to them, and often many others. Backing this up are a number of detailed financial controls which limit the way in which a firm can use the funds accruing to it. Finally, most key types of machinery and raw materials are allocated in accordance with the plan on a rationed basis rather than through the market. The amount of room for maneuver left to the Chinese or Russian plant manager, therefore, in theory at least, is negligible. All important decisions are centralized.

THEORY AND PRACTICE

There is a substantial difference between theory and practice in both countries, however.[15] Targets which, in the regulations, are given equal importance with others may, in fact, be ignored, and tight financial controls may be considerably more lax than they at first appear. The very number of controls necessitates a system of priorities whereby primary effort is put on achieving success in one or a limited number of areas, with the remainder receiving less attention or being left entirely to chance. In neither country, therefore, is control as tightly centralized in the hands of the planning authorities as the regulations imply. Furthermore, one can delineate significant differences between the degree of actual control in Communist China and the Soviet Union.

In the Soviet Union, although factory managers have some leeway in making decisions, centralized control has generally been extremely tight, and there has been no trend toward more decentralization as the economy has become more complex. This can be seen from the rapid increase in the number of commodities centrally planned and allocated on a rationed basis from about 250 in 1937 to 1,500 in the 1950's. A similar degree of complexity in Poland —where the number of such commodities was also approximately 1,500—has led to considerable discussion of and some experimentation with decentralized control through the price mechanism,[16] but not in the Soviet Union. There has been some experimentation with different forms of organization in the Soviet Union, such as the abolition of the industrial ministries whose control was on a nationwide basis and the switch to regional organizations whose control was confined to the one area but which cut across types of industries. The motivation behind moves such as this, however, has been as much a desire to have a degree of regional self-sufficiency so as to take some of the burden off the transport system caused by the tendency toward "gigantomania" in the construction of industrial plants as it has been a move toward decentralization. The major way in which the problem of complexity has been dealt with has not

[15] This is discussed at length in J. S. Berliner, *Factory and Manager in the USSR* (Cambridge: Harvard University Press, 1957), and D. Granick, *Management of the Industrial Firm in the USSR* (New York: Columbia University Press, 1954).

[16] J. M. Montias, *Central Planning in Poland* (New Haven and London: Yale University Press, 1962).

been reorganizations such as this but improvement of the planning apparatus itself. Recently, this has taken the form of looking into the possible advantages in the use of more mathematical techniques, particularly input-output analysis, which would make possible the use of computers.[17]

In China, in contrast, there has been considerable experimentation with various forms of decentralized control. On occasion, this has taken the form of greater use of the price mechanism and allocation through the market. One of the major problems of control over Chinese industry has been how to bring the tens of thousands of small-scale firms which use widely varying techniques under the direction of the central plan without hopelessly entangling them in administrative red tape and stifling their initiative.[18] In 1956, at the Eighth National Party Congress, it was decided to relax considerably marketing procedures so as to make it possible for these enterprises to buy and sell freely many items which had been previously rationed. Furthermore, in China, prices of producers' goods are set at a relatively high level,[19] unlike the Soviet Union, where they are only 5 per cent above average cost. This has enabled prices in this sector in China to continue to play some role in restricting demand, although that role has been considerably limited by the ready availability of funds to the individual enterprise from the budget and the People's Bank.

[17] H. S. Levine, "Input-Output Analysis and Soviet Planning," *American Economic Review, Papers and Proceedings,* Vol. 52, No. 2 (May 1962), pp. 127–137.

[18] There were 136,438 small-scale enterprises in Communist China in 1954. *Jen-min shou-ts'e, 1957 (People's Handbook)* (Peking: *Ta Kung Pao,* 1957), p. 428.

[19] Profits plus taxes on producers' goods industry in China were 43 per cent of average cost. Fan Jo-i, "A Brief Discussion of the Profit Rate on Capital," *Chi-hua ching-chi,* No. 8 (August 23, 1958), p. 28.

GREAT LEAP FORWARD

The most dramatic attempt to decentralize control over Chinese industry, however, took place in 1958–1959 during the Great Leap Forward and had nothing to do with a greater use of prices or the market mechanism. This move was not dictated so much by underlying economic conditions as it was by the impatience of the leadership with the pace of development, which, by any reasonable standards, was quite rapid. The belief that an even faster rate could be achieved by means of a transfer of control to the individual factory party committees was apparently principally based on the leadership's experience with guerrilla warfare, where victory was often achieved by giving maximum initiative to those at the scene of action while making sure through ideological indoctrination that that victory would not be achieved at the expense of more important objectives. What worked in guerrilla warfare, however, did not prove very effective for the economy. In industry, it led to blind attempts by all individual factories to expand output and capacity at a breakneck pace. This was to some degree possible by working both machines and men harder and longer hours, but there were severe limitations. A building might be expanded to make room for twice as much capacity, but the machinery in many cases still had to be imported, and this depended on the size of exports and not on party enthusiasm. There was also a tendency to produce goods simply to raise the index of physical output regardless of whether they were needed or not. The Great Leap form of organization, therefore, was much closer to anarchy than to decentralized control, so it is not surprising that, after two years, it began to be disbanded. The reforms of 1961 and 1962 have largely re-established centralized control, but whether this is a permanent decision or a temporary one designed to re-establish order before attempting another experiment in decentralization is impossible to say at this point.

THE LABOR MARKET

The one area where the Soviet Union has relied more heavily on indirect controls than Mainland China is the urban labor market. The great shortage of all types of labor in the Soviet Union made it difficult to enforce direct allocation of workers even during the brief periods when it was tried. The intensity of competition between industrial enterprises for whatever laborers were available was only brought under control by attacking the source of the demand for labor itself, namely the excess of funds available to the firms which could be used to bid up wages. In China, the great surplus of unskilled and semi-skilled labor and the small number of highly trained technicians make direct allocation between firms pointless in the case of the former and relatively easy in the case of the latter. In addition, the major problem with the urban labor market in China, as already mentioned, was to prevent excessive migration from the rural areas. Inasmuch as this was not primarily determined simply by the height of the lower-grade wages in the cities, it could only be stopped by direct means, such as requiring that permission be obtained from a number of authorities before undertaking a move.

This discussion by no means exhausts all the areas in the Soviet Union and China where the issue of decentralized versus centralized controls was met, but it is sufficient to make possible a few tentative conclusions. First of all, it is clear that many aspects of the formal organizational structure in China were copied from the Soviet Union, but that this structure was often used in different ways in the two countries. In particular, the size of the Chinese economy, when combined with its relative poverty and backwardness, dictated the use of somewhat more decentralized controls over production in both agriculture and industry. Secondly, ideological or political considerations have entered in, as evidenced by the Chinese experience with the Great Leap Forward. These may also play a role in the Soviet Union's refusal to move toward more decentralized controls as the economy becomes more complex.[20] Finally, different factor endowments and the relative surplus of labor in China have necessitated different types of controls over the labor market and, to some extent, in agriculture.[21] None of these differences, however, should cause one to lose sight of the many similarities and, particularly, the heavy reliance on centralized controls over the economy in both China and the Soviet Union when compared with all nations other than those of the Soviet East European bloc.

[20] What were essentially political considerations, for example, were a major factor in the Polish decisions from 1958 on to place heavier emphasis on direct controls. J. M. Montias, *Central Planning in Poland,* chap. 10.

[21] The surplus of labor in the Chinese countryside would have made the existence of Machine Tractor Stations an anomaly, for example, except in Manchuria.

Sino-Soviet Military Relations

By RAYMOND L. GARTHOFF

ABSTRACT: Military relations between the Soviet Union and Communist China were never as close as many have assumed, and since 1960 they have been virtually nonexistent. The Chinese have accepted a penalty to their military power as part of the cost of challenging Moscow's leadership in the Communist world. For the Soviets, the cost has been slight, though they have expended whatever leverage in mutual relations their selective military aid once gave them. In the postwar concluding phase of the Chinese civil war, Soviet support to the Chinese Communists was quite limited. During the Korean war, considerable supply of weapons was provided, though China was compelled to purchase this materiel. Only in the post-Stalin period was selective assistance given to building a Chinese capacity to produce its own conventional weapons and even more circumscribed support to nonweapons nuclear development and to modern aircraft and missile development. But, as a consequence of declining political relations, as earlier noted, even this assistance was virtually cut off in 1960. Moreover, the Soviets have clearly kept a close leash on military commitments to support Communist China. These limitations on weapons and commitments, limiting in turn Chinese freedom of action, have clearly been one of the sources of the Chinese impetus to acquire their own nuclear military power.

Raymond L. Garthoff, Ph.D., Washington, D. C., is a senior officer in the Department of State and Professorial Lecturer at the Institute for Sino-Soviet Studies, The George Washington University. He is author of Soviet Strategy in the Nuclear Age (1958 and 1962), Soviet Military Doctrine (1953), The Soviet Image of Future War (1959), and contributor to Russian Foreign Policy (1962), The Transformation of Russian Society (1961), other books, and many professional journals, writing especially in the fields of Soviet political and military affairs.

AS in the case of ideology, and of national interest broadly construed, military alliance and collaboration have proved to be factors both drawing together and dividing the Soviet Union and Communist China. Clearly, the military strand is but one in a complex pattern of relationships. Its frictions have served to be a secondary causative element in the development of the serious rift between the two powers, but, more significantly, it has been the victim of primarily political and ideological conflicts.

The course of Sino-Soviet military relations has passed through four more or less equal periods. First is the background period from the Soviet seizure of Manchuria in August 1945 to the establishment of Communist rule in Mainland China and the signing of the Sino-Soviet treaty of alliance in February 1950. A second period can be traced from that date through the Korean war until late 1954, following the visit of Khrushchev and Bulganin to Peking and their subsequent succession to power in Moscow in February 1955. From about the beginning of 1955 until mid-1960 followed a new period of growing but strained co-operation. Then, following the sudden virtual cutoff of Soviet military—and other— assistance in mid-1960, the current period has been distinguished by the general absence of military relations in any form. Each of these periods is sufficiently distinctive, and sufficiently significant, to merit our close attention.

CAUTIOUS AND LIMITED CO-OPERATION: 1945–1950

The full story of Soviet relations with the Chinese Communists during the postwar phase of the Chinese civil war is not yet clear, but its main features relevant to our present inquiry are known. Stalin cautiously reinsured Soviet influence by generally "correct" diplomatic dealings with the Nationalist government, while granting some assistance to the Communists. This Soviet policy of dealing with two hands may be explained by uncertainty on Stalin's part as to the outcome of the civil war. On the other hand, it is entirely possible that he wanted to keep China divided for a long period and, therefore, preferred to aid both sides in different ways. In any event, during the critical years from 1945 through 1948, Soviet military assistance was limited to giving the Chinese Communists a somewhat favored position in gaining strategic footholds and captured Japanese ordnance in Manchuria; political assistance was given initially to the Nationalist government by the 1945 Treaty of Friendship clearly recognizing it as the government of all China; economic "assistance" was limited to stripping Manchuria of its industrial assets at the expense of either and both of the Chinese rivals.

The chief Soviet objectives in declaring war on Japan and occupying Manchuria were: (1) to acquire a voice in the future of the North Pacific, including Japan, (2) to seize and incorporate into the Soviet Union Southern Sakhalin and the Kuriles, (3) to eliminate Japan and pre-empt Western presence on the North Asian continent, and (4) to re-establish former Russian influence and rail and base rights in Manchuria and consolidate the status of their Mongolian satrap. There is no good evidence that assistance to the Chinese Communists entered into this decision, and there is a wealth of evidence that Stalin expected the Nationalist government, hopefully weak and ineffective, to remain in control even in Manchuria. For this reason, he negotiated the 1945 treaty which assisted in meeting the above objectives at some cost to local Communist pretensions. The Soviet looting of Manchurian "reparations" is inconsistent with the contention that the Soviets handed over Manchuria to the Chinese Communists so that they could have a base to defeat the Nationalists. If that were the case, why destroy the major part of the great Mukden arsenals which could have given the Chinese Communists the wherewithal to fight? Finally, we have the evidence that Stalin in 1945 and 1946 urged the Chinese Communists to form a coalition with the Nationalists.[1] Mao did not, not only because he may have appreciated the opportunities better than did Stalin, but because his objective was to seize complete power and build a strong Communist China. The Soviet object was to wring concessions and influence for the Soviet Union from a weak China and to keep China weak through a nominal Nationalist rule in which the Soviets had powerful leverage through the Communists—and through other elements such as dissidents in Sinkiang and various war lords.

In this general context, the Soviets did permit the Chinese Communist Eighth Route Army to enter Manchuria, harassed—but did not prevent—the arrival of Chinese Nationalist troops, and permitted the Communists to "seize" captured Japanese military equipment and supplies in raids on Soviet "guarded" stocks. In all, it is reported that the Soviets captured from the Japanese about 300,000 rifles, nearly 5,000 machine guns, 1,226 artillery pieces, 369 tanks, and 925 aircraft. Much of the artillery and small arms, and some of the tanks and aircraft, were then acquired by the Chinese Communist forces in the spring of 1946 —marking their first tanks and combat aircraft in the whole civil war. The Soviets also released the ex-Manchukuo army personnel, a number of whom were recruited by the Communists. In November 1946, the Soviets withdrew from Manchuria, leaving the Chinese Nationalists in nominal control but the Communists in effective control of most of the region.[2]

There is no evidence of any further Soviet military assistance to the Chinese Communists during the four years of civil war. The Chinese Communist forces were equipped with a motley conglomeration of United States and Japanese produced weapons, mostly captured from the Nationalist forces. Chinese Communist claims for *gross* capture during the whole period from mid-1946 to mid-1950 is 3,160,000 rifles; 320,000 machine guns; 55,000 artillery pieces; 622 tanks and 389 armored cars; 189 military aircraft; and 200 (small) warships.[3] If we credit these figures, it will be evident that the Soviets permitted the Communists to seize only small amounts of tanks and aircraft in Manchuria, and, incidentally, the Chinese Nationalists took over much larger quantities of captured Japanese ordnance in 1945–1946 than did the Soviets—twice as many rifles, six times as many machine guns, and ten times as many artillery pieces.[4] This, plus the United States materiel originally supplied to the Nationalist armies, and not the Soviet Union, provided the military wherewithal for the Chinese Communist forces in winning the civil war.

[1] For example, Stalin informed Yugoslav party leaders that he had advised the Chinese Communists to enter a coalition government. See Vladimir Dedijer, *Tito* (New York, 1953), p. 322.

[2] These data are taken largely from Lt. Colonel Robert Rigg, *Red China's Fighting Hordes* (Harrisburg, 1952), pp. 100, 248, 251, 277, 297. Also, see Max Beloff, *Soviet Policy in the Far East, 1941–1951* (New York, 1953), pp. 20–64; F. F. Liu, *A Military History of Modern China, 1924–1949* (Princeton, 1956), pp. 227–229; General L. M. Chassin, *La conquete de la Chine par Mao Tse-tung* (Paris, 1952), *passim*.

[3] Rigg, *op. cit.*, p. 255.

[4] *Ibid.*, p. 276.

At the beginning of 1950 and victorious close of the civil war, the People's Liberation Army, as it had been renamed in 1948, was a massive, poorly equipped, and ill-balanced infantry force of about five million men, many of them late of the Nationalist or war-lord armies, formed loosely into four "field armies" with a total of 215 "divisions." [5] Air, naval, armored, and technical units were few and miscellaneous. When the retreating Nationalists stood their ground at Quemoy in 1949, the Chinese Communists were not even able to take that modestly defended offshore island.

BUILDING AN ALLIANCE: 1950–1954

On February 14, 1950, a Treaty of Friendship, Alliance, and Mutual Assistance between the Soviet Union and the People's Republic of China was signed in Moscow. An economic-development loan of $300 million from the Soviet Union was included in the agreements.[6] There were no published or known military provisions or protocols, but it is clear that arrangements were made at that time to institute formal military assistance in Soviet supplying of materiel and training. Under these arrangements, a Soviet military mission was established in Peking and an estimated 3,000 Soviet military advisors were sent to China to assist in organization and training.[7] Some, but not large numbers, of Chinese military men may also have been sent to the Soviet Union for specialized training.[8]

[5] See Harold C. Hinton, "Communist China's Military Posture," *Current History,* Vol. 43, No. 253 (September 1962), pp. 150–151.

[6] The full texts of the treaty and associated agreements are given as an appendix to Beloff, *op. cit.,* pp. 260–267.

[7] This estimated figure is given by Rigg, *op. cit.,* p. 302.

[8] Colonel Rigg notes reports that the Soviets unofficially provided training to some

Obsolescent Soviet LA-9 and LA-11 piston fighters and TU-2 twin piston-engine light bombers began to be provided to China in some hundreds. Thus, a program of military aid was begun.

In his exhaustive analysis of Chinese policy on the eve of the Korean war, Dr. Allen Whiting finds no signs of Chinese Communist participation in planning and preparing that conflict, nor until the summer of 1950 any preparation for possible participation in it.[9] The Soviets had been exclusively involved in building up the North Korean army and, evidently, in unleashing it. However, the unexpected United States intervention in support of the defenders, and the further unexpected success in crushing the North Korean forces in the autumn of 1950, led to what General MacArthur termed, with some justice, "an entirely new war." The Chinese entered the contest.

The Sino-Soviet military relationship also entered a new phase, as the Soviets had to rely on the Chinese to wage a war they had begun without the Chinese. It is likely that the Soviets were planning—and training—for Chinese acquisition of jet fighters apart from the Korean war. But, under the exigencies of the war, MIG fighters appeared in Manchuria in late October and entered combat against United States aircraft along the Yalu on November 1, 1950.[10] By December 1951, the Chinese Communists had about 700 MIG-15 fighters and 200 piston light bombers, concentrated in North China, and claimed a total air strength of 2,480 aircraft of all types.[11] By 1952 IL-28 jet light bombers were being

Communist airmen in the Soviet Union as early as 1947–1949, *op. cit.,* p. 321. If true, this is the one exception to nonassistance from 1946 to 1950.

[9] Allen S. Whiting, *China Crosses the Yalu* (New York, 1960), pp. iv-v *et passim*.

[10] *Ibid.,* p. 135.

[11] Rigg, *op. cit.,* pp. 323–324.

introduced, though they were not used in combat.[12] Later, a token number of TU-4's—B-29-type piston medium bombers—were transferred to Communist China, at about the end of the Korean war.

By 1951 military expenditures reportedly reached 48 per cent of the Chinese budget.[13] The Soviet military-aid program became and remained extensive, but it also was expensive. The Chinese were compelled to *purchase* this growing military assistance, and to incur heavy debts in the process. From 1950 to 1957, the value of such aid approximated about $2 billion, of which perhaps half was covered by Soviet credits.[14] During the brief era of relative freedom of expression in China in early 1957, General Lung Yun, a former dissident Nationalist but then a member of the Revolutionary Military Committee of the People's Republic of China and a vice-chairman of the National Defense Committee, publicly declared that it was "totally unfair for the People's Republic of China to bear all the expenses of the Korean War."[15] He noted that the United States had forgiven allied debts in World Wars I and II, while the Soviet Union would not. Finally, he also recalled how the Soviet army had dismantled and taken away Manchurian industry in 1946. Colonel Rigg reports campaigns in China in 1953 collecting money even from school children to buy Soviet tanks and aircraft.[16]

The Soviet assistance in building a more modern military establishment was essential to China. Modernization and mechanization placed requirements for military production and logistic and communications system which would otherwise have taken years. The Chinese had no choice but to accept Soviet terms.

While building Chinese military power, Stalin kept it fully dependent on the Soviet Union. Weapons were supplied, but not assistance in creating military production. Thus, China was at the least held on a leash of a few years—the MIGs and Ilyushins, and a few obsolescent Soviet submarines and destroyers, would have to be replaced in a few years, and their replacements could come only from the Soviet Union. While the Soviets could not directly prevent the Chinese Communists from building their own military industry, they could withhold their assistance and argue that it was more economical to buy Soviet-produced weapons. Also, by saddling the Chinese with outlays for military assistance as heavy as the Chinese could devote to their military requirements, they indirectly held back Chinese building of the foundation for an independent military establishment.

In addition to selling more modern weapons to China, Stalin used the occasion of the Korean war to press the Chinese in other ways. In particular, in September 1952, he forced a modification of the 1950 treaty to extend indefinitely the Soviet occupation of Port Arthur on the Yellow Sea.[17]

The death of Stalin had profound, but not immediate, effects on Sino-Soviet relations. The most immediate development was a convergence of Soviet

---

[12] The piston light bombers were used in combat but once; a flight of ten sent down the North Korean coast was intercepted by United States jet fighters and nine were destroyed.

[13] Rigg, "Red Army in Retreat," *Current History*, Vol. 32, No. 185 (January 1957), p. 3.

[14] Allen S. Whiting, " 'Contradictions' in the Moscow-Peking Axis," *Journal of Politics*, Vol. 20, No. 1 (February 1958), pp. 127–161.

[15] *Hsinhua*, June 18, 1957. See G. MacGregor, "Peiping General Criticizes Soviet on Seized Plants," *New York Times*, June 24, 1957.

[16] Rigg, *Current History*, January 1957, p. 3.

[17] See the text in Beloff, *op cit.*, pp. 265–266.

and Chinese interests in closing out the Korean war. But, beyond this, both recognized the need for some redefinition of their relationship. Accordingly, a high-level Soviet delegation visited Peking in October 1954.

PROGRESS AND STRAIN: 1954–1960

It was a major symbolic event to have the review of Sino-Soviet relations occur in Peking rather than Moscow. Khrushchev, Bulganin, Mikoyan, and Shvernik headed the delegation, reflecting the combined political, party, economic, and military interests involved. Agreements signed on October 11, 1954 included a reversal of the Stalin *diktat* of only two years earlier, and the Soviet Union agreed to withdraw from Port Arthur by May 31, 1955, turning over the Soviet installations there without compensation. A scientific-technical agreement was also signed. The provision of the 1950 treaty for joint exploitation of uranium resources in Sinkiang was revoked, with full control reverting to China as of January 1, 1955. No new military agreements were announced nor, apparently, reached.

In 1955 the Soviets withdrew from Port Arthur as promised and left the aircraft belonging to their units there, seeking in general to extend the impression of generosity. An additional agreement on co-operation in the peaceful applications of atomic energy was reached in 1955; also, the joint stock company to exploit uranium was dissolved as earlier agreed.[18] The following year, China joined other Communist states in entering the co-operative "Socialist" nonmilitary atomic research center at Dubna near Moscow—permitting the Soviets, incidentally, to siphon off the results of the best satellite and Chinese nuclear physicists.

The flow of Soviet modern weapons considerably diminished during the late 1950's, not as the result of a Soviet decision to choke it off but because the general air and short-term naval strength levels had been reached. In addition, though we are not privy to the agreements, it seems clear in retrospect that the Chinese gained acceptance in principal to the demand that modern defense industry be built up in China. Progress had been made by the Chinese alone in conventional basic land armaments such as small arms and artillery, but now, with Soviet help, a beginning was made in the partial construction and assembly of jet fighters, complete construction of light piston aircraft, and construction of tanks and of submarine and small patrol craft. By September 1956, the first jet fighters of Chinese "manufacture" were flown with some fanfare.[19] By the end of the 1950's, the Chinese Communist air force had some hundreds of MIG-17's and a few MIG-19's, as well as many older MIG-15's.

The Chinese Communist Army had, by the late 1950's, been substantially modernized into a force of reasonably well-equipped light infantry divisions.[20] Soviet training activities had been largely completed and phased out in the middle and late 1950's, and the military mission in Peking presumably turned more to problems of production facilities in more modern armaments and to co-ordination of military activities.

It should be noted that, throughout both the Stalin and post-Stalin periods, there has been no indication of co-ordinated training exercises or maneuvers between the Soviet and Chinese Communist armies, navies, or air forces. Apart from very limited direct Soviet support to the Chinese during the Korean war, there has been no real co-ordination of

[18] G. A. Modelski, *Atomic Energy in the Communist Bloc* (Melbourne, 1959), pp. 181–195.

[19] Rigg, *Current History,* January 1957, p. 5.
[20] *Ibid.,* p. 3.

their military operations or training, so far as we know. China is not in the Warsaw Pact, and there has been no bilateral equivalent in the Far East integrating air defenses and naval operations. Why? Clearly, such restraint on a militarily desirable exercise of alliance functions must have been caused by inhibiting political factors. We now know of some of these from the revealed exchange of political charges between the Soviet and Chinese Communist parties. In particular, a joint naval command in the Pacific foundered evidently between Soviet concern not to be drawn into possible Sino-American conflict over the Taiwan Straits and Chinese refusal to accept a subordinate role.[21] The same consideration of Chinese sensitivity over equality probably was responsible for failure to integrate fully air-defense systems.

Ultimately, the growing political estrangement of the Soviets and Chinese Communists would come to create even sharper effects on military relationships, but it should be noted that even in periods when the political surface was placid and harmonious there were severe limits on the nature and extent of military relationships.

During the period after 1954, important developments in military doctrine were occurring both in the Soviet Union and in Communist China. In both countries, there was belated recognition of the implications of nuclear war, but the consequences for each were very different. The Soviets had to adjust their concepts to weapons they had or were acquiring, while the Chinese military leaders were faced with the frustration of recognizing the decisive importance of weapons they did not possess.

In 1955 a number of Chinese military

men began to stress the importance of nuclear weapons and new military technology in general and to state specifically that China needed and would acquire "a sufficient quantity of the most modern materiel to arm the Chinese People's Liberation Army."[22] However, a divergence developed between those military leaders—especially in the general staff—who placed most emphasis on the immediate need for modern weapons and those in the ministry of defense—and political officers—who continued to emphasize the basic political-morale factors of a people's army, in the Maoist tradition.[23] This divergence was in part over doctrine and in part over policy: should Communist China acquire her own nuclear weapons, or rely on the Soviet Union? But either approach had to recognize the heavy dependence of China on the Soviet Union—either for Soviet nuclear protection and support or for Soviet assistance in developing Chinese capabilities.[24] As we have seen, beginning in 1955, the Soviets did in fact begin gradually to render assistance to the development of a modern Chinese military industry, thus lengthening the short leash Stalin had held on China's military power.

The next point of decision came in November 1957. The successful Soviet testing of an intercontinental ballistic missile and launching of the first artificial earth satellite encouraged the Chinese almost more than it did the Soviets, but it also underlined the gap between Chinese and Soviet capabilities. Then, in November, Mao Tse-tung—and a delegation of Chinese military

---

[21] See Edward Crankshaw, "Sino-Soviet Rift Held Very Deep," *The Washington Post*, February 12, 1961.

[22] Marshal Yeh Chien-ying, New China News Agency, Peking, July 27, 1955.

[23] See the detailed account of the debate in 1954–1957 in Alice L. Hsieh, *Communist China's Strategy in the Nuclear Era* (New York, 1962), pp. 15–75 (hereafter cited as *Communist China's Strategy*).

[24] *Ibid.*, pp. 72–75.

leaders—visited Moscow. On the basis of later indications, it appears that Mao used the occasion to seek a greater role for China in the Communist camp and that he requested nuclear weapons for China.[25] Among his colleagues visiting Moscow were the minister of defense, Marshal P'eng Teh-huai, and also the two leading army "modernizers," Marshal Yeh Chien-ying and General Su Yü, the chief of the general staff.[26] But the military mission was apparently unsuccessful, at least so far as nuclear warheads were concerned; some support may have been promised for development of missiles in China.[27]

As the facts of nuclear-missile warfare and the implications of Soviet refusal to provide nuclear weapons to China sank more deeply into the Chinese consciousness in 1958, significant policy disputes led to new decisions. During the spring and summer of 1958, a debate over military doctrine erupted, pitting the unreconstructed "modernizers," who stressed the urgent need for nuclear weapons and other advanced military technology, against the "conservatives," who stressed the importance of the basic political factors and massive military manpower and relied on eventual Chinese development of its own weapons needs.

As early as January, Marshal P'eng declared that the Chinese must "on the basis of *our national* industrialization systematically arm our army with new technical equipment. In the light of *our* industrial capacity, we can do so only gradually." [28] In May, the foreign minister, Marshal Chen Yi, remarked in an interview that "At that moment China does not own atomic weapons, but we shall have them in the future." [29] And, also in May, Air Force General Liu Ya-lou emphasized the need first to press priority economic build-up of the country, and then, on that basis, "*China's* working class and scientists will be able to make the most up-to-date aircraft and atomic bombs in the not distant future . . . atomic weapons and rockets made by the workers, engineers, and scientists of *our* country. . . ." [30]

This new line combined the importance of nuclear weapons with a major *Chinese* effort to design and construct them—Chinese "scientists," as well as "workers" and "engineers," were cited. However, this new line, in initial reaction to the Soviet refusal to supply nuclear weapons, did not last long. It placed too much emphasis on the need for early Chinese acquisition of nuclear weapons, which was simply not possible, despite vigorous efforts. Doctrinal confusion over balancing the decisive importance of something which they did not have with assertions of *current* Chinese strength was too great. The military leaders may also have pressed Mao too hard. In any case, a major conference called by the military committee of the party's Central Committee met from May 27 until July 22—two whole months of debate. Top party leaders—including Mao—addressed the conference, which reportedly was attended by 1,000 Chinese military officers. By the end of July, a new line had been adopted. Marshal Chu Teh spoke on July 31 of "defects" resulting from "tendencies toward an exclusive military viewpoint." [31] He said that

[25] *Ibid.*, p. 102; cf. pp. 76–109. See also Alice L. Hsieh, "China, Russia and the Bomb," *New Leader,* Vol. 43, No. 40 (October 17, 1960).

[26] *Ibid.* and cf. Donald Zagoria, *The Sino-Soviet Conflict, 1956–1961* (Princeton, 1962), pp. 169–171.

[27] *Ibid.* See also Hinton, *Current History,* September 1962, p. 153.

[28] *Ibid.*, pp. 109–110.

[29] *Ibid.*, pp. 106–107.

[30] *Ibid.*, p. 112. Cf. also Zagoria, *op. cit.*, p. 192.

[31] *Ibid.*, pp. 114 and 116. For discussion of the conference, see Zagoria, *op. cit.*, pp. 189–194.

the Chinese should study Soviet military experience, but by a "selective and creative" approach. The *Liberation Army Daily* on the next day explained that "a very few comrades" had "one-sidedly stressed the role of atomic weapons and modern military technology, and neglected the role of man."[32] Also on August 1, Marshal Ho Lung warned in *People's Daily* against relying on "outside aid" in solving China's military problems.[33] Yu Chao-li, in *Red Flag* on August 16, cited Mao on "the atomic bomb is a paper tiger," a theme quickly picked up by others.[34] Finally, on September 6, 1958, the Central Committee of the party adopted a resolution on mobilizing the whole male population into a "people's militia," a development explicitly tied to Mao Tse-tung's "strategic thinking on the people's war."[35] In October, General Su Yü was removed as chief of the general staff.

Thus, the Chinese were forced into gradually building up advanced weapons capabilities with minimal Soviet assistance while playing down the significance of these weapons which they did not yet have. There have been ample signs of undercurrents of military dissatisfaction with this solution.[36]

The impotency of the Chinese, and Soviet refusal to back them in any risky situation of Chinese interest, were only too clearly evident in the Quemoy crisis of August and September 1958.[37] It also appears that, at that time, the Chinese made another effort, with some success, to get at least limited Soviet concessions in military aid.

A new meeting of Mao and Khrushchev, perhaps brought about in part by Chinese plans for the Quemoy crisis, occurred at the end of July 1958. Marshals Malinovsky and P'eng Teh-huai were also present. Soon after, "leaks" in Warsaw disclosed Soviet-Chinese accords on increased economic and military assistance. The reports indicated that the Soviets had agreed to supply the Chinese with missiles, nuclear reactors, and possibly nuclear warheads. Missiles for defense against Taiwan were specifically mentioned. On the basis of later information, it is clear that nuclear warheads were not promised or supplied, but it is possible that Mao obtained limited Soviet commitments—just how circumscribed the Quemoy crisis would soon show!—and additional limited Soviet assistance to native development of defense and offensive missile programs and the Chinese non-weapons nuclear program.[38] This may have marked the last Sino-Soviet military agreement.

It should be noted that, as the Soviet Union became increasingly concerned with avoiding risks of a nuclear war and saw advantage in cultivating a *détente* with the United States, the Chinese Communists were becoming increasingly assertive in urging more active confrontation of the imperialists under the shadow of the Soviet missile and space achievements.

During 1958 and 1959, the Chinese continued to stress their determination to get nuclear weapons. At first, in 1958, the Chinese supported the idea of a nuclear-free zone in the Far East,

---

[32] *Ibid.*, p. 116.

[33] Zagoria, *op. cit.*, p. 193.

[34] Yu Chao-li, in *Hung ch'i (Red Flag)*, August 16, 1958. See also *Liberation Army Daily*, October 24, 1958, and *People's Daily*, November 12, 1958.

[35] *Hung ch'i (Red Flag)*, October 16, 1958.

[36] See A. Kashin, "Chinese Military Doctrine," *Bulletin of the Institute for the Study of the USSR* (Munich), Vol. 7, No. 11 (November 1960), pp. 39–44.

[37] See Hsieh, *Communist China's Strategy*, pp. 119–136.

[38] A. M. Rosenthal, "Warsaw Reports Soviet-China Pact," *New York Times*, August 7, 1958; Rosenthal, "Soviet Atom Arms To Go To Peiping, Warsaw Learns," *New York Times*, August 18, 1962.

but, when Khrushchev proposed this in a speech on January 27, 1959, the Chinese reaction was quite cool.[39] Rather, the Chinese seized an East German statement of January 26 that, if West Germany got nuclear missiles, they, too, would "request" them from *their* allies. The Chinese—alone of the other Communist states—commented that this would be "not only fully justified, but also *necessary*." [40] On January 21, 1960, the National People's Congress passed a resolution stressing not only that China would be bound by any disarmament agreement only with its express consent but also that it would accept no disarmament agreement in the negotiation of which it had not participated. The Soviets were clearly not entrusted or trusted to look out for Chinese politico-military interests.

In mid-1959 a startling new development in over-all Sino-Soviet relations occurred. From April 24 to June 13, 1959, Minister of Defense P'eng Teh-huai visited Eastern Europe—in Albania at the same time that Khrushchev visited. Marshal P'eng had not been one of the ardent "modernizers" in the mid-1950's, but he was well aware of the crucial importance of modern weapons. If he asked again for increased Soviet assistance, there is no evidence it gained anything. In June, Averell Harriman was told by Khrushchev that Russia had sent missiles—he did not say with nuclear warheads—to protect Communist China against Taiwan, but this appears to have been a figurative overstatement.[41] Suddenly, on September 17, 1959, the dismissal of Marshal P'eng Teh-huai and four vice-ministers was announced. P'eng

was charged with heading an "antiparty group." And, indeed, we have learned that he did directly challenge Mao at the Lushan Central Committee plenum in August 1959.[42] Most significant from the standpoint of our present inquiry, however, was the fact that P'eng had written a letter to the Soviet party attacking Chinese Communist policies. Khrushchev, in an unpublished speech at Bucharest in June 1960, criticized the Chinese Communists for removing P'eng for having communicated his views to the Communist party of the Soviet Union.[43] P'eng may have been disturbed by the fact that the growing breach with the Soviet Union jeopardized Soviet arms aid.[44] Meanwhile, another sign of the growing estrangement of the two Communist powers was the rehabilitation in April 1959 of former General Lung Yun, the outspoken critic in 1957 of Soviet military assistance.[45]

The deterioration of Sino-Soviet relations over the next year was rapid and finally erupted into the open in April 1960 with the publication of a scarcely veiled Chinese ideological attack on the Soviets. By July and August, the Soviets suddenly withdrew their 2,000 to 3,000 economic and military advisers and technicians. This action was drastic, sudden, and virtually complete.

THE RELATIONSHIP RUPTURED: 1960 TO THE PRESENT

In the three years since the sudden virtual cessation of Soviet military and economic assistance, there has been

---

[39] See Hsieh, *Communist China's Strategy*, pp. 103–109 and 155–161.

[40] Editorial, *Jen-min jih-pao*, February 4, 1959.

[41] Hsieh, *Communist China's Strategy*, p. 164.

[42] David A. Charles, "The Dismissal of Marshal P'eng Teh-huai," *The China Quarterly*, No. 8 (October–December, 1961), pp. 63 ff.

[43] *Ibid.*, pp. 64 and 74–75.

[44] *Ibid.*, p. 65.

[45] See Ronald Farquhar, "China Posts Go To 18 Rightists," *Washington Post*, April 18, 1959.

almost no Sino-Soviet military relationship of any kind. The effects, even in the short run, have been significant for the Chinese. Continued, though declining, Soviet export of petroleum products to China has been the chief indirect aid. One is tempted also, in describing Sino-Soviet military relations, to note reported clashes on the Sinkiang border in recent years.

Since 1960 the Chinese Communist armed forces have probably, in net, decreased in capability. In the few years immediately ahead, the Chinese will no doubt develop indigenous capacity to build some jet fighters, defensive surface to air missiles, radars, small warships, and possibly short-range rockets. In the latter half of the decade, they will doubtless develop nuclear warheads and medium-range missiles. But all these developments are much hindered by the virtual cessation of Soviet military and economic assistance in mid-1960 and continued nonassistance since that time. In particular, the Chinese have had to abandon for the time being their budding indigenous production of jet fighters and submarines and whatever plans they may have had for jet medium bombers. The numbers, and still more the proficiency, of the air forces have actually declined from attrition of materiel and shortage of fuel for proficiency training. The ground forces have presumably been little affected.

At present, the Chinese Communist army numbers about 2.5 million men, with about 115 infantry and two or three armored divisions.[46] The air forces total about 3,000 aircraft of all types, including about 2,000 jet fighters —nearly all older model MIG-15's and MIG-17's, with probably only a few MIG-19's—and a few hundred IL-28 jet light bombers.[47] Apart from a few TU-4 piston medium bombers, not new when given to the Chinese fully ten years ago, the Chinese have no long-range air forces. The Navy has about four destroyers, four destroyer escorts, thirty conventional attack submarines, and a modest number of patrol craft.[48] Probably not even all of these units are operational.

Apart from the material effects on the Chinese of the ending of Soviet aid, the very military alliance commitment has been placed in question. Soviet spokesman Titarenko, in a celebrated article in August 1960, mentioned China directly in a statement on the economic and military vulnerability of a Socialist state which had strayed outside the Socialist camp, was "isolated," and no longer engaged in "mutual cooperation." And, by the same token, he clearly implied that Soviet support to China in case of war was conditional.[49] Marshal Malinovsky, in January 1962, noted that Soviet strength would defend "those socialist states *friendly to us"*— a very blunt warning indeed.[50] *Pravda,* in January 1963, bitterly remarked that those criticizing the Soviet Union for the Cuban venture could not hold off the imperialists without the Soviet Union.[51] Other Soviet statements have, of course, said that the Soviet Union would defend any Socialist state, including China; the Soviets want to "deter" us. But the exceptions are revealing.

The Chinese, in turn, have had to recognize—as Li Fu-Ch'un put it, coincidentally on the very same day Titarenko's article was published in

---

[46] See Institute for Strategic Studies, *The Communist Bloc and the Western Alliances: The Military Balance, 1962–1963* (London, 1962), p. 8.

[47] *Ibid.* See also *China News* (Taiwan), July 10, 1962.

[48] *Ibid.*

[49] See Zagoria, *op. cit.,* pp. 335–336.

[50] Marshal R. Malinovsky, Tass, January 24, 1962.

[51] *Pravda* editorial, January 7, 1963.

August 1960—that China must "mainly rely on our own efforts" in the future.[52] And again, as Malinovsky was threatening the Chinese in 1962, Marshal Chen Yi was saying that all the Chinese problems including *"national* defense" could be solved by self-reliance.[53]

Unchained from considerations of the Chinese reaction, the Soviets opened new military assistance programs with modern armament to Indonesia and the Near East. Thanks to the Soviet Union, Indonesia now has a cruiser, TU-16 jet medium bombers, air defense and short-range missiles, and MIG-21 interceptors, while the Chinese do not. MIG-21's and TU-16's have been provided to several other neutrals. In a move particularly galling to the Chinese, the Soviets have now provided MIG-21's to India. The Soviets have apparently tried, unsuccessfully, to bribe the North Koreans to their side in the dispute within the Communist bloc with modern military aid. The Soviet Union and China signed separate military defense pacts with North Korea in July 1961. Some Chinese military men may hanker for military co-operation with the Soviet Union, but it is very doubtful if they even attempt to exert any influence on the political controversy.

THE FUTURE

In concluding, we can note one or two paramount features of the decline in Sino-Soviet military relations which may help us to understand, if not to predict, future developments.

It is clear that, throughout, the Soviets have not wished to lessen fundamental Chinese dependence on the Soviet Union, to give the Chinese Com-

munists a fulcrum for bargaining power vis-à-vis the Soviets, to raise Chinese prestige in the Communist movement or the world at large, or to increase the risks they themselves would run if the Chinese had capabilities which might tempt them to risk a conflict with the West. The Soviets recognize the dilemma they would then face of supporting China at unacceptable costs to the Soviet Union or of seeing Communist China be destroyed at irreparable cost to communism. Moreover, intensifying these concerns was the divergent Chinese Communist pressure for stronger support of revolutionary activity by indigenous Communists elsewhere as well as for more vigorous support of immediate Communist aims. The Soviets have defined their policy in terms of their own interests.

Consequently, it is not surprising that, in pursuing *their* objectives, the Chinese have been dissatisfied with Soviet policy. The Soviets may want a nuclear-free zone in the Far East to disarm both the United States and Communist China; the Chinese are unwilling to give up their aspirations to nuclear-great-power status, even if their "security" were otherwise ensured. The Soviet efforts in the mid-1950's to concede the most imperialistic of Stalin's extortions were not sufficient, neither was the grudging support apparently given from 1958 to early 1960 to the production of aircraft and creation of Chinese missiles.

The broader political causes of the Sino-Soviet dispute and widening split in the period since 1959 have intensified further military disassociation from the never intimate relationship of the 1950's. This development burdens and delays, but does not completely foreclose, Chinese military modernization. Clearly, the future course of Sino-Soviet military relations will depend

[52] Li Fu-Ch'un, *Hung ch'i (Red Flag),* August 16, 1960.

[53] Chen Yi, New China News Agency, January 5, 1962.

upon the political relations of the two powers. It seems farfetched to note the possibility of Sino-Soviet military *hostilities* if their conflict deepens and either feels vitally threatened by the other, yet, while improbable, even this extreme cannot be entirely excluded from the consideration of both parties. Complete reconciliation, with broad and deep alliance ties in all aspects of military preparation and planning—which would go far beyond anything achieved in the 1950's—seems no less remote and unlikely. The outlook is for a continuation of relative mutual military isolation and conditional alliance commitments.

Sino-Soviet Economic Relations, 1959–1962

By Oleg Hoeffding *

ABSTRACT: The peak in Sino-Soviet trade was reached in 1958–1959, when it accounted for half of China's total trade. It declined heavily in 1960–1962, as did China's trade with Eastern Europe. The decline reflected China's economic crisis as well as the Sino-Soviet conflict. Apart from the recall of Soviet experts in 1960, there is no clear evidence of overt Soviet economic warfare. The Soviet Union exerted severe economic pressure, but did so in the businesslike guise of cutting exports to China, in response to China's reduced ability to pay. However, the Soviet Union has tempered this closefisted attitude with a few semicharitable gestures. Commercial relations, although visibly strained by the political dispute, have remained formally correct. But the collapse of China's trade with the bloc, the severe curtailment of imports other than grain from the West in 1961–1963, and poor prospects of obtaining long-term credits in the West have deprived China of the opportunities she had prior to 1960 of harnessing foreign trade to the needs of her industrialization drive. Peking's all-round intransigence, for the time being, makes China virtually the only underdeveloped country not receiving economic aid from any source.

Oleg Hoeffding, Ph.D., Santa Monica, California, is an economist with The Rand Corporation. Previously, he was assistant professor of economics and senior fellow of the Russian Institute, Columbia University. During World War II, he worked in the Economic Warfare Division of the American Embassy in London. He is author of Soviet National Income and Product in 1928 (1954) and other publications on the Soviet economy.

* This paper is based on research performed for the United States Air Force under Project RAND and reported in other form. Views or conclusions it contains should not be interpreted as representing the official opinion or policy of the United States Air Force.

THE Soviet Union was the first country to extend the hand of fraternal aid to People's China. The construction of modern plants, despatch of experts, training of students—all this the Soviet Union did in the sincere desire to help China speed up the creation of a modern economy."

Thus, *Pravda,* on February 14, 1963, marking the thirteenth anniversary of the Sino-Soviet Treaty of Friendship, Alliance, and Mutual Assistance. Two weeks later, a very different view of the Soviet attitude to China was voiced by *Jen-min jih-pao:* In mid-1960, after the Bucharest meeting of the "fraternal parties": [1]

. . . Some comrades . . . lost no time in taking a series of grave steps applying economic and political pressure against China. Disregarding international practice, they perfidiously and unilaterally tore up agreements and contracts they had concluded with a fraternal country. These agreements and contracts are to be counted not in twos or in threes, or in scores, but in hundreds.

The "tearing up" that came first and promptly to the West's notice was the abrupt recall of thousands of Soviet specialists and technical advisers in summer 1960. [2]

What other agreements and contracts were torn up then, or since, is still a matter for conjecture. Soviet and Chinese "news management" has been so effective that it is extremely difficult to reconstruct in detail the course of economic relations since the emergence of acute strain in Sino-Soviet political and party relations late in 1959. Two points should be stressed before attempting a reconstruction.

[1] *Jen-min jih-pao* editorial, February 27, 1963.
[2] *New York Times,* August 15, 1960.

CHINA'S ECONOMIC CRISIS

The Sino-Soviet controversy has proceeded against the background of the economic crisis which still holds China in its throes, although possibly having passed its nadir in 1962. It is not easy to disentangle the impact of the crisis on Sino-Soviet economic relations from that of mutual hostility.

Soviet sources have consistently blamed the slump in trade on what they tactfully call China's "temporary economic difficulties." It would be as naive to accept this explanation as the alternative view that the slump reflects a ruthless near-blockade of China by the Soviet Union and its European satellites. Undoubtedly, the Chinese economic crisis provided Moscow with a pretext for, in effect, applying severe economic pressure, but also for disguising it as an entirely nonpolitical and businesslike scaling down of its exports to China, in response to the insolvency of a trade partner and debtor. But, even in a happier state of political relations, China's crisis—through its effects on supply of agricultural commodities and manufactured goods dependent on inputs from agriculture—would have profoundly affected Sino-Soviet trade—as it has, in fact, affected China's trade with the non-Communist world.

FORMAL RELATIONS PRESERVED

One should also dismiss the notion that something like a rupture of economic relations between China and the Soviet Union has occurred, let alone that Moscow has been waging unrestrained economic warfare against its ally. Actually, until mid-1963, at any rate, both sides have been careful to draw the line between "party relations" and economic "state relations" and not to allow the most acute deterioration of the former to bring about uncontrolled disruption of the latter. Even as the substance of Sino-Soviet trade was shrinking to a fraction of its past peak levels, care was taken to preserve the established routines and amenities of state trading: year after year, the annual trade negotiations have gone through their normal cycles, alternating between Moscow and Peking. Even though the cycles have tended to get longer, and have produced less and less in trade negotiated, the institutional framework has not been shattered. The same is true of established arrangements for technical, scientific, and cultural exchanges, which have been preserved in form, although undoubtedly much reduced in content.

In the light of this record, the "tearing up of hundreds of contracts" may be an emotionally charged and exaggerated figure of speech. The 1960 recall of the experts, and widespread withdrawal of Soviet technical and scientific aid that went with it, may have been an impulsive Soviet move that fully merited the Chinese epithet. Otherwise, as to trade and financial relations, at any rate, one gets the impression that the Chinese grievances stem not from agreements "torn up" but from old agreements harsh in the first place and literally enforced and from agreements newly negotiated—against the background of political tension and economic crisis—which must have struck the Chinese as niggardly, Shylocklike, and fratricidal rather than fraternal.

Two aspects of Soviet behavior also are inconsistent with any simple economic-warfare interpretation: First, as will be seen, as late as 1961–1962, the Soviets made token gestures to relieve China's food crisis. Second, study of the commodity composition of Soviet exports in 1960–1961 suggests that China was given the choice what to buy and what to forego under a much-reduced total-purchase ceiling. Most notably, Soviet oil exports had not been reduced by 1961. An oil embargo would have been an obvious move had the Soviet Union wanted to bring China to heel by economic warfare.

In short, when China's economic troubles were at their worst, it may have looked at times as if the Soviet heavyweight was willing to let his exhausted opponent take the count, while watching from his corner, but he never showed signs of jumping on his stomach or otherwise violating the rigorous Queensberry Rules which have so far governed Sino-Soviet "state relations."

Hear No Evil, Speak No Evil

True to that rule which bans the "bringing into the open" of strains and difficulties within the Communist camp, Soviet sources have maintained near-total silence on the deterioration of economic relations with China, as well as on her economic troubles. Thus, *Vneshniaia torgovlia,* the monthly journal of the Ministry of Foreign Trade, which had prominently featured the subject of trade with China while it was on the upgrade, published one single item on this subject in 1962. This was an uninformative communiqué on the signing of the annual trade protocol for 1962.[3] Otherwise, during the same year, the journal made only a few muted allusions to the decline of trade with China, in general surveys of Soviet and bloc foreign trade.

In effect, however, this curtain of silence has been a somewhat disingenuous sham. It has kept Soviet verbal comment to a minimum, but it has been completely negated by continued routine publication of the very complete and informative annual Soviet foreign-

[3] *Vneshniaia torgovlia,* No. 6 (1962), p. 5. The trade protocol was signed April 20, 1962.

trade statistics, as an eloquent record of the precipitous decline of trade with China from the 1959 peak. This record is summarized in the tables below.[4]

THE GREAT LEAP FORWARD

In 1958-1959, after eight years of fluctuating but impressive expansion, Sino-Soviet trade had responded vigorously to China's "Great Leap Forward." In two years, China's imports from the Soviet Union rose by 75 per cent, her exports by 49 per cent. China had regained first place among the Soviet Union's trade partners. The Soviet Union, in turn, came to account for nearly half of China's total trade. It also remained China's principal, and vital, source of imports of machinery and equipment, petroleum, and other goods which China would have found difficult to obtain elsewhere in the face of Western restrictions, the United States embargo, and shortage of foreign exchange.

The main motive force behind the trade expansion of 1958–1959 was the additional and urgent demand for capital equipment and raw materials generated by the Great Leap. The

[4] As cited in footnote (a) to Table 1. Data on Sino-Soviet trade in the text of this paper are drawn from these sources, unless otherwise indicated.

Soviet response to China's gargantuan appetite for imports was not ungenerous —or so it probably seemed to the Russians—although even then there were indications that the state of economic relations was far from cordial.[5]

Both in 1958 and 1959, the level of trade was considerably in excess of what had been provided for by the annual trade protocols for those years. The excess reflected Soviet willingness to meet supplementary Chinese shopping lists, presented in a helter-skelter fashion that must have been quite irksome to Soviet economic planners. In August 1958, and again in February 1959, the Soviet Union still proved willing to add substantially to its earlier commitments to support Chinese industrialization by selling more or less complete sets of equipment for industrial plants to be built with Soviet technical aid. Under two agreements concluded at those dates, the Soviet Union undertook to assist in this way construction of an additional 125 projects.

As shown in Table 2, the value of deliveries described in Soviet statistics

[5] For a study of Sino-Soviet economic relations prior to 1959 and the early signs of strain and deterioration, see the author's "Sino-Soviet Economic Relations in Recent Years," in Kurt London (ed.), *Unity and Contradiction* (New York, 1962), pp. 295–312.

TABLE 1—Sino-Soviet Trade, 1950–1961
(Million Rubles)[a]

	1950	1951	1952	1953	1954	1955	1956	1957	1958	1959	1960	1961
Soviet exports	350	431	499	628	684	674	660	490	571	859	735	331
Soviet imports	172	298	373	428	521	579	688	664	793	990	763	496
Balance[b]	178	133	126	200	163	94	−28	−174	−223	−131	−28	−166

[a] Values for all years are shown in "new" foreign-trade rubles, introduced January 1, 1961. Conversion at the official exchange rate, $1.00 = 0.90 rubles, will provide reasonable approximations of dollar values.

[b] Minus sign denotes Soviet import surplus. Minor discrepancies between balance shown and difference of items are due to rounding.

Sources: 1950–1954: *Vneshniaia torgovlia*, No. 10 (1959), pp. 2 ff; 1955–1959: *Vneshniaia torgovlia SSSR za 1955–1959 gody* (Moscow, 1961); 1960–1961: *Vneshniaia torgovlia SSSR za 1961 god* (Moscow, 1962).

TABLE 2—SINO-SOVIET TRADE BY MAJOR COMMODITY GROUPS, 1958–1961
(Million Rubles)

COMMODITY GROUP	1958	1959	1960	1961
SOVIET IMPORTS FROM CHINA (Total)[a]	793	990	763	496
Agricultural commodities (total)	351	403	236	45
Fibers, tobacco, oilseeds, and other raw materials	(147)	(212)	(126)	(30)
Foodstuffs of animal origin	(77)	(46)	(22)	(3)
Foodstuffs of vegetable origin	(128)	(144)	(89)	(12)
Fabrics, clothing, footwear	198	352	338	287
Other	244	236	189	164
SOVIET EXPORTS TO CHINA (Total)[a]	571	859	735	331
Machinery and equipment	286	538	454	97
"Complete plants" deliveries	(150)	(360)	(337)	(71)
Other	(137)	(178)	(117)	(26)
Iron and steel	55	43	53	31
Crude oil and petroleum products	83	106	102	109
Foodstuffs	1	1	—	57
Cereals	—	—	—	(16)
Sugar	1	1	—	(42)
Other	146	178	127	36

[a] Minor discrepancies between the totals shown and the sums of the items are due to rounding.
Sources: *Vneshniaia torgovlia SSSR za 1955–1959 gody* (Moscow, 1961) and *Vneshniaia torgovlia SSSR za 1961 god* (Moscow, 1962).

as "complete sets of equipment" reached a peak in 1959, accounting for 42 per cent of total exports to China.

Moscow, it is true, extended no credits to China to finance this import expansion. It made the Chinese pay promptly by concurrently stepping up their exports to the Soviet Union. However, Moscow showed itself accommodating by accepting payment, increasingly, in Chinese manufactured consumer goods, a class of goods traditionally low on the Soviet scale of import priorities. Table 2 shows that the principal items in this class—fabrics, clothing, and footwear—represented more than one third of total Soviet imports in 1959, running a close second to agricultural raw materials and foodstuffs which earlier had been the mainstay of China's exports to the Soviet Union. China would have been hard put to find other markets to trade such quantities of consumer goods for capital equipment vital to its industrialization ambitions.

IRRITANTS FOR PEKING

Soviet responsiveness to China's needs, however, had its reverse side in attitudes which the Chinese may have found predatory and cynical. Far from granting new credits, the Soviet Union insisted on punctilious discharge of China's debtor obligations. These resulted not only from the rather modest economic-aid loans of 1950–1954 but also from a variety of opaque transactions involving Soviet military aid, cession to China of Soviet military and naval-base facilities, and transfer of Soviet shares in what had been joint enterprises in the early 1950's. The total of China's debt has never been unequivocally disclosed. However, the size of China's export surpluses to the Soviet Union in 1957–1959, which largely represent debt-service payments in kind, suggests that the debt is large and burdensome (Table 1).

Soviet insistence on collecting the debt-service installments even in 1958–1959, when the need to finance its fast-mounting imports from the Soviet Union was straining China's export resources to the limit, would have been a source of serious grievance to Peking even if Moscow had not, at the same time, been showing striking and obviously self-seeking largess to other countries within and outside the bloc.

From 1958 on, Mongolia, North Vietnam, and North Korea were treated to a bounty of Soviet economic-development credits and also to waivers or deferments of payments on debts previously incurred, a favor never granted to China. In scale—when compared on a per-capita basis—this aid far exceeded anything the Soviet Union had given to China. In intent, it was outright bribery in the beginning Sino-Soviet contest for the allegiance of the Asian satellite regimes.

Outside the bloc, Soviet economic aid to Afro-Asian countries was also gathering momentum. This campaign, too, must have irked the Chinese. Not only did it signify Moscow's decision to back up with real economic resources what Peking regarded as misguided and heretical courting of "national bourgeois" regimes, while aid to China was being denied. It also goaded China into expanding her own competitive aid activities in Afro-Asia, thus adding to the strain on her resources.

Chinese displeasure at Soviet economic discrimination was not yet brought into the open directly. It was reflected, however, in the muted dialogue that was getting under way on the broad subject of uneven economic development in the Communist camp, and the obligations of its advanced and relatively wealthy members to assist the backward and poor ones. Peking, however obliquely, was charging Moscow with not living up to these obligations. Moscow insisted that aid and co-operation must be mutual and that it presupposed ideological and political unity, holding up the model of the economic co-ordination programs of the Council of Economic Mutual Assistance —which China never had joined. Soviet statements, with increasing candor, took the line that the Soviet Union would not retard its own economic development to help accelerate that of bloc partners engaged in heretical economic and social experiments. Ultimately, this line found its fullest—and, to Peking, most provocative—expression in the party program of 1961, which made it clear that the Soviet Union would not be diverted by obligations of "fraternal aid" from its majestic progress towards the "abundance" of full communism.

THE GREAT SLIDE BACKWARD

The first indications that economic relations were being seriously strained by political discord came early in 1960. In March, the Soviet Minister of Foreign Trade disclosed, obliquely but clearly, that negotiations towards a long-term trade agreement with China, in progress for more than a year, had been broken off. In April, by another clear implication, it was revealed that the trade protocol for 1960 envisaged a slight reduction in the volume of Sino-Soviet trade.[6] Then, as the interparty conflict was heading for its first open eruption at Bucharest, and the first indications of China's agricultural failures emerged, the curtain of silence fell. The startling news of the exodus of the Soviet experts was promptly and eagerly spread by the Yugoslav press

[6] Hoeffding, op. cit., pp. 298–301.

but totally suppressed in Soviet and Chinese sources.[7]

As the year progressed, it brought mounting evidence of the impact of China's agricultural crisis on her foreign trade. Exports of agricultural commodities to the West were sharply curtailed, and China was forced to turn for grain to Canada and Australia. All this justified curiosity as to how China was faring in trade with her principal partner. Neither Moscow nor Peking hurried to satisfy such curiosity. Nothing was said about either the course of trade in 1960 or trade intentions for 1961 until after the temporary patching up of party relations in December. In February 1961—unusually late—negotiations were started on trade for that year.[8] They were concluded in April, when it was finally admitted that trade had suffered a setback in 1960, attributed to the effect of "temporary food difficulties" on export resources of foodstuffs and other agricultural commodities.[9] However, the extent of the trade decline was not revealed until the annual volume of foreign-trade statistics appeared in August 1961 (Table 2). Total trade had dropped by about a fifth, considerably more than the 5 per cent decline envisaged by the 1960 trade protocol. However, this decline occurred from the unprecedented peak of 1959, and total trade had remained larger than in any year prior to 1958. China's exports to the Soviet Union had fallen more sharply than her imports. As expected, the export decline was mostly accounted for by agricultural commodities. Other exports—mainly consumer goods, ores, and metals—had stood up fairly well.

Although agricultural exports were cut nearly in half, China still had shipped some $250 million worth of such exports to the Soviet Union in her hour of need. The Soviet Union had supplied no food to China. In a semiapologetic vein, the Soviet Foreign Trade Minister said in a speech before the Chinese trade delegation in April 1961:[10] "1960 was a most unfavorable year meteorologically. In many countries, including the Soviet Union, some regions suffered badly from drought. Last year proved even more severe for China. . . ."

Yet, as China was committing some $300 million of hard-earned foreign exchange to grain purchases from the West, the Soviet Union had exported 6.8 million tons of grain to other countries in 1960 and was to export another 7.5 million tons in 1961.

There was no indication, however, that the Soviet Union had penalized or pressured China by arbitrarily cutting Soviet exports. In particular, exports of machinery and equipment remained high by any past standard save that of 1959, an exceptional year, and the decline in petroleum exports was minimal. It may well be that total Soviet exports were not reduced below the level agreed for 1960.

THE UNRELENTING BANKER

China, on the other hand, had clearly defaulted on her export and debtor obligations. Her export surplus in 1960 had dwindled to 28 million rubles. That this was far short of what had been planned and required to meet her 1960 debt-service payments was disclosed by

[7] Even now, Soviet publications have acknowledged this move only by a change in tense: Standard formulas such as "Soviet specialists are rendering invaluable aid in the building of China's industry" have been replaced by "Soviet specialists *have rendered*," and the like.

[8] *Pravda*, February 10, 1961.

[9] Communiqués on April 7, 1961 agreements, *Vneshniaia torgovlia*, No. 5 (1961), pp. 17–18.

[10] *Vneshniaia torgovlia*, No. 5 (1961), p. 13.

the announcement in April 1961 that China "had incurred a debt on account of trade operations in 1960" amounting to 288 million rubles.[11] This surprisingly large figure may imply that even in 1959 China had fallen behind on debt service and had been expected to make up the shortfall in 1960, by an exceptionally large export surplus. China was to repay this debt, free of interest, according to a schedule that may have represented an index of Chinese expectations at the time of the pace of their economic recovery: no payments in 1961, 8 million rubles in 1962, 50 in 1963, and 115 annually in 1964–1965. Nothing was said of remissions or deferments of China's other debts to the Soviet Union. This implied that even in 1961 China would be required to generate a large export surplus to the Soviet Union.

Inasmuch as the trade agreement for 1961 provided for elimination or curtailment of Chinese exports for a long list of important agricultural commodities, it was obvious that a major Chinese export surplus could result only from a drastic cut in Soviet exports to China. This was borne out by the trade returns for 1961. Thus, by merely standing on its rights as a creditor, the Soviet Union was imposing what in effect was indistinguishable from a partial embargo, combined with the exaction of a sizable volume of unrequited exports from the hard-pressed Chinese economy.

SEMICHARITABLE GESTURES

This tight-fisted Soviet stance was mitigated only by a gesture acknowledging China's food difficulties: 500,000 tons of Cuban sugar due to the Soviet Union was to be diverted to China in 1961, as an "interest-free loan" repay-

[11] *Ibid.,* p. 18.

able in 1964–1967, presumably in Cuban sugar due to China. The trade returns for 1961 showed that the value of this charity amounted to about one tenth of what China spent in that year on grain imports from the West. They also revealed that in 1961 the Soviet Union had sold China 300,000 tons of wheat, rye, and flour. This was not much compared to either the 6 million tons of cereals imported by China from non-bloc sources or the more than 7 million tons exported by the Soviet Union to other countries. But, interestingly, the Soviet Union charged China $60 per ton of wheat in this transaction, no more than China was paying for Canadian wheat, and about the same price as that charged for Soviet wheat to West European countries and Cuba. By contrast, East European satellites and North Korea were paying $69 to $75 for Soviet wheat.

1961: TRADE SLUMP GATHERS MOMENTUM

The drastic decline in trade presaged by the agreements of April 1961 was fully confirmed by the Soviet trade statistics for the year. In contrast to 1960, in order to produce the large favorable balance required from China for debt service, Soviet exports were cut more severely than imports, to a mere 45 per cent of the 1960 level, and their lowest point in the twelve-year history of Soviet trade with Communist China. China's exports declined by about one-third, with shipments of foodstuffs almost eliminated and those of other agricultural commodities cut to a minimum. Nonagricultural exports, however, also registered sizable reductions.

As in 1960, one had the impression that Moscow had left up to the Chinese the allocation of their sharply reduced total import allowance. Machinery and equipment imports—hitherto a high-priority item for China—were cut almost to one fifth of their 1960 value. A Soviet comment that this reflected a Chinese decision to reduce considerably the import of machinery "in connection with large imports of grain and of commodities needed for increasing farm production, and also a revision of investment plans" may not have been entirely disingenuous.[12] In 1961 Chinese economic policy, in fact, had turned its prime attention to the rehabilitation of agriculture and reduced industrial investment. Moreover, emergence of idle capacity in many industries had made imports of industrial equipment even less urgent. Perhaps the most telling sign that the Soviet Union had not engaged in outright economic warfare was the slight increase recorded in its 1961 petroleum exports, on which China depends to the tune of some 40 per cent of its total consumption.

These symptoms of Soviet restraint were the more noteworthy since China's foreign economic policy in 1961 seemed calculated to provoke rather than placate Moscow. It had defiantly extended aid to Albania to counter the virtual blockade imposed by the Soviet Union and its satellites. Early in the year, China withdrew from its "observer" role at the meetings of the Moscow-dominated Council of Economic Mutual Assistance and has boycotted them since. In June 1962, in a demonstrative countermove, Mongolia was admitted to the Council as the first and only Asian member.

Nor was China deterred by her economic plight from intensifying her aid campaign in Afro-Asia, in clear competition with the Soviet Union. In the course of the year, Chinese credits and grants were extended to Burma, Ceylon, Indonesia, Laos, Nepal, Ghana,

Guinea, Mali, and Nigeria. China also proceeded rapidly to build up trade with Cuba.[13]

CHINA DISENGAGES FROM BLOC TRADE

The decline in Sino-Soviet trade was accompanied by an even sharper contraction of China's trade with the European satellites, which previously had accounted for about one fifth of her total trade. In 1961 its volume fell to somewhere between 30 and 40 per cent of the 1960 level.[14] This reflected, mainly, China's strenuous efforts to husband her supply of export commodities for sale in Western markets in order to finance her massive grain purchases. This China succeeded in doing, by a vigorous export drive combined with drastic cuts in imports other than of grain and fertilizers and assisted by silver sales and short-term credits from Canada and Australia. The net result was a rapid and radical redeployment of China's foreign trade away from the bloc and toward the capitalist world. Bloc trade, at its peak, had accounted for some 80 per cent of China's total trade. In 1961 its share fell to about one half. It was to decline further in 1962.

TRADE IN 1962

The very meager information published in Soviet sources about the negotiations on the Sino-Soviet trade agreement for 1962 suggested that they proceeded unusually slowly and haltingly.

[12] *Vneshniaia torgovlia*, No. 11 (1962), p. 17.

[13] *Bulletin of Foreign Commercial Information, Supplement No. 4*, Moscow, May 1962; JPRS Translation No. 17,831, pp. 85 ff. This publication (whose circulation is very limited) contains the relatively most complete account of China's economic crisis to appear in Soviet sources.

[14] *Far Eastern Economic Review*, September 27, 1962, p. 595; *The Christian Science Monitor*, February 7, 1963.

After a preliminary "exchange of views" held as early as August 1961, it was agreed to start negotiations "at the expert level" in October. They did not get under way until late December 1961.[15] This delay may have been connected with the flare-up of the political controversy before and during the Twenty-second Congress of the Communist party of the Soviet Union.

Nevertheless, the protocol on 1962 trade was finally signed in April of that year. The fact that no indication was given whether trade was due to increase or decline implied the latter. The same could be inferred from the published lists of major commodities to be exchanged, which were unusually brief. No agricultural commodities except wool were mentioned among Chinese exports. Another notable omission was cotton fabrics, previously an important export item.

Somewhat ironically, this agreement, which marked China's further demotion to insignificant status among the Soviet Union's trade partners, preceded by only three weeks the signature of a Soviet trade pact with Cuba, the Soviet Union's latest ally, providing for a 40 per cent expansion of trade in 1962, to a total of $750 million.[16]

By present indications, Sino-Soviet trade in 1962 fell well below this figure. The official data are not yet available at the time of writing, but a further substantial decline has been reported.[17] This time, it is said to have affected petroleum products, an indication that China was driven to severe rationing of even the most essential imports from the Soviet Union.

[15] *Vneshniaia torgovlia,* No. 10 (1961), p. 15; *Izvestiia,* December 21, 1961.
[16] *Vneshniaia torgovlia,* No. 6 (1962), p. 7.
[17] *The New York Times,* Western edition, March 27, 1963. Total Sino-Soviet trade (exports plus imports) in 1962 amounted to approximately 615 million rubles, or $680 million. *Pravda,* July 14, 1963.

China Accelerates Debt Payments

Soviet sources have disclosed, however, that China, once again, was made to generate an export surplus to the Soviet Union in 1962, and apparently a larger one than had been agreed upon. This was the implication of an agreement signed April 20, 1963: "In accordance with the desire of the Chinese government," China was repaying part of the 1960 "trade debt" ahead of schedule. The advance payment was made out of a "balance in China's favor resulting from 1962 trade operations."[18] There was no explanation as to whether this extra export surplus had resulted from unscheduled additional exports by China or had been forced on her by Soviet withholding of exports previously agreed upon. In either event, the transaction amounted to the opposite of economic aid from the Soviet Union at a time when China was eagerly looking for credits in Western Europe and Japan.

Prospects for 1963

This agreement, however, and the trade protocol for 1963 signed simultaneously, proved that formal "state relations" in the economic sphere were weathering the storm which broke out in the party controversy early in 1963. Yet there were clear indications that the tenor and form of the trade negotiations had been affected by the dispute. In the two preceding rounds of negotiations—held in Moscow in 1961 and in Peking in 1962—both delegations were still headed by the respective foreign trade ministers, as had become customary. This was still true of the Soviet delegation in 1963, but the Chinese sent a deputy minister to Moscow. In 1961 and 1962, the visiting delegations had been received, respectively, by N. S. Khrushchev and Chou En-lai. In 1963

[18] *Pravda,* April 21, 1963.

it was Soviet Deputy Premier A. I. Mikoyan who received the Chinese delegation. The ice had evidently set.

The communiqué on the 1963 trade protocol was, again, highly uninformative and contained no hint that a revival of trade was in prospect. As in 1962, despite some improvement since then in China's agricultural situation, there was no reference to agricultural exports, save wool and—a trivial addition— apples and citrus fruit. On the Soviet export side, mention of tractors (export of which had been nearly discontinued in 1961) reflected continued Chinese concentration on the problems of her agriculture.

CHINA'S PREDICAMENT

With Sino-Soviet trade set for a third very lean year, and the rest of Chinese trade with the bloc cut to a minimum, China's position in the world economy is not an enviable one. In the early 1950's, she had in part chosen and in part been forced to throw in her lot with the economies of the Communist camp. In the course of a decade, she had evolved a pattern of trade with the bloc not inappropriate to her needs and resources during a period when a precarious balance of food output and consumption had enabled her to force rapid expansion of heavy industry.

The Soviet Union and Eastern Europe while showing no generosity, had nevertheless supplied the wherewithal of initial industrialization on an impressive scale. China, by trading raw materials and consumer goods for, mainly, machinery and equipment, had succeeded in harnessing not only her trade with the bloc but also that with the non-Communist world to the needs of her investment drive.

This pattern and function of trade crumbled rapidly with the onset of the agricultural crisis and the Sino-Soviet rift. It is idle to speculate whether the absence of the latter would have offered China an option other than turning for relief to the grain surpluses generated by the despised capitalist system. In fact, she had none, as the Soviet Union —with its own agriculture stagnant since 1958—did not divert its grain exports from East European and Western markets or free grain for China by curbing domestic consumption.

However, the holders of surplus grain were not in any giving mood, either, nor were they themselves among China's actual or potential export markets. Thus, China had to attempt to maximize exports to other markets in the West and to commit, in 1961–1963, a major share of the proceeds to paying for grain. Chinese performance of this triangular maneuver was impressively vigorous and agile, but it was an emergency operation which has not given China a place in the non-Communist network of trade that is either tenable or acceptable to herself in the longer run.

By mid-1963, China was attempting the logical next step toward returning her foreign trade to its past and preferred function of serving investment rather than consumption and was finding the going hard. With agricultural output apparently on the upgrade, and some prospect of soon restoring minimum self-sufficiency in food, China is now looking for sources of capital equipment in the West, evidently as a prelude to resuming industrial expansion. However, with China's foreign-exchange reserves depleted, export earnings but precariously maintained, and grain credits yet to be paid off, Western long-term credits are a prerequisite for major purchases of equipment and one that China, as yet, has had little success in realizing.

Businessmen in the West are eager to sell, but bankers cannot but legitimately doubt China's solvency. Governments, in conditions of general economic prosperity and confronted with large demands for economic aid from friendly and neutral countries, have little incentive to grant favors to a regime which, on its own insistence, is more genuinely hostile to capitalism than Moscow's.

For the time being, China's posture in the world economy remains the uncomfortable one of sitting between two stools. She has profoundly antagonized both centers of world power and both principal dispensers of politically motivated foreign aid. She shows no inclination to make political concessions in either direction as a price for kinder economic treatment. Instead, China is paying the price of intransigence by being the world's largest underdeveloped country and one of its poorest and virtually the only one not receiving economic aid from any source.

Factors of Unity and Factors of Conflict

By Richard Lowenthal

ABSTRACT: Russian and Chinese national interests tend toward opposition. The Sino-Soviet alliance is wholly due to seizure of power by Chinese Communists and to conflict with the same enemies. Economic, military, and diplomatic disparities have created a lopsided material dependence of Communist China on the Soviet Union, resulting in divergent views on priorities within the alliance, and have caused them to disagree on proper strategy in relation to the United States, anti-imperialist revolutionary movements, and independent neutral powers. Among states governed by totalitarian, ideological parties, these disagreements have naturally assumed the form of different interpretations of the common doctrine. Lacking other means of effective pressure on the Soviets, the Chinese have developed these differences into a systematic challenge to Soviet ideological authority. A Soviet attempt to evade this challenge and to preserve unity on the basis of toleration of inevitable differences and adjustment by compromise has failed; both sides have recognized the inevitability of factional schism for some time. They have built two rival Communist camps with separate policies. Underlying opposition of national interests is increasingly appearing, and doctrinal differences are hardening. Though a serious attempt to return to policy coordination is unlikely, the formal bond of the alliance may well continue as reinsurance against the common enemy so long as both countries are ruled by Communist party regimes.

Richard Lowenthal, Dr. phil., is Professor of International Relations at the Otto-Suhr-Institute of the Free University, West Berlin. He has previously worked as editorial writer on the London Observer and been a Research Associate at the Russian Research Center, Harvard. He is coauthor of The Sino-Soviet Dispute (1961) and author of Chruschtschow und der Weltkommunismus (1963) as well as of many contributions on relations among Communist governments and parties for American, British, and German publications.

ANY attempt to analyze the factors determining the foreign policies of Communist powers is bound to make use of two types of approach—that of "national interest" and that of "ideology." The two approaches are complementary in the strict sense that neither will yield precise, let alone satisfactory, results if pursued in isolation: National interest is subject to conflicting interpretations even within democratic states and assumes completely new aspects in the light of the ideology of a ruling totalitarian party, and ideological principles may entail widely differing consequences for foreign policy according to the national situation of the state whose rulers seek to apply them. Nevertheless, the two approaches correspond to two distinct groups of data that are relevant for the formation of foreign policy. The national-interest analysis may legitimately assemble all the elements in the situation of a state that are independent from the nature and ideas of its regime at the given moment—its geography, population, and resources, the power constellation surrounding it, the abilities and character of its people, and so on. The ideological analysis, on the other hand, should not only deal with the exegesis of the scriptures and programmatic documents of the ruling party but also seek to relate them to the regime's interest in self-preservation and to judge their relevance by that standard. Viewed in this way, the isolated pursuit of either approach may be useful and even necessary, not as an aim in itself, but as a preliminary step toward a realistic synthesis.

CHINESE AND RUSSIAN NATIONAL INTERESTS

If we apply this isolating method to the national interests of Russia and China, it appears highly unlikely that an alliance between Russia and a strong and united China would ever have arisen unless both states had come under Communist rule: Their "pure" national interests tend to oppose them. The interest of Russia as a great power might require a Chinese government strong enough to limit the encroachment of other powers on its territory, particularly during a period when Russia alone was not in a position to stop such encroachment, but it hardly requires a China that is a great power in its own right. The Soviets offered support to governments controlling part of China before 1927 and to a weak National government from 1936 to 1945 in order to limit the expansion of Japanese power on the Asian continent; they backed Mao Tse-tung after 1946 partly in order to limit the spread of American influence. But they did not then expect, and apparently did not desire, the creation of a strong China united under Communist rule: They maintained diplomatic relations with Chiang Kai-shek and even negotiated with him on the border provinces until the very eve of his expulsion from the mainland.

Conversely, Chinese national interest was opposed to interests of all the powers who had been exploiting Chinese weakness in a scramble for spheres of influence and privilege, including Russia, and, as British and French influence in East Asia declined, Russia came to rank second only to Japan as a danger to Chinese unity. Only the United States, because of its physical remoteness and its Open Door tradition, could appear as China's "natural" ally against the neighboring powers.

Even the Sino-Soviet alliance, created as an expression of the common "ideological" needs of two Communist regimes, did not end the role of "pure" national interest as a divisive factor. This showed itself in Stalin's attempt to maintain Russian privileges in Manchuria and Russian influence in Sinkiang, which was only dropped by his successors in 1954 in deference to Chinese pressure, and in later Chinese attempts to regain influence in the Mongolian People's Republic that were opposed by the Soviets, as well as in the recent bitter rivalry of both powers for control of the Communist regime in North Korea.

In trying to judge the importance of this factor of conflict and its trend of development, it may be said that it was acute when China was just emerging from prolonged civil war and international impotence, that it became dormant during the period when Chinese consolidation had been accepted by Russia as a fact but Chinese great-power ambitions had not yet begun seriously to manifest themselves, roughly between 1954 and 1957, and that it has since entered a new phase of virulence owing to the visible growth of these ambitions. The characteristic of that new phase is that the opposition of interests is no longer confined to the border regions from Korea to Sinkiang but has broadened into general Soviet opposition to the expansion of China as an Asian power and to its potential growth into a world power. Both the Russian policy of maintaining India as a counterpoise to China on the Asian continent and the Chinese effort to demonstrate India's impotence, while partly motivated by differences on Communist world strategy to be discussed below, are also manifestations of this direct opposition of national interests. The same applies to Moscow's evident determination to keep China out of the atomic club as long as possible. Finally, Russian opposition to the rapid growth of Chinese power is clearly one of the major factors limiting Soviet economic, military, and diplomatic aid to Communist China.

It follows that the opposition of na-

tional interests must become more acute the more the Chinese succeed in building up their independent power—unless and until they reach a point where Russia has to resign herself to a basic change in the relation of forces. The setbacks suffered by Peking in its attempts at rapid industrialization do not suggest that such a point will be reached soon, if at all, while its remarkable success in expanding its sphere of influence in Asia—among non-Communist no less than among Communist countries—indicates that the area of direct Sino-Soviet opposition may equally expand in the near future.

COMMON GOALS AND COMMON ENEMIES

The Russo-Chinese alliance, then, was originally wholly due to the ideological factor: It was concluded as a result of the conquest of power by the Chinese Communist party—a party which for reasons of principle as well as of self-preservation was determined to "lean to one side" in world affairs. The victorious Chinese Communists were not a satellite party—they were not led by Soviet agents, and they owed little to direct Soviet support—but their party structure and their ideas had been formed in the main on the Bolshevik model. They proposed to transform China in the Soviet image, if partly by different methods, and to co-operate with the Soviets in fostering the progress of "world revolution"—that is, in supporting the spread of Communist party rule to further countries. In struggling for this common goal, they were bound to encounter the opposition of the same enemies—the "imperialist" powers led by the United States. To this day, the common ideological goals used by both parties to legitimize their rule and the common enmities provoked by the pursuit of those goals remain the chief factors holding the alliance together.

It must be observed at once that, although the ideas and the structure of the Chinese Communist party regime were largely shaped by the Soviet model, as well as by the common Marxist-Leninist sources and the common needs of modern totalitarian power, they were never identical. Influenced possibly by the tradition of Chinese political thought with its stress on the skill and wisdom of the ruling group rather than on institutional forms, and certainly by the experience of surviving against overwhelming odds and triumphing over extreme hardships after decades of struggle, the Chinese Communists from the start put even greater emphasis than the Bolsheviks on the "subjective factor"—on the power of the revolutionary will, if combined with "correct thinking," to transform objective economic conditions and on the need to change the consciousness of the masses accordingly. The resulting differences in the style of work and the internal climate of the two ruling parties always contained a potential of ideological divergence, but they did not in fact lead to ideological conflict so long as their effects were confined to differences in the methods and pace used by either for revolutionizing their respective societies. Stalin, in contrast to his behavior in the Yugoslav case, never presumed to tell the Chinese how they should run their state, nor did Mao hint at any criticism of Soviet methods while Stalin lived. After his death, recognition of the right of each ruling Communist party to find the right institutional forms and the right pace for approaching the common goal in its particular conditions soon became part of official Soviet doctrine as laid down by Khrushchev. Hence it seems safe to say that the first Sino-Soviet ideological dispute on domestic problems—the debate on

the "People's communes" and the preconditions for moving to the "higher stage" of communism at the turn of 1958–1959—would not have broken out but for previous disagreements in the international field.

Nor can it be said that these international disagreements were purely ideological in their origin. The concept of world revolution does, of course, contain the basic ambiguity that it may mean the spread of Communist rule either by the territorial expansion of the Soviet fatherland or by the victory of independent revolutions. Stalin's limited and hesitant support for the Chinese Communists in their struggle for power was one expression of his firm commitment to the former interpretation. But he had accepted the accomplished fact of Mao's victory and, after his death, his heirs—N. S. Khrushchev in particular—had clearly shown their belief that a harmonious and parallel advance of independent Communist powers and movements was possible in principle. In fact, a considerable degree of harmonious co-operation was accomplished after 1954 and, most of all, during the severe ideological crisis that shook the Soviet bloc and the international Communist movement in 1956–1957. We are thus entitled to conclude that, despite the historically conditioned differences in ideological style, "pure ideology" has been mainly a factor of unity and that the "ideological disputes" have arisen from the impact of the common struggle against the West on the different national situations of the Soviet Union and Communist China and from their different interpretations of the ideology in the light of these different situations.

DIFFERENT SITUATIONS IN THE COMMON STRUGGLE

The relevant differences in the situations of the two powers concern their level of economic development, their military security, and their room for diplomatic maneuver. Given these differences, the common conflict with the Western alliance has resulted both in a rather one-sided material dependence of China on Russia and in different concepts of the strategy toward the United States, the colonial revolutionary movements, and the major uncommitted, excolonial nations that would be in their respective interests.

Economically, the Soviet Union has reached a stage of industrial development where further advance in any desired direction depends only on its own choice of priorities: It is in a position to achieve substantial improvements in its backward agriculture and in the standard of living of its people, or to continue the arms race at the desired pace, or to engage in massive development aid to its Communist allies or to uncommitted powers, though it cannot afford to do all these things at once. China is still in an early stage of her industrialization effort, which, for reasons of the lower starting level and the higher population pressure, appears considerably more difficult than even that of the Soviet Union under Stalin. A first attempt to achieve an industrial "leap forward" by original methods without massive foreign aid has collapsed; yet, because of the conflict with the West, no substantial capital aid can be expected from the advanced Western nations.

Militarily, the Soviet Union is one of the two world powers; owing to its possession of thermonuclear bombs and intercontinental means of delivery in adequate numbers, its leaders feel reasonably secure against deliberate attack from their enemies and consider that their national security could only be endangered by the unforeseen and unintended escalation of a local conflict. China has no independent deterrent and no near prospect of an effective one, as a few atomic bombs by themselves no longer fulfill this role. Without the broad basis of an all-round modern arms industry capable of steady technological advance, China may continue, as the leading regional power in Asia, to intimidate her underdeveloped neighbors but cannot become a world power capable of assuring its own security. Achievement of that status thus depends on the solution of her industrialization problem, which is uncertain in principle and certain to be slow at best.

Diplomatically, the Soviet government not only is almost universally recognized and holds a permanent seat in the Security Council of the United Nations but also is regarded by its opponents as a necessary partner for recurrent negotiations. Both the Soviet Union and the United States are aware that they have a common interest in avoiding nuclear war as well as opposite interests in the East-West conflict, and efforts to control the forms of the conflict by negotiation are the logical consequence of that awareness; they are facilitated by the fact that the areas in dispute between them, however important to one or both of them, do not form part of the national territory of either power. Communist China's government is not recognized by the United States and most of its allies and is kept out of the United Nations by their influence; moreover, its most direct dispute with the United States, concerning its protection of what the United States regards as the legitimate government of the Republic of China, is regarded by the Communists as the unlawful occupation by the United States of part of their national territory, the island of Taiwan. Hence, while, for the Soviets, diplomatic relations with the enemy are one of the natural forms of carrying on their conflict with him, they play almost no role in the Chinese arsenal.

LOPSIDED DEPENDENCE

The Soviet Union is, thus, the only country from which a Communist China can expect the capital aid that it desperately needs for its industrialization. It is the only country that can protect a Communist China from the supposed danger of an American or American-controlled attack or furnish it modern weapons for pushing its demands against American resistance. And it is the only great power that may be called upon to take care of the interests of Communist China in diplomatic negotiations with the enemy, particularly in the United Nations. In all these fields, the dependence is not only complete but also largely one way: Russia has no substantial need of Chinese economic co-operation; Chinese military strength makes at best an indirect contribution to Soviet security by diverting part of the enemy's energies and, above all, by preventing the establishment of a pro-American government at Russia's Far Eastern border; Chinese political influence with some Asian countries has proved at times useful, but by no means indispensable, to Soviet diplomacy.

Now it will easily be seen that, while mutual dependence among allies is a powerful bond of unity, one-sided—or at least strongly lopsided—dependence of the kind here described is a factor of unity and a cause of conflict at the same time, because it tends to produce sharp disagreement about the place of the weaker power's interests on the stronger power's list of priorities. Economically, the urgency of China's need for capital aid conflicts with the Russian inclination to put the arms race first, the improvement of living standards at home second, and even the wooing of uncommitted nations ahead of aid for China, which, being Communist, tends

to be taken for granted. Militarily, the Chinese demand for all-out Soviet support of the pressure against Taiwan conflicts with the Soviet sensitivity for risks of nuclear war and the consequent tactics of pursing any local offensive only to the point where the risk of escalation appears serious. Diplomatically, the Chinese insistence on being fully consulted about any negotiations between Russia and the American enemy conflicts with the Soviet desire at certain moments of crisis to achieve a relaxation of tension quickly, without much regard for Chinese consent or prestige. The result has been a series of disappointments for China in each of these fields.

DIFFERENCES OF STRATEGIC OUTLOOK

In addition to producing a lopsided dependence of Communist China on the Soviet Union with its attendant tensions, the different situations of the two major Communist powers have led them to see the outside world from different angles, and hence to develop different strategic ideas for their common struggle. In particular, the Soviets are more concerned to keep the risk of nuclear war under control, both because they have more to lose in a material sense and because they do in fact have more control over it. The Chinese, in view of the vastness of their country and population, of its comparatively poor development, and of their lack of an independent deterrent, are more inclined both to regard the risk as bearable and to feel that it does not depend on them. Similarly, it is natural for the Soviets to seek to co-ordinate the use of diplomacy in relations with non-Communist powers, both hostile and neutral, with the use of revolutionary movements. The greater limitation of Chinese diplomatic possibilities leads them to regard the maneuvers of Soviet diplomacy with skepticism and suspicion and to rely primarily, though not exclusively on the revolutionary weapon.

To the Soviets, the United States is both the leader of the enemy camp that must be broken up by a judicious mixture of nuclear blackmail, support for revolutionary movements, economic competition, and well-timed offers of negotiation and the partner in an effort to prevent the struggle from leading to a nuclear holocaust. To the Chinese Communists, the United States is also the leader of the enemy camp, but it is no partner in any diplomatic effort; instead, it is resented as the direct *national* enemy as well—the backer of the "counterrevolution" in a recent civil war, the bitterly hated opponent in the even more recent, sanguinary Korean war, the occupant of part of the national territory. In terms of Soviet demonology, the United States presents in the eyes of the Chinese Communists the interventionist powers of 1918–1920, the Nazi German invader, and the real United States of today—all rolled into one imperialist monster. As a result, the chance of obtaining anything from them by diplomacy appears as nil; the risk of provoking their military action appears as both inevitable and manageable— after all, the Peking regime has survived it before.

To the Soviets, the revolutionary movements in the colonial and semi-colonial countries—the only exploitable revolutionary movements that exist in the contemporary world—are both a source of strength to be tapped and a source of risks to be controlled: They are willing and, indeed, eager to support them, but they insist on their freedom to judge the precise point beyond which they cannot go. To the Chinese, who feel militarily less secure, the multiplication of armed conflicts in distant lands appears rather to diminish their direct peril because it may force the enemy to disperse his strength. Hence, their willingness to support such move-ments is limited only by their technical capacity—which, outside Asia, is in striking disproportion to their verbal militancy—not by any consideration of risk.

To the Soviets, it is a desirable objective to win over some of the uncommitted nations, temporarily by the promotion of conflict between those nations and some of the Western powers or permanently by the growth of Communist influence within their governments. But, failing that, even the wooing of genuinely neutral and independent nations by economic aid appears worth while from a Soviet point of view, not only in order to prevent these countries from sliding into the Western embrace, but also as part of their effort to influence the policy of their opponents by the pressure of world opinion inside as well as outside the United Nations: The steady campaigning to win neutral voices and votes on specific issues of the East-West conflict is one aspect of the Russian ability to conduct diplomacy in a continuous, world-wide field where a shift in any one element influences all others. To the Chinese, aid to neutrals appears justified only to the extent that they cease to be neutrals—either by getting involved in acute conflict with some Western power, or by coming under increasing Communist control from within, or by becoming part of Communist China's dependent buffer zone owing to her regional military preponderance. Aid for genuinely independent neutral states that feel free to accept support from both East and West appears to the Chinese Communists as a wanton waste of limited resources; attempts to use the machinery of the United Nations for achieving Communist-bloc objectives with the help of neutral votes are viewed by them as futile and self-defeating. In the special case of India, whose policy is regarded by Peking as the main obstacle to the expansion of its Asian buffer zone, all Soviet credits thus appear as direct aid to China's enemy—while, to the Soviets, China's attacks seem liable to push an important neutral power needlessly into the Western camp.

IDEOLOGICAL RIVALRY

Within an alliance, differences in the priority scales and the strategic outlook of the partners are normal; it is also normal that they are settled by repeated compromises so long as the conflict with the common enemy exceeds their importance. But, where the alliance is rooted exclusively in the common ideology of ruling totalitarian parties, the disagreements arising from their different situations naturally assume the form of different interpretations of that ideology. Once such an ideological dispute has come into the open, a pragmatic adjustment of the underlying policy differences becomes far more difficult. For, in a totalitarian-party regime, the authority of the leaders depends on general acceptance of their interpretation of the ideology; hence, any open challenge to the "correctness" of this interpretation amounts to a direct attack on that leadership and, above all, on the leader himself. It follows that, from the moment of such an open challenge, the common ideology that has united the allies becomes also a factor of serious conflict between them.

To avoid such effects, the partners of an ideological alliance will tend to take great care to keep their differences secret. And this was, indeed, the case with Russo-Chinese disagreements during most of 1958, which Western students have only been able to trace indirectly. Yet, because of the lopsided material dependence of Communist China on the Soviet Union, the Chinese Communists found that the Soviet leaders paid little attention to their secret representations. On the other hand, the crisis of 1956–1957 in the Soviet bloc and the role played by Mao Tse-tung's intact authority in overcoming it may have given Peking an idea that the Soviets in turn had become dependent on its ideological support for maintaining control of the world Communist movement. An ideological challenge in the forum of that movement, thus, must have appeared to the Chinese leaders as their one effective weapon for exerting pressure on their Soviet ally. This explains why they tried it indirectly and tentatively in late 1958 and with increasing boldness since the winter of 1959–1960.

The familiar debates on the possibility of the separate achievement of "full communism" by advanced countries, on the chances of "eliminating war" despite the continued existence of imperialism, on the character of imperialism as a "paper tiger" or a tiger with "real atomic teeth," on the need to subordinate national liberation movements to the "general line" of "peaceful coexistence" or to subordinate coexistence diplomacy to the "general line" of "anti-imperialist struggle," on relations with the "national bourgeoisie" in the excolonial countries, and on the chances of seizing power in some states by "peaceful methods" have been the result of that Chinese decision. The arguments show that, in raising their challenge, the Chinese Communists could not stop at simply translating their specific policy disagreements with the Soviets into ideological terms but had to turn them into parts of a coherent system based on their own revolutionary experience and on the structural characteristics of Chinese Communist thought derived from it. Those characteristics include the belief in the power of revolutionary determination aided by theory to overcome unfavorable material conditions, in the decisive role of people rather than arms technology in war, and in the principle of "uninterrupted revolution" both at home and abroad.

Even though the propaganda of this Sino-Trotskyite version of Marxism-Leninism was originally conceived merely as a means to exert pressure on Soviet foreign policy, its inherent logic implies a rival claim for ideological leadership of the alliance and the world Communist movement. Yet, such ideological rivalry, if maintained, must inevitably lead to schism; that outcome could only be avoided by the surrender of either side or by the common decision of both to retransfer the dispute from the ideological to the pragmatic plane where alone compromises are possible. Clearly, such a retransfer is in the interest of the Soviet Union as the stronger power, which would thus be freed from the constant ideological pressure of its weaker ally. The explicit Soviet renunciation of the "leading role" at the 1960 Moscow world conference of Communist parties amounted in effect to proposing this solution—an end of the ideological debate in favor of the preservation of unity by toleration of differences and pragmatic compromise. The interest of the Chinese Communists was less obvious: by accepting a return to pragmatism they would lose their best means of pressure on the Soviets, but, by rejecting it and courting a schism, they might lose all Soviet support—at least until the day when the Soviet leaders would capitulate and force the resignation of N. S. Khrushchev.

THE LOGIC OF SCHISM

Developments in the course of 1961, particularly the open quarrel over Albania and the Chinese defense of Stalin's memory, have made it obvious that the Soviet readiness to tolerate differences within the world movement stops at the borders of their sphere of

imperial control, while the Chinese Communists have given preference to the needs of continuing ideological struggle over the prospects of compromise. We can only guess from this behavior that they must have believed—and may still believe—in a chance of getting Khrushchev overthrown within a not too distant future. As a result of that choice, while both sides go on professing their devotion to the unity of the alliance and of the world movement, their respective concepts of unity have become mutually incompatible. The Chinese insist on restoring unity by an uncompromising, Leninist struggle for the purity of ideological principles; the Russians offer unity by toleration of differences among all bona fide Communists, including since 1962 the Yugoslavs. The Russians demand noninterference by either side in the parties and power spheres controlled by the other—a kind of Communist version of *cuius regio, eius religio;* the Chinese see their only chance in carrying the factional struggle into every stronghold of their opponents.

This means that factional schism has become a fact to the same extent that such a schism existed, in the pre-1914 Russian social-democratic movement, between Bolsheviks and Mensheviks: the formal preservation of a common framework and the profession of "common principles"—which are interpreted in sharply divergent ways—no longer prevent the organized ideological struggle between rival leaderships pursuing their separate policies in complete independence. Short of the fall of one of the leaders and his supporters followed by ideological surrender of his successors to the rival authority, such a development is irreversible, whatever "unity conferences" may be attempted for tactical reasons and under the prompting of the unhappy parties that would like to avoid a decision. But such surrender, unlikely in the nature of ideological struggles, becomes virtually impossible where the authority of the rival leaders is linked with the control of powerful states. Just because manipulation of the official ideology is a major source of power for any ruling Communist party, we must expect the schism to continue once it has reached that stage.

Yet the logic of the schism tends to make each side pursue increasingly independent policies and dig ever deeper foundations for their ideological opposition. In foreign policy, the Chinese have increasingly turned to creating their independent power sphere in Asia. They have secured the ideological allegiance of North Korea and North Vietnam; they have built up their buffer zone in Nepal, Cambodia, and Burma and broken effective Indian opposition to this development by military intimidation; they have appeared as active competitors with Soviet influence in Indonesia. The Soviets in turn, by continuing substantial economic aid to India at the height of the "border conflict," have given open and direct support to the enemies of their Chinese allies. Behind the differences of strategy in the common struggle against the West, which were the original cause of the ideological schism, the basic differences of "pure" national interest are thus coming to the surface once again.

In the ideological field, while either side may make outward tactical concessions to the wavering parties at certain moments, the inward elaboration of the rival doctrines tends to deepen the differences. The Soviets, forced into the "Menshevik" position, are putting increasing emphasis on the economic and technological preconditions for the transition to communism at home and the role of economic competition in ultimately deciding the conflict with the capitalist world, even quoting Lenin for the primacy of economic tasks after the

seizure of power.[1] The Chinese Communists, finding their road to industrialization temporarily blocked by lack of aid, their chance of power expansion concentrated in neighboring Asia, and their ideological attraction limited to the Communist parties and national revolutionary movements of the underdeveloped world, are getting further and further away from the Marxist belief in the mission of the industrial proletariat: They proclaim that the "focus of world contradictions" is today situated in Asia, Africa, and Latin America and that the victory of the national liberation movements in those continents will be *decisive* for the chances of the industrial working class in the advanced countries.[2] As Khrushchev comes to stress the Marxist elements in Lenin, the Chinese tend to snap the last links between their version of Leninism and classical Marxism.

PROSPECTS OF THE ALLIANCE

If it is true that the Sino-Soviet alliance is wholly due to the ideological solidarity of the ruling Communist parties, must we not expect the alliance to break up as the result of the ideological schism? Such a conclusion is tempting but not compelling for the simple reason that the schism has not removed the common conflict of both regimes with the non-Communist powers. Both the Soviet and Chinese Communists continue to regard the "imperialist" enemy as the only clear and present danger to their rule. By contrast, the Chinese Communists merely regard the present Soviet leaders

[1] See Khrushchev's speech to the plenum of the Central Committee of the Communist party of the Soviet Union on November 19, 1962, *Pravda*, November 20, 1962.

[2] "More on the Differences between Comrade Togliatti and Us," English translation of editorials in *Red Flag* (Peking), No. 3/4 (March 4, 1963), pp. 31–32, 45–46.

as an obstacle to the advance of world communism and the cause of insufficient support for their own objectives, while the Soviets may view the Chinese campaign as a danger to their authority and a hindrance to their policy but not as a physical threat to their power. The difference becomes clear if we make the assumption—admittedly improbable but not to be ruled out from the calculations of the Communist leaders—of a massive, American-supported landing by Chiang Kai-shek's forces on the mainland: the Soviets, for all their troubles with Mao Tse-tung, would clearly have to support him because of their vital interest in preventing the installation of a pro-American regime on their eastern border.

An important measure of common ideological interests thus clearly persists despite the ideological schism, but this seems sufficient only to maintain the alliance as a kind of mutual reinsurance against extreme—and objectively unlikely—situations of common danger. Far from ensuring a successful co-ordination of policies between the Communist allies, or even a serious attempt at such co-ordination, this "alliance in reserve" does not prevent the two leading Communist powers from seeking to build up two separate Communist camps with increasingly independent policies and increasingly different doctrines. Yet, so long as both are ruled by Communist party regimes, this final tenuous bond is unlikely to be snapped.

The Emergence of an Asian Communist Coalition

By A. M. HALPERN

ABSTRACT: Since the Moscow conference of Communist and Workers Parties in 1960, the Chinese People's Republic has acquired important support for its position in ideological op-position to the Soviet Union from a number of other parties, especially in Asia. The emergence of what amounts to an Asian Communist coalition enhances the practical possibility of a split in the world movement. A split, however, is contrary to the interests of the Asian parties. Their support for China reflects their individual interests and a polycentric trend. North Korea and North Vietnam both attach a high priority to national unification. They are encouraged by the Chinese and, in different degrees, restrained by the Soviet Union. This has brought their positions on imperialism closer to that of China. Both regimes have embarked on development plans intended to achieve structural changes in their economies, and both receive assistance from a number of bloc countries. The organizational demands of these plans have strengthened their opposition to revisionism and their support of national inde-pendence in the bloc. Somewhat parallel ideological develop-ments in the Japanese and Indonesian parties are traceable to a need to preserve organizational integrity. The viability of the coalition is dubious in case of a split but real and impor-tant if even minimum bloc solidarity is maintained.

A. M. Halpern, Ph.D., New York City, New York, is Research Fellow of the China Project at the Council on Foreign Relations. He was previously a staff member of the Rand Corporation, Advisor to the Education Division, CI and E Section, SCAP, and Assistant Professor of Anthropology at the University of Chicago. He is the author of Rand Research Memoranda on Far Eastern problems and has contributed articles on Chinese Communist affairs to several journals.

AS this article is being written, the signs of an impending climax in Sino-Soviet relations are unmistakably clear. In the early months of 1963, it also became clear that other Asian Communist regimes and parties had developed a special relationship to the Sino-Soviet controversy. Superficially, at any rate, it has come to appear that several Asian parties identify themselves with or otherwise support the Chinese case to such an extent that a fractioning of the international Communist movement may be a practical possibility. This development, however, would contravene the real interests of the major Asian parties. Some of these have, indeed, made serious efforts to mediate the Sino-Soviet conflict so as to forestall a choice which could only result in injury to themselves. A somewhat different line of analysis would take polycentrism as a starting point and consider whether its value has not been increasing in terms of the total strategy of Asian parties other than the Chinese.

The Moscow conference of eighty-one Communist parties in November-December 1960 established the context in which the trends examined here developed. The full history of the conference is evidently not yet written, for the Chinese have recently given broad hints that their version of the story is being held in reserve against the time when they may have use for it in their controversy with the Soviet Union. In the aftermath of the conference, the Chinese were in a weak position. They had had to accept an unsatisfactory compromise on the ideological issues which had been forced into public discussion by their initiative. They could and evidently did accept a quiescent role in foreign affairs for a certain length of time after the conference. But this could not satisfy them indefinitely.

In their effort to rebuild an influential position in Communist-bloc affairs, the most promising possibility was that of constructing a common front with other Asian parties. The form that such a front could take, however, and the degree of cohesion it could achieve, depended on the views and interests of China's prospective partners. Among these, the most important were the Democratic People's Republic of Korea and the Democratic Republic of Vietnam. In both cases, the regimes had economic and political goals to consider, of the greatest importance to themselves. While these goals were supported, even shared, by the Chinese People's Republic, it was not certain that the best strategy would be alignment with the Chinese in an anti-Soviet position.

The evidence to be considered includes North Korean and North Vietnamese treatment of the 1960 Moscow Statement, their respective seven-year (1961–1967) and five-year (1961–1965) plans, their demands for national unification, and their economic and diplomatic relations with the Soviet Union, the East European satellites, and the Chinese People's Republic. The patterns are different, but in 1963 there was convergence on ideological positions. For the major nongoverning Asian Communist parties, the Indonesian and the Japanese, the interests involved were of a different order, but there was a similar ideological development.

THE SITUATION OF NORTH KOREA

The Central Committee of the Korean Workers party must have met in plenary session almost immediately after the return of its delegation from the Moscow meeting. The delegation, led by Kim Il, returned to Pyongyang on December 3. On December 24, the text of a resolution on the Moscow meeting was published in *Nodong Sinmun*.[1] The position adopted by the Korean Workers party represented the extreme of militancy. It endorsed the stand its delegation had taken at Moscow. It emphasized national liberation struggles directed against imperialism— in the first instance, struggle against the United States in South Korea and, in addition, anti-imperialist movements in Cuba, Japan, Laos, Algeria, and the Congo. On the question of "defending peace," the language of the resolution needs no paraphrase:

War can be prevented and peace safeguarded *only* by steadily increasing the might of the socialist camp, actively developing the working class movement in the capitalist countries, further raising the flames of the national liberation struggle and organizing and mobilizing the popular masses in the struggle for defending peace, *only by putting pressure on and dealing blows* to the imperialist war incendiaries everywhere through the unity of all peace forces and the combination of all forms and methods of struggle.[2]

The resolution dealt with dogmatism as purely an internal matter, a danger to the organizational effectiveness of the Korean Workers party, which had, however, been overcome. It treated revisionism as a more serious threat, on both the international and the internal planes, and as a threat still in existence, so that it was necessary to "wage a struggle against even its slightest manifestation." In this and other North Korean statements over the following two-year period, the language employed is typically as outspoken as that of the Chinese, or even more so. It has not necessarily been accompanied, at least in international affairs, by equally forthright action.

In the realm of practical policy, the Democratic People's Republic of Korea apparently felt that it needed a clear understanding with the Soviet Union on the contribution the latter would make to the two matters of overriding importance to the former: national unification and economic development. On June 29, 1961 a North Korean party and government delegation led by Kim Il-song proceeded to Moscow, on the heels of a similar North Vietnamese delegation headed by Premier Pham Van Dong. The surrounding circumstances, the signing of a formal treaty, and the content of the treaty and its accompanying joint communiqué all suggest strongly that the initiative for this mission came from North Korea. What the North Korean demands were and whether they were satisfied can to some extent be deduced by comparing the documentation of the mission's visit to the Soviet Union with that of its visit, immediately afterwards, to the Chinese People's Republic.[3] China was willing to make an open-ended commitment, with fewer qualifications and a greater degree of mutuality, than was the Soviet Union.

National unification has been a prime North Korean objective for many years. The priority attributed to it as a near-future objective was raised in 1958, following the withdrawal of the Chinese People's Volunteers, and again after the collapse of the Rhee government in 1960. The accession of a military

[1] Korean Central News Agency, December 25, 1960. Note that Khrushchev's speech commenting on the meeting was delivered on January 6, 1961. The corresponding statement of the Central Committee of the Vietnam Workers party was published on January 12, 1961. The resolution of the ninth plenum of the Eighth Central Committee of the Chinese Communist party was adopted on January 18, 1961.

[2] Italics added.

[3] See Tass, July 6 and 10, 1961 for the Soviet Union-North Korean treaty and communiqué. See New China News Agency, July 11 and 15, 1961 for the Chinese-North Korean treaty and communiqué.

group to power in South Korea in early 1961 made the issue even more urgent. The language of both treaties on this point was identical, referring to unification on a "peaceful and democratic" basis. In the associated statements, the Soviet tendency was to support North-South negotiations, confederation, trade, and cultural co-operation. The Chinese tendency was to emphasize an imperialist threat to Korean unity, the involvement of Japan, and the integral relation of the Korean problem to an all-Asian resistance to the United States. The Fourth Congress of the Korean Workers party produced a declaration, "For the Peaceful Unification of the Country," which appealed for a popular uprising in South Korea, strikes, sabotage, boycotting of conscription, and the like.[4] Following this, the Democratic People's Republic of Korea has used all its propaganda facilities and political instrumentalities to attack General Park as an American puppet and to obstruct South Korean negotiations with Japan. On the question of unification as such, North Korea on several occasions in 1962, notably in Kim Il-song's speech to the Third Supreme People's Assembly,[5] advanced formal proposals for confederation, troop reduction and withdrawal of United States forces, free travel, and economic exchange between North and South as intermediate steps toward unification.

An exact assessment of what the North Koreans would like to do in regard to the South is hard to make from the evidence available. Their basic formulation is that the "liberation" of the South is essential to the completion of their revolution. This is regarded as an urgent mission, on which action should not be delayed. The Chinese support

them both on their definition of the situation and on all successive moves they have made. The major restraint is the sensitiveness of Korea in the international context, which attaches a high risk to any direct moves that would upset the *status quo*. The comparatively qualified support offered by the Soviet Union indicated a desire to restrain the North Koreans from doing anything rash. About the middle of January 1963, it appeared that the North Korean appeal for action by the South Korean population had been reduced to a recommendation for political agitation, using as slogans demands for civil liberties, aimed at replacing the Park government with a "democratic regime truly representing the interests of the people." This seems a mild prescription in the light of the emphasis placed by the fifth plenum of the Fourth Central Committee of the Korean Workers party on the immediate strengthening of "defense capacity" even at the expense of causing a "certain restriction to the development of the national economy." The same document reaffirmed the thesis that peace cannot be achieved by begging it of the imperialists but must be won by struggle. It also stressed the need for continued vigilance against the infiltration of revisionism in the party.[6]

On the economic side, the contribution of the Soviet Union and the European satellites to the North Korean Seven-Year Plan has not been negligible. In November 1960, the Soviet Union agreed to exempt the Democratic People's Republic of Korea from repayment of past loans amounting to 760 million (old) rubles and to extend the date of repayment for an additional 140 million rubles. In connection with the 1961 treaty, the Soviet Union reportedly agreed to further long-term

[4] Korean Central News Agency, September 17, 1961.

[5] Korean Central News Agency, October 23, 1962.

[6] See *Nodong Sinmun*, December 16, 1962, for the communiqué.

loans in support of the Seven-Year Plan. Soviet support apparently was to go primarily to North Korean mining and metallurgy, secondarily to the chemical industry. The first two areas have come to have a declining importance in North Korean foreign trade, offset to some extent by an increase in the export of chemical products. North Korea appears to be trying to develop an export pattern in which machines and finished goods will be increasingly stressed. For these, the Soviet Union does not seem to be an enthusiastic consumer.

As for implementation of existing agreements on scientific and technical co-operation and on commodity exchange, North Korean reports on semiannual protocols were exceedingly vague in 1962 and 1963 as compared with 1961. North Korean statements on appropriate occasions, such as the anniversaries of their 1949 economic and cultural co-operation agreement and their 1961 treaty with the Soviet Union, have supplied no significant details on the economic relationship. There has been a falling off of the kind of diplomatic contact represented by the exchange of special missions. A similar tendency is observable in North Korea's relations with the East European satellites. Trade and scientific exchanges have continued. The satellites may be more desirable partners in these respects than the Soviet Union. But there seems to have been no increase in the scale of exchange and, in some cases, such as Czechoslovakia, a probable decline.

In contrast, Sino-Korean relations have become closer and stronger, whether measured in terms of technical, cultural, and economic co-operation, frequency of semidiplomatic contacts, or the expression of mutual support and approval. Following the 1961 treaty, the outstanding exchanges of high-level delegations were a Chinese trade delega-

tion in January 1962, a Chinese National People's Congress delegation in April-May 1962, a return visit by a delegation of the Supreme People's Assembly of the Democratic People's Republic of Korea in June 1962, and a North Korean trade delegation in October-November 1962. As a result of these and other minor contacts, including some on the provincial level, China has become an increasingly important supplier of technical information and trained personnel in a variety of fields and with some degree of reciprocity.[7] In a trade agreement and an accompanying treaty of commerce and navigation signed on November 5, 1962, Sino-Korean trade relations were put on a long-term basis, adjusted to the duration of the North Korean Seven-Year Plan.[8]

The special importance of such co-operation to the Democratic People's Republic of Korea derives from the emphasis it places on the Seven-Year Plan. As shown in the report by Kim Il to the Fourth Congress of the Korean Workers party, this plan is designed to accomplish the critical transition of the North Korean economic structure. The stated purposes of the plan were to:

. . . complete socialist industrialization and the technical revolution . . . so as to equip all branches of the national economy with modern techniques, build a firm material and technical basis of socialism, and turn our country into a developed socialist industrial state. . . . Whereas in the previous plans the main emphasis was on building the skeleton of heavy industry . . . in the seven-year plan the main question is to reinforce, to put flesh to the skeleton, thus further

[7] The New China News Agency account of the latest protocol on scientific and technical co-operation, issued September 22, 1962, indicated the range but provides no figures.
[8] News communiqué released by New China News Agency, November 5, 1962.

strengthening the country's self-supporting economic system.[9]

Throughout 1962 North Korean statements about economic progress, which has actually been quite significant,[10] have increasingly stressed the necessity and desirability of self-reliance in executing the plan and have more and more clearly defined the goal as economic self-sufficiency. Chinese comment has been consistently favorable to these positions. The Chinese have asserted that North Korea's success has been brought about by the same qualities of correct leadership and consistent practice of mass-line methods as they themselves have enjoyed. Kim Il-song has been credited with making a creative application of Marxism-Leninism to the concrete conditions of his country, much as Mao did in China. Finally, in early 1963, an authoritative North Korean journal took the step of raising self-reliance to the level of a correct international revolutionary principle. The Democratic People's Republic of Korea now justifies independence in national planning as basic to the proper international division of labor in the Communist bloc. Having first established that "the decisive factor in the revolution of any country is its internal force," the journal concludes:

Dealing with the international division of labor, it is necessary first of all to take the economic construction of each country as the prerequisite. . . . This condition is all the more necessary because the purpose of international division of labor does not end in itself but in its stimulation and promotion of the economic growth of each country. Therefore, if we do not . . . develop an independent national economy,

we shall continue to be a great burden to the various fraternal countries. . . . Judging by all these realities, our party's policy of establishing an independent national economy . . . is entirely correct and is a thoroughly internationalist stand.[11]

THE SITUATION OF NORTH VIETNAM

The Vietnam Workers party took the 1960 Moscow statement seriously. On the return of its delegation, the Central Committee heard a lengthy report on the statement from Le Duan and issued a resolution.[12] Besides these, there were several long and thoughtful commentaries in the North Vietnamese press. A noteworthy point of the content of these writings was the presentation of peace as an objective which was actually attainable under present world conditions. Under these circumstances, the peace movement was represented as genuine, as no longer an agitational device adopted to educate the masses toward socialism. The statements also regarded both revisionism and dogmatism as dangers to the international Communist movement. Apart from these specific points, the Vietnam Workers party statements, in sharp contrast to the hasty, one-sided formulation of the Korean Workers party, treated the Moscow Statement as a satisfactory guide to action for the Communist countries, and specifically for the Democratic Republic of Vietnam, in an exceedingly complex international situation.

So far as their own objective of

[9] Korean Central News Agency, September 16, 1961.

[10] Far Eastern Economic Review, 1963 Yearbook contains a convenient summary of economic developments in North Korea and North Vietnam.

[11] "Socialist Revolution and Building of a New Life through Self-Reliance," Kulloja (Worker), No. 19 (1962). The journal is the organ of the Korean Workers party Central Committee. The article was quoted in extenso by New China News Agency, December 22, 1962.

[12] A long account of Le Duan's report was published in Hoc Tap, No. 1 (1961). The text of the Central Committee resolution was released by Vietnam New Agency, January 12, 1961.

national unification was concerned, the Moscow Statement imposed no unpalatable restraints on North Vietnam in regard to its actions in Laos and South Vietnam. The first cases of revived Viet Cong military activity occurred before the Moscow meeting. On December 20, 1960 the National Front for the Liberation of South Vietnam (NFLSV) was organized. The place of the NFLSV in North Vietnamese strategy remained somewhat indeterminate for about one year, but by early 1962 alternative political approaches to liberation of the South—through international diplomacy, for example—had been downgraded. The structure and platform of the NFLSV were fully revealed, and its status was built up by a series of tours of the Communist countries and by participation in the meetings of international front organizations.

In all its actions, military and political, in these disputed areas, the Democratic Republic of Vietnam seems to have enjoyed the consistent support of the whole Communist bloc. This may have been provided with somewhat greater enthusiasm by China and North Korea than by the European Communist countries; at least, Vietnam commanded relatively more attention in comparison with other international questions from Asian than from European Communists. The Chinese in particular reported in detail and endorsed every move, including numerous letters of protest to the International Control Commission, made by North Vietnam. It was only in 1963, when antagonism between the Pathet Lao and Laotian neutralists became sharp, that there was any indication that North Vietnam might feel unduly restrained by a Soviet desire to keep the Indo-Chinese situation under control.

Pham Van Dong's June–July 1961

mission to Asian and European Communist countries had, under these circumstances, a different purpose than Kim Il-song's. The difference can be simply measured. Where Kim Il-song needed to conclude treaties to put North Korea's relations with the Soviet Union and the Chinese People's Republic on a written legal basis, Pham Van Dong was satisfied with joint communiqués.[13] The primary purpose of the mission was undoubtedly, as P. J. Honey states,[14] to obtain further economic assistance in addition to the considerable amount already given earlier. This included cancellation of debts amounting to 430,000,000 new rubles and military aid valued at 220,000,000 new rubles in addition to loans promised in December 1960.

In May 1961 scientific and technical co-operation was put on a five-year basis, corresponding to the term of the North Vietnamese Five-Year Plan, with provision for the training of Vietnamese students in the Soviet Union and the supply of Soviet technicians to work in the Democratic Republic of Vietnam. Despite the occasional public recognition given to Soviet specialists, their number appears to be small. Soviet aid, however, is diversified, covering the development of state farms, supply of farm machinery, thermal and water-power facilities, the construction of the Hanoi engineering plant, and several light industrial and transportation projects. There has been continuing implementation of both economic and

[13] Texts of the Chinese-North Vietnamese communiqué were released by New China News Agency June 16; North Korean-North Vietnamese communiqué, by Korean Central News Agency June 22; Soviet Union-North Vietnamese communiqué, by Vietnam News Agency July 5, 1961.

[14] P. J. Honey, "Pham Van Dong's Tour," *China Quarterly*, No. 8 (October-December 1961).

scientific co-operation by periodic protocols.[15]

As against the apparently contracting scale of European satellite economic relations with North Korea, North Vietnamese trade has been reported as expanding. Protocols providing for an increased volume of exchange were signed by the Democratic Republic of Vietnam with Rumania, Hungary, and Czechoslovakia in March-May 1962 and with Poland, East Germany, and Bulgaria in addition to the other three in the first quarter of 1963. North Vietnam also has agreements on scientific and technical co-operation with some of these countries, notably Czechoslovakia, whose President Antonín Novotný included North Vietnam in the itinerary of his politically and economically important tour of Southeast Asia in January 1963.

Chinese, and to a lesser extent North Korean assistance, has also been important to the Democratic Republic of Vietnam. The North Vietnamese press has described in some detail the value to North Vietnam of Chinese financial assistance prior to 1961, amounting to 1.2 billion yuan, three quarters of which was in free grants. The basis of co-operation in 1961 and after was a long-term Chinese loan of 141,750,000 new rubles[16] to cover the building or expansion of twenty-eight industrial and transport enterprises during the period 1961–1967. The showcase project is the Thai Nguyen steel complex, reported by October 1962 to be well under way. Second to it is the Viet Tri industrial center, also well enough advanced in construction by the same date

---

[15] For example, an agreement signed on September 16, 1962 by Nguyen Duy Trinh and V. Dymshits, providing for the irrigation of 80,000 hectares of land and other matters, reported by Vietnam News Agency.

[16] Almost half of all bloc loans and almost half as much again as the Soviet loan for the period as of April 1961.

to be inspected with pride by the Chinese National People's Congress delegation to the Democratic Republic of Vietnam, headed by P'eng Chen. In both these projects, the contribution of Chinese personnel is said to be significant. Although there is no exact figure for the number of Chinese working in North Vietnam, Pham Van Dong in a speech in Peking referred to "thousands of experts," and other North Vietnamese sources have spoken of thousands of Vietnamese being trained in China.

Trade arrangements, said to be mutually beneficial, were further formalized by the conclusion of a treaty of commerce and navigation on December 5, 1962, a day before the signature of a North Korean-North Vietnamese trade protocol providing for mutual most-favored nation treatment. Few details of the operation of these agreements are known, but they can be taken as indications of increased mutual support among the three countries excluded from the Council for Economic Mutual Assistance.

In diplomatic contacts, the Democratic Republic of Vietnam has carefully kept all lines open. High-level Chinese missions to North Vietnam have included a military mission headed by Yeh Chien-ying (December 1961) and the National People's Congress delegation headed by P'eng Chen (September-October 1962). Besides these, there have been exchanges of visits by delegations of the respective friendship associations and a number of cultural visits. The Chinese People's Republic twice in 1962 received with fanfare delegations of the NFLSV, one headed by Huynh Van Tam in January and another headed by Nguyen Van Hieu in September-October. Vice-Premier Nguyen Duy Trinh, who was also chairman of the National Planning Board, made an unpublicized tour of

China from September 17 to October 5, 1962.

On the Soviet side, high-level missions to the Democratic Republic of Vietnam have included a Communist party delegation headed by B. N. Ponomarev (February 1962), a military delegation headed by General P. T. Batov (December 1962), and a delegation of the Supreme Soviet headed by Y. V. Andropov (January 1963). North Vietnamese visitors to Moscow during 1952 included Vo Nguyen Giap, Truong Chinh, and Nguyen Duy Trinh.

In terms of the objective of national unification, North Vietnam, though more circumspect in its ideological pronouncements, has had more scope for both military and political action than North Korea. The Indo-Chinese situation is, if only by a little, less sensitive than that of Korea. Soviet intervention in Laos did not inhibit action but, at least for a time, was to the North Vietnamese advantage. Ho Chi Minh's political and rhetorical style are very different from Kim Il-song's. But his comparative temperance should not obscure the depth of his conviction, which equals Kim Il-song's, that the liberation of the South is vital to the completion of his revolution. Seen in this light, the present state of things cannot be regarded with satisfaction by North Vietnam.

The North Vietnamese Five-Year Plan aims at a structural change of the economy as critical as that of the North Korean Seven-Year Plan—perhaps more critical, since the North Vietnamese economy is less advanced. The construction of basic heavy-industry facilities has the highest priority. On the whole, the North Vietnamese achievements do not match those of North Korea. The latter can plausibly claim to have solved its food problem; the former cannot. Expansion of foreign trade has become progressively im-

important to North Vietnam, though apparently more for the purpose of covering the cost of imported industrial materials than to supplement the food supply. In comments on the progress of the plan, emphasis on a well-rounded economy and on self-sufficiency has become more and more prominent. Much as in the case of North Korea, the Chinese have encouraged this attitude by their praise of Ho Chi Minh's leadership. Although no North Vietnamese statement quite approaches in explicitness the *Kulloja* article cited above, the trend toward a posture of national independence has been strong. In both cases, the organizational effort required to carry out the plans is intense. This has helped to lower the level of tolerance for revisionist tendencies in domestic affairs.

SUPPORT FOR CHINESE POSITIONS

North Korean support of Chinese People's Republic views and actions in 1961–1962 amounted virtually to identification. The degree to which automatic approval can be carried was illustrated by North Korean comment on the meeting of the Chinese National People's Congress in April 1962. The Chinese communiqués on the meeting were quite reserved, while the North Korean press represented it as a tremendous success. As another case in point, North Korean comment on Yugoslavia has closely paralleled Chinese comment, both in content and in timing. An attack on Tito was published in the May 28, 1962 number of the journal *Kukche Saenghwal (International Life)*, and in September the North Korean press began publishing a series of anti-Yugoslav articles. These were promptly relayed by New China News Agency.

The handling of Chinese international actions by the North Vietnamese press was considerably more selective. While supporting what were regarded as clearly Chinese rights—a United Nations seat, for example—North Vietnamese media have in general given less attention to Chinese issues and have tended to focus on cases where the Chinese have reached agreement with others, such as the Chinese friendship treaty with Indonesia and her border agreements with Burma, Pakistan, and Outer Mongolia. Thus, the Democratic Republic of Vietnam has consistently overstated the conciliatory aspects of China's posture and understated the more militantly demanding aspects. A test case was the differential handling of the Sino-Indian conflict. By the time this occurred, the Democratic People's Republic of Korea had so far identified with China that it could adopt no other tactic than to support, loudly, all details of the Chinese position. North Korean statements echoed the Chinese in denouncing the "Indian reactionaries" as tools of imperialism. North Vietnam seemed more ready to support the Chinese at the point where they offered to negotiate and withdrew their troops than in their more extreme anti-Indian pronouncements. North Vietnamese contacts with the outside world were still sufficient to enable Ho Chi Minh to correspond with Nehru, with perhaps some hope of affecting the situation.

In somewhat similar fashion, North Vietnam was in a position to attempt mediation of Sino-Soviet differences, while North Korea was not. In the chill that descended on the international Communist movement after Khrushchev's somewhat gratuitous attack on Albania at the Twenty-second Congress of the Communist party of the Soviet Union,[17] Ho Chi Minh was the best situated of Asian Communist leaders to mediate. His letter of January 1962 for a certain time seemed to be capable of achieving some success. Concurrently with the Chinese National People's Congress meeting of April, an exchange of letters between the Chinese and Soviet parties was initiated, and there were signs that, in return for a more moderate Chinese stance in both domestic and foreign affairs, Khrushchev might withdraw some of the sanctions he had earlier imposed on the Chinese.

Accounting for the renewed inflammation of the Sino-Soviet dispute after November 1962 is an exercise in guesswork. By resuming efforts for a *rapprochement* with Tito and by excluding China, North Korea, and North Vietnam from the Council for Economic Mutual Assistance, Khrushchev offered some provocation. Some aspects of China's domestic situation perhaps played a crucial role. By September 1962, possibly at an earlier point than had been anticipated, the Chinese felt that they had brought their domestic economic and political problems under control.[18] With the return of self-confidence, a major reason for continuing to tolerate inconclusive bargaining with Khrushchev would have then lost its force. This would be all the more so if Khrushchev's personal position had been thought to be weakened by domestic and foreign reverses.

On this analysis, the Cuban crisis of October-November 1962 would have been a pretext rather than a direct cause for Chinese attacks. Not that the

---

[17] Discussion of Asian Communist reactions to the Twenty-second Congress is slighted here in view of the treatment in R. A. Scalapino's "Moscow, Peking and the Communist Parties of Asia," *Foreign Affairs*,

January 1963. As the analysis made here shows, I cannot altogether accept "neutralism" or "nonalignment" as wholly applicable to the North Korean and North Vietnamese positions.

[18] See the communiqué of the tenth plenum of the Eighth Central Committee of the Chinese Communist party, New China News Agency, September 28, 1962.

crisis did not shock the Asian parties. Both North Korea and North Vietnam reacted in a highly negative way to Soviet handling of the situation. They did not, however, criticize the Soviets directly, but, by ignoring this aspect of the situation and concentrating on Castro's need for support and his right to defend himself against imperialism, they made their dissatisfaction plain in terms that reflected the value they place on their own national independence. This perception of what was involved was essentially the same as that of the Chinese. The counterattack on China by the European parties removed, for the time being, the possibility of mediation and forced the Asian parties to declare themselves.

For the Korean Workers party, no doctrinal change was necessary. Their one major statement on the matter was an appeal for international Communist unity, which would be meaningless without solidarity with the Chinese People's Republic. Their own national interest is revealed in two sentences:

What will become of our unity and what can be said of our solidarity if things take such a course in the socialist camp as one party and one country being isolated and ostracized yesterday and another party and another country being isolated and ostracized today? And if things go on like this, will not a certain other party and a certain other country be isolated and ostracized tomorrow? [19]

The North Vietnamese party, on the one hand, did have to clarify its doctrine and, on the other hand, retained a capacity for affecting the situation that was out of reach for the Korean Workers party. The ideological developments are contained in a series of arti-

cles, one published in November 1962, the others in February-March 1963. The November article, prepared for the anniversaries of the 1957 and 1960 Moscow declarations, stated a position of clear opposition to revisionism, demanded a strategy of struggle against imperialism, and adopted the Chinese emphasis on the definition of peaceful coexistence as "a form of class struggle between socialism and capitalism on a world scale." [20]

In their visits to Vietnam in January 1963, both Andropov and Novotný—who on this occasion acted in part as an agent of Khrushchev—presented in public their justifications of the Soviet handling on the Cuban situation. Their views were not adopted by the Vietnamese. Shortly thereafter, on February 10, the Political Bureau of the Vietnam Workers party issued a statement on the unity of the international Communist movement, of which the content was later elaborated in several authoritative articles.[21] These contain no ideological concessions to the Russians but incorporate the Chinese view of the vulnerability of imperialism and state as flatly as can be that, while the Soviet party remains the vanguard of international communism, China is absolutely essential to the Soviet camp.

[19] "Let Us Safeguard the Unity of the Socialist Camp and Strengthen the Solidarity of the International Communist Movement," editorial in *Nodong Sinmun*, January 29, 1963.

[20] Tran Tong, "Let Us Strengthen Unity and Resolutely Struggle for the Successful Achievement of Peace, National Independence, Democracy, and Socialism," *Hoc Tap*, No. 11 (1962).

[21] The Peking *People's Daily*, on March 12, 1963, printed the full texts of the Ho Chi Minh-Antonín Novotný joint communiqué, the Vietnam Workers party Politburo statement, a February 11 *Nhan Dan* editorial concerning the Politburo statement, and an article in *Hoc Tap*, No. 3 (1963), commemorating the eightieth anniversary of the death of Karl Marx. The extent of North Vietnamese support of China at this time is further shown by the fact that Vo Nguyen Giap and Le Duan, both considered among the Russian-oriented group in North Vietnamese leadership, published articles in this series.

The Vietnam Workers party goal is unity, and, if this can only be achieved by giving China her due, so be it. The one concession made to the Soviet view is that the Vietnamese treat the present ideological divergences as resulting from differences in the conditions of several countries—thus not, as the Chinese later argued, problems of ultimate principle. The Vietnam Workers party, then, regards it as the joint responsibility of the Soviet Union and China to discover a *modus vivendi*.

THE JAPANESE AND INDONESIAN PARTIES

Lack of space precludes a detailed examination of the positions taken by the Japanese and Indonesian Communist parties. As nongoverning parties, they do not have territorial or economic objectives of the same order as governing parties. Their local political situations and tactics, however, provide the basis for convergence of their ideological positions with the Chinese.

The Japanese Communist party's problem is that, after years of advocating a united front of all "progressive forces," it is now in sharp open competition with the Socialist party for influence on the labor movement and other mass organizations. The party has not been scoring great successes but has been forced into a defensive position. There have been defections and expulsions of leading personnel. In the most important instance, the defecting group broke with the party leadership on the question of whether the main enemy of Japanese progressive forces was "international monopoly capital," as the party line has held for some years, or "native monopoly capital." The defection strengthened the Socialist party at the expense of the Communist party. Under these circumstances, the organizational integrity of the Japanese Communist party was threatened, and the party leadership had no choice but to stand on a firm antirevisionist platform. The Sino-Soviet ideological controversy added somewhat to Japanese Communist party difficulties and the party tried to ignore or deny its existence for as long as it could. Khrushchev's de-Stalinization moves were also to the disadvantage of the Japanese Communist party. In contrast, the current Chinese Communist policy toward Japan, which one could describe with only a little facetiousness as recognition of the Japanese Communist party and of Japanese business combined with nonrecognition of the Japanese government and the non-Communist left, has been supportive of the Japanese Communist party leadership. When faced with the need to declare itself, it was almost inevitable that the Japanese Communist party would support China.

The position of the Indonesian Communist party (Partai Komunis Indonesia) is less difficult. Its basic strategy, recently reaffirmed, has been to promote a "democratic revolution," not a "socialist revolution." Its tactic has been to attract to itself the most nearly like-minded elements of the so-called "middle forces" in Indonesian politics. The success of this tactic depends a good deal on preserving unanimity within the party. Revisionist tendencies and de-Stalinization are at this time a greater danger to the party's solidarity than are their alternatives. The Sino-Soviet dispute apparently aroused some doubts among the Indonesian Communist party membership, not to the extent that might make splits imminent, but enough to make the leadership reaffirm a single line. The party in 1963 was more definitely in support of China than it had previously been but, like the Vietnamese party, showed a desire to remain in touch with both sides and to help mediate the quarrel.

CONCLUSION

In the space of two years, while the Sino-Soviet dispute has become deeper and more bitter, support for the Chinese position has attained greater proportions than could have been foreseen at the beginning of the period. In Asia, though there are parties, like the Outer Mongolian, which have clearly aligned themselves against China, there has developed what amounts to a virtual coalition of parties in favor. The coalition has arisen through a convergence of ideological positions, based on the individual interests of the respective parties. North Korea and North Vietnam have political and territorial ambitions wholly endorsed by the Chinese People's Republic and partly restrained by the Soviet Union—hence the appeal to them of China's uncompromising anti-imperialism and advocacy of struggle. Both regimes are promoting economic plans aimed at critical structural changes. They receive diversified support, in different proportions, from a number of bloc countries. China's support is perhaps more direct, more appropriate, and more unstinting than that of other countries. Apart from the sources of external support, both the Democratic People's Republic of Korea and the Democratic Republic of Vietnam have come to feel that their effort must be self-supporting and must aim at self-sufficiency—hence a growing emphasis on national independence, which spills over into defense of China's freedom from dictation. In both cases, also, the organizational effort required by the economic plans makes for the maintenance of political-psychological tension—hence antipathy to revisionism, especially in its internal manifestations. The Japanese and Indonesian Communist parties do not have as much at stake. The main issue in their cases is their internal organizational problems. These have been, to a certain extent, created or intensified by the Sino-Soviet dispute and by some of Khrushchev's policies. Thus, they, too, have had to move toward the anti-revisionist pole.

In its present form, the coalition is more against something than for something. It acts to protect its own interests and to protect the Chinese People's Republic against Soviet and European Communist attacks. But its real interest is in dispelling the source of trouble, not in exacerbating it. Those of the constituent members of the coalition who are able to do so offer themselves as mediators, and all of them, including the Chinese, avow an interest in unity.

The possibility of a split cannot be wholly ruled out. If it were to take place, and if the Chinese were to try to head a dissident international movement, the viability of the coalition would be tested under the most severe conditions imaginable. The question would be whether this protective anti-Soviet grouping could be transformed into an ideologically distinct and operationally solidary pro-Chinese coalition. This would be a coalition of a new nature. The sacrifices involved in forming it would be severe, and its field for constructive action in support of its members' objectives would be restricted.

The possibility of a really satisfactory *modus vivendi* between China and the Soviet Union at this time seems remote. But if some *modus vivendi*, permitting so much as the maintenance of a facade of world Communist unity, is arrived at, the viability of the pro-Chinese coalition would be enhanced. The grouping would not be absolutely dominated by China, but China would be its indispensable center. This in itself would constitute a significant alteration in the structure of world communism.

Russia, China, and the Underdeveloped Areas

By Harry Gelman

ABSTRACT: The divergence between Soviet and Chinese Communist policy toward the underdeveloped areas has derived largely from differing views of national interest. The advent of nuclear weapons has fostered a Soviet wish to control the risk of local-war clashes that might involve the Soviet Union in total war. For this and other reasons, the Soviets have attempted to reduce the emphasis given armed "anti-imperialist" struggles generally while continuing to encourage such violence in particular cases judged to be both profitable and of little risk. Moscow has also favored a cautious policy toward newly independent states, relying upon the gradual growth of Soviet political and economic influence to induce the ruling "national bourgeoisie" to accept estrangement from the West, dependence on the bloc, and eventual domination by the local Communist party. Communist China, on the other hand, regards militant action throughout the underdeveloped world as the principal weapon available to it to strike at and isolate the United States. Peking has, therefore, strongly opposed every Soviet policy which in the Chinese view might inhibit such militancy. The Chinese Communists have also posed, with some hypocrisy, as consistent defenders of the interests of Communist parties betrayed by the Soviet Union in its conciliation of the "national bourgeoisie."

Harry Gelman, M.A., Washington, D. C., is a student of Soviet and Chinese policy, educated at Cornell University, Brooklyn College, and the School of Slavonic and East European Studies of London University. He has published articles dealing with the effects of the Sino-Soviet conflict upon the Communist party of India in recent issues of Problems of Communism, and presented a paper on the same subject to the April 1962 meeting of the Association for Asian Studies which is shortly to be published in the compendium Communist Strategies in Asia (A Comparative Analysis of Governments and Parties).

SINCE at least 1958, the Soviet and Chinese Communist regimes have been pursuing divergent objectives toward the colonial and underdeveloped areas of the world, prompted in large measure by increasingly different views of the policies required by their national interests. With varying degrees of sincerity, each has interpreted and defended aspects of the line it has advocated as uniquely justified by Marxist-Leninist doctrine and as uniquely capable of securing the final triumph of the world Communist movement and the eternal happiness of the world's peoples. At the same time, each regime has condemned the policies of the other as deviations from Marxist-Leninist truth (either alterations of doctrine or failures to make the necessary alterations) caused by a selfish pursuit of national interests at the expense of those of the Communist movement. Although both Moscow and Peking have somewhat exaggerated the conscious perfidy of the fraternal antagonist for polemical purposes, each appears to be essentially correct about the other's motives.

Soviet attitudes toward the "national liberation movement" of the underdeveloped world appear to have evolved as the product of the interaction of two major factors: (1) the emergence of a nuclear-weapons technology which has engendered a Soviet desire to control the risk of local-war clashes that might lead to total war, and (2) the emergence from colonial status of new independent states led by a "national" bourgeoisie with neutral leanings that seem exploitable for Soviet foreign-policy purposes.

These considerations seem to have impelled Moscow toward a doctrine for national liberation movements that would both justify some reduction in the emphasis given to armed struggles in the underdeveloped world generally and allow the Soviet Union to use whatever degree of caution or boldness with regard to a particular armed struggle it might deem appropriate in the light of its appraisal of Western intentions, the balance of power, its own security interests, and the state of Soviet negotiations with the West. The Soviet solution has been to acknowledge a continuing but diminishing role for armed struggle, to make sweeping but ambiguous promises of assistance for such struggles, and to place heavy emphasis upon the use of a variety of other methods for advancing bloc interests in underdeveloped areas. These other methods will be discussed in detail below, but two points about them should be noted here: relatively slow-acting economic and indoctrination efforts are given great importance, and the national bourgeoisie ruling in underdeveloped countries is asserted to have, as a rule, a usefulness which will not soon be exhausted and which, therefore, should not be endangered by premature efforts by local Communists to come to power.

The Chinese Communist regime, on the other hand, regards militant action throughout the underdeveloped world as the principal weapon available to it to strike at and isolate the Western capitalist countries, particularly the United States, the power which backs an alternative Chinese government on Taiwan and which opposes the spread of Peking's influence in Asia. Peking has, therefore, opposed and denounced every Soviet policy or propaganda line which might, in its view, reduce the militancy of anti-Western movements—for example, the downgrading of armed struggle, the ascribing of good intentions to some Western statesmen, the emphasis upon the horrors of nuclear war, the suggestion that Soviet economic might will conquer "imperialism" in any case in the long run without risk. Peking depreciates the danger that world war may result from the escalation of military conflict in underdeveloped areas, it insists that maximum pressure against the West in these areas is both essential and decisive for the defeat of the West, and it appeals to the interests of all radical forces in underdeveloped areas, Communist or non-Communist, who wish to come to power over their "imperialist" or bourgeois enemies more rapidly than the Soviet timetable would allow.

Faced by these pressures, Moscow, in recent years, has had to seek a balance between its own conflicting interests; it has desired to preserve the essence of its relatively cautious and slow-paced policy toward the underdeveloped world while seeking to retain the support of radical groups which find the Chinese line more congenial. This has already proven extremely difficult, and it may, in fact, be impossible. The result thus far, as will be seen, has been a certain amount of wavering, self-contradiction, and ambiguity in Soviet statements on some subjects, a good deal of Soviet hypocrisy on other matters, and a few real concessions to the demands of Peking's audience. Because, however, the central elements of the Soviet strategy toward the underdeveloped world are apparently felt by the Soviet leadership to be essential to Soviet foreign policy and national security, they have not been abandoned under the Chinese attack, nor is this likely to happen.

THE SOVIET DOCTRINE OF STAGES

Soviet theory depicts the national liberation movement in each underdeveloped country as passing through discrete stages, each calling for different responses from the Communist bloc and the local Communist party and each a prerequisite for the next.

STAGE ONE: WINNING POLITICAL SOVEREIGNTY

In discussing the first phase, the period of the winning of political sovereignty, Soviet writings over the past four or five years have become increasingly concerned to defend the peaceful coexistence line against Chinese charges that it weakens both the will of colonial peoples to struggle for their independence and the ability of the bloc to aid that struggle.[1] These Chinese attacks were given impetus by a few published Soviet hints—most notably in the spring of 1960—that it would be undesirable for revolutionary struggles to be carried on so vigorously as to lead to a danger of world war.[2] Since 1960, under the pressure of Chinese competition, Soviet writers and spokesmen have tended to shy away from this dangerous subject and, indeed, have paid repeated tribute to the legitimacy of revolu-

[1] These Chinese charges have by now been voiced many hundreds of times in one form or another since the fall of 1959 in newspaper and journal articles, radio broadcasts, pamphlets, and speeches. The two most elaborate and authoritative presentations of the Chinese case are to be found in editorial department articles in the Chinese Communist party (CCP) Central Committee journal *Hung ch'i* (*Red Flag*): "Long Live Leninism," *Hung ch'i*, No. 8 (April 1960), and "More on the Differences Between Comrade Togliatti and Us," *Hung ch'i*, No. 3/4 (March 1963).

[2] See, for example, Khrushchev's statement before the United Nations General Assembly on September 23, 1960 on the need "to prevent the outbreak of new armed conflicts in Asia, Africa and Latin America as a result of clashes between the colonial powers and the peoples fighting for freedom and independence." *Pravda*, September 24, 1960. An article in a Soviet journal the previous spring had spoken of the need to "ensure a situation in which internal processes in particular countries do not lead to military clashes of the two diametrically opposite systems." A. Sovetov, "Leninist Foreign Policy and International Relations," *International Affairs*, No. 4 (April 1960).

tionary struggle of all types. As Peking has noted, however, Soviet writings have, from time to time, continued to make essentially the same point by persisting in the practice of referring to "war" in general as an evil to be abolished and of using this ambiguous term interchangeably with "world war."[3]

Peking has vehemently attacked intimations that armed struggles and bloc support for armed struggles should be bypassed or downgraded in favor of other means of struggle because of the dangers of escalation into total war. The People's Republic of China has maintained that regardless of whether "imperialism" can be deterred indefinitely from direct nuclear attack on the bloc, it cannot be deterred from incessant attempts at armed suppression of the national liberation movement which must inevitably evoke armed resistance. It has insisted that this violent struggle in the "intermediate areas" of the world must ultimately determine the fate of both the West and the bloc. And it has concluded that final victory cannot be guaranteed for either the colonial peoples or the bloc unless the bloc acts decisively to encourage armed uprisings and to defeat "imperialist armed suppression" wherever it occurs. Evasion of this "socialist" responsibility, Peking contends, can only encourage "imperialist aggression," weaken the militancy of the colonial peoples and their Communist parties, and increase—not lessen—the dangers of nuclear war.[4]

Thus, Peking rejects the argument toward which Moscow has repeatedly turned—namely that peaceful coexistence with the "imperialist" West is now possible because changes in the world military balance of power have made it increasingly possible to deter, or to "paralyze," as a *Kommunist* article declared in September 1960, "imperialist" military intervention to suppress revolutionary movements.[5] The Chinese Communists indeed see a possibil-

---

[3] Examples of this are to be found in the new Communist party of the Soviet Union (CPSU) Program (*Pravda,* November 2, 1961) and in the CPSU letter to the Chinese party dated March 30, 1963 (*Pravda,* April 3, 1963). The CCP in March 1963 attacked modern revisionists who "always talk about peace and war in general terms," who "only worry lest the 'sparks' of resistance by the oppressed nations . . . might lead to disaster and disturb their tranquility," and who "simply condemn these wars in an undiscriminating and arbitrary fashion." "More on the Differences Between Comrade Togliatti and Us," *op. cit.* In a *Jen-min jih-pao* (*People's Daily*) editorial a few days before this, Peking declared that, although the Soviets had "occasionally spoken of the necessity of supporting national liberation wars and people's revolutionary wars, they repeatedly stressed that 'a war under contemporary conditions would inevitably become a world war,' that 'even a tiny spark can cause a world conflagration,' and that it was necessary to 'oppose all kinds of wars.' This amounts to making no distinction between just and unjust wars and *to opposing wars of all kinds on the pretext of preventing a world war.*" (Emphasis added.) "Whence the Differences? A Reply to Comrade Thorez and Other Comrades," *Jen-min jih-pao* editorial, February 27, 1963.

[4] For a good example of this Chinese argument, see Yu Chao-li, "New Situation in the People's Struggle Throughout the World," *Hung ch'i,* No. 1 (January 1961). The Soviets, for their part, have, on occasion, flatly denied that the disappearance of colonialism will necessarily be decisive for the East-West struggle. See V. Matveyev, "Wars of Liberation and Diplomacy," *International Affairs,* No. 3 (March 1963), p. 71.

[5] A. Belyakov and F. Burlatskiy, "Lenin's Theory of Socialist Revolution and the Present Time," *Kommunist,* No. 13 (September 1960). A Soviet broadcast in Mandarin to China on March 30, 1962 similarly claimed that "under the conditions of peaceful coexistence, the people who are launching national liberation struggles are safe from being invaded by their former colonialists." This broadcast went so far as to say that "the liberation struggle waged by the people in the colonial and dependent countries . . . can be continued to the last *only* under conditions of peaceful coexistence." (Emphasis added.)

ity that the West can be deterred, not from attacking colonial peoples, but, rather, from escalating this inevitable "aggression" into an attack on the bloc and total war. The Chinese profess to believe that, in such cases, the West can be made to back down, provided that the Soviet Union will encourage all-out struggle and itself show a determined front.[6] Peking expresses concern lest a Soviet pretense that a blanket deterrence against "imperialist aggression" exists serve only to "paralyze" both popular resistance to "imperialism" and effective bloc support for such resistance.

For these reasons, the Chinese Communist regime declares that there can be "no peaceful coexistence between the oppressors and the oppressed."[7] Unlike Moscow—which uses the "peaceful coexistence" line particularly in its tactics toward the West—Peking has occasionally gone so far as to hint that its concept of "peaceful coexistence" applies primarily to some of the newly independent states, in name only to most

[6] It should be noted, however, that, during the Cuban crisis week of October 22–28, 1962, Chinese Communist propaganda, while of course vigorously anti-United States and pro-Castro, was nevertheless relatively circumspect and never went so far as to imply that the Soviet Union should take or threaten to take any specific course of military action toward the United States. Only after Khrushchev had backed down, and the People's Republic of China itself was therefore no longer threatened by the prospect of involvement in a world thermonuclear war, did Peking begin its violent denunciations of Khrushchev's "Munich" and greatly intensify its mass demonstrations in support of Cuba and its hysterical appeals for Cuban resistance to the last man. This suggests that Peking is by no means as certain that the West will always yield when met by force as it professes to be. It also suggests that there are large elements of hypocrisy in the Chinese Communist position.

[7] "Whence the Differences? A Reply to Comrade Thorez and Other Comrades," op. cit.

of the large Western powers, and not at all to the United States.[8] In this connection, Peking contends that, along with a Soviet tendency to inhibit militant struggle out of a cowardly fear of the consequences, there has been a tendency on the part of the Soviet Union to exaggerate the relative importance and value of negotiations with the West— thus in effect further encouraging neglect of Chinese national interests, which require sustained, not diminished pressure on the United States.[9] Similarly, Peking in its polemics has suggested— with questionable sincerity—that the

[8] Thus Mao Tun, in a speech to an Afro-Asian writers' conference in February 1962, emphasized the distinction between "principled" and unprincipled peaceful coexistence and explained that the former was set forth by "the Chinese people together with the other peoples of Asia and Africa" in the Five Principles of Bandung. Today, he said, such "principled peaceful coexistence" was being fostered by "the heroic struggles for national independence, democracy, and freedom which the peoples of Asia and Africa are waging"— implicitly, against the West. "Mao Tun Speech at Afro-Asian Writers' Conference," Jen-min jih-pao, February 14, 1962.

[9] Thus a CCP provincial secretary wrote in Jen-min jih-pao of October 20, 1960 that "to emphasize lopsidedly the meeting of leaders [of various countries] and to neglect revolutionary struggle of the masses . . . is a mistake." China Youth of August 1, 1960 contained an unusually frank statement of the Chinese belief that the sole bloc aim in negotiations with the West, or in any agreements reached, must be the use of "revolutionary tricks" to hasten the demise of imperialism. And, in its appeals to the interests of radical forces of underdeveloped areas, Peking has repeatedly intimated that it can represent them better than can Moscow because the People's Republic of China is not inhibited by the desire not to undermine negotiations with the West. On March 19, 1963, the New China News Agency quoted an Algerian journalist as telling a Peking meeting that "the revolution has in you its vanguard, an army 650 million strong," and that "from the beginning you have been among the few wholly and unconditionally at our side, because your state interests do not conflict with those of the colonial revolution."

Soviet Union naively regards total disarmament not merely as a slogan to rally the masses against "imperialism" but as a goal actually capable of achievement. The Soviet Union is therefore, according to Peking, nourishing an "unrealistic illusion" which can only disarm the people ideologically and further discourage the struggle against "imperialism." [10]

To all this, the Soviet Union has replied that its peaceful coexistence line does not discourage but assists the national liberation movement—in fact, that it is "only" under conditions of peaceful coexistence that successful national liberation struggles are possible.[11] Soviet spokesmen have added that the Soviet disarmament line is correct because total disarmament is allegedly a difficult but attainable goal [12] and because the achievement of this goal must mean the total demise of colonialism, for "imperialist" domination cannot last without the use of weapons.[13]

The Need for Armed Struggle

The Soviet preference for avoidance of direct military engagement with

Western forces in underdeveloped areas was accompanied, in 1959 and 1960, by a trend in Soviet writings toward limiting the over-all importance of and necessity for armed struggle in the national liberation movement, particularly during the first stage, the struggle for political independence.

Although the need for armed revolt in some cases was never disavowed and was sometimes vigorously affirmed, Soviet statements tended to suggest that the frequency of such cases was continuously declining—that nonviolent methods of gaining political independence were becoming more and more the rule because wars of colonial suppression by "imperialism" were themselves becoming progressively less frequent.[14]

Moscow at no time, however, ceased to applaud violence in underdeveloped areas in particular cases where it believed applause or even some degree of assistance to be profitable and of little risk either to Soviet security or to the Soviet foreign policy of the moment—especially so if Moscow also believed the violence to be inevitable in any case. This became particularly noticeable after the abandonment of the very soft Soviet line toward the West of late 1959 and early 1960 and after the onset of the massive Chinese attack on Soviet policy in 1960. Since 1961 Soviet statements belittling the over-all need for armed revolt against imperialism have become much less common, and the Soviet Union has conceded a verbal point to Peking by admitting the present "inevitability" of national liberation wars and "armed uprisings" in under-

---

[10] See the speech delivered by Liu Chang-sheng at the June 8, 1960 World Federation of Trade Unions meeting in Peking. Liu Chang-sheng, "On the Question of War and Peace," *Jen-min jih-pao,* June 9, 1960. In a report of a meeting of the Presidium of the World Peace Council broadcast by Peking radio on March 9, 1963, the Chinese delegate to this meeting was depicted as having told the council that "some persons who are advertising disarmament want to see the people who are waging struggles against imperialism and new and old colonialism give up their arms for self-defense and let imperialism do as it wishes."

[11] Soviet radio broadcast in Mandarin to China, April 3, 1962.

[12] See the Khrushchev speech in Moscow of October 20, 1960 (*Pravda,* October 21, 1960).

[13] Abdelkader El Ouahrani, "The Struggle for National Independence and Disarmament,"

World Marxist Review, Vol. 5, No. 6 (June 1962).

[14] A. Sovetov, "Leninist Foreign Policy and International Relations," *op. cit.;* A. Arzumanyan, "The October Revolution, Beginning of a New Era of World History," *Kommunist,* No. 16 (November 1960); Ye. Zhukov, "The Complete Collapse of Colonialism Is Inevitable," *Pravda,* January 5, 1961.

developed areas.[15] Moscow apparently interprets this to mean not, as Peking does, that armed uprisings must occur in every case but, rather, that, because imperialism is not yet fully deterred from armed suppression, armed uprisings must still inevitably sometimes occur. *Pravda* has reaffirmed a Soviet intention to "render any aid, including the delivery of modern weapons, to peoples who are beating off the attacks of the colonizers." [16] The 1960–1961 Soviet airlift to Laos furnished under the pretext of a formal request from Souvanna Phouma presumably was in this category.

When all this is noted, however, it remains true that Moscow continues to place far less emphasis upon the need for armed struggle in underdeveloped areas than does Peking and far more emphasis upon alternative methods of influencing events in those areas. One such method is use of the United Nations rostrum, which, as *Pravda* has stated, is the "particular" avenue favored by the Soviet Union for rendering "all possible support to the peoples waging the sacred struggle for their freedom." [17] Certainly it is the avenue whose use involves the least risk to the Soviet state. Peking has evidently noted that Moscow's employment of the United Nations forum to "expose" and "isolate" the imperialists has served to project an image of vigorous Soviet backing for anticolonial struggles while in fact merely substituting verbal for physical violence; in this sense, Khrushchev's banging of his shoe in the United Nation's General Assembly in 1960 was the deliberate use of braggadocio as an inexpensive substitute for action. In November 1960, Soviet propaganda implied that Khrushchev's mere act of introducing an anticolonial resolution in the United Nations was an example of Soviet "protection" of colonial peoples.[18] In contrast, the People's Republic of China has attacked the depiction of the United Nations as an institution capable of overthrowing colonialism.[19]

Another alternative method favored by the Soviet Union has been an appeal to the proletariat and other "progressive forces" of metropolitan colonizing countries to bring pressure upon their governments to end armed suppression of colonial peoples.[20] Soviet denunciations of the iniquities of punitive colonial wars have frequently included lengthy references to the sufferings caused by those wars to the proletariat of the metropolitan country itself—a point generally ignored by Peking. The Soviet stress upon the feasibility and importance of helping to abolish colonialism through political action in Europe has carried with it a tacit downgrading of the importance of armed struggle in the colonies. At the same time, it has seemed to shift a portion of

[15] N. S. Khrushchev, "For New Victories of the World Communist Movement," *Kommunist,* No. 1 (January 1961).

[16] "The Era of National Liberation," editorial in *Pravda,* December 26, 1962.

[17] *Ibid.*

[18] A. Davidson, "The Downfall of Colonialism in Africa," *International Affairs,* No. 11 (November 1960). Davidson stated that Khrushchev's introduction of the United Nations resolution was another Soviet demonstration of "its readiness to protect the rights of the African people."

[19] See, for example, the Chinese comments on the role of the United Nations in connection with the Cuban crisis of 1962: "The Fearless Cuban People Are the Most Powerful Strategic Weapon," *Jen-min jih-pao* editorial, November 5, 1962. See also the speech made by Liu Ning-i reporting on the Third Afro-Asian People's Solidarity Conference to a Peking rally: "Work Report of the Chief of the Chinese Delegation," *Jen-min jih-pao,* March 8, 1963.

[20] See, for example, the statement issued by Khrushchev in Moscow on December 27, 1960 commenting on the passage of an anticolonial resolution by the United Nations General Assembly: "Declaration of Comrade N. S. Khrushchev," *Pravda,* December 28, 1960.

the responsibility for ending colonialism away from the more militant—and possibly Peking-inclined—Communist parties of the underdeveloped areas toward the more reliable—and pro-Soviet—Communist parties of Europe.[21] As the geographical polarization of the world Communist movement between Moscow and Peking has proceeded, this factor has increased in importance and has found a corollary in Soviet attempts to use such older, Europe-based world-front organizations as the World Peace Council to oppose and offset growing Chinese influence in such bodies as the Afro-Asian People's Solidarity Organization.[22]

A third method preferred by Moscow to the support of armed struggle has been summed up in the assertion that economic rather than military battles are taking the "central place" as the old colonial structure gradually dis-

appears.[23] Peking has very limited capabilities for economic warfare and has a vested interest in preserving the primacy of armed struggle as a means of maintaining maximum pressure upon the United States. Accordingly, the Chinese Communists have charged that this Soviet attempt to shift the emphasis is tantamount to betrayal of the peoples of the remaining colonies and of nominally independent but actually "semi-colonial" areas such as Latin America.[24]

STAGE TWO: AFTER POLITICAL INDEPENDENCE

Soviet policy toward national liberation movements after the attainment of political independence divides this phase into two substages: (1) transition to the national democratic state, and (2) the subsequent transition to socialism. While Soviet theory insists that these substages are consecutive, it tends to blur the dividing line between them, implying that one must imperceptibly lead into the other.

The concept of the "national democratic state" was formally enunciated in the Moscow Statement of December 1960, in what *Pravda* the next day termed a "new contribution to Marxism-Leninism." The East German Politburo member Hermann Matern has publicly confirmed that this portion of the Statement was based on a Soviet draft.[25] The publication of this concept culminated a long tendency in Soviet writings and speeches to suggest the necessity of a transitional phase between the former colony's achievement of state sover-

---

[21] See, in this connection, the recent Chinese reproach to "the proletarian parties of the metropolitan imperialist countries" for daring to "flaunt their seniority before these people [of Asia, Africa, and Latin America], to put on lordly airs, to carp and cavil, like Comrade Thorez of France who arrogantly and disdainfully speaks of them as being 'young and inexperienced.'" "More on the Differences Between Comrade Togliatti and Us," *op. cit.*

[22] In an article reporting on the events of the Third Afro-Asian Solidarity Conference held in Tanganyika in February 1963, the Soviet representatives at that conference referred to the attempts of "certain individuals" to exclude from the conference delegates from both the European bloc states and the "international democratic organizations." The Soviet writers claimed that these attempts had failed, emphasized the "worthy contribution" to the work of the conference allegedly made by the World Peace Council, and decried efforts "to isolate this movement [the Afro-Asian Solidarity Organization] from the progressive forces of the rest of the world." M. Tursun-zade and L. Maksudov, "Strengthen Unity in the Struggle for National Independence, for Peace," *Pravda,* March 23, 1963.

[23] B. N. Ponomarev, "Some Problems of the Revolutionary Movement," *World Marxist Review,* Vol. 5, No. 12 (December 1962).

[24] "Whence the Differences? A Reply to Comrade Thorez and Other Comrades," *op. cit.*

[25] Hermann Matern, "The Moscow Resolutions Demonstrate the New State of the World," *Neues Deutschland,* December 23, 1960.

eignty under bourgeois leadership and its final emergence as a bloc member under the dictatorship of the proletariat.

Although many of the features envisaged for the "national democratic state" bear considerable resemblance to the program for a transitional state form in colonial countries put forward by Mao Tse-tung in 1940 in his "On New Democracy," there is one striking difference. As the Italian Communist party has publicly noted, Mao "stressed very explicitly that the broad alliance of classes" envisaged in his program "must be directed by the labor movement and by the Communist party." [26] This is not the case with the new Soviet concept. Present Chinese policy has therefore appeared hostile to the gradualistic and evolutionary interpretation the Soviet Union has given to the emergence of the national democratic state and suspicious lest the new concept be used to justify both a further indefinite delay in the attainment of Communist hegemony and a tolerant attitude toward individual bourgeois leaders favored by Moscow but opposed by Peking for reasons of national interest. Although Peking signed the Moscow Statement in which this concept appeared, subsequent Chinese writings—in contrast to Soviet comment—have been notably reticent about it and, on at least one occasion, have implicitly attacked it.[27]

[26] See the article by "Asiaticus" in the Italian Communist party weekly *Rinascita* (*Rebirth*), Rome, January 27, 1963.

[27] Tung Pi-wu in a speech on October 9, 1961 remarked that "there is no country in which the national and democratic revolution can achieve complete victory under the leadership of the bourgeoisie; neither the plan for a bourgeois republic *nor that for any other form of bourgeois state* can enable these countries to embark on the road of completely independent development." (Emphasis added.) New China News Agency, October 9, 1961. The allusion to "any other form" seemed clearly directed at the new form

As explained in the December 1960 Moscow Statement and in subsequent Soviet comment, a national democratic state will be one which has fulfilled four chief prerequisites: (1) the adoption of an "anti-imperialist" foreign policy; (2) the winning of complete economic and cultural independence from the "imperialist" world and the assumption of close economic ties with the bloc; (3) the rise of the state sector to a predominant position in the economy; and (4) the achievement of a list of "democratic reforms" and "democratic freedoms," two of the most important of which are land reform and—implicitly—unfettered freedom of activity for the Communist party.

Soviet writings have frequently implied that these goals have importance in the order named and are to be achieved through the efforts of a broad united "anti-imperialist front" embracing "all patriotic strata" of the country concerned. Despite certain periodic Soviet manifestations of impatience with the national bourgeoisie and sallies in defense of local Communist parties under attack, it has long been the Soviet position that so long as tendencies in the first three directions can be observed—and particularly the first one—local Communist parties should not regard the absence thus far of substantial "democratic reforms"—that is, concessions to themselves—as grounds for precipitating matters through armed revolt.[28]

Although Soviet comment is ambiguous regarding the relative status of the national bourgeoisie and the proletariat after the attainment of the national

being promoted by Moscow, the national democratic state.

[28] See "The National Liberation Movement at the Present Stage," editorial in *Kommunist*, No. 13 (September 1962). See also Ye. Zhukov, "Significant Factor of Our Time," *Pravda*, August 26, 1960.

democratic state, it implies that the Communist party may not yet have achieved direct control but will probably occupy a position of influence in a state still ostensibly led by "progressive" bourgeois figures. The calculated vagueness which has continued to surround this concept thus allows Communist parties to accept, for a transitional period of undetermined length, an alliance in which the Communist party exercises total, major, or rather limited control over the national bourgeoisie, depending on the readiness to compromise of the party concerned or the wishes of its advisers from the Communist party of the Soviet Union. It is intimated, however, that once this position has been achieved, the subsequent phase of transition to direct Communist leadership and bloc membership will be easy, and possibly bloodless.[29] In other words, the "bourgeois state machine" will be gradually transformed by Communist infiltration, rather than abruptly "broken" in the classical Leninist manner.

This notion of a gradual, imperceptible taming of the national bourgeoisie, facilitating an eventual peaceful Communist assumption of power in underdeveloped countries, has been basic to Soviet thinking for several years. Soviet writings have drawn a fundamental distinction between "state-monopoly capitalism" in mature Western capitalist countries and "state capitalism" in underdeveloped countries. Unlike the former, the latter has been found to have "progressive" potentialities, given the proper alignment of class forces.[30]

Soviet writers, while always recognizing what both Moscow and Peking have termed the "dual, vacillating nature" of the national bourgeoisie, have frequently expressed the optimistic assumption that overriding economic forces, together with pressure from the proletariat and peasantry, would, in the end, compel the national bourgeoisie to accept economic and political estrangement from the West and increasing dependence on the bloc.[31] These tendencies were expected to weaken "imperialism's" world economic position, to hasten the day of bloc economic superiority over the capitalist world, and thus to accelerate the slide of the underdeveloped countries toward "socialism."

Finally, the advent of the national democratic state and then of Communist domination was somehow to be facilitated by the attraction to be felt by bourgeois leaders toward the "positive example" of Soviet methods and achievements and the leanings of some national bourgeois figures toward ideas they have termed "Socialist." Soviet writers have not always sharply emphasized the irreconcilability of some of these ideas with Marxism, and, even

---

[29] See, for example, B. N. Ponomarev, "On the State of National Democracy," *Kommunist*, May 1961; see also G. Starushenko, "On National Democracies," *Pravda*, January 25, 1963.

[30] See the Soviet textbook *Osnovy Marksizma-Leninizma* (*Fundamentals of Marxism-Leninism*) (Moscow, 1959), Chapter 16, "The National Liberation Movement of the Peoples Against Colonialism." See also the concluding remarks by A. M. Rumyantsev, chief editor of the *World Marxist Review*, in a discussion organized by the journal in December 1962: "The Socialist World System and the National-Liberation Movement," *World Marxist Review*, Vol. 6, No. 3 (March 1963).

[31] In January 1963 one Soviet article therefore attacked the "dogmatic notion that in our time the dominating tendency in the evolution of the national bourgeoisie is permanent conservatism and rapprochement with internal and foreign reaction." Those who have held this view, the article declared, have proceeded from an erroneous "denial of the anti-imperialist potency of the national bourgeoisie and from a general underestimation of the democratic and patriotic forces." I. Pavlov and I. B. Red'ko, *Narody Assi i Afriki* (*Peoples of Asia and Africa*) (Moscow), No. 1 (January-February 1963).

when they have done so, they have frequently also stressed the "progressive" nature of these bourgeois inclinations.[32]

THE CHINESE POSITION

Chinese Communist propaganda has denounced the notion that an evolution toward "socialism" may be facilitated under even the nominal leadership of "progressive" members of the bourgeoisie. Peking has seemed particularly exercised by the reiterated Soviet contention that state capitalism in the newly independent countries, given favorable conditions, may prepare the ground for a gradual and peaceful transition to "socialism."[33] The Chinese People's Republic has repeatedly indicated lack of faith in the long-term "revolutionary potentialities" of the national bourgeoisie when not firmly led and controlled by the proletariat. It has insisted that an eventual violent armed revolution, led by the proletariat and resulting in the total obliteration of all parts of the "bourgeois state machine," is essential to the advent of "socialism" in all countries, without exception, where the proletariat has not previously seized hegemony during the "anti-imperialist" struggle for political independence.[34] Chinese writings make it clear that such an eventual violent upheaval can be avoided in newly independent underdeveloped countries only if the local Communist party has previously followed the "thoroughly

anti-imperialist revolutionary road established by the Chinese people,"[35] whereby "the leadership of the revolution was assumed by the proletariat and not by the bourgeoisie" before independence.[36]

The working class thus established a firm alliance with the peasants, brought the antifeudal revolution to its final end, destroyed once and for all the very foundation of imperialist rule in China, and on those reliable foundations opened up a way for the subsequent transition from the democratic revolution to the socialist revolution.[37]

For its part, Moscow, while agreeing on the desirability of early Communist domination of the national liberation movement, has treated this as an unlikely event in most underdeveloped areas and has apparently built its policy on the expectation of radical bourgeois or *petit bourgeois* leadership of the struggle for independence in the great majority of cases. Soviet propaganda has suggested that it is the duty of Communist parties before independence is achieved to co-operate with the particular anti-"imperialist" tactics— whether violent or nonviolent—adopted by non-Communist leaders of broad liberation fronts; in pursuing such co-operation, the party would, at the same time, preserve its independent structure and expand its influence as far as possible among workers and peasants, so as to facilitate the exertion of greater pressure on the bourgeois leadership after independence has been attained.

In fact, despite the generalized Chinese Communist complaints about the overly tolerant Soviet attitude toward

[32] See, for example, G. Skorov, "Some Economic Questions of the Decay of the Colonial System," *Mirovaia ekonomika i mezhdunarodnye otnosheniia (World Economics and International Relations)*, No. 4 (April 1958).

[33] See "What Kind of Stuff Is Nehru's Much-Advertised Socialism," anonymous article in *Hung ch'i,* No. 7 (1963).

[34] See "A Basic Summing Up of Experience Gained in the Victory of the Chinese People's Revolution," editorial-department article in *Hung ch'i,* No. 20–21 (November 1960).

[35] Wang Chia-hsiang, "The International Significance of the Chinese People's Victory," *Hung ch'i,* No. 19 (October 1959).

[36] Peking home service radio, January 24, 1960.

[37] Wang Chia-hsiang, "The International Significance of the Chinese People's Victory," *op. cit.*

the national bourgeoisie, in overt dealings with specific newly independent nations that have not followed the "Chinese path" and are consequently now ruled by the national bourgeoisie, the criteria used by Chinese foreign policy have not differed significantly from those used by the Soviet Union. For Peking, the significant point has never been the posture of a ruling national bourgeoisie toward its own Communists but, rather, its posture toward the Chinese People's Republic. Underdeveloped states that are strongly aligned with the Chinese Nationalist government or that belong to military alliances with the United States—for example, Thailand—are discovered to be ruled by reactionary forces suitable to be overthrown; underdeveloped states that are believed to show a conciliatory attitude toward Peking—for example, Cambodia, Burma, Ceylon—are not so described. The only outstanding leader of the Asian national bourgeoisie who has been subjected to all-out public attack by Peking as a pawn of imperialism has been Nehru, and, of all the Communist parties of the underdeveloped world, only the Indian Communist party has been publicly chastised by the Chinese Communist party for its restrained attitude toward its government. The many past "betrayals" of India to "imperialism" by both Nehru and the Indian Communist party were retroactively discovered by Peking, however, only after a fundamental clash of national interests between India and the People's Republic of China had been made manifest and the Indian Communist party had declined to support Peking.[38] Moreover, despite

Peking's claims to represent the interests of underdeveloped peoples betrayed by Soviet caution, the Chinese public reaction to the execution of Iraqi Communists by the new Iraqi government in February 1963 has been much more restrained than that of Moscow. The Iraqi Communist party, of course, has been a vehement supporter of the Communist party of the Soviet Union in public polemics with the Chinese party in recent years, while the new Iraqi government continues to recognize the Chinese People's Republic and to offer every prospect of normal relations with it.

Some Problems Faced by Soviet Policy

Despite this evidence of Chinese Communist hypocrisy, it is apparent that the Soviets have experienced considerable difficulty in recent years both in countering Chinese arguments to the Communist and other radical forces of the underdeveloped areas and in reconciling Soviet doctrine with the trend of events in the real world.   First, the Soviet Union, which had evidently initially wished to preserve Cuba as the best example of a "national democratic state," has had at last to yield to Castro's wishes to have Cuba recognized as "building socialism"—and thereby, by implication, to be entitled to the Soviet protection which has, in the past at least, been a perquisite of bloc status.[39]   Secondly, the Com-

[38] "More on Nehru's Philosophy in the Light of the Sino-Indian Boundary Question," *Jen-min jih-pao* editorial-department article, October 27, 1962; compare with the line on Nehru taken in the first article on this subject, "Nehru's Philosophy in the Light of the

Sino-Indian Boundary Question," *Jen-min jih-pao* editorial-department article, May 6, 1959. For the most forthright statement of the Chinese Communist party case against the Indian Communist party, see "A Mirror for Revisionists," *Jen-min jih-pao* editorial, March 9, 1963.

[39] The East German official Matern testified in *Neues Deutschland* of December 23, 1960 that the Cuban delegate to the 1960 Moscow conference had objected to the original Soviet formula for the "national democratic

munist party of the Soviet Union, in defending its position against Chinese attack, has had to go further than heretofore in condemnation of measures taken against Communist parties by newly installed governments of the national bourgeoisie; particularly so, as noted in the case of Iraq, when the Communist party in question has recently been a loyal supporter of Moscow against Peking.[40] Thirdly, some Soviet writers during the last two years have shown considerably less confidence than heretofore that the growth of the state sector and of state capitalism in newly independent countries will necessarily facilitate the Communist advent to power; there has been more of a tendency to hedge and to stress the vital importance of the growth of Communist influence over the peasantry as a means of keeping pressure upon the national bourgeoisie and preventing "state-monopoly capital" from seizing control of the state-owned sector of the economy.[41] Fourthly, Soviet spokesmen over the last year have become increasingly concerned to defend Soviet economic-aid policy against the Chinese argument that, as one Soviet writer put

it, "the aid of the socialist states to economically underdeveloped countries objectively leads to the preservation in these countries of the status quo or even strengthens the forces of reaction."[42] And, finally, Soviet statements, particularly since the fall of 1962, have become more and more explicit in denunciation of Chinese efforts to win over the underdeveloped nations of world to Chinese influence—and to exclude Soviet influence—through appeals to racial and geographical arguments.[43]

In all this, the main lines of Soviet policy as they have developed under Khrushchev have not thus far been fundamentally altered. Insofar as it is grounded in the needs of the Soviet state as seen by the dominant leadership, the slower-acting and more cautious Soviet doctrine toward the underdeveloped world is not likely to be abandoned, although it may continue to be amended. Similarly, insofar as the dominant Chinese leaders continue to see the pushing of a more forward strategy in the underdeveloped world as essential to their interests in the confrontation with the West and especially with the United States, Peking is not likely to cease this endeavor.

---

state." Although Soviet writers have never explicitly stated that Cuba—or for that matter, any country—was now a national democratic state, this was strongly hinted in Ponomarev's April 1961 *Kommunist* article already cited. The Soviet recognition of Castro's regime as "building socialism" on a par with the bloc was formalized in the Soviet May Day slogans for 1963. *Pravda,* April 8, 1963.

[40] For a good example of the many such Soviet protests in the past year, see "Contrary to the Interests of the Peoples," an Observer article in *Pravda,* January 22, 1963.

[41] One such more cautious estimate on the role of state capitalism in these countries is furnished by Y. Rozaliyev, "State Capitalism in Asia and Africa," *International Affairs,* No. 2 (February 1963).

[42] Rumyantsev, comment in discussion "The Socialist World System and the National-Liberation Movement," *op. cit.* Rumyantsev announced that such a view has nothing in common with Marxism-Leninism.

[43] The Soviet Union Communist party letter to the Chinese Communist party of March 30, 1963 (*Pravda,* April 3, 1963) thus insisted that proletarian unity must be based on "class anti-imperialist solidarity, and not nationality, color, or geographical principles." Rumyantsev, in "The Socialist World System and the National-Liberation Movement," *op. cit.,* similarly warned against the views of "those who invoke Kipling's 'East and West Will Never Meet,' that is, who reduce everything to geographic or ethnographic differences."

European Communism and the Sino-Soviet Schism

By William E. Griffith

ABSTRACT: East European communism has two subgroups: the more moderate Yugoslavs, Poles, and Hungarians and the more rigid East Germans, Czechoslovaks, Rumanians, and Bulgarians—plus the pro-Chinese Albanians. West Europe has two mass Communist parties, the semirevisionist Italians and the rigid French, and many other small, sectarian ones. The effect of the Sino-Soviet schism has been decisive only in Albania, which, out of fear of Yugoslavia, has deserted Moscow for Peking, and primary only in Yugoslavia, where it furthered but did not primarily cause the new Soviet-Yugoslav *rapprochement*. Elsewhere throughout Europe, Communist parties have remained pro-Soviet. Even so, by giving party leaderships more room for maneuver, the schism has significantly contributed to, although not primarily determined, the consolidation of Polish moderation, the extension of liberalization in Hungary, and ideological revisionism and reformism in Italian communism. In the long run, it seems likely to further still more increasing differentiation and moderation throughout European communism.

William E. Griffith, Ph.D., Cambridge, Massachusetts, is Director of the International Communism Project at the Center for International Studies, Massachusetts Institute of Technology, and Lecturer in Politics at Massachusetts Institute of Technology and at the Fletcher School of Law and Diplomacy. He is author of Albania and the Sino-Soviet Rift (1963) and of articles on East European communism and Sino-Soviet relations.

IN the East European countries—aside from Albania and Yugoslavia—one can discern two Communist subgroups: the more moderate Polish and Hungarian leaderships and the more rigid East German, Czechoslovak, Rumanian, and Bulgarian. In West Europe, the two mass Communist parties, the Italian and French, differ greatly but have some important similarities, and there are also small to minuscule Communist parties in the other West European states.

By the spring of 1963, the effect of the Sino-Soviet schism upon the European Communist parties [1] had been decisive only in Albania and major only in Yugoslavia; elsewhere it was secondary, greatly overshadowed by continuing Soviet influence and by internal factors in each country and party. In East Europe, it, in part, caused Moscow to increase economic co-ordination through the Council for Mutual Economic Aid (CMEA); in West Europe, it was less influential than the continuing impact of Soviet de-Stalinization—itself, however, one of the factors in the schism.

Four preliminary points should be made. Firstly, since the seriousness of the Sino-Soviet dispute first became widely known in 1960, there has been no significant change in the allegiance of any European Communist party, with the only partial exception of the Soviet-Yugoslav *rapprochement:* Albania has remained under Chinese influence and protection, and the other European Communist parties have remained substantially faithful to the Soviet Union. Secondly, the dispute became intense, and the allegiance of European Communist parties clear, by 1959 at the latest.[2] Thirdly, differentiation among the European Communist parties is both less and more than one might think: except Albania, they all—including the semirevisionist Italians—remain ultimately faithful to Moscow, but, within this allegiance, there are many subtle variants and groupings. Fourthly, whether or not the future will bring—as I think probable—a formal, public Sino-Soviet break, one already exists in fact: the "Sino-Soviet bloc," to use Marx's graphic phrase, has already been "thrown on the rubbish-heap of history."

ALBANIA

For the first time since the Mongols, a European state is under the influence of a major Far Eastern power. Even more significant, not only does China's continued support of Albania demonstrate to its sympathizers the worldwide nature of Peking's ambitions, but the Peking-Tirana axis so shamelessly defies Khrushchev and so strikingly demonstrates the limits of his power that it represents a major factor in the Sino-Soviet schism. I have elsewhere [3]

[1] Donald S. Zagoria, *The Sino-Soviet Conflict* (Princeton, 1961); Zbigniew K. Brzezinski, *The Soviet Bloc, Unity and Conflict* (2nd ed.; New York: Praeger, 1961); Geoffrey Hudson, Richard Lowenthal, and Roderick MacFarquhar, *The Sino-Soviet Dispute* (New York: Praeger, 1961); Alexander Dallin and Jonathan Harris (eds.), *Diversity in International Communism* (New York: Columbia, 1963); William E. Griffith, *Albania and the Sino-Soviet Rift* (Cambridge, Mass.: Massachusetts Institute of Technology, 1963); Walter Laqueur and Leopold Labedz (eds.), *Polycentrism* (New York: Praeger, 1962); a special number of *Problems of Communism,* Vol. 11, No. 3 (May–June 1962); William E. Griffith (ed.), *European Communism and the Sino-Soviet Rift,* a symposium in 2 volumes, to be published by the Massachusetts Institute of Technology Press in 1963–1964. Current developments are covered in *Survey, China Quarterly, Problems of Communism, East Europe, Est et ouest,* and *Osteuropa.*

[2] David A. Charles, "The Dismissal of Marshal P'eng Teh-huai," *The China Quarterly,* No. 8 (October–December 1961), pp. 63–76.

[3] Griffith, *Albania and the Sino-Soviet Rift, op. cit.*

analyzed at length the origins and course of Soviet-Albania relations; in brief, the primary cause for Albania's defiance of the Soviet Union was the justified fear of its leaders that they would be turned over by Khrushchev to their hated and feared Yugoslav neighbors. Even without the Sino-Soviet dispute this menace might well have faced them, as it did in 1948, when they were saved from probable liquidation by their Yugoslav protectors by Stalin's break with Tito, and in 1956, when the Hungarian revolution probably saved them from the same fate. When in 1957 the dispute began and the Chinese chose to make Yugoslavia one of their points of attack, the Albanian leader Hoxha's choice, although desperate, was clear, and so far it has proven, from his viewpoint, quite justified.

The Albanian Communist leadership is "native"—that is, they did not take power as *émigrés* returning from Moscow—hardened in wartime guerrilla fighting, Western-educated, solidified by massive, bloody purges, and made up of "intellectuals in arms" in a poor, underdeveloped country. Like Tito, Ho Chiminh, and Mao Tse-tung, Hoxha was never a Moscow agent; he combines traditional Balkan fury with a fanatical internationalism so typical of small, publicized rulers. Hoxha's break with Khrushchev was greatly facilitated by Albania's geographical isolation from the Red Army and by its assurance of Chinese aid; yet his real protection remains the historic inability of his neighbors, Yugoslavia, Greece, and Italy, to agree upon the distribution of the Albanian spoils. His future seems relatively good. Only in the unlikely case of general reconciliation between Khrushchev and Mao would he be sacrificed by the Chinese, and even then he could, and probably would, turn to the West rather than to Khrushchev or Tito for support. As in other aspects of the dispute, however, one general caveat is necessary: Khrushchev's and Mao's successors, like Stalin's, may well attempt a reconciliation, one even with only temporary and probably deceptive prospects for success. Unless and until this happens, however, China's outpost in the Adriatic seems at least more stable than Khrushchev's in the Caribbean.

YUGOSLAVIA

Soviet-Yugoslav relations have recently seen an increasing public *rapprochement*. By the spring of 1963, Yugoslavia was formally recognized by Khrushchev as a "socialist state" and as a member of the "socialist commonwealth." This latter, however, was much looser than its previous incarnation, the "socialist camp," had been in 1953 or even in 1956, and Yugoslavia's return to Soviet grace did not, at least at first, involve either total ideological agreement or membership in CMEA or the Warsaw Pact.

Since 1955 Khrushchev's determination on an ultimate *rapprochement* with Tito, although varying, has always been a constant in Soviet policy. Strategic considerations, the desire to end one of Stalin's greatest anachronisms, and community of interests determine Khrushchev's pro-Yugoslav policy; the 1956 Polish and Hungarian events only temporarily interrupted it; and Mao's 1957 decision to make "Yugoslav revisionism" an instrument against Khrushchev accelerated, although it neither decisively nor even primarily determined, Khrushchev's renewed public courting of the Yugoslavs in 1960–1962. Tito's assiduous and successful cultivation of relations with the neutralist underdeveloped countries had made him a more attractive ally for Khrushchev.

On the other hand, by 1961 Yugoslav economics and politics were in a state which made Tito anxious for Soviet aid.

The economy, which in 1959–1960 seemed booming, was by 1960–1961 in another of its recurrent crises. More seriously, the unity and effectiveness of the Yugoslav Communist apparatus was increasingly menaced by the revival of nationalities tension and the looming struggle for succession to the seventy-year-old Yugoslav leader. Furthermore, the increasing integration of the Common Market to its west and of CMEA to its east threatened Yugoslavia with economic and political isolation, and its hostility to and fear of West Germany naturally attracted it to Moscow's anti-German policies. Finally, Tito and his associates were internationalist Communists who had always hoped and expected to return, if possible on their terms, to the international Communist movement, and by 1962 the Sino-Soviet dispute and Khrushchev's post-1956 acceptance of differentiation and local autonomy in East Europe had removed most of the obstacles to their return. They could now retain their internal independence and the possibility, should Soviet policy turn against them, of resuming a more independent posture.

Thus, to alleviate his domestic crisis and to ease a *rapprochement* with Khrushchev, Tito undertook a large-scale reversal of much of the internal liberalization of the late fifties, and, although not abandoning it at home, he ceased stressing the international validity of his deviant Communist ideology. Khrushchev in turn accepted the restoration of full Soviet-Yugoslav party and state relations in spite of the continued existence of major ideological differences, a major step toward the relativization of ideology. Although Tito did not immediately try to play in the Balkans and in East Europe a role like his 1955–1956 role, his *rapprochement* with Moscow further worsened Soviet-Albanian relations, improved Yugoslav relations with its historically violent anti-Yugoslav neighbor, Bulgaria, and gave another ally to the more moderate East European Communist leaderships.

EAST EUROPE: THE MODERATES

After 1956 Gomułka slowly stabilized his rightist, domesticist regime and thus improved his relations with Khrushchev, the more so when the Sino-Soviet dispute made Moscow need allies, not only satellites, against Peking. When Red Army tanks brought Kádár to power in Hungary in November 1956, the West thought him a mere Soviet Quisling, but, after ruthlessly eliminating his opponents on the right, he gradually eliminated those on the left as well, a dual purge which culminated after the Soviet Twenty-second Congress in October 1961 in the final defeat of his last extremist opponents. Since then, Kádár has rapidly forced forward a controlled liberalization; in some respects, Budapest is now a freer city than Warsaw. Like Gomułka, he has been a sure ally to Khrushchev against the Chinese. Poland and Hungary have consistently displayed the maximum sympathy for Yugoslavia which Moscow would at any time permit, and more liberal Polish Communists have shown considerable sympathy for Italian Communist developments.

Although in 1956–1957 and again in 1958–1959 there were faint signs of pro-Chinese sympathy in Poland and Hungary, this sympathy was in no way shared by the Polish or Hungarian leaders. From the beginning of the public Sino-Soviet dispute, Gomułka and Kádár took not only a strongly anti-Chinese and pro-Soviet line but one which also stressed considerably more than did the more rigid East European leaders the desirability of domestic autonomy for each Communist party. Unlike Tito, neither has international ambitions; like him, both came from the native rather than the Moscovite faction of their parties; but both came to power by the Red Army and both ruled in countries with strong cohesive intelligentsias bound to Western culture, features which in 1956 caused the elite and mass opposition without which neither would have come to power. Even so, neither Poles nor Hungarians wanted another and inevitably unsuccessful revolution against Moscow, and both, therefore, accepted something like the nineteenth-century co-operation with Russia and Austria, while their rulers were willing to relax the more irrational aspects of Stalinist rule. Gomułka went much farther, particularly in his continued toleration of the collapse of agricultural collectivization; his improved relations with Khrushchev, resulting in part from the Sino-Soviet dispute, brought an official Soviet endorsement of continuation of private proprietorship in Polish agriculture, as of Kádár's unorthodox 1962 slogan "he who is not against us is with us."

Yet both Gomułka's and Kádár's attitudes toward the Sino-Soviet dispute remain ambivalent. Both profit from its existence and intensification and, therefore, probably do not want to see it completely resolved; yet, both have reconsolidated their control over their parties and countries on the basis of concentration on economic construction rather than ideological engagement, and neither, therefore, wants the dispute to sow new seeds of discord in his territory. Furthermore, because an open and total Sino-Soviet rupture might well initially increase Soviet desire to tighten control over East Europe, neither probably desires an open Sino-Soviet rupture. There is some evidence that Gomułka tried hard before and during the January 1963 East German party congress to persuade Khrushchev to moderate his fury against the Chinese.

EAST EUROPE: THE EXTREMISTS

The leaderships in East Berlin, Prague, Bucharest, and Sofia are all rigid and extremist in policy and neo-Stalinist in sympathies but, with the partial exception of Rumania, totally pro-Soviet in practice. Their countries have neither the strong anti-Russian, religious nationalism of Poland and Hungary nor a cohesive pro-Western intelligentsia.

East Germany—the German Democratic Republic—is, for the overwhelming majority of its people, neither German nor democratic, neither a nation nor a state, but a Soviet colony ruled by a group of Russian Quislings; its head, Walter Ulbricht, is the most hated Communist chief in Europe. Czechoslovakia is not a historic state and is still beset with Czech-Slovak rivalry, and its democratic traditions, although made dormant by lack of a spirit of resistance, prevent majority support for the regime. Germany and Czechoslovakia before 1933 had mass Communist parties, but these are now strongly bureaucratized, and their intelligentsias have neither the tradition of resistance nor the cohesiveness to menace their regimes. There were significant signs of pro-Chinese sympathy in both parties in 1958 and 1959, but the total pro-Soviet policy of their leaders, whose lack of popular support makes Moscow's backing imperative for their survival, stifled them overnight in 1960. The dependence of the East German and Czech leaders on Moscow makes it safe for Khrushchev to rely upon them for total support against Peking, and his need for their support and his realization that the East German and Czech regimes are so weak that only a form of neo-Stalinism can guarantee their security, plus his general post-1956 policy of increased autonomy for

East European leaders, have so far assured their continuation in power.

Bulgaria has a mass-based Communist party of traditionally extremist tendencies; its intelligentsia is weak, and its Byzantine and Ottoman past precludes long traditions of resistance; its people are traditionally pro-Russian. Nevertheless, its pre-1956 ruler, Chervenkov, whom Khrushchev purged as a concession to Tito, in 1958–1959 demonstrated the most extensive and documented pro-Chinese tendencies of any prominent East European Communist. His final degradation in 1962 was a part of the victory of Khrushchev's creature Zhivkov over his opponents, but it also may have been partially due to his extremist and pro-Chinese sympathies. Like Albanians, Bulgarians are traditionally anti-Yugoslav, and this alone would force Khrushchev, as long as he carries out a pro-Yugoslav policy, to have a totally reliable and therefore probably unpopular and weak proconsul in Sofia. Yet, Soviet economic aid and Bulgarian Slavophile traditions have so far eased this problem, and the oft-purged Bulgarian leadership will probably, in the near future, be totally loyal to Khrushchev and, therefore, hostile to Peking.

Until the last few months, one would have said much the same about Rumania. True, Gheorghiu-Dej and his associates, like Gomułka and Kádár, came from the native rather than the Moscovite faction in their party, and Rumanians are violently anti-Russian because of their ties with Western culture and their irredentist longing for the recovery of Bessarabia. But communism in Rumania was always extremely weak, and the Byzantine and Ottoman heritage of its Phanariot rulers and the weakness and lack of any tradition of resistance of the Rumanian intelligentsia have helped to keep Rumania safely under Soviet control. There is no serious evidence of past or present pro-Chinese sympathies in the Rumanian party, and Gheorghiu-Dej's pro-Soviet and anti-Chinese position has been as reliable as that of Ulbricht, Novotný, and Zhivkov. Yet recently, there have been fairly convincing reports of some Rumanian opposition to Soviet economic integration moves within CMEA, coupled with increased Rumanian trade with West Europe and occasional signs of cultural deviation. Rumania's record of economic growth is unique in East Europe, and its rulers may be gradually developing some feeling of confidence in their own resources, a sentiment undoubtedly reinforced by Khrushchev's gradual loosening of total control. It seems likely that Rumania, still primarily a raw material producing rather than an industrial country, would inevitably differ with any Soviet policy of total economic integration of East Europe which would tend to freeze it at its present industrial level and structure, but it seems doubtful that Bucharest will flatly defy Moscow and even more doubtful that, if it did, it would turn to Peking for support.

The East European line-up on the Sino-Soviet dispute is, therefore, neither uniform nor simple. On policy issues such as de-Stalinization and the *rapprochement* with Yugoslavia, Gomułka and Kádár are closer to Khrushchev than to Mao; the contrary is probably true, did they dare to express their views, of the other East European leaders. On the desirability of a public break between Moscow and Peking and of an extremely hostile policy toward Albania, the line-up is reversed: Gomułka and Kádár fear these would limit their flexibility, and the more rigid Communist leaders feel that they would profit from the resultant tightening up of interparty and interstate ties with Moscow. The more rigid leaders are, therefore, more pro-Moscow, and hence more hostile to Peking and Tirana, than the more moderate ones. Their weakness combines with their fanaticism to assure their more centralist view of optimum Moscow-East European relations. Yet, Gomułka's and Kádár's relative popular support as compared with the weakness of the others makes Khrushchev feel that the former, if less docile, are stable and more reliable allies.

The probable worsening of the Sino-Soviet schism makes it likely that differentiation in East Europe will increase still further in the future. Ideological relativization, internal autonomy, and economic strains all combine to indicate that, although Peking's influence there is unlikely to increase, Moscow's is likely to become less all-pervasive.

WEST EUROPE: THE MASS PARTIES

Prewar West Central Europe had only four mass Communist parties: in France, Italy, Germany, and Czechoslovakia. The German party was destroyed by Hitlerism and the war and only artificially re-established in the Soviet Zone after 1945. The Czechoslovak party, in power after 1948, became increasingly bureaucratized and sterile. The French party, although less strong than immediately after the war, and subsequently further weakened by Gaullist stability and the settlement of the Algerian war, is still of major significance; its bureaucratized leadership headed by Maurice Thorez is much the same as before 1939. The Italian Communist party was also weakened by the collapse of the postwar popular-front experiment and by the 1956 Polish and Hungarian events. However, its leadership has in its head Palmiro Togliatti, one of the most flexible and tactically brilliant Communist leaders in the world today, and it still remains in uneasy and partial alliance with Nenni's Socialists, thereby main-

taining its hold on some local governments, especially in central Italy.

Both the French and Italian parties were confronted with the political consolidation and very high economic growth rate characteristic of their countries, as of the other Common Market states, in the late fifties and early sixties. For the Italian Communists, this was particularly serious, because it produced the beginnings of semiaffluence for the northern Italian workers and a mass migration of hundreds of thousands of Italian peasants to the factories of the Po valley. Italian Communist policy was popular front, its ideology was increasingly revisionist, it claimed considerable autonomy from Moscow and seemed not to hesitate occasionally to differ with it, and its role in the Sino-Soviet dispute seemed to align it to the right of the Soviet Union. The French party, on the other hand, was as loyal to Moscow as the East German or Czechoslovak. It faithfully followed every convolution of the Moscow line and was used by Khrushchev perhaps more than any other party as an instrument against the Chinese.

Although its leaders would have preferred the certainties of Stalinism to the flexibility and unpredictability of Khrushchev, they were, above all, faithful servants of the Kremlin. Yet, in the French party, aside from its fundamental and total loyalty to Moscow, there was another reason, one shared with the Italians, why serious pro-Chinese sentiment was unlikely. The Chinese appeal primarily to underdeveloped countries, above all to their intellectuals; the burgeoning prosperity of France and Italy smothered any potential breeding ground, except among the most alienated and fanatical intellectuals, for pro-Chinese sentiment.

Unlike Thorez, Togliatti was always a genuine gradualist; in 1948, under Stalin's pressure, he reluctantly abandoned his popular-front policy, only to return to it as soon as possible after Stalin's death. Through his continuing local alliance with the Nenni Socialists, many Communists long held office on the local level and wanted to keep on doing so. The consequent necessity of maintaining alliance with the Socialists drove Italian communism to the right, and the equal necessity of keeping a clear dividing line between them and the Socialists provided a built-in limitation on their resultant revisionist tendencies. Togliatti has consistently favored a *rapprochement* with Yugoslavia—Thorez opposed it as long as Moscow permitted. There was no serious policy or organizational base for pro-Chinese sentiment in Italian communism. Even had there been, Togliatti's relative moderation never extended to the two key factors which kept the Italian party under control: his determination never to break with Moscow and to support it on all basic issues, and his equal determination to preserve the authoritarian structure of the Italian party. The increasing deviations in the Italian party in late 1961 came into public view: the right-wing revisionists led by Amendola, the left-wing neo-Stalinists led by Scoccimaro, and the youthful, anti-Stalinist internationalist leftists around *Nuova Generazione*. Neither of the latter two were pro-Chinese, Scoccimaro because of his extreme pro-Soviet organizational tendencies and the *Nuova Generazione* group because Chinese views resembled Stalin's dogmatism. The French party had at least potentially the same tendencies, but the only one of them which came into public view—the 1963 opposition within the Communist Student Federation—was, like *Nuova Generazione*, closer to Trotskyism than to Maoism. By clever manipulation, Togliatti held all the deviations in the Italian party relatively under control.

Although he often appeared to take such a right-wing position as to make one wonder if he were not acting independently of and perhaps in opposition to Moscow, it usually turned out that either he had been expressing a Soviet position which only later became public or when, as in 1961 over polycentrism, Moscow expressed opposition to one of his theories, he promptly abandoned it. In 1956 and again in 1961, the rigid French Communists had strongly criticized, with Moscow's support, Italian communism's deviations, but, by late 1962, Togliatti and Thorez, both praised by Moscow and denounced by Peking, seemed on better terms.

In short, then, the only pro-Chinese sentiment which existed in French and Italian communism was among small, isolated groups without any serious influence on the parties, organization, or policies. Although there were certainly tendencies on the right wing of Italian communism which could not be pleasing to Moscow, and although the international effect of Italian revisionist ideology might eventually cause Moscow serious trouble, Khrushchev found Togliatti, like Gomułka, a highly desirable ally against the Chinese and was willing to accept some Italian domestic deviations as long as fundamental loyalty to Moscow was not questioned. On the other hand, Thorez's rigidity, like Ulbricht's and Novotný's, was, for the Soviet leader, overshadowed by his unquestioning loyalty to Moscow.

WEST EUROPE: THE SMALLER PARTIES

Outside Italy and France, West European communism is micro- rather than macrocosmic; Communist parties are mere sects. Small, poor, isolated from the main course of the life of their countries, increasingly irrelevant to the upsurge in West European prosperity, considered by the vast mass of the population to be agents of Moscow, these parties are prone to deviation, particularly when they ineffectually compete with a mass social-democratic party, often in power, alone or in coalition. Their leaderships, for decades wholly dependent on Moscow for ideology and support, are bureaucratized and stultified, their pronouncements automatic echoes of the Kremlin line. More recently, they were often disoriented and sometimes split by the impact of de-Stalinization, the Soviet *rapprochement* with Yugoslavia, the 1956 Polish and Hungarian events, and the Sino-Soviet dispute. In 1956 the Soviet crushing of the Hungarian revolution caused the withdrawal, as from the French and Italian parties, of many young intellectuals—in England, for example, of some people who made up the New Left. Everywhere the left wing of the mass social-democratic party was always an available and not too foreign refuge for the average non-apparatchik intellectual. On the other hand, Khrushchev's reformist tendencies were inevitably anathema to their other type of deviant, the extreme leftist. In any sectarian Communist party which has no chance to come to power and which is completely alienated from its society, fanatical, purist, leftist sectarianism is a chronic, structural disease. Stalinism was a guaranteed vaccine against its serious spread; Khrushchev's reformism encouraged it as much as it did Togliatti's moderation.

Consequently, there developed in some of these small parties genuine Chinese sympathizers, numerically no larger than those in the French or Italian, but more prominent in relation to the small size of the parties in question. For a time, the leaders of the Norwegian Communist party seemed almost pro-Chinese: they traveled to Peking as well as to Moscow and made some pro-Chinese statements. However, as the Sino-Soviet dispute progressively worsened in late 1962, they returned to, if indeed they had ever left, their pro-Soviet allegiance. The leader of the Danish Communist party, Axel Larsen, had defected with many of his followers after the 1956 events; his weakened successors, like the Swedish Communists, remained safely pro-Soviet. The Finnish Communist party was larger in size but so hampered by anti-Soviet sentiment in the country and by Khrushchev's favor to Kekkonen and so dogmatic in spirit that it had no alternative but a pro-Soviet policy. The small illegal West German party was, at the top, an arm of Ulbricht and, therefore, pro-Soviet. Some of its harassed members, however, like some of the isolated British Communists, showed ineffectual sympathy for the Chinese. The Belgian and Swiss Communist leadership came under the influence of Togliatti rather than of Thorez, in part because of the prosperity of their countries; the Belgians even expelled a small pro-Chinese minority headed by the chief of the Brussels Communist organization. The Spanish and Portuguese Communists, illegal at home and with their leaderships in Moscow, were inevitably pro-Soviet. The increasing probability that Salazar and Franco could not last much longer tended to push them, for internal reasons, toward a popular-front policy, thus making it more unlikely that they would be pro-Chinese. The Greek Communist party was illegal and its leadership in emigration and, therefore, safely pro-Soviet; unlike any other, it effectively controlled a legal mass popular-front party in Greece. However, Greece's increased prosperity, association with the Common Market, and anti-Albanian policy made it probable that they would move, if anywhere, to the right rather than the left—that is, toward Togliatti rather than toward Mao.

EFFECTS OF THE COMMON MARKET

The West European Communist parties were also confronted with the burgeoning prosperity of the European Economic Community (EEC), a phenomenon contrary to Marxist-Leninist doctrine, menacing to the Soviet Union, and threatening to extremist Communist policies. The same was true to a lesser extent of the East European Communist parties and the Soviet Union itself and, above all, of Yugoslavia. Until early 1962 Soviet, East European, and West European Communist hostility to EEC, with the exception of the Italians, had been complete and extreme. The Italian Communists and, even more, the left-wing trade-union federation, Confederazione Generale Italiana del Lavoro (CGIL), which had a Communist majority but a Nenni Socialist minority, had begun to insist that international Communist policy on EEC and also on co-operation with non-Communist trade unions be reviewed. The new Italian Communist position resembled the Western policy of "gradual evolution" in East Europe: working within the system for "in-system" changes. For the Italian Communists and the CGIL, denunciations of the EEC and non-Communist trade unions do no one any good, least of all the Communists; they have insisted, therefore, that Communists should try to gain some trade-union representation within the EEC and should co-operate much more broadly with non-Communist trade unions. Initially, only the Yugoslavs and, to some extent, the Poles supported these ideas. The Chinese and their allies naturally and violently opposed them; the Soviets were, at best, neutral. However, with the prospect of British entry into the EEC, and presumably in part as a result of Italian, Polish, and Yugoslav influence, the Soviets, in the summer of 1962, modified their position to one of not quite total hostility. The Poles, Hungarians, and Yugoslavs had political as well as economic reasons for wishing to preserve their present extensive trade with West Europe, and even the rigid Czechs apparently felt the same. As was to be expected, the French Communists and the other West European parties—except the Belgians and Swiss—strongly opposed Italian "revisionism." However, in late 1962 and early 1963, the Italians, under pressure from the Nenni Socialists, made it clear that, if necessary, they would go ahead alone, and Moscow and the West European parties reluctantly agreed. The CGIL decided, with the formal approval of the others but without their participation, to set up its own office at EEC headquarters in Brussels.

CONCLUSION

With the exception of Albania, China has gained no foothold in European communism. Nevertheless, by giving the party leaderships more room for maneuver, the Sino-Soviet schism has significantly contributed toward, although not decisively determined, the consolidation of Polish moderation, the extension of liberalization in Hungary, and ideological revisionism in Italian communism. In the long run, it seems likely to further still more increasing differentiation and moderation in much of European communism.

Russia and China View the United States

By Alexander Dallin

ABSTRACT: Soviet Russia and Communist China see the United States in significantly different ways. The present divergence can be related to antecedents such as the enmity between the United States and the Chinese Communists before their seizure of power and the nonrecognition of the present regime by the United States. More important, the quest of the Peking regime for national "unification"—including Taiwan—and for great-power status—both opposed by the United States—have no analogue in the Soviet Union. The significant differences between Chinese and Soviet perceptions arose after November 1957, when Peking and Moscow began to pursue conflicting strategies. Moscow rather uncertainly strove for a *détente* with the United States; Peking insisted on the continued need for "struggle" and "action." The differences were entirely in keeping with the broader Sino-Soviet gulf regarding the nature of thermonuclear war and the prospects of "peaceful coexistence." Peking has been frustrated by Soviet failure to give military support to China against the United States and has amply publicized the inconsistencies of Soviet policy toward the United States. Neither the Soviet Union nor Communist China can compel the other to adopt its views and policies regarding the United States. To the United States, it matters greatly which of the two Communist powers and strategies emerges victorious.

Alexander Dallin, Ph.D., New York City, New York, is Professor of International Relations, Columbia University, and currently Director of its Russian Institute. Among other works, he is author of The Soviet Union at the United Nations (1962) and editor of Diversity in International Communism (1963).

153

IN a lengthy statement, ostensibly addressed to their Italian comrades, the Chinese Communists in March 1963 acknowledged:

. . . It is obvious that differences of principle exist in the international Communist movement today as to how to appraise and how to deal with U. S. imperialism, the arch-enemy of the peoples of the world.[1]

Even a cursory perusal of recent statements does indeed reveal significant differences between the Soviet and Chinese images of the United States, its goals, and its capabilities and between their prescriptions for coping with it.

Making some allowance for Peking's proclivity to give an "unfair" account of the Soviet position, one finds confirmation for the divergence in remarks such as these:

Those [in Moscow] who slanderously attack the Chinese Communist Party allege that our unremitting exposure of imperialism and especially of the policies of aggression and war of U. S. imperialism, show our disbelief in the possibility of averting a world war; actually what these people oppose is the exposure of imperialism. . . . They prettify U. S. imperialism in one hundred and one ways and spread among the masses of the people illusions about imperialism, and especially about U. S. imperialism.[2]

ANTECEDENTS

Some predisposing factors antedate the current Sino-Soviet rift. It has been correctly argued that the Communists' victory in itself constituted a major defeat for half a century of American policy in Asia: The reciprocal relation of American failures and Communist successes in China set the stage for what ensued. In an interview with Anna Louise Strong, held in August 1946 and repeatedly quoted by the current leadership since 1960, Mao Tse-tung made a number of comments which remain valid in his eyes. On the one hand, he argued, the United States is out to maximize its conquests. On the other hand, it does not threaten the Socialist camp directly, if only because it must first dispose of the rest of the non-Communist world, which was labeled a vast "intermediate zone."[3]

Mao was thus able to tell the Soviet Union that a more vigorous stand would not invite war with the United States— a point Peking has not failed to reiterate.[4]

Victory did not significantly alter the Communists' attitude toward the United States. On the contrary, it instilled in the Peking leadership a sense of pride in its isolation, reinforced by American and United Nations nonrecognition of the mainland regime, and it found therein further cause for suspicion of the outside world. The Korean war was fought, by the Chinese, as a "resist America" campaign.

[1] "More on the Differences Between Comrade Togliatti and Us," *Hung-ch'i*, No. 3/4 (1963); English translation in *Peking Review*, No. 10/11 (March 15, 1963).

[2] "The Differences Between Comrade Togliatti and Us," *Jen-min jih-pao* (Peking), December 31, 1962; English translation in *Peking Review*, No. 1 (January 4, 1963).

[3] Mao Tse-tung, *Selected Works* (in English) (Peking, 1961), Vol. 4, pp. 99–100. This concept helps "explain" the alleged American tendency toward aggrandizement, which includes an encirclement of China (from Japan, South Korea, Taiwan, South Vietnam, Thailand), but puts the showdown into the indefinite future. True, "as everybody knows, what the U. S. ruling clique calls the 'national purpose' is to achieve world domination." Yet (in harmony with the Chinese view of local wars) Peking insists that "seizure of the 'intermediate zone' plays an increasingly important role in U. S. global strategy." *Jen-min jih-pao*, January 21, 1963.

[4] *Selections from China Mainland Magazines* (Hong Kong), No. 233 (October 31, 1960), cited in Donald S. Zagoria, *The Sino-Soviet Conflict, 1956–1961* (Princeton, 1962), p. 404.

At least three major sources of Sino-American enmity are commonly recognized to have been apparent in China prior to the fundamental shift in policy in 1957–1958: the quest for national "unification," especially the claim to Taiwan and the offshore islands; a drive for prestige and recognition as a great power; a commitment to further the cause of communism at home and abroad. Traditional and "ideological" facets thus combined, on the Chinese side, to prepare the ground for the growth of intense anti-Americanism.

On the Soviet side, at least the first two of these three compulsions were lacking. If anything, the ubiquitous hostility toward imperialism had on several occasions been moderated by the fact that Russia and America appeared to share, if not interests, then enemies, in Europe and in the Far East. As one of the Big Three in 1941–1946, the Soviet Union gained that aura and legitimation which the Chinese Communists lacked. Yet, in the following years, Moscow, much as the Chinese comrades, properly identified Washington as its first and most dangerous foe. There was nothing "inevitable" about the parting of their ways.

In the post-Stalin decade, the picture became significantly more blurred. First, the inherent tensions in the traditional Bolshevik love-hate for the "citadel of capitalism" became more apparent as the search for new answers and new policies began after Stalin's death. Second, Moscow soon began to modify some of its stereotypes—either explicitly (for instance, on violence) or by omission (for instance, on the prospects of economic crises)—securing, on the whole, a more realistic assessment of the world environment. And, third, the changes, in the Soviet Union and in the Communist movement at large, created and then sanctioned a measure of diversity in Communist attitudes unprecedented in the past generation.

CONFLICT OR COEXISTENCE?

After a variety of crises, the search for new solutions was still on when events in the fall of 1957 spurred a profound reassessment by both Moscow and Peking. Having consolidated his own position, Khrushchev viewed the latest accomplishments—notably, the intercontinental ballistic missiles and space satellites—as indicators of Russia's new might and as a wise investment that would automatically pay rich dividends. To the Chinese leaders, by contrast, these developments seemed to produce new opportunities for action. While Moscow agreed that it had at last achieved near-parity in effective nuclear and deterrent power and thus undermined the United States "position of strength," the wind of rosy optimism which swept the Soviet capital led to the assertion that "a new stage of coexistence" had begun. The Chinese Communist line, on the contrary, saw "the east wind prevailing over the west wind" in a perspective of greater revolutionary potentials and enthusiasm. Essentially, Peking pressed for a "forward" policy, while Moscow sought a *détente;* one prepared to rely on men and will, the other on history and power-in-being; one responded to "left" and the other to "right" impulses and formulas in the Communist world.

There was some truth in the Chinese charges of Soviet inconsistency. Moscow no longer had simple or single answers. In Soviet analysis, too, the United States was *the* major antagonist. Yet it was also (as Moscow put it at times) the major partner—the other superpower, the other major industrial state, the only one behind which the Soviet Union lagged. Unlike the Chinese, Moscow sensed some identification—precisely thanks to the rivalry the two were engaged in. At times, Soviet leaders no doubt recognized the fact that the two superpowers—unlike the Chinese—were both "modern"—and perhaps also "Western" and "white." In 1959–1960 and intermittently since then, Soviet media have developed the notion that the United States was not ruled by "madmen" and "maniacs" but that there were powerful "men of reason" in Washington.

Now the Chinese asked of Moscow what it believed or planned: "With regard to the U. S. imperialists, one day you will call them pirates and the next you say they are concerned for peace. . . ." After agreeing to the so-called Moscow Statement, which in December 1960 recognized that "U. S. imperialism is the chief bulwark of world reaction and . . . an enemy of the people of the whole world," the Soviet leaders, Peking charged, maintained "that the destiny of mankind depended on 'cooperation,' 'confidence' and 'agreement' between the heads of the two powers, the United States and the Soviet Union." [5]

The difference was more profound, perhaps, than either protagonist knew. As one American expert wrote, "much of recent Soviet foreign policy toward the United States appears to be based on the calculation that forces at work within American society are bent on achieving a *modus vivendi* with the USSR and are willing to pay a relatively high price for it." [6] Especially during and after the Khrushchev visit to the United States, in 1959–1960, Soviet statements abounded in references to the "peaceful" American people, with whom the Soviet people wish to live in "friendship." Even later, in April 1962, Khrushchev told an American editor that, except for the difference in the two systems:

We really have no cause for serious quarrels. Nowhere do our interests directly clash, either on territorial or on economic questions. The Soviet Union and the United States are both countries that are excellently provided with natural resources and possess large populations and well-developed industry and science. . . .[7]

To Peking, such views were bound to sound like treason. The "modern revisionists" in Moscow were, in Chinese eyes, guilty of many things, of which their view of the United States was but one. Here was only one, but one important instance of broad differences in world view—differences which also encompassed the East-West dilemma, the inevitability of war, alternative ways of economic development, and the nature of the colonial world.

Doctrine and Reappraisal

The Chinese position, since 1958, combines some elements of the earlier Maoist argument with echoes of the rigid Stalinist view. A unique aspect of the Soviet scene, under Khrushchev, by contrast, is a timid diversity and at times uncertainty of comments emanating from within the Soviet Union. One may find in Soviet speeches and publications reiteration of certain concepts which are held by Peking; more significantly, one also finds instances in which the present Soviet leadership repudiates or ignores these views. By the logic of the two positions, the Chinese argument is more systematic, more consistent, and more extreme; the Soviet argument, torn between doctrinal assumptions and realistic reappraisals.

The common point of departure is the assessment of "imperialism." Pe-

[5] "More on the Differences," *loc. cit.*
[6] Zbigniew Brzezinski, *Ideology and Power in Soviet Politics* (New York, 1962), p. 105.

[7] Khrushchev interview with Gardner Cowles, *Pravda,* April 27 1962.

king adheres to the orthodox view that "imperialism is by nature predatory. . . . When its policy of plunder meets with obstacles which cannot be surmounted by 'peaceful' means, it resorts to war." [8] While Moscow does not dispute this proposition "in principle," Peking in turn does not use it to dispute explicitly the Khrushchevian tenet that 'wars are no longer to be considered "inevitable" even while "imperialism" survives. But Peking did insist that the warlike nature of imperialism was immutable, hinting, in 1962–1963, that "some persons" had dangerous illusions about it.

Despite the verbal concessions to the Chinese in the "compromise" Moscow Statement of December 1960, Moscow rarely went so far as to argue—as Peking did—that American imperialism is "the most vicious enemy of peace . . . the most ferocious and most cunning enemy of the peace-loving peoples of the world." In Chinese eyes, the Russians were guilty of not exposing and assailing the United States and, instead, of talking seriously—"strategically," and not merely "tactically" —of hazardous matters like disarmament. "These [Soviet] friends, when discussing disarmament, talk very little or not at all of the facts of U. S. expansion of armaments and preparation for war. . . ." [9] At the center of the debate was, then, the Chinese contention that nothing had led, indeed nothing could lead, to a change in the essence of American objectives—or of imperialism in general—and the Soviet reply that a qualitative change had occurred in the international situation, for a variety of reasons, such as the greater might of the "socialist camp" and the destructiveness of thermonuclear weapons. To any reasonable person this made global wars "unthinkable." [10]

Time and again, Peking warned Moscow that the United States still wanted and expected war: the professions of the Eisenhower administration were not to be trusted; the Kennedy administration was bound to be as bad as its predecessor—in fact, worse. [11] As for Khrushchev's and his followers' illusions, Peking retorted with venom:

[8] Yu Chao-li, "On Imperialism as the Source of War in Modern Times," *Hung-ch'i*, No. 7 (April 1, 1960).

[9] Liao Cheng-shih, speech at World Peace Council meeting in Stockholm, December 16, 1961. The theme is further developed in "The Differences Between Comrade Togliatti and Us," *loc. cit.*

[10] When Khrushchev visited the United States, in September 1959, Peking commented that "in view of the U. S. cold war record and its aggressions of all kinds in the past," its intentions should be judged "not by its words but by its deeds." *Jen-min jih-pao*, September 29, 1959. The following spring, Peking devoted lengthy articles to the question, "Is There Any Change in U. S. Foreign Policy?"—only to conclude that, while there was "a certain change of methods," the "substance" of American objectives remained the same. The argument pointed to American efforts to break out of its "isolation" and to "gain time, restore military predominance, and tighten up control over its 'allies.'" Tsui Ch'i and T'an Wen-jui, "Comment on the Present Foreign Policy of the United States," *Shih-chieh Chih-shih*, No. 6 (March 20, 1960).

[11] For an exposition of Chinese views of the Kennedy administration, see Mei Yi, "Kennedy and his Clique," *Shih-chieh Chih-shih*, No. 3 (February 3, 1961), which described the Kennedy election as "a victory for the Rockefeller financial group in the struggle among the various financial groups for the control of the [U.S.] government" and Lyndon Johnson's place on the ticket as a victory of certain financial, oil, and arms interests. In fact, it made every member of the cabinet and White House inner circle a puppet of some monopoly interests. See also Huang Kang, "A Few Things About Kennedy," *Hung-ch'i*, No. 13 (July 1, 1961); Chen Yü, "Kennedy's 'Brain Trust,'" *Shih-chieh Chih-shih*, No. 14 (July 25, 1961), which finds: "The fact that Kennedy employs these so-called college professors, experts, and scholars shows that his tactics are more sinister and vicious" than those of his predecessor.

It will be recalled that three years ago, following the "Camp David talks," some persons in the international Communist movement talked a good deal about Eisenhower's sincere desire for peace, saying that this ringleader of U. S. imperialism was just as concerned about peace as we were. . . . Now we again hear people saying that Kennedy is even more concerned about world peace than Eisenhower was and that Kennedy showed his concern for the maintenance of peace during the Caribbean crisis.

One would like to ask: Is this way of embellishing U. S. imperialism the correct policy for defending world peace? The intrusion into the Soviet Union of spy planes sent by the Eisenhower administration, the hundred-and-one acts of aggression around the world by U. S. imperialism, and its threats to world peace—have these not repeatedly confirmed the truth that the ringleaders of U. S. imperialism are no angels of peace but monsters of war? And are not these people who try time and again to prettify imperialism deliberately deceiving the people of the world? [12]

How could Mao and his followers reconcile the image of a United States madly arming and preparing for war with their insistence that a tougher policy did not amount to "brinkmanship"? The answer was Mao's "paper tiger" formula. As the Chinese told their American comrades on December

[12] "The Differences Between Comrade Togliatti and Us," *loc. cit.* See also Zagoria, *op. cit.,* p. 240 ff, and *Jen-min jih-pao,* June 13, 1960. On the Kennedy administration, see also *Jen-min jih-pao,* December 1, 1961; English translation in *Peking Review,* No. 49 (December 8, 1961), which concluded that the United States had "sustained a series of disastrous defeats," and, because of the uneven development of capitalism and the struggle among the imperialist countries, the entire imperialist world was "slithering further down the slope of disintegration." The Kennedy administration was accused of "preparing for both all-out nuclear war and limited wars of various types." See also Alexander Dallin and Others (eds.), *Diversity in International Communism* (New York, 1963), pp. 213–214, 222–226, 234–236.

10, 1959, "On the surface, this enemy [the United States] seems strong, but actually it is hollow and feeble. . . . The situation in the United States, in which the new forces are still inferior and the decaying forces have the upper hand, is definitely a temporary phenomenon, which must change to the opposite."

Here was a morale-building lesson which the Chinese Communists had brought with them to power from civil-war days. As Mao reiterated in November 1957, "Over a long period we formulated the concept that strategically we should despise all our enemies, but that tactically we should take them seriously." This applied to the United States, to imperialism in general, and to the atom bomb.

When Peking sought to invoke this thesis during the Cuban crisis of October 1962—presumably to demonstrate that Moscow was guilty of unnecessary cowardice, having retreated in the face of United States threats—Khrushchev felt compelled to take open issue with the "paper tiger" theme. Accusing unnamed would-be Marxist-Leninists of trying to provoke a thermonuclear clash between the Soviet Union and the United States, in which these *provocateurs* would "sit it out," he went on to argue that "imperialism is now no longer what it used to be. . . . If it is a 'paper tiger' now, those who say this know that this 'paper' tiger has atomic teeth." [13]

But the Chinese Communists indignantly reaffirmed their formula, insisting that it was "of great importance for the question of whether the revolutionary people will dare to wage a struggle, dare to make a revolution, dare to seize victory"; it was important also to "destroy the arrogance of the enemy" and to instill "revolutionary

[13] Nikita Khrushchev, report to the Supreme Soviet of the Soviet Union, December 12, 1962, in *Pravda,* December 13, 1962.

determination and confidence, revolutionary vision and staunchness" in the masses.[14] The two capitals were speaking different tongues.

In the same speech defending his Cuban policy, Khrushchev had referred to the "reasonable" men in Washington. Here was another area of Sino-Soviet disagreement. While Soviet publications and, at times, leading figures continue to resort to the primitive stereotypes of monopoly rule, politicians as tools of economic interests, and crude exploitation, the total image of the United States as conveyed by a Khrushchev or Adzhubei reflects some sense of meaningful diversity in American life, in which individual actors, such as the President, are their own masters; in which depressions no longer figure as inevitable phenomena; in which, Moscow argues, even disarmament could be absorbed by the existing system without serious dislocations; and in which a tug-of-war is being fought between "lunatics" and "wild men," who are prepared to "go down with music," to start a thermonuclear war, and the "men of reason," who put survival ahead of the achievement of American objectives.

The Soviet image, as it has evolved, suffers from considerable ambiguities and contradictions.[15] But the gap between it and the Chinese picture of America is so striking that Peking inquired whether Moscow still believed in the Leninist theory of the state, which posits that the entire state apparatus is " the tool of monopoly capital for class rule."

And if so, how can there be a president independent of monopoly capital; how can

there be a Pentagon independent of the White House; and how can there be two opposing centers [one, moderate; the other, "ultra"] in Washington?

Those who portray President Kennedy as "sensible," Peking added, are presumably "serving as willing apologists for U. S. imperialism and helping it to deceive the people of the world." [16]

IMPLICATIONS

References, since 1962, to the "willing" or "deliberate" assistance which Khrushchev was lending the imperialists hinted at a new and perhaps fundamental element in the Sino-Soviet debate. Paradoxically, the Chinese argument that American-Soviet contradictions are *not* paramount [17] in the present stage of world affairs makes more credible to its proponents the idea that the United States and the Soviet Union may be working toward an accommodation detrimental to the cause of communism and, more particularly, to the cause of China. The old suspicion of the "outsider" was rekindled when, in mid-1958, precisely when Peking was executing its shift toward a "leftist" policy, Khrushchev proposed to solve the Middle Eastern crisis by a summit meeting which would have included Nehru and Hammarskjold but not Mao Tse-tung.[18]

The Chinese Communists readily applied their sweeping skepticism about

[14] "The Differences Between Comrade Togliatti and Us," *loc. cit.*

[15] For an astute attempt to analyze the Soviet view, see Nathan Leites, "The Kremlin Horizon," RAND Memorandum RM-3506-ISA (March 1963).

[16] "More on the Differences," *loc. cit.*

[17] While Moscow has insisted that "the chief contradiction of our epoch is the contradiction between socialism and capitalism" (Boris Ponomarev, "With the Name of Lenin. . . ," *Pravda*, April 23, 1963), Peking has "pointed out that the real and direct contradictions of the world [after the Second World War] were the growing internal contradictions of the capitalist world itself" (Yu Chao-li, *op. cit.*). See also Mao's *Imperialism and All Reactionary Cliques are Paper Tigers* (Peking, 1958).

[18] See Zagoria, *op. cit.*, pp. 199–206.

negotiations with the leading imperialists to the specific context of impromptu summitry. Peking would henceforth remind unnamed comrades that the problems dividing the two worlds were so basic that it was both naive and treasonous to believe in the ability of a handful of men to overcome or resolve them.

Chinese suspicions of Moscow's outlook are likely to have been reinforced by Soviet pronouncements regarding the decisive nature of Soviet-American agreements. Gromyko, speaking in December 1962, was but one of several to point out, after the Cuban crisis:

. . . how closely associated the destinies of the world are today with Soviet-American relations. It is an historically established fact that without understanding between the USSR and the USA not a single serious international conflict can be settled, no agreement can be reached on any important international problem. . . . If the USSR and the USA pool their efforts to iron out the conflicts and complications which arise in these regions, the emerging flames of war die down and the tension subsides.[19]

Peking's answer was plain: The view that "every matter under the sun can be settled if the two 'great men' sit together" smacked of "great-power chauvinism" and of "power politics," and was alien to Marxism-Leninism.[20] Evidently with the Cuban crisis in mind, a prominent spokesman for the Chinese regime told an Afro-Asian conference in Moshi, Tanganyika:

The attempt to decide major problems of the world and to manipulate the destinies of mankind by one or two countries will certainly end in utter failure and be condemned by history. The coun-

tries of Asia and Africa as well as all peoples are firmly opposed to the big powers bullying, oppressing, and giving orders to smaller countries.[21]

For years China has maintained that it would not let the Soviet Union negotiate binding agreements for it—for instance, on nuclear testing. The very real fear of a closed Soviet-American "nuclear club," from which Communist China was barred, added fuel to the suspicions which alienated Peking from Moscow. Thus, the "hot line" agreement in the spring of 1963 was apt to be viewed by the Chinese as further evidence of Soviet subservience to the West and by Moscow as incidentally strengthening the Soviet hand by demonstrating to Peking that Moscow had options regarding its foreign policy, while presumably Peking had none.[22]

Out of these fears and suspicions, then, there also emerged an ideological element: the identification by Peking of the Soviet line as an exemplar of "modern revisionism," which "objectively" helps the imperialist camp. With good Bolshevik logic, it found the chain linking Khrushchev with Tito and Tito in turn with Washington. The communiqué released following the tenth plenum of the Central Committee of the Chinese Communist party (September 28, 1962) did indeed speak of modern revisionists who "betray the cause of communism ever more shamelessly and give aid and comfort to the plans of imperialism." *Pravda* omitted this passage from its version of the communiqué.

---

[19] Andrei Gromyko, speech before the Supreme Soviet of the Soviet Union, *Pravda*, December 14, 1962.

[20] "More on the Differences," *loc. cit.*

[21] Liu Ning-yi, "Unite to Fight Against Imperialism," February 4, 1963; English translation in *Peking Review,* No. 7 (February 15, 1963).

[22] Peking interpreted Kennedy's American University speech precisely in this fashion, as part of "a most cunning and vicious move in his 'peace strategy.' " *Jen-min jih-pao,* June 22, 1963.

"UNITY OF THEORY AND PRACTICE"

Richard Lowenthal has suggested that the potential rivalry of the two powers could become actual only when concrete policy disagreements arose which took the debates out of the realm of abstractions. As it happens, it has been precisely around relations with the United States that the divergences have crystallized since 1958. On a succession of issues, from Taiwan, over Soviet-American summitry, to the Congo and Cuba, the problem has been how the Communists must handle the United States. Each of the two positions here assumes a good deal of coherence and consistency. The Chinese aversion to serious negotiations with the enemy and to efforts to achieve a *détente* with the United States is entirely in keeping with the general world view and the view of modern war, in particular, as held in Peking. Similarly, the Soviet effort to avoid a showdown, the orientation towards a build-up of economic and military might over time, and a willingness to arrive—at least for the time being—at a *modus vivendi* with the West is in harmony with broader assumptions made in Moscow about the drift of world affairs.

Here the attitude toward war becomes significant again. True to itself, Peking argues that nuclear weapons—any more than other changes in military technology—cannot change basic and durable historical laws. It denies the Soviet thesis that, in the nuclear age, war is no longer the continuation of politics and reasserts the classic distinction between just and unjust wars. Moreover, Peking was prepared to argue, even after nuclear war life would go on, with communism inevitably victorious.[23]

Moscow's firm rejection of this and other instances of "dangerous ultra-revolutionary pyrotechnics" in turn implied a search "for sensible agreements with all who demonstrate that they take a realistic approach to the present alignment of forces and who understand what the consequences of a thermo-nuclear war would be."[24] Here the arguments had a direct bearing on actual conduct. Since 1958, if not earlier, Peking has variously sought to apply pressure on Moscow to help it secure its objectives abroad. But it must have realized, with a good deal of frustration, that it had no effective leverage to compel the Soviet Union to do what China wished—least of all, to commit Soviet armed forces to assist in the seizure of Taiwan.

Peking needed Soviet assistance to attain its goals. Yet, by seeking to compel Moscow to back Peking's political strategy, it contributed to the rift between them without thereby advancing its own ends. While Peking was no doubt outraged by Soviet "cowardice" —be it in Laos or in Cuba—it was futile for the Chinese to argue that a policy of greater risks was certain not to provoke war with the United States and that local wars need not escalate into general, nuclear conflicts. Moscow was sure it knew better.

CONSTANTS AND VARIABLES

There are few obvious limits to Sino-Soviet divergences regarding the United States. The only thing, perhaps, that could make the Sino-Soviet military alliance operative would be a United States attempt to replace the Communist regime in China with a pro-American government: if the alternative to the present system is an extension of United States power along the perimeter of the Soviet Union, Moscow would be prepared to intervene in force.

---

[23] *E.g.,* "The Differences Between Comrade Togliatti and Us," *loc. cit.*

[24] B. N. Ponomarev, "With the Name of Lenin," *loc. cit.*

Beyond this most unlikely contingency, the prospects are uncertain. The political fundamentalism in Peking is by no means immutable, and its eventual moderation could contribute to a *détente* in the Far East. But, it is important to note, even short of such a radical change, the Chinese leadership has not been "fanatical" or "irrational" in its policy. It has repeatedly recognized superior force when confronted with it, and, as in Korea, it has been prepared to "compromise" when necessary. More recently, it has sought to involve the Soviet Union in various operations but has carefully observed its own rules of conflict management to keep out of involvements in India, Laos, or Vietnam, which might provoke United States intervention in force.

One may point to three major components to describe the divergence of outlook discussed above. (1) China has certain national goals—such as the quest for territorial "unification" and for international acceptance—for which Russia has no equivalent needs. (2) China sees the world—and appeals—from the vantage point of an underdeveloped country. Thus it naturally strives to identify with other "have-nots"; its anti-imperialist animus logically turns its point against the United States. In many respects—the rational, but not the racial—this is a valid Leninist approach. Yet, the Soviet Union, which pursued a somewhat similar policy in earlier days, increasingly seems to have outgrown such an outlook, even though it professes to champion the cause of the new states. (3) Finally, the Sino-Soviet alignment today happens to coincide with the division of international communism into "left" and "right" movements, each advocating strategies scarcely susceptible of reconciliation with the other's. While none of these three elements need remain static, there appears to be little prospect for an early or substantial change of heart.

Either of the two great Communist powers can, but neither needs to, present a grave challenge to the United States. Either may, under different circumstances, become the more dangerous or the more difficult to cope with. Yet the future remains "open-ended": All permutations remain possible, and, at some future stage, any two of the three—Russia, China, United States—may find parallel interests in restraining or isolating the third on this or that cause.

Recent events have helped to dispose of a widespread American myth which invites political indolence, namely, the assumption that the Sino-Soviet dispute has no direct bearing on the United States because it is "a family quarrel."[25] Quite the contrary, the attitudes and policies of the two powers toward the United States are a central issue in their rift, and, within limits, the United States, by its own response and behavior, can perhaps affect the course or balance of the dispute, whose outcome must not be a matter of indifference to this country.

[25] This article was written before the eruption of Sino-Soviet differences in July 1963. In its "open letter" of July 14, 1963, the Central Committee of the Communist party of the Soviet Union charged that the Chinese leaders "consider it to their advantage to preserve and intensify international tension, especially in the relations between the USSR and the USA." The Chinese People's Republic refused to adhere to the partial nuclear test ban treaty, charging officially (in its Statement of July 31) that Soviet sponsorship of the treaty amounted to "capitulation to U. S. imperialism" and "allying with the United States to oppose China." The Soviet reply (*Pravda*, August 4, 1963) in turn accused Peking of lining up with the "madmen" in Washington, Bonn, and Paris in abetting thermonuclear war.

Some Recent Developments in Socialization Theory and Research

By William H. Sewell *

THE scientific study of socialization—the processes by which individuals selectively acquire the skills, knowledge, attitudes, values, and motives current in the groups of which they are or will become members—is of rather recent origin, despite the fact that throughout human history man has been concerned with the question of how the human animal is transmuted into a human being. The earliest contributions to the field came mainly from philosophers, psychologists, and sociologists who were intrigued with the problem but who had little other than their own insights and observations upon which to base their explanations. With the development of experimental psychology, interest in the scientific study of child development began both in Europe and America. This fact, coupled with the growth of public interest in child-rearing, gave rise to the establishment of a number of child-welfare research stations and child-study centers in the United States,

especially after 1920.[1] These centers instituted descriptive and experimental studies which were carried out by educators, pediatricians, and home economists—usually under the leadership of a psychologist. For a number of years they have provided a great flow of detailed information on characteristics of children, particularly their mental and physical growth. But until relatively recently they have given comparatively little emphasis to emotional and social aspects of development. The field of child development has continued to prosper, and many contributions to current socialization research have come from those who are professionally identified with this field.

Much of the more recent work on socialization, however, has other sources

[1] For an authoritative statement of the history by one of the leading participants in this development, see Lawrence K. Frank, "The Beginnings of Child Development and Family Life Education in the Twentieth Century," *Merrill-Palmer Quarterly,* Vol. 8 (October 1962), pp. 1–28.

William H. Sewell, Ph.D., Madison, Wisconsin, is Professor of Sociology at the University of Wisconsin. He has published extensively on research methodology and social psychology. He is particularly well known for his work on infant training and personality and his studies of social class and personality of the child. His most recent book, coauthored with Oluf M. Davidsen, is Scandinavian Students on an American Campus (1961).

* The writer wishes to thank William H. Sewell, III, Ellen W. Sewell, Vimal P. Shah, and Renee Bash for bibliographical assistance.

of intellectual stimulation and support; probably the first and foremost of these has been the psychoanalytic movement. Psychoanalytic theory made its way into American psychology and was used increasingly in the study of personality and child psychology.[2] Freud's theories on the importance of the early life experiences for subsequent personality structure was and continues to be a major force in socialization theory and research. A second force of great importance was the development of behavior theory in psychology and particularly the elaboration of theories of social learning. The psychologists brought to the field of socialization not only a rather substantial body of empirically based theories to be tested but also a rich tradition of experimental method which was to supply much-needed rigor to investigations in the field. A third major force was social anthropology which, as a result of many years of careful ethnographic research in primitive societies, had clearly documented the role of socialization as a mechanism of culture transmission and suggested that culturally determined child-rearing systems might help explain "national character" or "modal personality." A fourth force, but not one of great strength until quite recently, has been sociology, with its emphasis on the importance of social structure in the development of human behavior—stressing particularly the family, the school, the community, primary groups, voluntary associations, and the social-class structure.

The convergence of these forces, in the early forties to the mid-fifties, with the older developmental emphasis has resulted in a tremendous outpouring of speculative writing, theoretical essays, research articles, and monographs on socialization, most of which have focused on the intellectual, emotional, and social development of the young child.[3] Socialization has come to be one of the principal areas of convergence between psychologists, anthropologists, and sociologists. It also constitutes an important area of specialization in the rapidly developing field of social psychology.

Before attempting to discuss developments in the field of socialization during the past five years, it will be useful to indicate briefly some of the major concerns and emphases current in the ten or fifteen years preceding this period. Irwin L. Child in his comprehensive summary of theory and research in the field of socialization, published in 1954, gives primary attention to the antecedents of specific systems of behavior.[4] The systems most emphasized were oral, anal, excretory, sexual, and aggressive behavior and, to a lesser extent, dependence, achievement, affection, and fear. These systems, especially the first five, are derived mainly from psychoanalytic theory. The antecedent variables emphasized in rela-

[2] Kurt Lewin, Henry A. Murray, John Dollard, Neil Miller, O. Hobart Mowrer, and Robert Sears, to mention some of the well-known leaders in the field, helped to give the psychoanalytic view academic respectability by conducting research in part guided by psychoanalytic theories and by integrating various psychoanalytic views with behavior theory.

[3] Fortunately, there are currently several bibliographical aids to this literature, including: *Child Development Abstracts and Bibliography* published by The Society for Research on Child Development, *Psychological Abstracts* published by the American Psychological Association, *Sociological Abstracts* published by Sociological Abstracts, Inc., and the *Annual Review of Psychology* published by Annual Reviews, Inc., at Stanford California. A valuable source on current research is *Research Relating to Children: Studies in Progress* published periodically by the U. S. Children's Bureau in Washington, D. C.

[4] Irwin L. Child, "Socialization," in Gardner Lindzey (ed.), *Handbook of Social Psychology* (Cambridge, Mass.: Addison-Wesley, 1954), pp. 655–692.

tion to this set of consequent variables were primary disciplines for handling sex, excretory, and oral drives—that is, various aspects of feeding and weaning, toilet-training, and punishment practices. These all deal with the stages of psychosexual development thought by Freud to be so crucial in their effect on later personality. Other matters treated in the review included the relation between: age at socialization and dependence and achievement orientation; discontinuity in socialization and psychological conflict; techniques of reward and punishment and anxiety, fear, guilt, and identification; and social class and child-rearing practices. The conclusion reached by Child after reviewing approximately one hundred such studies was:

Systematic research on socialization guided by the interpretive inferences of clinicians and ethnographers, has already succeeded in identifying a number of variables that appear to be of importance as influences on the later behavior of the individual who is socialized. A considerable body of tentative knowledge has been developed about these influences . . . every finding cited in this chapter is necessarily subject to some kind of explanation other than the one presented here. . . . In short, the existing body of research findings, while impressive as a whole, is not very solid in detail.[5]

A more critical observer would perhaps have concluded by this time or possibly a few years later that socialization research guided by the psychoanalytic approach had been quite barren in terms of its empirical findings. In any event, there seems little doubt that the psychoanalytic approach dominated the study of socialization and to a marked extent inhibited other approaches. The study of the modes by which parents and other socialization agents deal with the needs not so directly derivable from

5 *Ibid.* p. 685.

libidinal drives was relatively neglected. Moreover, the influence of social structure variables on either socialization practices or subsequent behavior was largely overlooked or was limited largely to the differences in the way the social classes handled infant-training. There was considerable neglect of problems of role-learning. Finally, many of the studies suffered from small and poorly designed samples, inadequate data-gathering techniques, rather loose handling of data analysis, and a tendency to make generalizations well beyond the limits supportable by their data.

THE ROLE APPROACH

The developments in theory and research on socialization during the past five years that the writer finds interesting and thinks are important inevitably consist of personal selections; another observer with another orientation might well stress quite other developments or might not even see the trends which to this observer seem clear. What is intended here is not an inclusive review of the literature on the topic of socialization, in the tradition of the annual reviews on child development produced in psychology or education, but, rather, a statement of a few new directions in socialization research with only passing notice to the older traditions in the field. This will, of course, mean that certain important aspects of socialization research will not be covered. Three of these areas which will not be considered are animal socialization, the traditional child-development fields such as growth and maturation, language development, perceptual development, learning, and cognitive development, and the cross-cultural studies of socialization in the personality and cultural tradition.[6] Cross-cultural studies will

6 Authoritative reviews on all but the first and last of these topics will be found in Harold W. Stevenson (ed.), *Child Psychology:*

be treated in another paper in this series dealing with culture and personality.

What, then, are the important new developments in socialization theory and research in the past five years? The one which seems most striking to this observer is the extent to which socialization research and thinking has been influenced by social-role and social-systems theory. While the study of social-role has a long and honored past in sociology and a more recent past in psychology and anthropology, its influence on socialization research has been comparatively recent. Possibly in part because of the rather disappointing empirical results of the studies guided by psychoanalytic thinking in the prior period, in part due to developments in sociological theory, social psychologists working in the field of socialization have shown a greatly renewed interest in role theory as a link between social structure and behavior. Some credit for this renewed interest must go to a hardy group of sociologists trained at the University of Chicago, who kept the torch of symbolic-interaction theory burning for more than three decades after it had been handed to them by George Herbert Mead, its principal proponent.[7] Credit also goes to Talcott Parsons who has given impetus to the recent development of role theory. His interest arose naturally out of his attempts to produce a conceptual scheme for the analysis of the structure and process of social systems, focusing on the system of institutionalized roles.[8] His position is further elaborated in his writings on family structure and the socialization of the child, which presents a detailed analysis of the child's internalization of roles as he passes through various stages of psychosexual development and integration into the family system.[9] Because this work was written well before the period to be covered in this paper, and because Parsons' writings are likely to be well known to most readers, no attempt will be made to summarize his complex argument here other than to point out that he places great stress on psychoanalytic ideas of developmental crises.

More recently, a theory of socialization stressing role-learning has been elaborated by Orville G. Brim, Jr.[10] He draws heavily on interactionist ideas but also emphasizes the social-system context. Socialization is defined as a process of learning by which an individual is prepared to meet the requirements that society has set for his behavior in a variety of social situations. These requirements always attach to

---

The Sixty-Second Yearbook of the National Society for the Study of Education (Chicago: University of Chicago Press, 1963). For other coverage, see John C. Wright and Jerome Kagan (ed.), "Basic Cognitive Processes in Children," *Monographs of the Society for Research in Child Development,* Vol. 28 (1963); and J. P. Scott, "The Process of Primary Socialization in Canine and Human Infants," *Monographs of the Society for Research in Child Development,* Vol. 28 (1963).

[7] Among those strongly identified with the interactionist tradition are Herbert Blumer, Leonard S. Cottrell, Jr., Robert E. L. Faris, Everett C. Hughes, Alfred Lindesmith, Anselm L. Strauss, Arnold Rose, Ralph Turner, Neil Gross, Tomatsu Shibutani, and Irwin Goffman.

[8] Talcott Parsons, *The Social System* (Glencoe: The Free Press, 1951).

[9] Talcott Parsons and Robert F. Bales, *Family, Socialization and Interaction Process* (Glencoe: The Free Press, 1955).

[10] The most complete statement of his position yet published is his "Personality Development as Role-Learning," in Ira Iscoe and Harold Stevenson, *Personality Development in Children* (Austin: University of Texas Press, 1960), pp. 127–159. Other sources are his "The Parent-Child Relation as a Social System: I. Parent and Child Roles," *Child Development,* Vol. 28 (September 1957), pp. 343–346; and Orville G. Brim, Jr., David C. Glass, David E. Lavin, Norman Goodman, *Personality and Decision Process* (Stanford: Stanford University Press, 1962).

one or another of the positions or statuses in either the larger society or some smaller social system. The required behavior—including habits, beliefs, attitudes, and motives—in a given position is considered to be an individual's prescribed role, and the requirements themselves are the role prescriptions. Thus, there are sets of reciprocal requirements regulating the behavior of individuals toward each other depending on their positions in the system. One learns these reciprocal requirements from interacting with others in a variety of social situations and by gradually developing the ability to take the role of the other. His knowledge of these social situations, his ability to discharge successfully his role in each situation, and his motivation to perform up to the level which the situation requires are all variables explaining individual differences in behavior. The social structure regulates to a large degree the child's exposure to various aspects of the culture and, consequently, what he will learn. The absence of certain positions in the social structure will result in deficiencies in the child's socialization to the roles these positions represent. Any particular role relationship will vary with the particular culture or subculture in which it takes place and, of course, with the personal characteristics of the specific individuals occupying given statuses, with whom the child interacts. Variations in the culture and in the characteristics of the socializing agent will result in variations in child-rearing practices, leading to personality differences. Brim also discusses the importance of anticipatory socialization, the crucial role of language in the socialization process, the importance of role playing in the learning of roles, and the development of the conception of self.

This approach suggests at least some different orientations to familiar problems, including greater attention to the ways in which parents teach the child to be aware of different roles, the influence of the parents' perception of the social structure on what they pass on to the child, the areas of differentiation in social structure which parents ignore or insist that the child learn, the modalities used in communicating with the child, the nature of the interaction of the child with significant persons in the social structure, the influence of the personal qualities of the socializing agents, the influence of the sex of the socializing agent and the sex of the child on what is learned, the effect of the absence of certain role models on role learning, the ways socialization processes are influenced by family structures—not only the age, sex, and size characteristics but also other less apparent aspects such as the power differential between generations and the instrumental-expressive relations between the sexes—the ways in which social systems other than the family affect the socialization processes, the consistency in the performance of the individual across roles, and the extent to which socialization is oriented toward future roles. These are some of the many concerns suggested by a social role-social systems approach to socialization.[11]

It would be gratifying if it could be reported that much systematic empirical

[11] For recent discussions of the interactionist position, see Frederick Elkin, *The Child and Society* (New York: Random House, 1960), and Tomatsu Shibutani, *Society and Personality* (Englewood Cliffs, N. J.: Prentice-Hall, 1961). See also Arnold Rose, "A Systematic Summary of Symbolic Interaction Theory," in Arnold Rose (ed.), *Human Behavior and Social Processes* (Boston: Houghton Mifflin, 1962), pp. 3–19; Anselm L. Strauss (ed.), *The Social Psychology of George Herbert Mead* (Chicago: University of Chicago Press, 1956); and George Herbert Mead, *Mind, Self and Society* (Chicago: University of Chicago Press, 1934).

work had been done on these and related problems arising out of recent developments in role and social-systems theory. This is not entirely true. Some good beginnings have been made, and a number of studies guided by these ideas are now under way. In fact, relatively few studies of socialization now completely ignore role and social structure variables.

Role-learning among children

There are a number of studies which have emphasized social role-learning in children. These include Brim's study of sex role-learning within two-child families in which he set forth general propositions describing role-learning in terms of interaction with others, including taking the role of the other. From these propositions he derived the hypotheses that children who have a sibling of the opposite sex will have more personality traits of the opposite sex than will children whose sibling is of the same sex and that the effect will be greater for younger than for older siblings.[12] The results of the analysis confirmed both hypotheses. Another important study using the role and social-structure idea is Elder's research on parental power legitimation in which he found that adolescents are more likely to use their parents as role models if the parents explain their rules when asked to do so and that the attractiveness of parents as role models is less among both autocratic and permissive parents than among democratic parents.[13] Also relevant is the McCords' study of the effects of parental role

models.[14] They found that the influence of a criminal father on the criminality of the son is dependent on the explicit values of the parents and the affectional and control structure of the family system. Maccoby's studies of the learning of social roles are also pertinent.[15] She describes the process by which children learn roles through role-taking in childhood and tests hypotheses about the influence of the parental model on the child's tendency to be a rule enforcer in activities involving peers. She found that if the mother had been generally restrictive in her dealings with the child in early childhood her boy would tend to be a rule enforcer; for girls the relationship did not hold, but punishment was related to rule-enforcement behavior. Mussen and Distler jointly and Mussen individually have investigated the effects of the father-son relationships on the development of attitudes appropriate to the male role and have found that the fathers who carry out both nurturing and controlling functions, and do so with warmth and rewards, are likely to be effective role models for their sons.[16] Lynn and Sawrey report on the differential effects of the absence of the father on the role behavior of children,

---

[12] Orville G. Brim, Jr., "Family Structure and Sex Role Learning by Children: A Further Analysis of Helen Koch's Data," *Sociometry*, Vol. 21 (September 1958), pp. 343–364.

[13] Glen H. Elder, Jr., "Parental Power Legitimation and its Effects on the Adolescent," *Sociometry*, Vol. 26 (March 1963), pp. 50–65.

[14] William McCord and Joan McCord, "Effects of Parental Role Model on Criminality," *Journal of Social Issues*, Vol. 14 (1958), pp. 66–75.

[15] Eleanor E. Maccoby, "Role-Taking in Childhood and its Consequences for Social Learning," *Child Development*, Vol. 30 (June 1959), pp. 239–252; and "The Taking of Adult Roles in Middle Childhood," *Journal of Abnormal and Social Psychology*, Vol. 63 (November 1961), pp. 493–503.

[16] Paul H. Mussen and Luther Distler, "Masculinity, Identity, and Father-Son Relationships, *Journal of Abnormal and Social Psychology*, Vol. 59 (November 1959), pp. 350–356; and Paul H. Mussen, "Some Antecedents and Consequences of Masculine Sex Typing in Adolescent Boys," *Psychological Monographs*, Vol. 75 (1961), pp. 1–24.

finding, among other things, that father-absent children showed poorer peer adjustment.[17] They also exhibited a higher degree of dependence, pseudo maturity, and idealization of the father. Hoffman's investigation of the relationship between the father's role in the family and the peer-group adjustments of the child concludes that, if the father is the primary agent of control, the children will become assertive and aggressive.[18] Other studies of social role-learning emphasizing social-systems variables include: Hartley's studies of the sex-role concepts of children and of sex-role pressure in the socialization of the male child,[19] the study by the McCords and Thurber on the effects of parental absence on the role behavior of male children,[20] Stotland and Hillmer's experimental study of identification and self-esteem,[21] and the study by Hoffman and associates of the effects

of the child's experiences on his school role.[22] It should be noted also that Winch has elaborated and is currently testing a series of interesting hypotheses about identification which rely heavily on the learning of social roles in the context of the family system.[23] Lynn's paper in which he uses a social-systems approach to develop a theory of sex differences in identification development and in which he reviews data relevant to his formulation should also be mentioned.[24] Whiting has presented a theory of resource mediation and learning by identification which has grown out of his research at Harvard over the past ten years.[25] Finally, Slater has published a critique on Parsons' theory of differentiation in the nuclear family,[26] and Bronfenbrenner has made a critical analysis of Freud's and Parsons' theories of identification.[27]

Social class

Studies of social class and socialization also reflect the trend toward social-system and social-role approaches. Studies recently reviewed by Bronfenbrenner [28] and by Sewell [29] indicate that

[17] David B. Lynn and William L. Sawrey, "The Effects of Father-Absence on Norwegian Boys and Girls," *Journal of Abnormal and Social Psychology*, Vol. 59 (September 1959), pp. 258–262.

[18] Louis W. Hoffman, "The Father's Role in the Family and the Child's Peer-Group Adjustment," *Merrill-Palmer Quarterly*, Vol. 7 (April 1961), pp. 97–105.

[19] Ruth E. Hartley, "Sex-Role Among Elementary School-Age Girls," *Marriage and Family Living*, Vol. 21 (February 1959), pp. 59–64; "Sex Role Pressure and the Socialization of the Male Child," *Psychological Reports*, Vol. 5 (September 1959), pp. 457–468; "Children's Conceptions of Male and Female Roles," *Merrill-Palmer Quarterly*, Vol. 6 (January 1960), pp. 83–91; "Some Implications of Current Changes in Sex Role Patterns," *Merrill-Palmer Quarterly*, Vol. 6 (April 1960), pp. 153–164.

[20] Joan McCord, William McCord, and Emily Thurber, "Some Effects of Paternal Absence on Male Children," *Journal of Abnormal and Social Psychology*, Vol. 64 (May 1962), pp. 361–369.

[21] Ezra Stotland and Max L. Hillmer, Jr., "Identification, Authoritarian Defensiveness, and Self-Esteem," *Journal of Abnormal and Social Psychology*, Vol. 64 (May 1962), pp. 334–342.

[22] Lois W. Hoffman, Sidney Rosen, and Ronald Lippitt, "Parental Coerciveness, Child Autonomy, and Child's Role at School," *Sociometry*, Vol. 23 (March 1960), pp. 15–22.

[23] Robert F. Winch, *Identification and Its Familial Determinates* (New York: Bobbs-Merrill, 1962).

[24] David B. Lynn, "Sex Differences in Identification Development," *Sociometry*, Vol. 24 (December 1961), pp. 372–384.

[25] John W. M. Whiting, "Resource Mediation and Learning by Identification," in Iscoe and Stevenson, *op. cit.*, pp. 112–126.

[26] Philip E. Slater, "Parental Role Differentiation," *American Journal of Sociology*, Vol. 67 (November 1961), pp. 296–308.

[27] Urie Bronfenbrenner, "Freudian Theories of Identification and their Derivatives," *Child Development*, Vol. 31 (March 1960), pp. 15–40.

[28] Urie Bronfenbrenner, "Socialization and Social Class through Time and Space," in Eleanor Maccoby, Theodore Newcomb, and

the earlier emphasis on social-class differences was mainly on specific child-rearing practices. All of these studies emphasized social-class differences in toilet-training and weaning and a limited number of other specific infant-care techniques. Moreover, their findings were often inconsistent and contrary. Bronfenbrenner was able to discern differential trends in the training practices of lower- and middle-class mothers which he felt indicated that any previous gap between the classes was narrowing. Sewell in his review of the literature on social class and childhood personality found that most of the earlier studies had concentrated on general measures of adjustment or on constellations of neurotic symptoms rather than on more meaningful personality variables. What empirical evidence there was did not support the popular notion that middle-class children are more neurotic or less adjusted than lower-class children.

During the past five years, studies of social class and socialization have had, for the most part, a different emphasis. They have been concerned with such things as differences in the quality of family relationships, patterns of affection and authority, conceptions of parenthood, parents' expectations for the child, and other aspects of parent-child relationships. Kohn's studies of social class in relation to parental values, authority, and the allocation of parental responsibilities are good illustrations of the trend.[30] In these studies,

he finds that middle-class parents emphasize internalized standards of conduct, including honesty and self-control, while working-class parents stress respectability, including obedience, neatness, and cleanliness. Responses to misbehaviors also differ: middle-class parents respond to misbehavior in terms of the child's intent and take into account his motives and feelings, while lower-class parents focus on the child's actions and respond according to their perception of the seriousness of the act. He also finds that working-class mothers expect the father to constrain and punish the child to a more marked extent than do middle-class mothers. Bronson and associates have been concerned with patterns of affection and authority in two generations and find that, in the middle class, parental patterns have not been as rigidly defined as in the lower-class family.[31] They also report that shifts are taking place over time in the companionship and authority relationship of working-class mothers with companionship being more emphasized than formerly. They also find that working-class mothers have always exercised more authority than middle-class mothers but that middle-class mothers are taking on more of the authority function in recent years. Rosen's work should be mentioned because it shows that independence training, achievement motive, and achievement values are all positively corre-

Eugene Hartley (eds.), *Readings in Social Psychology* (New York: Henry Holt and Co., 1958), pp. 400–425; and "The Changing American Child—A Speculative Analysis," *Journal of Social Issues,* Vol. 17 (1961), pp. 6–18.

[29] William H. Sewell, "Social Class and Childhood Personality," *Sociometry,* Vol. 24 (December 1961), pp. 340–356.

[30] Melvin L. Kohn, "Social Class and Parental Values," *American Journal of Soci-*

ology, Vol. 64 (January 1959), pp. 337–351; and "Social Class and the Exercise of Parental Authority," *American Sociological Review,* Vol. 24 (June 1959), pp. 352–366; and Melvin L. Kohn and Eleanor E. Carroll, "Social Class and the Allocation of Parental Responsibilities," *Sociometry,* Vol. 23 (December 1960), pp. 372–392.

[31] Wanda C. Bronson, Edith S. Katten, and Norman Livson, "Patterns of Authority and Affection in Two Generations," *Journal of Abnormal and Social Psychology,* Vol. 58 (March 1959), pp. 143–152.

lated with the social-class position of the child's family.[32] Middle-class parents in their child-rearing put pressure on their children to succeed, teach their children to believe in success, and create conditions making success possible. The Miller and Swanson studies of social class and personality are important in that they not only examined social-class differences in child-training but further differentiated their subjects by whether or not they came from families in the bureaucratic or entrepreneurial settings and related these variables to their ways of resolving conflict and to their mechanisms of defense.[33] Numerous predictions were made about how social class and the nature of the setting either singly or in combination would influence child-rearing and subsequent styles of coping with conflict. Some of these hypotheses were partially confirmed and others were not. There is not space to discuss their rather diverse findings, but at least they have suggested some promising dimensions for consideration in research on socialization. Other recent studies of social class and socialization which reflect some of the trends already noted may be mentioned. These include the work of Tuma and Livson on socioeconomic status and attitudes toward authority,[34] Kantor and associates on social class and maternal attitude

toward the child,[35] the research of Burchinal and associates on the personality adjustment of children from various social classes,[36] the study by Sewell and Haller on factors in the relationship between social status and childhood personality,[37] and the study by Boek and associates on social class and child-care practices.[38]

Social structure

Recently a number of studies have appeared in which family-structure variables are examined in relation to socialization outcomes in children. One of these is Strodtbeck's study of the influence of family interaction in Jewish and Italian families on their sons' achievement values.[39] Using power as his antecedent variable, he found a negative correlation between father's power in the family and the achievement-value score of the son. Since he

[32] Bernard C. Rosen, "Race, Ethnicity, and the Achievement Syndrome," *American Sociological Review,* Vol. 24 (February 1959), pp. 47–60; and "Family Structure and Achievement Motivation," *American Sociological Review,* Vol. 26 (August 1961), pp. 574–585.

[33] Daniel R. Miller and Guy E. Swanson, *The Changing American Parent* (New York: John Wiley and Sons, 1958); and *Inner Conflict and Defense* (New York: Henry Holt and Co., 1960).

[34] Elias Tuma and Norman Livson, "Family Socioeconomic Status and Adolescent Attitudes to Authority," *Child Development,* Vol. 31 (June 1960), pp. 387–399.

[35] Mildred B. Kantor, John C. Glidewell, Ivan N. Mensh, Herbert R. Domke, and Margaret C. L. Gildea, "Socioeconomic Level and Maternal Attitudes toward Parent-Child Relationships," *Human Organization,* Vol. 16 (Winter 1958), pp. 44–48.

[36] Lee G. Burchinal, Bruce Gardiner, and Glen R. Hawkes, "Children's Personality Adjustment and the Socioeconomic Status of their Families," *Journal of Genetic Psychology,* Vol. 92 (June 1958), pp. 144–159; and Lee G. Burchinal, "Social Status, Measured Intelligence, Achievement, and Personality Adjustment of Rural Iowa Girls," *Sociometry,* Vol. 22 (March 1959) pp. 75–80.

[37] William H. Sewell and Archie O. Haller, Jr., "Factors in the Relationship Between Social Status and the Personality Adjustment of the Child," *American Sociological Review,* Vol. 24 (August 1959), pp. 511–520.

[38] Walter E. Boek, Marvin B. Sussman, and Alfred Yankauer, "Social Class and Child Care Practices," *Marriage and Family Living,* Vol. 20 (November 1958), pp. 326–333.

[39] Fred L. Strodtbeck, "Family Interaction, Values, and Achievement," in David C. McClelland, Alfred L. Baldwin, Urie Bronfenbrenner, and Fred L. Strodtbeck, *Talent and Society* (New York: D. Van Nostrand Co., 1958), pp. 135–194.

also found that Italian fathers tended to be more powerful than Jewish fathers and that Jewish boys tended to have higher achievement values than Italian boys, he uses this finding as a possible explanation of the higher social mobility of Jews. Rosen and D'Andrade, in an observational study designed to examine the origins of achievement motivation, found that boys high in *n* Achievement tended to be independent of their fathers in problem-solving situations but tended not to be independent of their mothers.[40] Both mothers and fathers of boys high in *n* Achievement tended to display more warmth than did parents of boys low in *n* Achievement. Straus, in a study of conjugal power structure, found that autonomic families—families in which husband and wife are roughly equal in power—produced sons with higher achievement values, lower anxiety, and lower rejection of parents than families in which either parent was dominant or in which the parents were in conflict.[41] Differences between the types of families on a fourth dimension—the boys' school grades—were in the same direction but not significant. In a study of structural variations in child-rearing, Elder found that lower-class, less-educated, and Catholic parents, and parents with large families, tended to be more authoritarian in their relationship with their adolescent children than middle-class, well-educated, and Protestant parents, and parents with small families.[42] Adolescents subjected to

either extremely authoritarian child-rearing patterns or to extremely permissive patterns tended to feel their parents were less fair and tended to feel more rejected by their parents than those adolescents subjected to democratic patterns of child-rearing.

Other studies of the influence of social structure on socialization outcomes include Becker's study of the effect of family-structure variables on the teacher-pupil relationship,[43] Yarrow's study of child-rearing in families of working and nonworking mothers,[44] the study by Lippitt and Gold of classroom social structure as it relates to school performance, social adjustment, and self-conception of children,[45] Cohen's,[46] Miller's,[47] and the Matza and Sykes[48] studies of various aspects of social structure in relation to juvenile delinquency, Schachter's study of the effect of birth order on affiliative

---

[40] Bernard C. Rosen and Roy D'Andrade, "The Psychological Origins of Achievement Motviation," *Sociometry,* Vol. 22 (September 1959), pp. 185–218. See also the references in footnote 32.

[41] Murray A. Straus, "Conjugal Power Structure and Adolescent Personality," *Marriage and Family Living,* Vol. 24 (February 1962), pp. 17–25.

[42] Glen H. Elder, Jr., "Structural Variations in the Child Rearing Relationship,"

Sociometry, Vol. 25 (September 1962), pp. 241–262.

[43] Howard S. Becker, "Social Class and Teacher-Pupil Relationships," in Edwin R. Carr and Blaine E. Mercer (eds.), *Education and the Social Order* (New York: Rinehart and Co., Inc., 1957), pp. 273–285.

[44] Marian Radke Yarrow, Phyllis Scott, Louise DeLeeuw, and Christine Heinig, "Child-rearing in Families of Working and Nonworking Mothers," *Sociometry,* Vol. 25 (June 1962), pp. 122–140; and Lois W. Hoffman, "Effect of Maternal Employment on the Child," *Child Development,* Vol. 32 (March 1961), pp. 167–197.

[45] Ronald Lippitt and Martin Gold, "Classroom Social Structure as a Mental Health Problem," *Journal of Social Issues,* Vol. 15 (1959), pp. 40–49.

[46] Albert K. Cohen, *Delinquent Boys* (Glencoe, Illinois: Free Press, 1955).

[47] Walter Miller, "Lower-Class Culture as a Generating Milieu of Gang Delinquency," *Journal of Social Issues,* Vol. 14 (1958), pp. 5–19.

[48] David Matza and Gresham Sykes, "Juvenile Delinquency and Subterranean Values," *American Sociological Review,* Vol. 26 (October 1961), pp. 712–719.

behavior,[49] Sears' follow-up study of the effects of early socialization on aggression in middle childhood,[50] Peck's study of family patterns and adolescent personality,[51] the Peck and Havighurst study of character development in Prairie City,[52] and Koch's article on siblings' attitudes toward each other and toward their parents.[53] Finally, Yarrow's review of studies of maternal deprivation should be mentioned.[54]

This, of course, is by no means a complete list of the studies which in part or in whole reflect the trend toward consideration of social-system and

social-role variables (a number of the studies cited throughout this review would be equally good examples, especially those cited in connection with adolescence and socialization to occupational roles); nor would it be correct to infer that all these studies have been guided exclusively by social-system or social-role ideas—several of them have had their central inspiration from other theories. Nevertheless, all of them to a considerable degree reflect the increasing emphasis on social-role and social-systems variables.

LATER SOCIALIZATION

A second recent development in socialization thinking and research has been the increased interest in socialization in periods other than childhood.[55] This interest is closely related to the development of a role-theory approach and flows directly from it. Thus, if socialization is role learning—in the sense that it refers to the process by which the individual acquires the skills, knowledge, attitudes, values, and motives necessary for performance of social roles—it follows that in any but the most static societies the individual cannot possibly be prepared during childhood for the complex roles that he will be called upon to play at later periods in his life. This is not to deny the fundamental importance of childhood socialization but only to assert that role-learning is a continuous process

[49] Stanley Schachter, *The Psychology of Affiliation* (Stanford, California: Stanford University Press, 1959).

[50] Robert R. Sears, "Relation of Early Socialization Experiences to Aggression in Middle Childhood," *Journal of Abnormal and Social Psychology,* Vol. 63 (November 1961), pp. 466–492.

[51] Robert F. Peck, "Family Patterns Correlated with Adolescent Personality Structure," *Journal of Social and Abnormal Psychology,* Vol. 57 (November 1958), pp. 347–350.

[52] Robert F. Peck and Robert J. Havighurst, *The Psychology of Character Development* (New York: Wiley, 1960). See also Robert R. Sears, "The Growth of Conscience," in Iscoe and Stevenson, *op. cit.,* pp. 92–111.

[53] Helen L. Koch, "The Relation of Certain Formal Attributes of Siblings to Attitudes Held Toward Each Other and Toward Their Parents," *Monographs of the Society for Research in Child Development,* Vol. 25 (1960), pp. 1–124.

[54] Leon J. Yarrow, "Maternal Deprivation: Toward an Empirical and Conceptual Reevaluation," *Psychological Bulletin,* Vol. 58 (November 1961), pp. 459–490; and "Research in Dimensions of Early Maternal Care," *Merill-Palmer Quarterly,* Vol. 9 (April 1963), pp. 101–114; and Lawrence Castler, "Maternal Deprivation: A Critical Review of the Literature," *Monographs of the Society for Research in Child Development,* Vol. 26 (1961), pp. 1–64. For reviews of research on other aspects of infancy, see William Kessen, "Research in the Psychological Development of Children," *ibid.,* pp. 83–94; and B. M. Foss (ed.), *The Determinants of Human Behavior* (New York: Wiley, 1961).

[55] This emphasis was highlighted in a recent Social Science Research Council conference on socialization throughout the life cycle (May 17–19, 1963). The preliminary papers presented included the following: Orville G. Brim, Jr., "Socialization Through the Life Cycle"; Murray A. Straus, "Childhood Socialization"; Charles E. Bidwell, "Pre-Adult Socialization"; Irving Rosow, "Forms and Functions of Adult Socialization"; Yonina Talmon, "Comparative Analysis of Adult Socialization"; Howard S. Becker, "Personal Change in Adult Life."

throughout life and that the individual must not only learn new roles and abandon old ones as he passes through various status sequences in his life cycle but that he will also have to learn new roles as he experiences social mobility and as disruptive changes take place in the society.

Perhaps the most direct evidence of the trend toward greater concern for later socialization is indicated by the increased attention given in recent years to adolescent socialization. Although the social psychology of adolescence has long been a concern of social scientists, it is only recently that much attention has been given to this period as one in which important socialization processes take place. Role theory and social-systems analysis are evident in much of present-day work in this field. Parsons' article on the school class as a social system is the classic statement on the manner in which first teachers and then peers become increasingly important as agents of socialization, while parents and family diminish in influence as the child passes through the school system and finds his place in society. This occurs in part through selection mechanisms that operate in the school and peer social systems.[56] Although authorities have debated the question of whether or not there is a distinctive youth culture, there seems to be no disagreement with the notion that the adolescent period is one in which some childhood habits and roles must be abandoned while new roles appropriate to sex and age must be learned or that the school and peer groups are the most important socialization agencies at this time.[57] Coleman's study of adolescents

in ten high schools in the Chicago area not only is the most complete empirical study of adolescent values available but also clearly documents the extent to which peers rather than parents become the important reference figures for high-school youth.[58] Jones, using data from the California Growth Study, shows that the school and the peer group, in their collaboration to promote their common goals, are powerful and pervasive forces in the socialization of the adolescent. Her studies also indicate how these forces differentially influence youth from varying social backgrounds.[59] A study by Bronfenbrenner, Devereux, and Suci describes the relations between parental and adolescent behavior, taking into account sex of child, sex of parent, level of parental power, and the socioeconomic position of the family. They examined various aspects of parent-child relationships, such as "perceived parental power," "adolescent competence," "expressive rejection," "affection," and "affiliative companionship," and found that girls receive more affection, praise, and companionship; by contrast, boys are

ology of Education (Homewood, Ill.: The Dorsey Press, 1962), pp. 106–109; Ernest A. Smith, American Youth Culture: Group Life in Teen Age Society (Glencoe: Free Press, 1962); and Edgar Z. Friedenberg, The Vanishing Adolescent (New York: Dell Laurel Editions, 1962).

[58] James S. Coleman, The Adolescent Society (Glencoe: The Free Press, 1962). See also Richard L. Simpson, "The School, the Peer Group, and Adolescent Development," Journal of Educational Psychology, Vol. 32 (September 1958), pp. 37–41; and James S. Coleman, "Academic Achievement and the Structure of Competition," Harvard Educational Review, Vol. 29 (Fall 1959); pp. 330–351; Robert D. Hess, "The Adolescent: His Society," Review of Educational Research, Vol. 30 (February 1960), pp. 5–12.

[59] Mary C. Jones, "A Study of Socialization Patterns at the High School Level," Journal of Genetic Psychology, Vol. 93 (1958), pp. 87–111.

[56] Talcott Parsons, "The School Class as a Social System: Some of Its Functions in American Society," Harvard Educational Review, Vol. 29 (Fall 1959), pp. 297–318.

[57] Robert R. Bell, "The Adolescent Subculture," in Robert R. Bell (ed.), The Soci-

subjected to more physical punishment and achievement demands. In general, both extremes of either affection or discipline were deleterious for all children; girls were especially susceptible to the detrimental influence of overprotection; boys to the ill effects of insufficient parental discipline and support.[60] This study has been replicated in Germany with basically similar results. Wilson has shown that the social climate of the high school has a decisive influence on the level of educational aspirations of boys from various social classes.[61] Harris has summarized evidence on the part that work plays in the socialization of adolescents, showing its importance to the development of responsibility, self-development, and a favorable self-image.[62] A study by Straus has shown the widespread concern of parents with providing meaningful work role-learning experiences for their adolescent sons.[63] The effect that social-

ization in lower-class and slum subcultures has on delinquent behavior has been the subject of considerable research interest but is most completely documented in the work of Cloward and Ohlin.[64] Bandura and Waters have studied the relation between child-training and adolescent aggression.[65] Reiss has examined the educational norms of normal and delinquent adolescents in relation to their positions in the social structure.[66] Rosenberg has assessed the influence of consonance or dissonance in religious affiliation on self-esteem and psychosomatic symptoms in adolescence.[67] Many other studies could be mentioned, but this sampling and some of the studies cited in the previous section illustrate the wide range of concerns and offer evidence of the stress currently being placed on adolescent socialization.

When attention shifts from adolescent to adult socialization, there is no comparable body of knowledge. Even

[60] Urie Bronfenbrenner, "Toward a Theoretical Model for the Analysis of Parent-Child Relationships in a Social Context," in John C. Glidewell, *Parental Attitudes and Child Behavior* (Illinois: Charles C Thomas, 1961), pp. 90–109; E. C. Devereux, Urie Bronfenbrenner, and G. J. Suci, "Patterns of Parent Behavior in the United States of America and the Federal Republic of Germany: A Cross-National Comparison," *International Social Science Journal,* Vol. 14 (Unesco: Reprint, 1963), pp. 1–20.

[61] Alan B. Wilson, "Residential Segregation of Social Classes and Aspiration of High School Boys," *American Sociological Review,* Vol. 24 (December 1959), pp. 836–845. For evidence on peer-group influences, see Archie O. Haller and C. E. Butterworth, "Peer Influences on Levels of Occupational and Educational Aspirations," *Social Forces,* Vol. 38 (May 1960), pp. 287–295.

[62] Dale B. Harris, "Work and the Adolescent Transition to Maturity," *Teachers College Record,* Vol. 63 (March 1961), pp. 146–153.

[63] Murray A. Straus, "Work Roles and Financial Responsibility in the Socialization of Farm, Fringe, and Town Boys," *Rural Sociology,* Vol. 27 (September 1962), pp. 257–274.

[64] Richard A. Cloward and Lloyd E. Ohlin, *Delinquency and Opportunity* (Glencoe: The Free Press, 1960). See also: Albert K. Cohen and James F. Short, Jr., "Research in Delinquent Subcultures," *Journal of Social Issues,* Vol. 14 (1958), pp. 20–37; Walter B. Miller, "Lower Class Culture as a Generating Milieu of Gang Delinquency," *Journal of Social Issues,* Vol. 14 (1958), pp. 5–19; Albert J. Reiss, Jr., and Albert Lewis Rhodes, "The Distribution of Juvenile Delinquency in the Social Class Structure," *American Sociological Review,* Vol. 26 (October 1961), pp. 653–661.

[65] Albert Bandura and Richard H. Waters, *Adolescent Aggression* (New York: Ronald Press, 1959).

[66] Albert J. Reiss, "Are Educational Norms and Goals of Conforming, Truant, and Delinquent Adolescents Influenced by Group Position in American Society," *Journal of Negro Education,* Vol. 28 (Summer 1959), pp. 309–333. See also his "Social Integration of Queers and Peers," *Social Problems,* Vol. 9 (January 1961), pp. 103–120.

[67] Morris Rosenberg, "The Dissonant Religious Context and Emotional Disturbance," *American Journal of Sociology,* Vol. 68 (July 1962), pp. 1–10.

on the descriptive level, what is known on adult socialization is rather scant—especially in comparison with what is known on childhood and adolescence. Practically no good research on socialization into the marital role exists—despite the fact that numerous books on marriage and family contain "insightful advice" on adjustment to the marriage partner. There is some research on family life education indicating some dimensions of the problem of adult role-learning and suggesting some of the techniques that have been most successful in getting parents to modify old or to adopt new child-rearing practices.[68] Some good beginnings have been made in recent years in the study of socialization to occupational roles. These studies grow out of a long tradition of research on careers by sociologists.[69] Becker and his colleagues have provided the most complete study yet available on socialization to a professional role in their research on the medical student.[70] Their study shows how the social selection process operates to determine who will enter medical school and documents the ways in which the students'

perspectives change as they progress through the years of training until they finally emerge from medical school with appropriate skills and a sense of identity with their profession but with still unresolved dilemmas on a number of issues crucial to their future role as doctors. Lortie, in his study of lawyers, finds that the most important phase of socialization for the practice of law is the sorting and sifting process, which takes place during the first year or so after completion of law school and determines the position the attorney will occupy in the system of legal work.[71] It is probably not necessary to do more than mention the many studies of socialization to different occupational roles that have been done in the past five years to indicate the wide scope of interest in occupational socialization. Corwin has studied role conception and identity in nursing,[72] Westby has investigated the socialization of the symphony musician,[73] Taylor and Pellegrin have studied the professionalization of the life-insurance salesman,[74] the Simpsons have examined the process by which the psychiatric attendant acquires an identity with his work,[75]

[68] Orville G. Brim, Jr., *Education for Child Rearing* (New York: Russell Sage Foundation, 1959).

[69] A good deal of this interest has been stimulated by Everett C. Hughes, who has long been interested in the part occupational roles play in the lives of men. See his *Men and Their Work* (Glencoe: Free Press, 1958) for his writings on several occupational roles.

[70] Howard S. Becker, Everett C. Hughes, Blanche Greer, and Anselm L. Strauss, *Boys in White: Student Culture in Medical School* (Chicago: University of Chicago Press, 1961); and Howard S. Becker and Blanche Greer, "The Fate of Idealism in Medical School," *American Sociological Review*, Vol. 23 (February 1958), pp. 50–56. See also Samuel W. Bloom, "The Process of Becoming a Physician," THE ANNALS, Vol. 346 (March 1963), pp. 77–87; and Anselm L. Strauss, *Mirrors and Masks* (Glencoe: Free Press, 1959).

[71] Dan C. Lortie, "Laymen to Lawmen: Law School, Careers, and Professional Socialization," *Harvard Educational Review,* Vol. 29 (Fall 1959), pp. 352–369.

[72] Ronald G. Corwin, "Role Conceptions and Career Aspiration: A Study of Identity in Nursing," *Sociological Quarterly* (April 1961), pp. 69–86; and Hans O. Mauksch, "Becoming a Nurse: A Selective View," THE ANNALS, Vol. 346 (March 1963), pp. 88–98.

[73] David L. Westby, "The Career Experience of the Symphony Musician," *Social Forces,* Vol. 38 (March 1960), pp. 223–229.

[74] M. Lee Taylor and Ronald J. Pellegrin, "Professionalization, Its Functions and Dysfunctions for the Life Insurance Occupation," *Social Forces,* Vol. 38 (December 1960), pp. 110–114.

[75] Richard L. Simpson and Ida H. Simpson, "The Psychiatric Attendant: Development of an Occupational Self-Image in a Low Status

Eulau and associates have investigated the political socialization of legislators,[76] and Braude has studied the ways in which the rabbi comes to develop an acceptable professional identity.[77] This list could be expanded to cover other professional and semiprofessional roles, but it would not include studies of socialization to skilled trades or to the many semiskilled and unskilled jobs that make up a large proportion of the occupational roles in society. Strangely enough, these occupations for the most part have escaped the recent concerns of sociologists.[78]

Work on other aspects of adult socialization has been quite limited and is mainly directed at socialization to old-age roles and to new statuses in institutional settings. Numerous articles and books have been published on the problems of adjustment to old age and the adjustments of patients and inmates to hospitals, mental institutions, prisons, and homes for the aged. There is no need to consider most of this work in this review because, for the most part, it does not employ a socialization approach. A notable exception is Goffman's book on the social situation of

mental patients and other inmates.[79] Deutscher reports an interesting study on the ways in which parents prepare themselves for what he calls postparental life.[80] This is the stage in the family cycle following the marriage and departure of children from the parental home. He shows that anticipatory socialization through playing at the postparental role in situations analogous to it and by developing attitudes favorable to the anticipated role makes this a much less traumatic period than most writers on the family had expected. Cavan's article on role adjustment in old age is provocative.[81] She attempts to show how old persons can develop adequate self-conceptions at various stages of old age such as retirement, widowhood, and grandparenthood through participation in groups which permit and encourage them to play roles having group support and approval and thus to reformulate their self-conceptions in relation to their new statuses. A promising theory has been advanced by Cummings and associates which holds that aging is primarily a process of disengagement in which the individual participates in a process of mutual withdrawal with others in his social system.[82] From research thus far completed, it appears that this process begins in later middle age with a shift in self-perception which reflects the beginning of anticipatory socializa-

---

Occupation," *American Sociological Review,* Vol. 24 (June 1959), pp. 389–392.

[76] Heinz Eulau, William Buchanan, LeRoy Ferguson, and John C. Wahlke, "The Political Socialization of American State Legislators," *Midwest Journal of Political Science,* Vol. 3 (May 1959), pp. 188–206.

[77] Lee Braude, "Professional Autonomy and the Role of the Layman," *Social Forces,* Vol. 39 (May 1961), pp. 297–301.

[78] The strong sense of identity with the occupational role that characterizes professionals is clearly not shared by industrial workers. For evidence on this point, compare Charles E. Bidwell, "The Young Professional in the Army: A Study of Occupational Identity," *American Sociological Review,* Vol. 26 (June 1961), pp. 360–372; and Robert Dubin, "Industrial Workers' Worlds: A Study of the Central Life Interests of Industrial Workers," in Rose, *op. cit.,* pp. 247–266.

[79] Erving Goffman, *Asylums* (New York: Doubleday and Co., 1961).

[80] Irwin Deutscher, "Socialization for Postparental Life," in Rose, *op. cit.,* pp. 506–525.

[81] Ruth S. Cavan, "Self and Role in Adjustment During Old Age," in Rose, *op. cit.,* 526–536.

[82] Elaine Cummings, Lois R. Dean, David Newell, and Isabel McCaffrey, "Disengagement—A Tentative Theory of Ageing," *Sociometry,* Vol. 23 (March 1960), pp. 15–21; and Elaine Cummings and William E. Henry, *Growing Old: The Process of Disengagement* (New York: Basic Books, 1961).

tion to aged roles. This shift is accompanied by a restriction on amount and variety of interactions undertaken and on the quality of interaction with others. Finally, a self-centered and idiosyncratic set of behaviors come to characterize the aged. Much more research needs to be done to test this formulation, but at least it appears to offer some possibilities as a guide for future research in adult socialization. Parsons argues in a recent essay that the process of disengagement implies an increased capacity for disinterested judgment and that society should take this capacity into account in making a positive redefinition of the aged role.[83] Payne, in a study of the process of aging, finds that old people, when faced with important decisions, turn to middle-aged adults for value support and information. He argues that this constitutes a role reversal whereby adult children become agents of socialization for their aged parents.[84] Other relevant writings bearing on the problem of adult socialization are Streib's article on family patterns in retirement,[85] Thompson's study of preretirement and adjustment,[86] and Talmon's study of retirement in a planned society.[87] There are also some suggestions on socialization

to the sick role.[88] Litman, has made a study of the process by which the self-conceptions are modified immediately after crippling accidents or illnesses, as the individual passes through a long period of rehabilitation and finally learns roles appropriate for one with his handicaps.[89] Perhaps the best example of the study of socialization in an institutional context is Wheeler's study of the complex processes by which the reformatory inmate is socialized to the role of prisoner and then resocialized as he moves out of the correctional community.[90] Other studies could be mentioned, but these are perhaps sufficient to show that some attention is being given to adult socialization. Obviously, research is only now beginning to come to grips with such key issues as the following: the extent to which socialization to adult roles differs from socialization in childhood (does later socialization involve primarily the learning of quite specific skills and values as contrasted to childhood socialization, which is concerned more with the control of primary drives and the internalization of general values and attitudes?); the kinds of techniques which are useful in the socialization of adults; the possible limitations placed on later socialization by the lasting effects of early socialization; the influence of the differing interactional structure

[83] Talcott Parsons, "Toward A Healthy Maturity," *Journal of Health and Human Behavior,* Vol. 1 (Fall 1960), pp. 163–173.

[84] Raymond Payne, "Some Theoretical Approaches to the Sociology of Ageing," *Social Forces,* Vol. 38 (May 1960), pp. 359–362.

[85] Gordon Streib, "Family Patterns and Retirement," *Journal of Social Issues,* Vol. 14 (1958), pp. 46–60. See also Gordon F. Streib, Wayne E. Thompson, and Edward A. Suchman, "The Cornell Study of Occupational Retirement," *ibid.,* pp. 3–17.

[86] Wayne E. Thompson, "Pre-Retirement Anticipation and Adjustment in Retirement," *Journal of Social Issues,* Vol. 14 (1958), pp. 35–45.

[87] Yonina Talmon, "Ageing in Israel: A Planned Society," *American Journal of Sociology,* Vol. 67 (November 1961), pp. 284–295.

[88] See particularly David Mechanic and Edmund H. Volkart, "Stress, Illness Behavior, and the Sick Role," *American Sociological Review,* Vol. 26 (February 1961), pp. 51–58; and David Mechanic, "The Concept of Illness Behavior," *Journal of Chronic Diseases,* Vol. 15 (February 1962), pp. 189–194. A comprehensive statement is found in Talcott Parsons, *The Social System* (Glencoe: The Free Press, 1951), pp. 439–447.

[89] Theodore J. Litman, "Self Conception and Physical Rehabilitation," in Rose, *op. cit.,* pp. 550–574.

[90] Stanton Wheeler, "Socialization in Correctional Communities," *American Sociological Review,* Vol. 26 (October 1961), pp. 697–712.

of various groups on the adult socialization processes; the extent to which there is anticipatory socialization for later stages in the life cycle; the factors preventing some individuals from responding to adult socialization; and the manner in which the individual learns to cope with conflicting role demands. Future work must give attention to these and related problems before we will know much about adult socialization on other than a descriptive level.

METHODOLOGICAL ADVANCES

The third important recent trend in socialization work, and one which is not necessarily related to the two developments previously discussed, is toward increased sophistication in the design and execution of research. This trend is reflected in the growing concern about methodological matters shown by research workers in the field. This is evidenced by the recent publication of a handbook on methods of research sponsored by the Committee on Child Development of the National Academy of Sciences-National Research Council.[91] About half of the chapters in the compendium deal with matters directly relevant to socialization research, including interviewing, projective techniques, attitude and value measurement, the assessment of motivation and affect, the appraisal of personality characteristics, the study of children's groups, the study of interpersonal behavior, anthropological techniques, the measurement of family-life variables, and laboratory experimental methods. All are written by experts and reflect the strides made in the development of research methods in recent years. This

methodological concern is also demonstrated by the amount of effort workers in the field are devoting to the development and testing of research instruments. A listing of this work would require more space than can be allotted, but some excellent examples can be given. One of the most widely used tools is the Parent Attitude Research Instrument, developed by Schaefer and Bell, which in its factor-analyzed version produces three factors: authoritarian control, hostility-rejection, and democratic attitude toward child-rearing.[92] Another instrument developed by Williams, called the PALS (parental authority-love statements), purports to evaluate the parents' behavior and attitudes from the child's point of view.[93] Calogeras has related TAT (thematic apperception test) responses to questionnaire and interview responses and finds that they produce comparable intrafamilial attitude scores.[94] Milton has factor analyzed the intercorrelation among child-rearing variables and finds stable factors including: strictness, adjustment, warmth, responsible child-training orientation, aggression, and punitiveness.[95] Straus has developed a questionnaire for assessing family interaction.[96] Bell has published a critical

[91] Paul Mussen (ed.), *Handbook of Research Methods in Child Development* (New York: Wiley, 1960).

[92] Earl S. Schaefer and Richard Q. Bell, "Development of a Parental Attitude Research Instrument," *Child Development,* Vol. 29 (June 1958), pp. 339–362.

[93] Walter C. Williams, "The PALS Tests: A Technique for Children to Evaluate Both Parents," *Journal of Consulting Psychology,* Vol. 22 (December 1958), pp. 487–495.

[94] Roy C. Calogeras, "Some Relationships between Fantasy and Self-report Behavior," *Genetic Psychology Monographs,* Vol. 58 (November 1958), pp. 273–325.

[95] George A. Milton, "A Factor Analytic Study of Child-Rearing Behaviors," *Child Development,* Vol. 29 (June 1958), pp. 381–392.

[96] Murray A. Straus, *Family Interaction Schedule* (Minneapolis: Minnesota Family Study Center, 1963).

paper on the methodological problem of retrospective parental attitude questionnaires.[97] Lesser has demonstrated that aggressive responses on the TAT are convertible to Guttman scales.[98] Sarason's group has produced evidence on the validity of the Test Anxiety Scale for Children.[99] Schaefer has developed circumplex models for maternal behavior and for the emotional and social behavior of the child.[100] He uses love-hostility and autonomy-control as the bipolar dimension in the maternal behavior model and love-hostility and extroversion-introversion in the model for the child. The models seem to be related to each other on the love-hostility dimension. Maccoby, in a thoughtful article, has discussed the choice of variables in socialization research, pointing out that standard vari-

[97] Richard Q. Bell, "Retrospective Attitude Studies of Parent-child Relations," *Child Development*, Vol. 29 (June 1958), pp. 323–338.

[98] Gerald S. Lesser, "Application of Guttman's Scaling Method to Aggressive Fantasy in Children," *Educational and Psychological Measurement*, Vol. 18 (Autumn 1958), pp. 543–551.

[99] Seymour B. Sarason, Kenneth Davidson, Frederick F. Lighthall, and Richard R. Waite, "Rorschach Behavior and Performance of High and Low Anxious Children," *Child Development*, Vol. 29 (June 1958), pp. 277–286, and "Classroom Observations of High and Low Anxious Children," *ibid.*, pp. 287–296; and Charlotte Fox, Kenneth Davidson, Frederick F. Lighthall, Richard R. Waite, and Seymour B. Sarason, "Human Figure Drawings of High and Low Anxious Children," *ibid.*, pp. 297–302; and Irving Sarnoff, Frederick F. Lighthall, Richard R. Waite, Kenneth Davidson, and Seymour B. Sarason, "A Cross-cultural Study of Anxiety among American and English School Children," *Journal of Educational Psychology*, Vol. 49 (March 1958), pp. 129–136.

[100] Earl S. Schaefer, "Converging Conceptual Models for Maternal Behavior and for Child Behavior," in John C. Glidewell (ed.), *Parental Attitudes and Child Behavior* (Illinois: Charles C Thomas, 1961), pp. 124–146.

ables employed in laboratory studies—or for that matter in various theories—undergo a great deal of modification in real-life situations and that subtle differences in the definition of a variable can affect the nature of the behavior predicted from it.[101] She further argues that the same socialization practice may well have different effects in different cultural situations.

Experiments are less common in socialization research than in some areas of child development or social psychology, but there are examples, among the studies reviewed, of both laboratory experiments and experiments in the family setting.[102] Most studies of socialization depend either on observational, questionnaire, or interviewing techniques for their data, but it is only fair to say that much less attention is paid to sampling than to data-gathering and data-analysis techniques.[103] A notable exception is Elder's study which had a large and well-designed sample, permitting controlled analysis.[104]

Increasingly, students of socialization are coming to the realization that studies in a social-systems context require much more complicated designs than the "single variable approach," which was so common formerly. This has led to a more careful choice of

[101] Eleanor E. Maccoby, "The Choice of Variables in the Study of Socialization," *Sociometry*, Vol. 24 (December 1961), pp. 357–371.

[102] For examples, see: Schachter, *op. cit.*, Strodtbeck, *op. cit.*, and Rosen and D'Andrade, *op. cit.*

[103] For a critique of questionnaire and interview techniques and a suggested program emphasizing observational techniques, see Marion R. Yarrow, "Problems in Parent-Child Research," *Child Development*, Vol. 34 (July 1963), pp. 215–226.

[104] Glen H. Elder, Jr., "Parental Power Legitimation and Its Effect on the Adolescent," *Sociometry*, Vol. 26 (March 1963), pp. 50–65.

variables to conform to the theory guiding the research. The Straus study previously cited is a good example of this.[105] Using conjugal power as his independent variable, he classified families into four types on the basis of distribution of power between the parents and related these types to his dependent variables, which were four adolescent personality attributes chosen to correspond with Parsons' "functional imperatives." Previously formulated hypotheses were then tested by appropriate statistical procedures. Another interesting observation is that there are now a few studies that have a programmatic and interdisciplinary character rarely found in socialization research in the past. One of the best examples is the work of the Cornell group on the relationship between authority and affection in the family and leadership and responsibility in children.[106] When a preliminary study came up with puzzling results, they re-analyzed their data, introducing more controls. They found curvilinear relationships with different optimal levels for the sexes. A theoretical model was constructed which accounted for the parent-child relationships. This has since been tested on German as well as American samples and is being revised as new empirical data indicate the need for modification. Although not all studies come up to the standards of these last two, many of those reviewed are equally well designed. Finally, a word should be said about the generalization made by the authors of recent studies. While to this reviewer there still seems to be a tendency to over-generalize the results from limited studies, this is much less true today than in preceding periods. Socialization research cannot be said to be as rigorous as that in some other branches of social psychology, but it is becoming increasingly respectable.

[105] Murray A. Straus, "Conjugal Power Structure and Adolescent Personality," *Marriage and Family Living*, Vol. 24 (February 1962), pp. 17–25.

[106] For the references, see footnote 60.

Book Department

INTERNATIONAL RELATIONS

CORAL BELL. *Negotiation from Strength: A Study in the Politics of Power.* Pp. viii, 248, iv. New York: Alfred A. Knopf, 1963. $4.95.

This book examines the Western policy of "negotiation from strength" and concludes that it has failed. The author, an economist, teacher, and former member of the Australian Foreign Service, analyzes the steps taken by Western policy-makers following the organization of the North Atlantic Treaty Organization in 1950 and finds that "strength was no more seriously sought than negotiation." Her contention is that goals of military strength sought by the planners were never attained, not because the West lacked the economic means, but because it lacked the will and fiber to provide them short of actual war; and John Foster Dulles opposed negotiation with Russia not so much because it was likely to be unproductive as because it tended to produce *detente* and created a condition in which it "becomes impossible for democracies to maintain a posture of strength." Time, she says, obviously has proved to be militarily against the West because the United States, as chief center of Western power, has lost the invulnerability to Russian destruction which she had at the beginning. The chances of negotiated settlement have dwindled, and "accommodations by default or tacit acquiescence" are more likely in the future—indeed, already evident in eastern Europe and perhaps East Germany.

There is a semantic distinction in the use of the word "policy" in discussion of international affairs which has never been dichotomized satisfactorily. "Policy" is used to refer to the stated objectives of a nation as well as to its actual conduct *vis-a-vis* other nations. Policy, as objective, necessarily undergoes refinement in the conduct, for the reaction of other nations not only affects implementation but invariably enriches the original idea.

During the period examined by Dr. Bell it was fashionable journalistic practice to approach each innovation in American foreign policy in a spirit of suspecting the worst. Most writers appeared more interested in scoring critical debating points than in seeking to understand the purpose of innovation. Thus Dr. Bell takes the conventional look down her nose at what she describes as the Dulles "policy" of massive retaliation, seeing no link between the genesis of that idea and the "policy of the deterrent," which is more firmly imbedded in Western strategy today than any other "policy." If, as she concludes, deterrence has created no more than a balance of terror under which we are headed for accommodation with the Russians by default, one might still feel thankful that it has saved us to date from negotiating from weakness. Dr. Bell joins a school of postwar writers on foreign affairs who are too steeped in gloom for their own good.

JOHN ROBINSON BEAL
Bureau Chief
Time, Incorporated
Ottawa

LEONARD BEATON and JOHN MADDOX. *The Spread of Nuclear Weapons.* Pp. xi, 216. New York: Frederick A. Praeger, 1962. $4.50.

This is an important book. Americans, large numbers of them, should read it. It deserves to be extensively reviewed—at greater length than is at my disposal. "One of the important conclusions of this study," write Beaton and Maddox, "is that the spread of nuclear weapons is by no means inevitable. Though many countries are technically equipped for the manufacture of nuclear weapons, comparatively few have chosen to do so. Indeed only China (and she very ambiguously) has indicated that she will obtain nuclear power independently . . . the spread of nuclear weapons is obviously not as inexorable even as the spread of the juke-box."

The authors, military and scientific correspondents for the *Guardian,* respectively, first examine the technical problems confronting nations in search of an independent nuclear capability and the types of assistance "established" nuclear powers can provide. A series of nine case studies then follows, ranging from Great Britain and France through China and India to Switzerland and Israel. In each instance proper but oft-neglected stress is laid on the variety of pressures put upon governments not to make a self-fulfilling prophecy out of the inevitability argument.

Until quite recently, too many American students of international affairs accepted without question the scientific prognostication which Beaton and Maddox successfully refute. Worse, they played "games" which posited the existence of several nuclear powers in order to construct elaborate "theories" of so-called multiple deterrence. Worst, they derived conclusions regarding advantages the United States supposedly could derive from pushing along the process of proliferation with timely technical and material aid. Even if the spread of nuclear capabilities were inevitable, it would still be reckless to assume that what would some day come about would be good. The authors of *The Spread of Nuclear Weapons* are not led astray in the same way. They show that the beneficence of existing nuclear nations will have been largely responsible if proliferation does indeed take place. From this carefully documented conclusion they draw the logical policy inferences: "Serious consideration should be given to the continuing need to base nuclear weapons in large numbers on foreign soil," and, even more important, "serious consideration should be given to restrictions on delivery systems to countries unwilling to give an undertaking to restrict themselves to conventional warheads."

The Institute for Strategic Studies in London should also be congratulated for sponsoring this timely study.

EDGAR S. FURNISS, JR.
Mershon Professor of Political Science
Ohio State University

Personnel for the New Diplomacy. Report of the Committee on Foreign Affairs Personnel. Pp. xi, 161. Washington, D. C.: Carnegie Endowment for International Peace, 1962. $2.95.

The growing magnitude and complexity of this nation's external responsibilities caused the Secretary of State, in August 1961, to initiate a new study of the selection, training, and career development of foreign service personnel. A carefully selected and experienced committee of twelve, assisted by a competent staff, submitted the present report some sixteen months later. In the interim, the committee and staff covered a great deal of ground, visiting overseas posts in all parts of the world, digesting specially prepared studies or "working papers," reviewing government bureaucratic practices, and appraising existing legislation applying to foreign service agencies. The resulting report is a model of condensation and exposition, admirably suited to serve as a guide to substantial improvement in the entire foreign service structure.

The committee's frame of reference did not extend to the activities abroad of the Department of Defense, the Central Intelligence Agency, the Arms Control and Disarmament Agency, and the Peace Corps or to other overseas governmental activities outside of the Department of State and its wholly-contained Agency for International Development and United States Information Agency. Within this purview, the committee found it necessary to study the role of the Secretary in the Department of State and the relationships between policy formulation and program development in estimating the human resources required to carry out policies and programs. Special attention was given to executive and professional personnel in the belief that requirements in these two categories were the most crucial.

The committee's findings are set forth in terms of the dimensions of the new diplomacy, a framework for foreign affairs personnel management, the kinds and attributes of the personnel required, and the kinds of education and training requisite for effective service in foreign affairs. Analyses of the numerous situations examined are accompanied by specific recommendations for change and improvement. The report concludes with a summary of new legislation and administrative action needed for a foreign service whose effectiveness might be commensurate with today's needs. Among the improvements advocated with some urgency is a greater degree of uniformity in the treatment and training of the "family of services" within the Department of State. As to better training, the report strongly recommends the creation of a new National Foreign Affairs College, to replace the Foreign Service Institute, open to trainees from the various civilian and military agencies having foreign affairs programs. This major proposal envisages the presence of a core faculty together with area and other specialists and the maintenance of liaison with the leading universities.

HALFORD L. HOSKINS
Senior Specialist in
  International Relations
Legislative Reference Service
Library of Congress

ROBERT BLUM (Ed.). *Cultural Affairs and Foreign Relations.* Pp. viii, 177. Englewood Cliffs, N. J.: Prentice-Hall, for the American Assembly, Columbia University, 1963. $3.95.

The readers of the five essays which comprise the bulk of this volume can hardly fail to be impressed by the scale to which relations among nations in the fields loosely called "cultural" have grown, as well as by the rich diversity of channels and vehicles through which such relations are today carried on. The very variety of devices whereby the cultural resources of this and other countries have been tapped attests to an inventiveness in social affairs which must nearly match that current in the hard sciences. The development is the more remarkable in the United States, which has during most of its history been an importer rather than an exporter of "culture," as the essay by Philip H. Coombs emphasizes. Although this country had started a small cultural relations program with a limited objective before World War II, our real efforts did not get under way until about fifteen years ago. Several of the Western countries had a long head start, and, in some respects, they still maintain a considerable lead. And Russia has, of course, moved into the field with tremendous vigor. Yet, the United States, in the face of an isolationist tradition, of an almost total lack of experience, and of a pluralistic and permissive polity has attained a respectable posture.

Self-congratulation was hardly the purpose of these papers nor of the Arden House meetings for which they were prepared. They trace the postwar history of international relations and exchange in fields of science, the visual arts, the

The Atlas of Britain and Northern Ireland

Planned and directed by D. P. BICKMORE **and** M. A. SHAW. *Prepared by the Cartographic Department of the Clarendon Press.* Virtually all the material resources of England, Scotland, Wales, and Northern Ireland are mapped in this truly breath-taking atlas. Through new cartographic techniques, facts and physical characteristics are graphically portrayed in this volume's 200 pages of maps (some in as many as twelve colors). Sections on geology, seacoasts, climate, and water are followed by others on agriculture, fisheries, demography, industry, and world trade. Regional maps convey additional information. The *Atlas* contains a 24-page gazetteer, an introduction, and copious notes. $15\frac{1}{2} \times 20\frac{1}{2}''$ $100.00

The Kurdish Republic of 1946

By WILLIAM EAGLETON, JR. The Kurdish Republic of Mahabad was short-lived; when Soviet occupation troops withdrew, it collapsed. Because so much documentary material was destroyed in the debacle, Mr. Eagleton's account is based on interviews with Kurdish, Turkish, Persian and Arabian survivors of the Iranian executions. His book shed light on Soviet involvement, on relationships between Kurds and Azerbaijani, on Kurdish nationalism, and on the personalities of Kurdish leaders.
Illustrated. $4.80

The Organization of a Community Development Programme

By PETER DU SAUTOY. From his experience in Ghana as Director of Social Welfare and Community Development, Mr. Du Sautoy outlines ways of developing a community program in an emerging nation. He discusses national and local governmental encouragement, urban problems, extension education, personnel training, and the results of such a development program. Appendices contain various departmental forms and much information of practical value to the field worker, whose interests the author keeps constantly in mind. $3.40

Studies in Frontier History
Collected Papers, 1928–1958

By OWEN LATTIMORE. These collected essays and other papers form the largest contribution by a recognized authority to the study of the area surrounding the great Chinese land mass. Divided into six sections—the Inner Asian Frontier, Sinkiang, Mongolia, Manchuria and China, national minorities, and social history—the book affords a broad view of the author's developing concept of pastoral nomadism. $12.00

Oxford University Press / New York 16, N. Y.

theater, music, student and professor exchange, literature, and the humanities, and lay particular emphasis upon problems of human development through education in underdeveloped lands. But the intent is to criticize, to raise questions, and to prescribe for the future. The contributors share a conviction in the crucial importance of cultural relations in the world and an urgent feeling that the United States, through both its governmental and its private resources, must do a great deal more and do it a great deal better. Suggestions of what to expand and what to change dot many of the pages, and some are expressed in a more generalized way in the recommendations of the American Assembly itself, which are appended.

These essays contain a surprising amount of information in a relatively small space. They are too "hard-packed" to be very easy for the reader, and, as is probably inevitable in this kind of collection, there is some duplication. This reviewer would have preferred fewer statistics on educational exchange, for example, and more discussion of some of the underlying issues —such as the overlapping and sometimes conflicting purposes of cultural programs, whether as a weapon in the Cold War, or an instrument of social development, or the general advancement of human knowledge, or American cultural advancement. He would have preferred a modest reduction in the pages on co-operation in the hard sciences and some treatment of the important and tremendously difficult problems of interchange and co-operation in the social sciences, which are almost overlooked. The volume would have profited also from more exploration of some of the real mechanical difficulties of administration—of budgets, organization, and personnel.

But this is a highly informative and thought-provoking book. The American Assembly has, as is its habit, contributed greatly to the cultural and educational equipment of thoughtful Americans.

FREDERICK C. MOSHER
Professor of Political Science
University of California
Berkeley

SAMUEL FLAGG BEMIS. *American Foreign Policy and the Blessings of Liberty and Other Essays.* Pp. 423. New Haven: Yale University Press, 1963. $10.00.

Samuel Flagg Bemis is the dean of university scholars of American foreign policy, and the present volume of his essays collected over a period of nearly forty-five years is under the appreciative sponsorship of his university's press. Here are seventeen of his occasional essays, including his presidential address before the American Historical Association in December 1961. Whether of early or late vintage these writings are good, and as worthy of publication as his many books. Naturally several of the essays concern his chief scholarly interests—the diplomacy of the founding era of American nationality, or the diplomacy of John Quincy Adams. There is a longish essay—75 pages—on "Early Diplomatic Missions from Buenos Aires to the United States, 1811–24." The book concludes with an essay proposing a joint Congressional resolution to allow intervention by the United States in the Western Hemisphere, perhaps in Cuba, if activities of communism there should endanger the independence of the United States.

The reader of these essays will notice the depth of research and study behind them, and it is especially this hard labor in the manuscript collections and the archives which so often distinguishes the author's work from that of his fellow historians. Bemis has never been a scholar who generalized from the studies of his fellows, but throughout his career has been a leader in going to the archives and collections, not merely in his own country but abroad. These collected essays show his indefatigable energy for truly original research, happily still continuing since his recent retirement at Yale.

They also show a high literary ability, and honesty and objectivity, qualities essential for a first-rank scholar. Bemis makes the British secret service during the American Revolution an exciting operation. In another essay he admits both the virtues and crotchets of the Adams family, with some humorous if appreciative comments on the personality of Henry Adams II, the cautious but kindly keeper of the family papers twenty years ago who gradually allowed Bemis access and at one notable juncture left the key with him.

All in all, a most interesting and valuable collection.

ROBERT H. FERRELL

Indiana University

DAVID M. PLETCHER. *The Awkward Years: American Foreign Relations under Garfield and Arthur.* Pp. xvi, 381. Columbia: University of Missouri Press, 1962. $7.50.

This is a study of a neglected decade of American international relations, the 1880's. The most notable figure is James G. Blaine, who was appointed Secretary of State by President Garfield in 1881, served briefly under President Arthur, and was reappointed by President Benjamin Harrison in 1889. Significantly the indexes of standard surveys of international relations list Blaine meagerly if at all. His tenure in 1881 was brief, because of Garfield's death six and a half months after inauguration, and he resigned soon after Arthur's succession. However, he clung to the office after Arthur had appointed his successor, Frelinghuysen, busy with policies that might commit his successor, policies which, however, Frelinghuysen promptly junked.

Blaine was hampered by an insatiable appetite for the presidency which occasionally induced him to "wave the bloody shirt" and "twist the British Lion's tail." Moreover his impetuous temperament led him to conduct diplomacy by fits and starts. His attempts to resolve the Pacific War between Chili and Peru over possession of the rich guano deposits was rendered almost impossible by the crisis-provoking ineptitude of the Latin-American "diplomats" the patronage system compelled American presidents to select. A year after his resignation Blaine was to betray his Anglophobia before a congressional committee by saying, "It is a perfect mistake to speak of it as a Chilean war on Peru. It is an English war on Peru with Chili as the instrument."

Professor Pletcher aptly epitomizes the diplomatic ineptitude of the period: "Thus, for example, Blaine proposed his peace Congress, which depended for success on Latin-American stability and good will at the very moment of his most tactless intervention in the war in the Pacific. As for Frelinghuysen's policies, Senator Bayard pointed out that the Nicaragua treaty would lead the government to spend millions of dollars on an interocean canal, while, at the same time, the reciprocity treaties reduced the revenue. Others objected that both Blaine and Frelinghuysen intended to elbow Europe out of the central isthmus but that Frelinghuysen showed no reluctance to play a role in the Congo where Americans had fewer interests than in Central America."

It was a decade with an illusion of grand national prestige in the face of the post-Civil War neglect of the means of national defense. From naval power that, in the mid-1860's, put the United States first, the decline by the 1880's taxes the reader's credulity when, for example, a leaky warship, the "Ashuelot," sank in the China sea in fair weather with the loss of eleven sailors. It was soberly asserted that, in three weeks, the navy of Chili could sweep American commerce from the Pacific and attack San Francisco without significant hindrance by American warships. And after long debate an indifferent Congress compromised the controversy between wooden sailing warships and proposed ironclads by authorizing construction of two steel cruisers carrying full sail power.

This reviewer fondly wishes that somehow the results of Professor Pletcher's prodigious researches might have been so organized as to stand out as a picture in bold outline.

WILFRED E. BINKLEY

Professor of Political Science
Ohio Northern University

GEORGE MODELSKI (Ed.). *SEATO: Six Studies.* Pp. xxxiii, 302. Melbourne: F. W. Cheshire, 1962. No price.

This work is the result of a research project initiated in early 1958 by the Department of International Relations of the Australian National University. Four of the authors were on the staff of this institution, and the fifth holds a doctorate from it. Each presents a self-contained analysis of a selected topic, but all of the chapters view the Southeast Asia Treaty Organization (SEATO) as a Western big-power arrangement for the small states of Southeast Asia. George Modelski, the editor, is also responsible for the chapters dealing with the function and organization of SEATO and with the Asian participants in this organization. He notes (pp. 21–28) SEATO's lack of a career service; its limited financial resources—$1,000,000 per annum; and its extreme caution, at times bordering "on timidity." Although the events of early 1962 seemed to vindicate SEATO's purposes, the Laotian crisis did pose the problem of how to cope with a foreign-supported civil war. Disagreement among the—non-Asian—Big Three members on this first crucial issue "immobilized SEATO, and virtually robbed it of its usefulness" (p. 5).

One chapter, written by the late Professor Leicester C. Webb, deals with Australia and SEATO. This contribution provides important insights into the origins of Australia's interest in SEATO. R. Gavin Boyd discusses China's attempt to obstruct SEATO and its encouragement of neutralism in the countries of South and Southeast Asia. A penetrating analysis of India's very negative reaction is provided by Mrs. R. Brissenden. Pakistan's involvement is an obvious explanation of the Indian response, but she points out in addition that India was not prepared to share the view of China held by the United States. The year 1954, moreover, had initiated a "soft" period rather than a "tough" one in Sino-Indian relations (p. 228). Mrs. Brissenden, rather significantly in light of subsequent developments, predicts (p. 243) that a future Indian Minister of External Affairs may well give "a more positive commitment to the notion of some organized collective form of defence" of the South Asian region.

Warren P. Hogan wrote the concluding chapter, which deals with the overwhelming role of the great powers in Asian trade relationships. He observes that not only is the contribution of Asian trade to world trade decreasing but also the terms of trade for Asian countries. To put the trading picture in perspective, Dr. Hogan notes that Soviet Union trade with Asian countries is, in the aggregate, still below 1938 levels and that the contribution of Japan, Hongkong, and Malaya surpasses by far the combined total of all other Asian countries—excluding those of the Communist bloc.

This study provides the reader with more than its title indicates and is a valuable contribution to an understanding of the international relations of the area. A question could be raised as to whether it has presented enough of SEATO itself. Some of the chapters provide important background to a broader understanding of SEATO, but a concluding chapter pulling the various threads together might have brought the role of SEATO in this part of the world into clear focus. A degree of unevenness in the use of the latest available material and statistical data is probably unavoidable in a multiauthor project.

PAUL W. VAN DER VEUR
Senior Research Fellow
Australian National University

EVAN LUARD. *Britain and China.* Pp. 256. Baltimore: Johns Hopkins Press, 1962. $5.00.

This, the first of a series of books dealing with contemporary British foreign policy, directs itself to an area towards which Britons and Americans alike have shown more than the usual ineptness of foreign officers and less than the usual penetration of scholars. The very topic of China has been subjected to a succession of intellectual fads, in which the imagination of Western policy-makers and policy-talkers has been for generations perhaps as significant in intercultural relationships as the actual facts of what has been going on. During World War II, for example, it was possible to speak of Chiang Kai-shek for some years as an archangelic statesman and within twelve months to dismiss him as a diabolical reactionary.

The value of Dr. Luard's book is that it is neither an attempt to explode myths nor an effort to marshal facts about China itself. Not a critique, it is a direct account of British foreign relations with China, particularly as concerns the years following World War II. Accurate as a record of actual British policy, it is valuable also as a record of the opinion of many influential Britons and Americans. Britain has, in fact, adopted policies which, while not accepted by the United States government, have been recommended by a considerable segment of vocal American opinion.

Britain and China emphasizes the fact that trade has been the governing consideration of British policy since the first direct contact between the two countries in the seventeenth century. The book, quite naturally, does not concern itself with the fact, somewhat bizarre when seen in relation to British preoccupation with commerce, that American opinion has been based largely on considerations ranging from international good will to *Realpolitik*. To this reviewer, it would appear that ideas and policies concerning China and very possibly other non-Western countries have emerged from a climate of educated opinion—as opposed to popular opinion—and that the reasons given for ideas and policies have, in effect, been rationalizations after the fact of personal and group acceptance of the particular content of a cultural climate, however fickle the climate may be.

Dr. Luard makes no such assumptions. He points out, to be sure, that "In fact, British trade with China has never in its history been more than two and a half per cent of total U. K. trade. Today it represents about .07 per cent." He recognizes, moreover, that "International relations today are dominated more than all else by ideological considerations." The fact remains, however, that British opinion crystallized itself into policy through emphasis on the all-importance of "trade," curiously enough an activity viewed personally with opprobrium by many of the governing Britons who encouraged it as national and international policy.

When Dr. Luard moves into the area of "ideological considerations," he nonetheless records opinions little different from those reflecting concern for the carriage of goods: in current terms, an accommodation to the Red China government and an effort to bring the pressure of international opinion to bear on its behavior, through such means as improved East-West communication and admission of the Red government into the United Nations. Undiscussed are the possibilities that Peking may wish only to take advantage of an accommodation while remaining unmoved by any pressure, and that the leaders of Red China may have already involved their government in political and economic contradictions that could undermine its position. Like many other valuable studies of Western relations with Eastern countries, this book suggests the importance of nonrational factors in arriving at positions or policies concerning international affairs.

HERRYMON MAURER
Consultant in Cultural Anthropology
Bureau of Research in Psychiatry and
    Neurology
State of New Jersey

ALEXANDER DALLIN. *The Soviet Union at the United Nations: An Inquiry Into Soviet Motives and Objectives.* Pp. viii, 244. New York: Frederick A. Praeger, 1962. $5.75 clothbound; $1.95 paperbound.

This book should be read by all serious students either of the United Nations or of the Soviet Union. The author sets forth Soviet attitudes toward international law, international organization, the specialized agencies, and disarmament and the total image of the United Nations among both the Soviet people and the official Soviet representatives in the United Nations.

He emphasizes that these attitudes and images have not been static. Opposition

to world government and insistence on national sovereignty, nonintervention, Soviet great power position and the veto, and somewhat inconsistently, to equality of states and self-determination of colonies have been continuous. Initial opposition to the League of Nations as "enemy headquarters" was, however, modified when the Soviet Union entered that organization. In the United Nations, the Soviet position changed from Stalin's initial tolerance to positive opposition when the United Nations appeared to be an instrument of the West in the Cold War, culminating in the Korean hostilities. In the "thaw" after the death of Stalin, Khrushchev conceived the United Nations as an instrument of "peaceful coexistence," during the Suez episode and, increasingly, in spite of Hungary, during disarmament negotiations and the 'Spirit of Camp David," until the summit conference of 1960 was shattered by the U-2 incident and Soviet hopes in central Africa were shattered by the United Nations Congo policy. The belief that the United Nations can be useful during the period of coexistence has, however, continued.

After considering the pros and cons in detail, Dallin comes to the conclusion that Khrushchev probably wants disarmament but fears that Western demands for inspection and control of the "balance of terror" during an indefinite first stage of disarmament might facilitate Western aggression. The Soviets have, it is true, manifested willingness to accept some international inspection and have become less opposed to international policing once the world is disarmed, but, according to Dallin, the outlook is not favorable.

The author gives much attention to the Troika proposal which he thinks, if adopted, would ruin the United Nations. His pessimistic conclusion, that the Soviet government could not easily retreat from its position on this matter, has not been born out, since the Soviet Union accepted a permanent term for U Thant after the book was published. In this connection, the author concludes that the threefold view of the world was merely tactical to win the unaligned states, and has not

actually superseded the dual view of the world inherent in a revolution, whether French, Russian, or Chinese, which expects to become universal. He notes that the latter opinion has, as George Kennan pointed out, tended to be a self-fulfilling prophecy (p. 198) because the antirevolutionists usually accept the revolutionists' appraisal of themselves and facilitate their organization by organizing against them.

All of the great powers, and some of the lesser, have departed from their Charter obligations when they thought immediate national interest required (p. 199). All have conserved the United Nations as an instrument of national policy rather than as an instrument to assure peaceful coexistence, to settle conflicts, to control competition, and to develop co-operation. The Soviet Union has appeared more intransigent, because its revolution was more recent and it has been in a minority. Both of these conditions have, to some extent, been cured by time, and the Soviet Union has tended to become a better United Nations member, though more vocal in its confidence that history is on the side of its ideology. Since Stalin began to talk of communism in one country, Soviet policy, both in the United Nations and elsewhere, has become more Russian and less Communistic. The author's listing of Russian goals in the United Nations resembles those of all sovereign states (p. 192) suggesting "selective co-operation" rather than the "maximizing of United Nations authority." The latter aim, as recognized by Professor Maurice Bourquin, will have to await a greater "feeling" by the people of the world of "the unity of mankind" (p. 200).

QUINCY WRIGHT
Visiting Professor
Columbia University

INIS L. CLAUDE. *Power and International Relations.* Pp. x, 310. New York: Random House, 1962. No price.

In his new book Professor Claude reexamines the theoretical underpinnings of the field of international politics. The product of his labors deserves the most attentive reading. The book falls roughly into three equal parts: the first third of the book is a painstaking and penetrating review of the concept of the balance of power; the second portion deals with collective security and the relationship between it and the balance of power; the final third of the book discusses world government, that is, a situation where a monopoly of power is present on the world scene.

In analyzing these three possible solutions to the problem of maintaining world peace and stability, the author throws into serious question some of the fundamentals of present theory in international politics. Particularly arresting is a masterful exposition of the theoretical, factual, and linguistic faults and failures of the balance-of-power concept. The reader will find this portion of the enquiry devastating.

Also highly interesting is Claude's reinterpretation of Woodrow Wilson's role as chief author and proponent of collective security. The material presented suggests a Woodrow Wilson we are unaccustomed to finding in the frequent accounts of the man and his role in international affairs. Here there is a strong suggestion that Woodrow Wilson was a hard-bitten realist, a master political strategist—who knew well the value, the role, and the use of power—trying to ease the United States into the position of world leadership which its power position dictated for it. It must be admitted that the picture of Wilson's efforts and motives which Mr. Claude presents is far more consistent with the career of a political personality rising from an assistant professorship at Bryn Mawr to the presidency of the United States and leadership of the allies in World War I than the picture of an inept idealist in world affairs that historians and political scientists have usually presented.

Perhaps most important of all, Mr. Claude's book contains the implication that the argument between "idealists" and "realists" that has occupied so much attention in the field of international relations has been, in fact, a wasteful argument, and that new categories of distinctions are necessary. This is a book to stimulate new thought, and one can only hope that it will be widely read.

A. F. K. ORGANSKI
Professor of Political Science
Brooklyn College
City University of New York

AMERICAN GOVERNMENT AND HISTORY

SIDNEY KRAUS (Ed.). *The Great Debates: Background — Perspective — Effects*. Pp. 439. Bloomington: Indiana University Press, 1962. $7.95.

A distinctive feature of the 1960 presidential campaign was the direct confrontation of the two major candidates in a series of television appearances. Although these occasions were commonly referred to as "debates," they did not conform strictly to a debate procedure. The two principals did not challenge each other, but rather responded to a series of questions propounded by impartial, or at least bipartisan, panels. Since there has been some criticism of the networks because of this procedure, it is only fair to say that it was the candidates themselves who insisted on this technique rather than that of an outright debate.

This symposium by a group of broadcasting and public opinion experts analyzes the series of programs from almost every conceivable angle. The general consensus seems to be that on balance Kennedy profited more than Nixon from the four appearances, partly because Kennedy was less well-known than Nixon at the outset and gained more than the latter from the publicity. The first debate, in particular, according to the experts, gave a definite edge to Kennedy, although the later meetings were much more evenly balanced. There was some negotiation regarding a fifth program, but the plans were dropped at the last minute.

The technical details in connection with the staging of these affairs were amazingly complex. Every possible effort was made to avoid any appearance of favoring one candidate over another. The networks incurred heavy expense in putting the programs on the air, and there was, of course, no commercial sponsorship, although one network did raise the question in a tentative way. The Federal Communications Commission law had to be amended temporarily in regard to equal time so that minor party candidates could not take advantage of the situation.

Much of the book is devoted to intensive statistical analysis, mostly by way of polling, to determine the effects of the programs. Many charts and diagrams are used to show to what extent the "debates" affected voting, how the programs affected the "images" of the candidates and so forth. These visual media are interesting but not too convincing because, as the compilers themselves state candidly, the samplings are too small.

Despite much difference of opinion among these contributors, there was pretty general agreement that the programs were, on the whole, worth-while, although there were numerous suggestions as to changes in any subsequent series. It was pointed out that such a procedure at least forces partisans to listen to both sides of the party question, although there was considerable skepticism as to how many opinions were actually modified.

J. H. LEEK

University of Oklahoma

ALPHEUS THOMAS MASON. *The Supreme Court: Palladium of Freedom.* Pp. 207. Ann Arbor: University of Michigan Press, 1962. $4.95.

Once more the Supreme Court has become the subject of public controversy. Its critics argue that the Court has seriously weakened the nation by engaging in acts of judicial supremacy. They claim that by substituting its own judgment for that of the people's representatives, it has acted like a superlegislature. Its defenders, both inside and outside the Court, have tended to argue either that judicial self-restraint is the best doctrine to follow or that judicial activism is truer to the meaning of judicial review.

Professor Mason attempts to illuminate the present controversy over judicial review by a careful scrutiny of what was said and done during the Colonial period, at the Constitutional Convention, and up to the decision in *Marbury* v. *Madison.* He demonstrates that there was widespread support of judicial review as a guardian of individual rights, affording a corrective for conditions that might provoke revolution. But the historical record does not provide conclusive answers to the questions which are at the center of the controversy over the Court: what kind of power does the Court have? how much? and in what areas?

A search for answers to these questions in the history of the Court substantiates Corwin's judgment that "judicial review represents an attempt by American Democracy to cover its bet." For since the days of Jay and Marshall, the power of the Court has been used to legitimize public power and to safeguard individual rights against governmental arbitrariness. Mason believes that neither the doctrine of self-restraint nor judicial activism is sufficient by itself to guide the Court in reconciling liberty and order. He thinks that restraint in the use of the Court's power to settle socioeconomic issues is practicable and desirable because the majority should not be stopped from experimenting with social and economic arrangements. When mistakes are made, new majorities will come forward to correct them. But the Court must be more active when overbearing majorities tamper with civil liberties. When the power of the government is used to render ineffective the democratic processes for publicizing and correcting the majority's mistakes, the Court has a special responsibility to remove these legislative impediments to the operation of a working democracy. Only in this way does the Court effectively perform its dual role: by protecting minority rights it keeps open the channels by which majorities can legitimately command popular support.

The Supreme Court is a timely book, presenting a sound reconsideration of the Court's role in a democracy. It can be read with profit both by those who seek social reform through legal action and by those who oppose reform as against community consensus.

HENRY M. HOLLAND, JR.
Associate Professor of Government
State University College
Geneseo
New York

WILLIAM C. HAVARD and LOREN P. BETH. *The Politics of Mis-Representation: Rural-Urban Conflict in the Florida Legislature.* Pp. xiii, 293. Baton Rouge: Louisiana State University Press, 1962. $5.00.

This study of the legislature of Florida is unusually well written and offers a broad panorama of political and organizational interpretation. The authors, now respectively in Louisiana and Massachusetts, were faculty colleagues in the Department of Political Science at the University of Florida. They approach their subject with high ideals and with the point of view that public action should be responsive to majority will. "If we have appeared hypercritical at times," they write (p. 242), "we can only plead our calling: when the academician ceases to be a gadfly in a one-party (or 'no'-party) state, who is left to perform the vital function of criticism?" Their critical analysis ranges over the background of Florida politics, apportionment, selection and membership of the legislature, its organization, its practices in the transaction of business, lobbying, and legislative-executive relations.

"The legislature is not representative according to . . . proportionality of population. . . . The current political style of the state depends to a great extent upon a legislature which settles general issues by trading votes for local concessions, on legislators whose main service is as political brokers for their constituencies and for selected economic interests, and on a dispersal of both executive and legislative authority so that effective patterns of institutional leadership and a majority consensus are precluded from politics. . . . Much of the organization and procedure of the Florida legislature has been pressed into the service of the political groups which have become dominant through the geographical system of apportionment. . . . In Florida the election is a more or less disagreeable means of entry into the real world of politics, which consists almost exclusively of the personal relations among those who have been admitted to the inner circle. . . . Without a party or factional organization which he can look to for support and guidance (and can influence reciprocally), the slender new legislative reed can soon be bent in the direction in which the legislative leaders wish. . . . The organization of the legislature is also malleable and has been shaped to the demands of the system . . . neither do its processes permit much confidence in its rationality" (pp. 242–245). The absence of clear gubernatorial leadership, in part because of the strength of an elective cabinet, and the problems of coming to grips with state responsibilities are also examined.

The authors' suggested remedies (pp. 250–252) are principally institutional reforms, but they recognize also (pp. 253–254) the need for party government. They issue no clarion call, however, for a two-party system. They have dealt well with the pathology of Florida legislative politics. Time or other studies will reveal whether they may have underpainted the basic and potential strength and promise of the legislature in political accommodation and in the molding of consensus.

FRANKLIN L. BURDETTE
Professor and Director
Bureau of Governmental Research
University of Maryland

BURL NOGGLE. *Teapot Dome: Oil and Politics in the 1920's.* Pp. ix, 234. Baton Rouge: Louisiana State University Press, 1962. $6.00.

The tribulations of the Harding Administration have become identified in political folklore with the leases of the Naval oil reserves in the Teapot Dome area, and the investigations subsequently conducted with such zeal and fairness by the Senate Committee on Public Lands and Surveys are vivid examples of the usefulness of such inquiries. The scandal has

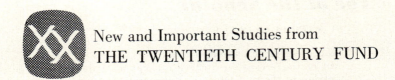

become a modern morality play, with scalawags in office receiving money for betraying the public interest and courageous Senators exposing the shameless action. But there is more to the affair than the exposure of wrong-doing, and Mr. Noggle, with the perseverance of a Senator Walsh, has gone into the background of the leases, which he shows to be a phase of the prolonged conflict between conservationists and their opponents for the control of public lands and forests.

The details of the background have been supplied by the papers of Harry A. Slattery, one of the little-known figures of the controversy, who operated offstage, pulling the right strings and seeing the right people to make things happen. Slattery was a dedicated conservationist, a former secretary of their trade association, and later, under the New Deal, he served briefly as Undersecretary of the Interior and administrator of the Rural Electrification Administration. The story of the part played by the conservation lobby in the political process is well done, and we learn of their vigil before the 1920 political conventions, of their efforts to commit Harding to a conservationist platform and to influence the appointment of the Secretary of the Interior. The nomination of Senator Fall was a shocker, but the conservationists mobilized political support to frustrate his design on the Forest Service. The early issues were routine, and Governor Pinchot, the conservation leader, we are told, was "still unable to see the oil for the forests." But oil was in the air; Senator La Follette was persuaded to introduce a resolution of inquiry, and Fall resigned his post after two years in office.

Mr. Noggle is intrigued by the political "fallout," as it were, of the investigation; some reputations were lost, and among the innocent victims was W. G. McAdoo, whose political career was blighted because it was his misfortune to have had Edward L. Doheney for a client. President Coolidge comes out very well indeed: he kept his job and his reputation, and we are delighted to learn that he slyly invited Mr. Slattery to the White House to be briefed on just what was going on in Washington.

ROLAND YOUNG
Professor of Political Science
Northwestern University

JOSEPH L. MORRISON. *Josephus Daniels Says . . . : An Editor's Political Odyssey from Bryan to Wilson and F. D. R., 1894–1913.* Pp. x, 339. Chapel Hill: University of North Carolina Press, 1962. $7.50.

Josephus Daniels Says . . . is a worthy addition to the growing list of excellent biographies and monographs that, taken together, constitute the best existing body of literature on the history of any single American state since the Reconstruction period. The present volume is not and was not meant to be a personal biography, although Daniels lives vividly in all his warmth and personal greatness in these pages. Dr. Morrison's book is, rather, a study of Daniels' training, growth, and leadership in journalism and politics between 1882 and 1913. It was a turbulent era in North Carolina, and the "Tar Heel Editor" was inevitably in the thick of almost every fight—the Populist revolt, the campaign to disfranchise Negroes, the fight for public education, battles for railroads and trusts, and the movement for Wilson's nomination in 1912. This book shows clearly enough why Daniels was a powerful force long before he carved his niche in national history as Secretary of the Navy in the Wilson administration and as President Franklin Roosevelt's Ambassador to Mexico.

A brief review cannot possibly do full justice to the merits of this book. Perhaps the most important thing to say is that the author has been fair, objective, and properly critical. He has also shed much new light on controverted episodes, particularly the incident involving Professor John Spencer Bassett at Trinity College in 1903 and the three-cornered fight for the senatorial nomination in 1912 among Furnifold M. Simmons, William W. Kitchin, and Walter Clark. The author has given us what is, along with

Dewey M. Grantham's biography of Hoke Smith of Georgia, the best account of the dilemmas and frustrations that plagued Progressives in the South in the first decade of this century, and one of the best analyses of the political metamorphosis that transformed many southern agrarians into Progressives. Finally, Dr. Morrison has made an important contribution to the history of modern American journalism in his excellent chapters on Daniels and the Raleigh *News and Observer*.

This book parallels Daniels' first volume in his own memoirs, *Tar Heel Editor*. Dr. Morrison resisted the temptation, if ever he felt it, to rely upon his subject for facts and interpretations. His account is based on prodigious research in newspapers and manuscript collections, and he makes no statements that cannot be supported by contemporary evidence. The result is solid history and an important contribution to recent American history.

ARTHUR S. LINK

Princeton University

JOHN HOPE FRANKLIN. *The Emancipation Proclamation*. Pp. x, 181. Garden City, N. Y.: Doubleday, 1963. $3.50.

The author begins his discussion with a chapter entitled "The Precedents and the Pressures," in which he deals with the nineteenth-century forces in various parts of the world working against the institution of slavery and also with the techniques and methods used to implement the legal destruction of the institution. Logically, there follows an account of the confused attitude in the North toward the slavery question during the early stages of the war, with emphasis upon Lincoln's plans for compensated emancipation plus colonization and upon the forces that ultimately brought the President to the issuance of the Proclamation. Though the advice given to Lincoln is by no means neglected, primary attention is paid to the evolution of the document in his mind.

The checkered response to the Proclamation is effectively presented. Some received it enthusiastically, others strongly denounced it, and others appeared to await future implications before registering positive judgments. The author appears to feel that the President's action harmed the Republicans more than it helped them in the congressional elections of 1862, though he points out that other issues weakened them in those elections.

Although the Proclamation is viewed as both a moral pronouncement and one designed to help win the war, emphasis is placed upon the former of these after the definitive document, somewhat revised, was issued January 1, 1863. A new purpose—emancipation—was now involved in the struggle, with the result that European sentiment became less friendly to the South and more so to the North. Good evidence on this point is, however, advisedly tempered by suggestions of growing European interest in northern wheat and Union victories. "Only gradually," states the author, "as Union victories gave support to the Proclamation, did its effect on European attitude become clear" (p. 78). The definitive Proclamation, which provided for the employment of slaves as soldiers, is claimed to have still further weakened their loyalty and aroused their enthusiasm because it now gave them a definitive purpose for which to fight.

In this generally good analytical work, two points might have received more emphasis. Lincoln's pre-Civil War moral views on slavery are properly included, but his political and social views on that problem are neglected. And the references to the connection between the Confiscation Act of July 17, 1862, and the President's Proclamation leave this reviewer, at least, rather confused as to just what the relationship was between those documents, somewhat different in scope and nature.

HENRY H. SIMMS

Professor of History
Ohio State University

PAGE SMITH. *John Adams*, Vol. 1: *1735–1784*; Vol. 2: *1784–1826*. Pp. xx, 1170. New York: Doubleday, 1962. $14.50.

If Samuel Johnson had his Boswell, John Adams now has his Smith. Of course, there are contrasts: Boswell was Johnson's contemporary and confidant while Smith lives two centuries later than Adams. Adams, however, bridged the chronological gap as best he could by keeping a copious diary, by writing an autobiography, by saving tens of thousands of letters, and by preserving other biographical materials. Indeed, no one, not even Jefferson, among the founding fathers preserved for posterity more completely the efforts of a fruitful and long life of public service than did John Adams. Until recently none of the Adams Papers were available. Professor Smith, among the first scholars to use them, has certainly written the definitive biography of the second President of the United States.

And yet as excellent as this book is, it is not without blemish. This reviewer, at least, wishes that the author had treated more at length and convincingly the crisis of the Alien and Sedition Acts and the Kentucky and Virginia Resolutions. Moreover, at times Professor Smith seems to hurry along in his narrative when a pause for a succinct interpretation of Adams' arguments here or a brief stop to reveal his subject's mental workings there, would have added in the complete presentation of John Adams and would have given the reader a more thorough knowledge of one of the hitherto lesser known of the founding fathers. Especially perhaps would many readers like more interpretation about the quarter-century that John Adams lived after he left the presidency and during which he carried on a voluminous correspondence. But why quibble over the few minor dark spots on a brilliantly executed canvas?

Dr. Smith has written with imagination and sympathy toward his subject although his work is in no sense a eulogy. Indeed, Adams himself left in his autobiography, his diary, and his letters ample evidence of his own shortcomings. He was awkward, aloof, cold, haughty, quarrelsome, vain, ambitious, highly sensitive, even self-righteous—to name some of the more obvious character defects. To offset such unfortunate traits as these, Adams was courageous, faithful, honest, intelligent, sincere, tenacious, trustworthy and vigorous. All of these personality traits and

more, the author shows in his scholarly treatment. Others have discussed Adams' public career with varying degrees of success, but none has given posterity the complete picture. Here for the first time is set forth in ample detail the lasting love affair between John Adams and Abigail. Not only were these two married for many years, but they were lovers throughout their lives. Here was one of the most successful marriages imaginable.

What will be the primary consequence of Professor Smith's monumental study of our first Massachusetts-born President? Obviously, some of the more critical conclusions about John Adams will be corrected. Adams will rise in esteem among students of American history and more especially among scholars of the presidency. But Adams, even with the aid of this splendid tribute, will not become one of our half-dozen really great Presidents. His stature will be enlarged and he will be more appreciated: this will be the net result of Professor Smith's efforts, and this is no small achievement for a biographer. Awarded the Kenneth Roberts prize, Mr. Smith is destined for greater recognition for this superbly written book. Both publisher and author are to be congratulated on a task well done.

GEORGE OSBORN
Professor of Social Science
University of Florida

BENJAMIN FRANKLIN. *The Papers of Benjamin Franklin,* Vol. 6: *April 1, 1755 through September 30, 1756.* Edited by Leonard W. Labaree, in association with Ralph L. Ketcham, and assisted by Helen C. Boatfield and Helene H. Fineman. Pp. xxix, 581. New Haven: Yale University Press, 1963. $10.00.

This volume centers around the beginning of Indian warfare on the Pennsylvania frontier in 1755 and 1756. In it, Franklin played a dominant role both as a legislator and as a military officer. After Braddock's tragic defeat on July 9, 1755, the governor asked the assembly to raise funds and forces. The assembly answered with a bill including the taxing of the proprietary property, which the governor's instructions forbade him to sign. Franklin, as committeeman, in the name of the assembly answered that he believed the people would not sacrifice their liberty for a little temporary defense support. From early August to the last of November, the assembly, under his influence, held out until the proprietors offered £5000 toward defense, and a crowd of frontiersmen came to town demanding help, many having lost their homes, their crops, and their families. The assembly now passed a bill that the governor could sign, for it accepted the gift in place of taxation of proprietary property. With an additional grant of £55,000 a defense program began.

This whole episode was typical of Franklin's way of specious arguing, not from principle previously held, but from his view of a given problem. His stand was that, though the governor was instructed against signing such bills, he should, in the light of the great need, disobey them for the sake of a higher duty. He considered the proprietor first as just one of the property holders, then like the lords in England. But actually the proprietor represented the king who established proprietaries as palatinates, usually with the power of the Bishop of Durham, saving only the sovereignty of the king, though the Penn charter did not contain the Durham clause. Franklin had no argument which would hold against the proprietor, for the charter even gave him the authority to assume control in time of emergency, except in regard to the property of the inhabitants. Moreover, for the proprietor to have conceded the point, along with assembly claims to sole power in money affairs, would have given that body the power to destroy the proprietor and his province, the same principle involved in the *McCulloch* v. *Maryland* case in the nineteenth century when the latter tried to tax the national bank branch.

Once defense plans were started, Franklin got himself into the thick of fort-building and arming inhabitants, and eventually served as commander of the forces around Philadelphia, all of which could not have been easy for an inexperienced man of fifty. There seems to be today a changing conception of the editing of such papers as Franklin's, as though it were done more to give the general reader a comprehensive idea of what happened, filling in the gaps of the sources with history fragments, than to provide the research scholar with firsthand primary source material. This is the method used in this project. It would, however, make the collection more useful to novice scholars doing theses and honor papers if relatively little explaining were done than if the whole subject is worked out for them. Such a pattern of editing would also greatly reduce the expense.

Like the other volumes which have appeared in the series, this one is all that one could ask for in scholarship, while the contemporary scene, graphically pictured, makes the volume so interesting that one is led to sit down with it and read it from cover to cover like a novel, in spite of the occasional lengthy instrusions of historical narrative in the headnotes.

VIOLA F. BARNES
Professor of History, Emeritus
Mount Holyoke College

WILLIAM KELLAWAY. *The New England Company, 1649–1776: Missionary Society to the American Indians.* Pp. 303. New York: Barnes and Noble, 1962. $8.50.

Mr. Kellaway has provided us with a valuable account which serves to emphasize again the many close relationships between New England colonies and mother country through the seventeenth and eighteenth centuries. Again we become aware of the close identity in England between Nonconformist zeal and commercial interests. The Society for the Propagation of the Gospel in New England came into being by Act of the Long Parliament in 1649. It was a response to demands from the frontier areas for assistance in the necessary work of conversion and civilizing of the Indians and an expression, too, of individual enterprise which would have brought such an organization into being, even had the "first fruits" of missionary zeal not already been apparent. Publicity and fund-raising went together.

Here the author surveys the pamphlet literature which preceded and followed the Society's forming. Throughout the Interregnum, the Society had the encouragement of government, but at the Restoration it suffered the vicissitudes of uncertain politics and a threat to the property holdings which were its chief source of revenue. In 1660 it was incorporated by charter as a company, familiarly known as the New England Company. Notable among those " 'godly, able citizens' " who devoted their talents to more than one endeavor was its first governor, the scientist, Robert Boyle—a moderate Anglican sympathetic to Nonconformist views and having the necessary influence to enable it to surmount alterations in religious attitudes.

The author gives a detailed account of the work of the Company in England. Membership ran in families and, following Boyle's advice, was composed of men well-versed in "economical affairs." After 1759, they were also of unconcealed dissenting character. Across the Atlantic, commissioners managed the funds coming from England. Here we find well-known names: Winthrop, Mather, Hutchinson or, at a later period, Mayhew, Hancock, Oliver. But we are introduced to a new aspect of their work.

Three chapters the author devotes to those who spread the gospel, from the memorable John Eliot and Jonathan Edwards, to that last small group still at work when the Company decided in 1786 that it could no longer "exercise its trusts out of the King's dominions," and transferred its efforts to Canada, where it continues today. The painstaking work of translation of Bible and religious tracts is set forth in a chapter on "The Indian Library."

Mr. Kellaway lists the location and extent of his manuscript sources and includes an index which lists Company members, commissioners, and missionaries, with the dates of their service.

Frank J. Klingberg
Professor of History, Emeritus
University of California
Los Angeles

Theodore Draper. *Castro's Revolution: Myths and Realities.* Pp. vi, 211. New York: Frederick A. Praeger, 1962. $4.50.

This is a revision of three essays which originally appeared in *Encounter*. The first demolishes some of the myths and misconceptions about the Cuban revolution which won it the sympathy of many intellectuals in other countries—myths and misconceptions that were propagated both by apologists who knew they were false and by observers misled by revolutionary propaganda or by their own imaginations. Castro's policies, as they developed, not only betrayed those who fought the revolution with him, but cruelly disillusioned many of his supporters abroad.

The second essay, "How NOT to Overthrow Castro," helps to explain the fiasco of the Bay of Pigs. Mr. Draper thinks that some American officials were not sufficiently aware of the implications of the ideological differences within the Cuban exile community or of the need to make sure of the support of the underground in Cuba. Last-minute efforts to deal with both problems had no result because both the Americans and the Cuban leaders in the training camps thought that the invasion must take place before Castro received further supplies of Communist arms. The Revolutionary Council, which was set up by the principal exile groups in March 1961, seems to have been treated rather disdainfully by those in charge of the invasion.

In general, the author is somewhat critical of the policy of the United States. He does not believe that disloyalty or ineptitude at Washington helped Castro to defeat Machado, or, as another group have asserted, that the State Department refused Castro aid and thus forced him to turn to Russia. On the other hand, he characterizes the policy of the Eisenhower administration as "at best, cautious and indecisive." He does not discuss the reasons why more aggressive action seemed inadvisable or suggest what effective action, short of armed intervention, was practicable.

The third essay, on "Castro and Communism," is especially interesting. Though Castro in some of his speeches has asserted that he was always a Marxist at heart, his attitude, as Mr. Draper shows, has been curiously ambivalent. On several occasions he has admitted, with a humility that seems curiously out of character, that he has only gradually come to an understanding of what communism really means. Mr. Draper doubts whether his conversion is yet complete, and thinks that Castro's inherent instability makes it hazardous to predict his future course.

DANA G. MUNRO
William Stewart Tod
   Professor of History, Emeritus
Princeton University

EUROPEAN GOVERNMENT AND HISTORY

A. M. MCBRIAR. *Fabian Socialism and English Politics, 1884–1918.* Pp. x, 387. New York: Cambridge University Press, 1962. $9.50.

Dr. McBriar's book satisfies a very real need: that for an assessment of the Fabians neither too smoothly "authorised history," nor denigratory of a remarkable body of men and women. It has its flashes of wit in the academic Fabian manner, but, while not too insufferably austere, it never descends to the still more insufferable flippancy which an external view of so serious-minded a company often evokes. The book is exactly what it sets out to be: a review, sympathetic but balanced and critical, of just what Fabian influence amounted to, whether in its original stronghold of Progressive politics on the London County Council—a body after all fully equal, in 1900, to many a sovereign state in the United Nations in

1960—or in the declining Liberal and the rising Labour parties.

There can be no gainsaying the meticulous and yet modest scholarship of the book, and its organization is clear and logical. The general conclusion is what one might expect: pervasive as Fabian influence was, and on occasion significant, on the whole it was neither originally creative nor decisive in actual situations. Given the English empirical tradition and sociopolitical structure, something like this would have happened had the particular Fabians never come together in their particular society, but as codifiers and expositors of a *Zeitgeist* they played an invaluable role. Most surprising and revealing of the general findings, perhaps, is the astonishing insularity of the Fabian world view—if indeed that is not a contradiction in terms: to us, conditioned to see the twenty years 1894–1914 as a march to Armageddon, it is astonishing to see how little this group of educated, intelligent, and well-informed people seem to have noticed what was happening. Their almost offensive preoccupation with the immediately practical served their future reputation ill in this respect, not to mention the ambiguity of some of their flirtations: Rosebery's was the wrong horse to back.

Dr. McBriar tells the Fabian story with erudition and some elegance, but perhaps with something of the defects of the Fabian virtues. If one has a complaint, it is that the story is too thinly colored and too impersonal. It is true that we need no irrelevant scandals about the extra-—or intra-?—mural activities of H. G. Wells, and in the austerest pages the personality of Bernard Shaw simply cannot be kept down, but, while Hubert Bland and Sydney Webb come through, justice is scarcely done to Beatrice. One would have liked also some consideration of the Fabian aftermath: after all, if the Communists did capture the Fabian Research Department, party writers like Emile Burns and Page Arnot retained some Fabian empiricism and suavity. But such complaints, perhaps personal to this reviewer, cannot detract from the real and

Kindly mention THE ANNALS *when writing to advertisers*

considerable achievement of the book: a solid and excellently balanced survey of a political movement remarkable in its origins and its development, and even in its very English ordinariness.

O. H. K. SPATE

Australian National University
Canberra

C. A. R. CROSLAND. *The Conservative Enemy: A Programme of Radical Reform for the 1960's.* Pp. 251. New York: Schocken, 1963. $4.95.

This book is a series of essays which do constitute an excellent, well-argued program for radical reform in Britain as seen by a Labour Member of Parliament who is a vigorous right-wing Socialist. But its title seems a bit unfortunate, and from its program there are strange omissions. *The Conservative Enemy* suggests a kind of hostility that one does not find in the book. The "New Left" in his own party, specifically the other Crossland, with an extra "s," seem to him to be about as much "the enemy" as the Conservatives.

By and large, this reviewer would go along with Mr. Crosland's reforms, most of which are applicable in principle to America, and all of which shed light on the British economic and political situation. His radical reforms—and many of them are radical—might be considered in this country less as a somewhat revisionist statement of socialism than as a more thoughtful expansion of what we call—not too accurately—advanced "liberalism," than Americans of a non-Socialist left usually give it. But I should welcome him as a Socialist comrade who cogently suggests means to Socialist ends involving less socialization of ownership, and less emphasis on it, than was once the Socialist custom. He plays down the class struggle as central and exalts what is or ought to be the role of the consumer. He talks—and documents—vigorous common sense on heavy inheritance taxation, the role of mass media, advertising, the use of land and urban planning, and the status of labor unions and corporations. But he scarcely alludes to matters like the Common

Market, disarmament, or foreign policy generally. He specifically gives disarmament a low place on his list of priorities in Socialist issues in Britain. This may conform to the fact that Britain depends so largely on American defense and spends, relatively, so little. Its defense policies have not bred so large a military-industrial complex as Eisenhower warned us against.

But it is a great weakness in so substantial a book that it does not discuss socialism and peace or a Socialist foreign policy for Britain. The author does show his awareness that Socialist principles and Socialist ethics must find expression in the great ascent of nations emerging out of deep poverty, but this awareness is not manifest on the informed and suggestive level of other of his issues, and it is not related to a comprehensive program for peace. He ignores almost wholly the struggle in his own party on nuclear disarmament and its influence in the world. Automation also seems to present to him no such problem as it seems to present in the United States.

In short, the book is better as a program against Conservatives in Britain than as a significant inquiry into the role of socialism in our interdependent world.

NORMAN THOMAS

New York City

ROBERT HEUSSLER. *Yesterday's Rulers: The Making of the British Colonial Service.* Pp. xxvi, 260. Syracuse, N. Y.: Syracuse University Press, 1963. $5.75.

Dr. Heussler has written an account of the British colonial service that is sympathetic in the exact sense of the word; he has tried to understand how things were done and why they were done as they were. His interest is in selection and training and how they affected the colonial empire and its aftermath; this is in no sense intended to be a history of the colonial service, and there is not much about what colonial officers actually did. But there is considerable detail about the way they were chosen. For this, Dr. Heussler has supplemented his written sources by interviews with all the right people, and his analysis is both workman-like and perceptive.

He is mildly surprised that selection should have been so much a matter of personal contacts and therefore so frankly based on a form of education that was available only to the "privileged classes." But—with what to one bred in the system seems remarkable good sense—he bases his judgments on the class structure and assumptions of the period he is writing about, not of today. He describes the ideals and spirit of the British public schools and of Oxford, seeing rightly that the colonial service grew from them, and missing, I think, only one major point—made with sledge-hammer overemotion in an early Kipling story, *The Flag of their Country*—that while service, patriotism, responsibility, paternal rule over others might be the ideals of Governors and Headmasters, boys openly mocked at them or were embarrassed at their mention, while inwardly accepting them. The Colonial Service aimed at the ideal product of this set of values, the man who had won school and college colors, had taken "a good second" in Classics, above all had been head of his house and president of the junior common room. Such men were often prepared to live in extreme discomfort and loneliness, and to administer primitive tribes with admirable justice and paternal affection; at first not always sympathetic to "the educated native," they showed surprising adaptability in the last phase of preparation for independence, taking orders from African ministers who were often eager to reverse their policies and whom they were bound to regard as inexperienced. This was perhaps their chief glory.

Looking at the British Empire at the mement of its greatest physical extent, Dr. Heussler finds some truth in the cliché about absent-mindedness, in its administration if not in its acquisition. There is no theory of empire, as with the French; management of the great sprawling ramshackle congeries might be discussed in London and Oxford, but—as Dr. Heussler points out—if any decision was reached, it was likely to melt away in the course of transmission to the circumference and to be disregarded or reinterpreted on the spot. To one intimately concerned with India, and much more detachedly with Africa, one of the oddest and most revealing things about the whole business is the complete disregard in Africa of Indian experience. That the two overseas empires had nothing whatever to learn from each other was so fundamental an assumption that it was never even questioned; in all his researches, Dr. Heussler found no mention of the training college started by Wellesley in Calcutta in 1800, of Hailey-bury as an Indian Civil Service training college from 1806 to 1859, of the brief experiment in selection by examination in 1833, of its abandonment and resumption in 1856, of the constant changes in age of recruitment for the Indian Civil Service thereafter. Yet surely there was something to be learned from so much discussion, experiment, and experience.

Dr. Heussler concludes—and I agree—that the chief memorial to the Colonial Service, and indeed to British rule, will be not institutions but personal memories and the example of district officers. His book is an important prologue to the full history of the Colonial Service which needs to be written.

PHILIP MASON

Director
Institute of Race Relations
London

STANLEY HOFFMANN, CHARLES P. KINDLE-BERGER, LAURENCE WYLIE, JESSE R. PITTS, JEAN-BAPTISTE DUROSELLE, and FRANÇOIS GOGUEL. *In Search of France*. Pp. xiii, 443. Cambridge, Mass.: Harvard University Press, 1963. $8.95.

Recently an American poet and critic reviewing the work of another poet suggested that his poetry would be improved if he took the risk of using words other than "heart," "love," and "death." Students of modern France must take a similar risk and learn to discuss the Republic without using such exhausted concepts as that of the "bourgeois" and France's *élan vital*. The six contributors to this valuable book have in the main avoided the tired and thin metaphors conventional in the history of France. This is especially true of Stanley Hoffmann's acute one-hundred-page analysis of the "Paradoxes of the French Political Community." Charles Kindleberger's examination of "The Postwar Resurgence of the French Economy" brilliantly exposes the limits of the accepted explanations for France's economic pace in the past and her present spectacular economic growth, while Laurence Wylie's original and fresh treatment of the communities of Chanzeaux and Roussillon from the viewpoint of "Social Change at the Grass Roots" is unsurpassed for its concreteness, breadth, realism, and life.

Jesse R. Pitts's "Continuity and Change in Bourgeois France" is, unfortunately, much less successful. His sociological essay, depending upon such concepts as that of the "nuclear family," "peer groups," "delinquent communities," and "do-good communities," gives the impression that the same essay would have been written if the author's subject had been a society other than that of France. Professor Jean-Baptiste Duroselle reviewing the "Changes in French Foreign Policy since 1945" presents France as more passive and "introversive" in attitude than the customary image of the nation suggests. He shares the pride of his countrymen in France's continuing civilizing "mission" and notes that the budget for "cultural relations" is never challenged. Finally François Goguel, Secretary General of the French Senate, attempts a balanced judgment of the "Six Authors in Search of a National Character."

All the contributors to this good collection are in agreement that France's future is obscure, paradoxical and, most likely, a troubled one. General de Gaulle is thought to have fashioned little that will be institutionally permanent. It is also properly felt that France's political parties will experience, after the General's departure, grave difficulties in creating a vital role for themselves in the political life of their nation.

It is to be regretted that none of the authors have considered in any detail the embarrassing question as to the quality of freedom existing in contemporary France. The role of the police, their constant presence, perhaps unequaled in France's history, must be part of any accurate picture of the Fifth Republic. Professors Hoffmann and Kindleberger have soundly developed the contemporary French trust in planification. Yet all of the authors have shied away from the implications of this trust. There is in modern France an ill-concealed feeling of sophistication and condescension toward governments and societies that identify themselves as democracies in spirit and form. France's disenchantment with the democratic revolution of the West may well be the final and unhappy ending to the dreams of a new future for mankind that began so promisingly in 1789.

EDWARD T. GARGAN
Professor of History
Wesleyan University

OTTO PFLANZE. *Bismarck and the Development of Germany: The Period of Unification, 1815–1871.* Pp. 510. Princeton: Princeton University Press, 1963. $10.00.

The career of Prince Otto von Bismarck has been a source of deep and continual interest to the historical mind for over a century. Since his rise to power in 1862, a flood of research and speculation has been devoted to his achievements and shortcomings, especially in Germany, where his credits and debits have been audited and reaudited by innumerable writers. The debacle of 1945 released a new generation of critics, who have turned to his personality and his work in their search for clues that might explain the "German catastrophe." Professor Pflanze's book has benefited from this wealth of material; the author has studied not only the tremendous bulk of source material dealing with the unification, but also the many controversial interpretations given to the architect of the Second Empire. The result is most satisfying. No other work, at least in English, offers the reader so complete a picture of German politics between 1862 and 1871, combined with so sound a judgment on the historical implications of the facts presented.

Professor Pflanze's book is not a biography in the traditional sense; it is more in the nature of a political biography. The human element—an absorbing subject in the case of Bismarck—is relegated to second place; the events, either influenced or shaped by the Chancellor, occupy first place. Professor Pflanze admires the diplomatic skill by means of which Bismarck bent every occurrence in these critical years to his advantage. He notes that Bismarck approached every problem, whether great or small, with a series of alternatives up his sleeve, a method which gave his transactions great flexibility, but also cast over them the shadow of shiftiness and ambiguity.

The dexterity with which he pursued his goal against both domestic and international opposition is, indeed, an extraordinary spectacle. However, Dr. Pflanze is aware that Bismarck cannot be classified merely as a diplomatic virtuoso. He remains the dominating statesman of the European state-system from 1862 to 1890, and this fact leads us to a further question: What kind of statesman was he? Professor Pflanze views him as essentially a Prussian. His rise to power and his entire policy of unification were determined by a Prussian desire for aggrandizement. He relied on Prussian militarism and Hohenzollern authoritarianism as his basic weapons. German nationalism must, therefore, be considered a less important ingredient in Bismarck's political program. This is not to say that Professor Pflanze agrees with Rothfels and others that Bismarck was a man alien to his time. On the contrary, he says, "It is utterly incorrect to depict Bismarck as a man out of his age." Pflanze sees him rather as a statesman who used moral and ideological forces as means, not ends.

In support of his thesis, Professor Pflanze describes German nationalism prior to 1870 as weak and lethargic, a judgment which can hardly be justified by the attitude of the German people during the Franco-Prussian war, and which is certainly refuted by the excesses of national-

ism to which the Germans—like most Europeans—gave themselves over before the first world war. Pflanze calls Bismarck the political surgeon who amputated nationalism from liberalism, and conservatism from legitimism. The result of his surgery was a new synthesis in German political attitudes compounded of nationalism, militarism, and authoritarianism. This reviewer concurs with Professor Pflanze's indictment, if indictment it is meant to be, and is also in agreement with his appraisal of Bismarck's fight against liberalism and constitutionalism. Bismarck's sense of ethical responsibility was, we must admit, no substitute for legal and institutional checks on the use and abuse of power. This reviewer, however, differs from Professor Pflanze in the evaluation of the international situation. In view of the blindness of the Austrian leadership, what solution other than the *Kleindeutsche* would have been possible?

It is tragically ironic that Bismarck himself became the victim of Hohenzollern authoritarianism in 1890, as did the German people in 1914. Professor Pflanze's narrative of the German unification reveals an intimate knowledge of the complexity of party life, of parliamentary alignments, and of court intrigues in the period prior to 1871. The second volume of *Bismarck and the Development of Germany* is anticipated with great interest.

GERHARD MASUR
Professor and Chairman
Department of History
Sweet Briar College
Virginia

ALFRED J. RIEBER. *Stalin and the French Communist Party, 1941–1947*. Pp. xiv, 395. New York: Columbia University Press, 1962. $7.50.

Mr. Rieber's book deals with an important subject, and readers should not be put off either by its inordinate length or by its inaccurate title. What Stalin's own relations, if any, were with the French Communist party, we do not and cannot know; as Mr. Rieber points out we have hardly any information even on the more general question as to the methods, if any, by which the Soviet Communist party attempted to guide the conduct of their French comrades. What we have here is a particular instance of a general problem, the requirement that all foreign Communist parties should use their position to fortify their own grip on the institutions of the country in which they operate, and to serve the interest of the world Communist movement as defined by the Soviet leadership. Sometimes these two aspects of their task conflict with adverse consequences, either for Soviet policy, or for the party, or for both.

Mr. Rieber has little to add to the knowledge we already possess about the wartime dilemmas of French communism either before the Nazi attack on Russia or during the Resistance period. His real subject begins with the Liberation and the Communist role in the "tripartite" governments that followed it. In his view, the Russians hoped that events in France would follow the Czechoslovak model, and for this to happen the Communists must not allow themselves to be jockeyed into opposition. This made them take up positions on internal policy—wages for instance—and on colonial questions which were difficult to reconcile with their class position or doctrinal commitment.

Even more important were questions of foreign policy. The Soviet aims in Germany were difficult to square with France's needs, and the Soviet Union did not think France's support important enough to justify modifying its own views. On the questions of the Saar, the Rhineland, and the Ruhr, it was difficult for the French Communists to avoid getting out of step —though the Soviet Government does not seem to have taken this too hard.

In fact, the Soviet leaders were clear that what would decide the political evolution of Europe was the balance between the Great Powers; if the Anglo-Saxons were determined to stay in western Europe there was no prospect of Communist victory. By their own handling of the situations they hardened this determination. They concentrated upon consolidating their hold upon eastern Europe and eastern Germany. The French could only

meet their own immediate requirements by aligning themselves with the United States and Britain. The "tripartite" regime in France had no further *raison d'être*.

Insofar as the story can be followed from external sources, Mr. Rieber makes a good job of it. His book lacks the human dimension. No attempt is made to penetrate below the surface of diplomacy and politics. Of the drama and passion of the time there is no trace. His thorough bibliography does not contain a single novel.

MAX BELOFF
Gladstone Professor of Government
and Public Administration
All Souls College
University of Oxford

JOHN KOSA. *Two Generations of Soviet Man: A Study in the Psychology of Communism.* Pp. viii, 214. Chapel Hill: University of North Carolina Press, 1962. $5.00.

A variety of approaches have been used in attempting to order the data of modern communism. In this study, the author treats communism as an updated, Marxian version of Oriental despotism. Its essence he believes to be the imposition by a power monopoly of all norms, goals, and values. Assuming that the Russian Communist leaders planned from the very beginning to create "Soviet men"—people who accept sincerely the demands of the "Red Superego"—he postulates that by 1945 a generation of such men had indeed been molded in Soviet Russia. The regime then set about to prove that its formula had universal application by implementing it in the satellite nations. This is the second of the generations mentioned in the title and the one with which the author is principally concerned. Maintaining that the "party state . . . [has no] function more important than the over-all enforcement of the superego," he applies the method of social psychology and devotes most of his book to a description of the character of the Red superego, the methods it uses to achieve its aims, and the reaction of the population.

Will the Communist experiment succeed? The author believes it may. With the help of Khrushchev's greater flexibility in method, the Communists have been able to manipulate the beliefs even of nations that lack an uninterrupted tradition of pariah psychology and, unless the trend be reversed, a second generation of Soviet men may be created as quickly as the first. "We are approaching the era of the manipulated man," the author concludes. Coexistence is impossible, war fearful to contemplate. But it may be possible for the West to convert its opponent peacefully, and to this task he summons the forces of democracy.

There are serious difficulties in the way of accepting this work as an important contribution to our understanding of communism. Much depends on the validity of the conceptual framework, but the Oriental despotism theme is by no means convincingly demonstrated. There are other serious shortcomings. The author generalizes far beyond his evidence, reveals little sense of historical development, and fails to reckon satisfactorily with the implications of a superego that demands perfect identification but is willing in practice to accept much less. The book is worth reading chiefly for its suggestive insights into personal reactions, especially of the intelligentsia, to the kind of demands made on belief and behavior in a Communist state.

NATHAN SMITH
Associate Professor and Chairman
Department of History and Political
Science
Washington College
Chestertown
Maryland

THEODORE E. KRUGLAK. *The Two Faces of TASS.* Pp. 263. Minneapolis: University of Minnesota Press, 1962. $5.00.

The official news agency of the Soviet Union, TASS, has frequently been described in the halls and the committee rooms of Congress as "the official liar of the Soviet Government," "the cover for Soviet military intelligence," and worse. No one, says the author of this study, has a kind word for TASS, except American news agency executives. They have been

exchanging news and services with TASS and its predecessor for forty years, and they know that, despite frequent difficulties, this is a form of coexistence that has worked to mutual advantage.

How it has done so and what some of the difficulties are, are discussed in Theodore Kruglak's book, the first serious inquiry into the history and operation of the Soviet news organization. The author, formerly professor of journalism and provost of Long Island University and, more recently, director of the Leysin American School in Switzerland, has succeeded admirably in describing the evolution of the agency, its relationship with its government, its foreign branches, and the way in which they are staffed, while at the same time analyzing its principles of operation, the techniques used in the gathering and dissemination of news, and the distinction which its staff members make between "hard news" and "features" —or propaganda. He is critical of the general assumption that TASS is a cover for espionage, describing the cases that are usually cited to support this view but concluding that most TASS men are genuine newspapermen engaged in their trade and with no time for cloak and dagger activities—in which, indeed, experience shows they are not particularly gifted. He expresses the belief that the Soviet government has not sought to employ TASS as a spy service for the last decade.

The most fascinating chapters in Mr. Kruglak's account, apart from those that deal with TASS's early directors and their unhappy fate in the period of the purges, have to do with the way in which TASS newsmen report news from the United States and how the transmitted news is doctored for home readers and, conversely, the way in which the agency beams news of the Soviet Union abroad. The image of the United States that emerges from TASS reports is a distorted one, but not necessarily, Mr. Kruglak argues, because of deliberate misrepresentation. It is the result rather of an emphasis upon political news and an almost total lack of coverage of American cultural, scientific, and educational achievements. The image of the Soviet Union is no more objective, because in projecting it TASS acts less as a news agency than as a sort of information service like the United States Information Agency, "determined to impress the world with the accomplishments of the nation, rather than compete with other international news agencies in reporting all the news."

GORDON A. CRAIG
Stanford University

JAMES BOWEN. *Soviet Education: Anton Makarenko and the Years of Experiment.* Pp. xi, 232. Madison: University of Wisconsin Press, 1962. $5.00.

American educators who are familiar with Anton Makarenko's trilogy *The Road to Life*—a translation of the Russian *Pedagogischeskaya Poema*—are almost certain to be intrigued with the author's origins, ideological commitment to Soviet communism, and personal history. *The Road to Life* is an impressive account of one of the truly significant pedagogical experiments of the twentieth century.

In his slim and lucid volume, Bowen has undertaken three tasks. Makarenko's somewhat checkered career in seeking to rehabilitate Russia's postrevolutionary *besprizorniki*—war waifs and delinquents —is adequately sketched. We come to see Makarenko as an outstanding educational pioneer, something of a maverick, dedicated to youth, possessing an intuitive feel for what is genuine in human relationships, and with the true educator's flair for style.

Bowen's second task is to present us with synoptic and analytic accounts of Makarenko's chief writings. Here the treatment is much too brief and unintegrated to be considered definitive, although it is refreshing to find a non-Soviet scholar handling what is essentially strange and alien material in such an eminently fair and necessarily cautious manner.

Finally, the author attempts an assessment of Makarenko as educational philosopher and theoretician. This is the most demanding task of all, and it is no reflec-

tion on Bowen that he is unable to do the topic justice in the limited space at his command. Thus, it is perhaps misleading to say of Makarenko that he was "unsophisticated in higher thought," or to reduce the deeply poetic and philosophical side of his nature to a quite ordinary mystical intuition. Academic philosophizing and the higher thought are not necessarily equivalents, and while Makarenko was not a trained philosopher as was Dewey, there are many passages in Makarenko's writings which prove his ability to maneuver skillfully in the realm of lofty and austere ideas.

Bowen does come to grips with the chief problem presented by Makarenko as theoretician and empiricist. This is the problem of erecting a philosophy of education on the premise that man's collective needs and aspirations must determine his individual consciousness. From this followed the pedagogical problem of creating a system of self-perpetuating challenges which would elicit not only the stoic group loyalty of youth, but also their creative, imaginative, and personal yearnings. Makarenko was far from successful in solving these problems, and he faced certain untenable and even ominous contradictions which he was unable to resolve before his untimely death in 1939.

It is to be hoped that the appearance of Bowen's book—as well as Frederic Lilge's 1958 monograph, *Anton Semyonovitch Makarenko: An Analysis of His Educational Ideas in the Context of Soviet Society*—will initiate serious discussions among American educators on the applicability of Makarenko's views to our own pressing educational problems. Most of us would probably reject Makarenko's basic philosophical and psychological premises. But certainly in working with culturally deprived and delinquent children, to cite only one example, Makarenko may have much to teach us.

IVOR KRAFT
United States Department of Health,
Education and Welfare

J. K. ZAWODNY. *Death in the Forest: The Story of the Katyn Forest Massacre.*

Pp. xviii, 275. Notre Dame, Ind.: University of Notre Dame Press, 1962. $6.50.

The fate of Poland during World War II was more tragic than that of the other Allied nations. The first victim of the war, she was defeated within four weeks, and then, in accordance with the Stalin-Hitler Pact, was occupied by her two powerful totalitarian neighbors. This book deals with one of the ghastliest events of this double-barreled occupation, the disappearance of about 15,000 Polish prisoners of war.

After the German invasion of the Soviet Union, in accordance with a Soviet-Polish pact, Polish prisoners held in Russia were to be released and form a new Polish army. But of the 250,000 prisoners, 15,000 were missing; of 14 Polish generals only 2 were released, and of 300 high-ranking officers only 6. Numerous attempts of the Polish government-in-exile to find them were fruitless. High Soviet officials, including Stalin, gave evasive answers. When the Germans seized the area of Smolensk, not far from the Polish border, they discovered in the nearby Katyn Forest mass graves in which about 4,500 men in Polish uniforms were buried. The bodies, with hands tied by ropes behind their backs and with bullets in their necks, lay in ten to twelve layers one on top of the other. The ropes were of Russian, and the bullets of German, manufacture. The Germans accused the Russians of the murder of the prisoners and maintained that German bullets of this make had been sold to the Soviet Union and the Baltic States prior to 1939. Moscow indignantly denied the charge.

Dr. Zawodny has made a thorough study of the material pertaining to this case and has earnestly tried to find an unbiased answer to the tangled question of who committed the mass murder. He has combined factual and political analysis of the material, realizing, as have earlier students of the case, that both Germany and the Soviet Union might have been prompted by the same motive: the desire to exterminate Polish intellectuals, who constituted the majority of the officer corps

and were the potential leaders of a Polish fight for independence. The percentage of officers among the missing men was strikingly high.

In an attempt to prove their innocence, the Germans invited three commissions—a Polish Red Cross commission, an independent international commission of specialists from twelve countries, and a German Medical-Judiciary Commission—to investigate the matter. Hundreds of bodies were exhumed, autopsies were made, and numerous identification papers, letters, and photographs were found. Identification papers showed that among the victims were several hundred lawyers, hundreds of teachers, twenty-one university professors, and many physicians and journalists. The three German-sponsored commissions found that the mass murder had been committed in the spring of 1940 when Katyn was in Russian hands. But a special Soviet investigation commission, formed after the reoccupation of the region by the Soviet Union, decided that it had been committed in the fall of 1941 when Katyn was occupied by Germany.

Among the Allies, suspicion of the Soviet government was strong. But the Soviet Union was then enjoying high prestige owing to the magnificent war effort of the Russian army, and the Allied leaders were reluctant to charge Moscow with so hideous a war crime. Churchill put strong pressure on the Polish government-in-exile to abandon charges against the Soviet Union which might split the unity of the Allies at a crucial time. Dr. Zawodny stresses the remarkable fact that at the Nuremberg trials the Soviet Union charged Germany with the Katyn murders, but did not press the charges, obviously out of fear that an investigation might lead to unpleasant results. As to the Western Allies at Nuremberg, Churchill has stated in his memoirs that "it was decided by the Western governments concerned that the issue should be avoided, and the crime of Katyn was never probed in detail." But in 1952 a Select Committee of the United States Congress probed the case and issued a 2,000-page report that was not inhibited by such considerations and put the blame squarely on the Soviet Union.

Dr. Zawodny's presentation and analysis of the material throws important light on the case and proves Soviet guilt. The Katyn problem may now be considered solved, but the fate of the 10,500 still-missing Poles remains unknown.

SIMON WOLIN
Inter-University Project on the
  History of Menshevism
New York City

ROMAN DEBICKI. *Foreign Policy of Poland, 1919–39: From the Rebirth of the Polish Republic to World War II.* Pp. xi, 192. New York: Frederick A. Praeger, 1962. $5.50.

Coming to the present work fresh from Herbert Kaplan's recent (1962) chronicle of the steps leading up to the First Partition, one can but wonder how, in the twenty years from 1919 to 1939, Poland could have had the courage even to try to ward off what, from the beginning, could clearly be seen as the inevitable. In the two decades before 1772, when the Polish state was partitioned for the first time, three Powers had been waiting to perform the act of dismemberment. In the period of Debicki's study there were but two, Austria, which had been the first to "grab" the other time, having ceased to be a Power. That was the only difference, the number of partitioners. Everything else was the same.

Fully aware of the common purpose animating its two neighbors, we see the Polish state, nevertheless, dedicating itself to the task of warding off the inevitable doom, in the hope that by the time the day arrived two things would have happened to block the neighbors' designs. For one thing, by then Poland would be reckoned by both sides, Germany and the Soviet Union alike, as of greater value independent and intact, and serving as bridge and barrier between themselves, than she would be dismantled and therefore implacably irredentist. For another, by then Poland would have made so many friends abroad, that designs for dismemberment on the part of either neighbor would seem fool-

hardy, if not insane, as by then the Polish cause would have become identified inextricably with the general cause of stability and peace. To implement the ideals embodied in these two hopes became the object of Polish foreign policy from the beginning to the end of the twenty inter-war years. This Debicki makes plain: means differed, the end and goal remained the same.

Although recognized as a state early in 1919, Poland did not know until four years later in what her territory consisted, as it was not determined until March 1923, when at last the eastern frontier was confirmed by the Council of Ambassadors. Aleksander Skrzyński was Foreign Minister, and his policy as adopted at once was that of "equal balance" as between the two neighbors, Germany and the Soviet Union, on whose whims the life of the state depended. Naturally, he sought to win friends abroad, as did his successor, August Zaleski, Piłsudski's man in the Foreign Office following the coup of 1926, and their efforts bore fruit in the acceptance of Poland as a nonpermanent but renewable member of the Council of the League of Nations, following Germany's election to the Council in the autumn of 1926. The strategic position was employed conspicuously by Piłsudski a year later, in December 1927, when he faced the war-mongering Valdemaras of Lithuania in Geneva, with the question, "War—or peace?" and thus averted an incident which could have led to a general conflagration.

Toward the East, the policy of "equal balance" was implemented as early as in 1929, with the signing of the Litvinov Protocol and later by the Pact of Non-Aggression with the Soviet Union concluded on January 25, 1932. Toward the western neighbor, relations were stabilized by the Ten Year Non-Aggression Pact of January 26, 1934. Before signing this, Hitler had measured Piłsudski's temper in two "eyeball to eyeball" encounters in the waters around Danzig, and had not pressed the point, biding his time for picking off Poland until he had disposed first of Austria. Piłsudski, and his Minister Józef Beck, hoped by the Pact to gain time sufficient for the day when Hitler would strike, gravely miscalculating in this the speed with which Hitler would complete his revolution, and paying for the Pact with serious loss of prestige abroad.

Professor Debicki was an officer in his country's foreign service during the whole life of the Polish state, and is now on the staff of Georgetown University, with access to every source of material on the period of his study. He has used not only all official files but in addition many of those "stray documents outside the traditional diplomatic archives" which the historian of our era must consult if he is to understand interwar history, so many deals having been arranged and concluded in secret and by personal contact. As a result, his chronicle is authoritative and detailed, a sad reminder of twenty years in the life of a country which would have liked, and indeed tried, to "go it together" with other like-minded and peace-loving countries, but which in the end found it had always to "go it alone."

MARION MOORE COLEMAN
Cheshire
Connecticut

RICHARD F. STAAR. *Poland, 1944–1962: The Sovietization of a Captive People.* Pp. xviii, 300. Baton Rouge: Louisiana State University Press, 1962. $7.50.

This volume represents an ambitious attempt to describe the present structure and development of the political system of Poland. However, while the study contains much valuable information about the constitutional system and the organization of political institutions—the party as well as some "pressure groups"—it falls short of the author's intention "to indicate some of the sources which provide a key to the political structure of Eastern Europe" (p. vii).

Above all, the author's view of governmental and political dynamics of East European countries is somewhat one-sided. According to Staar, "policy since 1944 has been almost completely determined by the Kremlin. The basic motivating force behind this influence is a desire to transform the socio-political system of Poland into

one as closely like the Soviet prototype as possible" (p. 5). He sees Poland presently "in the third stage of development U.S.S.R. style . . . begun in October 1956" (p. 271). As a result, today, "the political structure of the country is actually based on the U.S.S.R. prototype . . . most tangibly portrayed through the adoption of a Stalin-type constitution." In international politics "Poland can hardly claim to have a policy of its own" and "the regime in Warsaw is a puppet of the Kremlin and, as such, loyally supports the latter" (p. 277).

In terms of this analysis the "Sovietization" of Poland has been an unbroken and unidirectional process since 1945, the end-product of which is seen as a replica of the Soviet system. The author practically ignores the political upheaval of October 1956, and regards its aftermath merely as a new stage of "Sovietization." In the author's view, today, just as a decade ago, Communist control over Poland is "virtually absolute" (p. 1) and the lack of personal freedom striking. This is, of course, true by the political standards of liberal democracy, but Communist systems should be, above all, studied in their own terms. Yet, the author does not make any attempt to compare Polish politics with the politics of other East European countries. In the absence of such an analysis the most important aspects of Polish communism remain unexplored, and little is being added to our knowledge of political change under conditions of totalitarian control.

ANDREW C. JANOS
Research Associate
Center of International Studies
Princeton University

ANDREW GLADDING WHITESIDE. *Austrian National Socialism before 1918.* Pp. 143. The Hague: Martinus Nijhoff, 1962. 11.75 D. guilders.

This review is being written in Salzburg on a historic anniversary, thirty years after Hitler's *"Machtergreifung,"* January 30, 1933. Twenty-five years ago Hitler occupied Austria via the *Anschluss.* Certain Austrians, as members of the *"Hitlerbewegung,"* played an important role in this event. It had several antecedents, both in fact and in ideology. Whiteside throws new light on one of these, though he admits that, while there are similarities between the German National Socialist Party and the Austrian, the nature and extent of their connection have not been sufficiently investigated by him (p. 121).

Yet, this much is certain and significant: of the Austrian National Socialist Party of the Monarchy, some leaders continued their work in the succession states. Riehl was active in the young Austrian Republic. In fact, he acted as executive secretary of a high-sounding office, the Interstate Chancellery, established to keep the fragmented prewar movement together. Significantly, the new Nationalsozialistische Deutsche Arbeiterpartei (NSDAP), founded in Munich in 1919, eagerly joined the Chancellery. Riehl even claimed credit for the adoption of the Swastika (1920) as the Nazi emblem. The Chancellery and affiliates agitated henceforth for *Anschluss*. It held two of its annual plenary sessions in Salzburg (1920, 1923). Hitler attended the first. After his release from Landsberg prison in 1924, he got complete control of the Chancellery; Riehl was ousted. By 1926 Hitler had succeeded in a thorough purge of all who had favored autonomy for the Austrian party.

Whence came this Austrian National Socialist Party? What were its aims? Whiteside answers by taking a careful sojourn into intellectual history, the political backgrounds and the industrial transformation of the Habsburg Monarchy, the peculiar problems of worker migrations, and eventual clashes in the Bohemian industrial districts. In 1904, at Trautenau in Bohemia, a party named the "Deutsche Arbeiterpartei" was organized. Its members called themselves *Nationalsozialisten*. The ultimate sources of their mental framework must be looked for in the intellectual, behavioral, and economic changes of the nineteenth century. The psychological climate favored radical political and economic ideas. The increasingly bitter antagonism between German and Czech workers promoted chauvinistic nationalism. Detailed statistics and quota-

tions illustrate the emergence of a new "mystique." The weakness of Austrian parliamentarianism (p. 118) is seen as a major cause for the spread of that "mystique." The author's insight concerning the role of national borderlands in creating ideologies seems significant. The phenomenon deserves further attention and examination in other places as well.

Whiteside's study, like Burghardt's *Borderland*, gives evidence of important research and lucid work being tackled by American scholars on Austrian affairs. Burghardt and Whiteside offer scholarly insights into "borderland sociology," as I like to call it, uncovering behavioral patterns valid in other areas as well.

ERNST F. WINTER

Salzburg—New York

GLANVILLE DOWNEY. *Ancient Antioch*. Pp. xvi, 295. Princeton: Princeton University Press, 1963. $7.50.

This book is a condensation of Mr. Downey's more extensive study, *A History of Antioch in Syria from Seleucus to the Arab Conquest* (1960). The essential notes and bibliography of the original have been included. The author surveys Antioch's history from its foundation in 300 B.C. by Seleucus I. Nicator, a successor of Alexander the Great, to its final capture by the Arabs in A.D. 638.

Under the Seleucid kings of Syria, Antioch not only became the administrative and cultural center of their vast empire, but also exerted a decisive influence on the international politics of the Hellenistic age. After the Roman conquest of Syria in 65 B.C., commercial interests in Rome and the lavish patronage of Augustus and Tiberius revived Antioch's prosperity and influence. During the second and third centuries A.D., the city became strategically important as the base for Rome's eastward expansion against Persia. Its position as the largest Greek metropolis in the Semitic world also made it the scene of the conflict and synthesis of Greek and Oriental elements in Christianity.

Mr. Downey describes Antioch's literary, philosophical, and religious achievements in sketches of such figures as Libanius, Julian the Apostate, St. Ignatius, St. John Chrysostom, and St. Symeon the Stylite. The artistic and architectural achievements are presented in an excellent set of maps and photographs of the city's remains. Of particular interest is a new chapter dealing with the magnificent mosaic floors uncovered in recent excavations. Metalwork, such as the famous chalice of Antioch, is also given careful treatment.

It is perhaps regrettable that the author has chosen to include a number of events which occurred in Antioch without adequately explaining their bearing upon the history of the city. Thus he describes the impressive succession of Roman conquerors of Syria: Pompey, Caesar, and Antony, without giving us a clear picture of the effects of their conquests on the Antiochenes. A tendency of the author to present sequences of unrelated incidents has further weakened the narrative. Such criticism applies primarily to Mr. Downey's treatment of pagan Antioch for which, it must be admitted, the ancient sources are, at best, fragmentary. This difficulty is largely overcome in his treatment of Antioch as a Christian city where a fuller historical tradition survives. Here, Mr. Downey's narrative is more complete and coherent.

For the nonspecialist, however, the author has provided a valuable introduction to an important phase of Classical civilization which has been badly neglected by modern scholarship. Mr. Downey has more than compensated for the defects of his narrative by offering a picture of the immense variety and vitality of Antioch's achievements.

ROBERT A. HADLEY
University of Pennsylvania

ASIA AND AFRICA

CHANG CHUNG-LI. *The Income of the Chinese Gentry*. Pp. xvii, 369. Seattle: University of Washington Press, 1962. $7.75.

Let me be ungenerous first. I hate books that are mistitled. This book is about the income of the nineteenth-century Chinese gentry just as Professor Chang's previous volume, as indicated in its subtitle, was about nineteenth-century Chinese gentry rather than the Chinese gentry in general. This is the sort of important matter which is primarily explicable in terms of the exigencies of book-selling and the ready seducibility of scholars. Finally, on this tack, I do not know how one can know as much as Professor Chang does and not use imagination more.

Beyond these qualifications I feel that the intellectual world owes Professor Chang a great debt. He has given us another of those terribly important, first order approximations in scholarship. Before his work all of us talked sooner or later about the income of the Chinese gentry either during the nineteenth century or before. Now he has given us a large-scale presentation. The design of this volume may ruin your eyes, but it packs far more information into its four hundred pages than you would expect to find of more carefully marshalled data. Furthermore, the sources of these data, however varied, are carefully identified for those capable of pursuing these matters into their original lair.

The income of the gentry is divided into two main categories: public services and teaching, and land ownership and mercantile activities. The former is broken down into four subcategories: (1) office, (2) gentry functions, (3) secretarial services, and (4) teaching. In a supplementary section, not well developed analytically, another category, "Income from Other Services," is attached. For most of the gentry, most of the time, teaching was bread and butter, though of course not the most spectacular source of large fortunes. Professor Chang makes us well aware of the importance of the teaching functions to the gentry in respects other than those having to do with their sources of income.

However much one may care to argue about individual points, and regardless of titles and plaints about more creativity, fu-

Leadership in Communist China

By JOHN WILSON LEWIS, *Cornell University*

THIS is a comprehensive analysis of leadership doctrines and techniques devised and employed in the party's rise to power before 1949 and used since then. It emphasizes the period of the rise and fall of "great leap" optimism, 1958–1962. The first major analysis of the Chinese Communist political system, this book is an important contribution to knowledge of the theory and practice by which the elite guide the Chinese populace into "proper" thoughts and actions.

318 pages, charts, tables, $5.00

Major Governments of Asia

SECOND EDITION

Edited by GEORGE McT. KAHIN, *Cornell University*

IN each of the five sections—on China by Harold C. Hinton, Japan by Nobutaka Ike, India by Norman D. Palmer, Pakistan by Keith Callard and Richard S. Wheeler, and Indonesia by George McT. Kahin—the political development and contemporary governmental system of the state are ably described by a specialist who has done extensive research and writing on the country he discusses. The authors present many new and hitherto unavailable data and analyses which will interest specialists. The entire book has been revised and brought up to date.

728 pages, maps, charts, tables, $10.00

Five African States

RESPONSES TO DIVERSITY

The CONGO, DAHOMEY, the CAMEROUN FEDERAL REPUBLIC,
the RHODESIAS and NYASALAND, SOUTH AFRICA
Edited by GWENDOLEN M. CARTER, *Smith College*

IT would be difficult to find five African states more varied in background and characteristics than the ones in this volume. Yet all are strained by counterpressures toward internal division and toward unity. In this book, Edouard Bustin, Virginia Thompson, Victor T. Le Vine, Herbert J. Spiro, and Thomas Karis give insights into forces present in all of Africa and in fact characteristic of developing states.

728 pages, frontis., maps, tables, $10.00

 CORNELL UNIVERSITY PRESS

Ithaca, New York

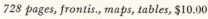

Kindly mention THE ANNALS *when writing to advertisers*

The Association for Asian Studies

Publications

The Journal of Asian Studies. This is the leading American scholarly quarterly covering research in all of the disciplines of the social sciences and humanities on countries of East Southeast, and South Asia from Japan to Pakistan.

The Bibliography of Asian Studies. In addition to four regular issues of articles and book reviews a special fifth number, the *Bibliography* of Asian Studies is published annually in September. It contains several thousand titles of books and articles published in Western languages during the preceding year and is an invaluable reference tool for both the specialist and the non-specialist.

Monographs and Papers. The Association has published ten scholarly monographs dealing with a wide variety of disciplines and areas. It plans to continue this program and in addition to publish a new series of substantial research papers.

Newsletter. A quarterly publicaton containing news of the profession, informaton about research and teaching programs and materials, and notices of scholarly meetings is distributed to the membership.

Subscription and Membership. The annual subscription rates, including the *Bibliography*, is $10 (domestic and foreign postage included); the *Bibliography* separately is $4. Membership in the Association, which includes the *Journal, Bibliography,* and the Association's *Newsletter,* is $10 (regular) and $5 (student). Subscription and memberships may be entered through the Secretariat of the Association at the address below.

Association for Asian Studies, Inc.
P.O. Box 606, Ann Arbor, Michigan

ture work in this field will start from Chang Chung-li's. It is a thorough, massive, and careful enough first approximation so that all future treatment must consist of statements which refute, confirm, or qualify some set of the statements presented here. He has given us a basis for more cumulative work than we had before he helped us. Finally, despite the special nature of the period on which he wrote, given the very strong and stable elements of Chinese society, I would be willing to lay very good odds indeed that this first order approximation will serve us exceedingly well in many if not most other periods of Chinese history as well as the one for which it was written.

MARION J. LEVY, JR.
Princeton University

CHALMERS A. JOHNSON. *Peasant Nationalism and Communist Power: The Emergence of Revolutionary China, 1937–1945.* Pp. xii, 256. Stanford, Calif.: Stanford University Press, 1962. $5.75.

Mr. Johnson has in his book attempted to use a description of the Communist organization of guerrilla warefare against the Japanese in World War II as a basis for analyzing the character of Chinese communism. The major part of the book gives a detailed history of the situation in China that resulted from the Japanese attack and the breakdown of order, and led to the development of Communist guerrilla organizations and the Communist takeover of vast rural areas in North and Central China. This war story is based in the main upon the secret archives of the Japanese army in China, which have now become available. From this study of the growth of Communist power during the war, the author draws his conclusions about the character of Chinese communism, which in his view has become a "national communism" based on the "social mobilization" of the Chinese masses. In the author's view, such "social mobilization of the masses" is characteristic of the modern national state, whereas nineteenth-century nationalism was based on a narrow intellectual and bourgeois

support. By mobilizing the "peasant masses," the Chinese Communists succeeded in giving modern China its "national Communist ideology." As a comparison, the author refers to the establishment of communism in Yugoslavia, which he describes as a result of wartime peasant mobilization, and includes a whole chapter on the Yugoslavian story, based on secondary material.

The value of this book is in its detailed description of the story of guerrilla warfare in China and the use made of it by the Communists in expanding their power. The tremendous gain made by the Communists during the war by exploiting the situation created by the Japanese is well known, but Mr. Johnson has provided a great deal of detailed historical material concerning this Communist growth which is of foremost importance to an understanding of the course of the Communist victory in China. This is the central part of the book. But the theoretical conclusions that the author develops from this story in his first and concluding chapters remain highly debatable. The term "alliance," which he uses to describe the relationship between the Communists and the peasants, remains totally undefined, and this is perhaps the most decisive weakness of the author's assumptions. Mr. Johnson does not at all concern himself with the Communist purpose in this so-called alliance. He identifies this purpose with "nationalism" without saying more about nationalism than to give what he calls a functional definition under which nationalism is realized through the "social mobilization" of "the masses."

Mr. Johnson takes issue with an earlier statement of mine—which he slightly twists—in which I pointed out the fallacy of regarding the Chinese Communists' policy as an expression of the peasant will or of regarding the Communist leader as a "peasant leader." Mr. Johnson holds that the Communist party did not act so much "for the sake of the peasantry" as "on the side of the peasantry," and this by implication seems to be his interpretation of "alliance." Nothing is said about the fact that the Communists did not remain "on the side" of the peasantry, but, if anything, placed themselves above the peasants and used them not for peasant, but for their own, Communist, purposes.

It is very true that during the war the Chinese Communists, like the Communists in Yugoslavia, in the Soviet Union, and everywhere else, concealed, or put in cold storage, their Communist goals and tried to claim the role of nationalist leaders. But this temporary Communist tactic ended after the war, and in China, as elsewhere, the Communists followed their over-all Communist purposes within the framework of Marxism-Leninism which aim at goals that are more than a "national myth" or an "ideological gestalt" of "nationalist impulses." This Communist policy is as little dealt with in this book as is the whole framework of Marxism-Leninism, and there is no logical connection between the documented part of the book and its vague assertions of an "alliance" and of a "national myth," which remain undefined.

FRANZ MICHAEL
Professor of Chinese History
and Government
Far Eastern and Russian Institute
University of Washington

EDGAR SNOW. *The Other Side of the River: Red China Today.* Pp. xvi, 810. New York: Random House, 1962. $10.00.

This second great "scoop" in Snow's career is unquestionably a must for all who wish to understand mainland China today, whether layman or specialist. The world first met Mao Tse-tung in *Red Star over China* through Snow's long interviews with him in a Yenan cave in late 1936, following the Reds' Long March and just prior to the dramatic capture of Chiang Kai-shek at Sian and the reconstitution of the United Front between the Chinese Nationalists and Communists that braced the country against the coming Japanese onslaught. Snow meets Mao again in 1960, but this time in a palace. The first book reported a smuggled passage at great peril; the second, a journey with independent means and the permission of both the United States and the People's Republic of China. Again the timing was fortunate; Snow had been barred from the Soviet Union during Stalin's lifetime because of a "premature" (1949) prediction of Sino-Soviet differences. They were becoming overt in 1960, and the dust was just settling on the illusions of the Great Leap Forward. Snow contrasts the bustling city and country life he saw in even remote areas with the fantastic stories of widespread starvation reported by respectable journalists at home. American Sinologists are amassing documentary material and piles of conflicting refugee reports, but are working at the disadvantage of an almost total lack of "field studies." Every eye-witness account has some value, but no other American has Snow's unique background or high contacts.

One suspects that Snow considers himself something of a modern De Tocqueville. He inquires into all the most controversial aspects of Chinese life in some 86 concise chapters, which include descriptions of the continuing rural and delayed urban communes, impressive industrial construction, the lack of "slave labor," the real torment of thought reform, "statistics," the reasons for the "hundred flowers" campaign, the new puritanism, imitative ballet, stereotyped literature, the reconciliation of national minorities, Sino-Soviet differences, and the closeness and significance of China producing a nuclear bomb. Yet he constantly sets down the limitations of his observations: his nationality, his mediocre command of the language, and the "built-in" censorship of Chinese Communist society, to say nothing of the vastness of his subject—one-fifth of mankind. While Snow attempts to put into the American idiom the way in which the Chinese Communists see their problems and the world, he is clearly distressed at the dogmatic view of the United States held by both the Chinese leaders and masses. The title from Pascal conveys the message that unless the people on each side of the river— the Pacific—can come to communicate, their unreal images of each other could lead to disastrous conflict.

For the expert here is unrivalled reporting; for the student, background material and leads to scholarly research; for the policy-minded, a repast of controversial —and often original—food for thought. The organization, appendix, bibliography, and especially the detailed index render this large volume easily manageable.

GEORGE O. TOTTEN
Associate Professor of Political Science
University of Rhode Island

KYUNG CHO CHUNG. *New Korea: New Land of the Morning Calm.* Pp. x, 274. New York: The Macmillan Company, 1962. $6.00.

This volume makes a very limited contribution to the understanding of old or "new" Korea or Koreans. In many respects—all unwittingly, I am sure—the author does a positive disservice to his own people and to his English-speaking friends, who may seek to rely upon some of his statements or the interpretation he has given of events, persons, or circumstances he describes. Though the book was intended to do a great deal of good, the author may well have done the reverse by his slavish use of many sources which are suspect or at least partially discredited by serious scholars and objective interpreters of the Korean scene.

The book is an uneven patchwork of facts, alleged facts, opinions, and views of other people which the author has put together in an editorial sense with some skill. Quotation marks are used not at all, or rarely, even when he borrows whole paragraphs and sections of another man's writing—including, in Chapter II, whole sections of my own interpretation of Korea's heritage. It is not that Mr. Chung does not acknowledge these sources—beginning on page 265- -but rather that no one knows where the author does his own writing and when he borrows the words of his source. And some of these sources are highly suspect in their frequently one-sided interpretation of men and events— for example, his use of Richard C. Allen's unauthorized biography, *Korea's Syngmann Rhee,* as a prime source; the *Voice of Korea,* and the *Korean Republic* as others. The present time—when many nations are struggling under the yoke of a "new banditry," the reign of political opportunism—is not a period when historical or political evaluations can be made with ease. However, Mr. Chung does not use even the basic precautions of the horseback scholar. Though he apparently does not suspect them himself, many of his sources are suspect—whether right, or left, or just pure partisan propaganda.

This young man might have great promise as a chronicler of events if he had acquired the discipline of a scholar, or had had the good fortune to work under one in the production of this book. It is with regret that I have to comment adversely on this latest venture of an author who has produced, with all its limitations, a useful and generally factual book titled *Korea Tomorrow,* published in 1956. It would have been better if this new book had not been published—it will only further confuse a highly confusing and difficult period of history. but its acceptance will be transitory, if at all.

GEORGE FOX MOTT
Washington, D. C.

T. R. FEHRENBACH. *This Kind of War: A Study in Unpreparedness.* Pp. xii, 688. New York: The Macmillan Company, 1963. $10.00.

The war in Korea was, in the author's phrase, "a war of policy"—one in which the objectives, and limits, set by policy replaced the accustomed aim of simple military victory as the end in itself. He appreciates that the aim of our intervention was to turn back Communist aggression, and was successful. But he also recognizes the difficulty of communicating to the American people this limited purpose of our long and limited commitment. He notes the need to be ready to fight other limited "wars of policy" in the coming decades, and he wants the American people to understand this need. This is the political message of the book, and a sound one, but the chief distinction of the work is the author's personal message.

War is very impersonal in its broad sweep, but it is also intensely personal.

The author, a veteran of World War II, was recalled to service in Korea where he held platoon and company commands and battalion staff duty. This is not the usual historian's study, nor the general's memoir of moving of divisions on the chessboard of political terrain. It is a soldier's story of war, a foxhole-eye view, and it is a good one. It would be too much to term Fehrenbach's book a classic, but it has drama and vivid ability to recall or evoke an impression of the war as experienced in the front lines. It is based largely on personal narratives, operation records, and similar accounts. As the author readily admits, "portions of this book may be more hearsay than history"—but the image conveyed by the book as a whole is history. In describing the broad political context of the war, and of the strategic decisions as made in Washington and Tokyo, the author's impressionistic—though generally informed and certainly conscientious—style may be less successful than in the major parts of the book where the reader slogs across Korea with the GI's.

Finally, there is a message about grand strategy derived from Mr. Fehrenbach's interlacing of the purposes and the harsh details of the war in Korea: wars or crusades of total victory and extermination may turn to the new nuclear and push-button weaponry to destroy the land, "but if you desire to defend it, protect it, and keep it for civilization, you must do this on the ground, the way the Roman legions did, by putting your young men into the mud."

RAYMOND L. GARTHOFF
Institute of Sino-Soviet Studies
George Washington University

D. INSOR. *Thailand: A Political, Social, and Economic Analysis.* Pp. 188. New York: Frederick A. Praeger, 1963. $5.75.

The pages are few, but there is a little bit of everything in this book, with an index to find them: descriptions of Bangkok, up-country areas and towns, temples, varieties of religion and politics, foreign affairs, intrigue, the Chinese minority, and various economic features. The book has many virtues which might be noted,

and perhaps the most striking is the quality of eye-witness reporting on places, people, and events. This reviewer found one or two paragraphs in the book worth the price of the whole, for example, the item (p. 77) describing how General Phao in his heavy-handed way challenged Democratic Party leader Khuang, to a cockfight on the Pramane Ground to see who was more democratic, and Khuang's slashing response which was so typical of the man, "Let Phao have a cockfight with someone born in the year of the Cock"—that is, Pibun who was Prime Minister and Phao's political boss. This is the authentic atmosphere of Thai politics which few catch.

The book is marred by some unnecessary moralizing, by some apodictic statements that stop the reader dead in the middle of a consonant, and by some translations which are not translations. For instance, the moralizing in favor of representative democracy on pages 111–115 might be regarded by some readers as either naive or ethnocentric. The second paragraph of the Foreword contains the flat statement that the "study of politics is of necessity somewhat abstract and de-personalized—though this applies less to Thailand than to the West." After twenty-one years in the hurly-burly of Washington's corpuscular politics, this statement so hypnotized the reviewer that it took another twenty-four hours to move on to paragraph four where a lesser road block to forward reading was encountered in the translation of *Nai Luang* as "the lord within (the Palace)." Actually it refers to the master or lord of the governmental services, the bureaucrats being traditionally known as *kha luang* and the chief of state as their lord or *nai luang*. But this is a small thing, as is the interpretation of *kan muang* as meaning the "business of the city," leading this writer to the conclusion that only in the city of Bangkok is politics taken seriously, and then only by a few. True enough a *muang* may be a city, but in this context it has the larger frame of reference of the whole nation such as it has when associated with the word *Thai* in the words *muang Thai* or the "Thai nation" not the "Thai city." A phrase frequently encountered in Thai documents reads *kan muang kan bokkhrong* or "politics and government."

This reviewer takes exception also to a number of statements which hardly seem supported by the evidence. An example occurs in the discussion of the Buddhist religion and Buddhist peoples where the writer commented that "They [the Buddhist peoples] have not prevented wars, of course, any more than Christianity has done, but at least there have never been Buddhist wars—or persecutions either." The bloody history of Thai-Burmese-Mon wars with the depopulation of whole provinces provides an excellent setting in which to sit and contemplate this statement in Yogi detachment. But as this reviewer remarked earlier, these are perhaps small flaws and can be papered over with the excellencies of the other pages which have an eye-witness quality.

KENNETH P. LANDON
Associate Dean for Area Studies
School of Language and Area Studies
Foreign Service Institute
United States Department of State

BURTON BENEDICT. *Indians in a Plural Society: A Report on Mauritius.* Pp. 167. London: Her Majesty's Stationery Office, 1961. 25 s.

The system of indentured labor, which followed the abolition of slavery, was responsible for the migration of a large number of Indians in the nineteenth century. Recruiting agencies in India hired people to work on plantations and farms in different parts of the British Empire. Although these people were contracted for a specific term, it was often stipulated in their agreement that they could settle down in the colonies after the expiry of their contract. The movement of indentured laborers was followed by a voluntary migration of other Indians, mainly merchants, traders and technicians, on their own. Today, we find large colonies of these Indians and their descendants in Burma, Malaya, Fiji, Hong-Kong, Canada, the United States, the West Indies, South and East Africa, and Mauritius. Everywhere the Indians constitute a distinct community. In most places, the dominant group in the host society has not encouraged them to get absorbed in the country of their adoption, nor have the Indian settlers shown any inclination to shed their sociocultural identity.

The study under review relates to the "plural society" in Mauritius. This "sugar" island has an interesting colonial history, having passed through the hands of the Dutch and the French to the British. Indians had already reached Mauritius during the period of its French occupation, 1715–1814 A.D. We are told in this report that in 1806 there were 6,162 Indian slaves—about 10 per cent of the island's total slave population. These were drawn mainly from the French colonies in Peninsular India and worked as domestics, artisans, masons, and weavers. In Mauritius, slavery was abolished in 1835, and the flow of indentured labourers from India to Mauritius started the same year. In 1835, Indians constituted a minute proportion of the population, but, by 1861, two-thirds of the island's population was Indian, which proportion is maintained up to the present.

Besides Indians, the island is inhabited by Englishmen; Franco-Mauritians—Mauritians of French descent and accepted as "white"; Creoles—Mauritians of a mixed African or Indian and European descent; Muslims; and Chinese. The book, however, is devoted mainly to the Indian section of Mauritian society. Creole, the French *patois*, is the *lingua franca* of this island. At one time, the Franco-Mauritians represented the economically and politically dominant community of the island. Next in importance were the Creoles, followed by the Gujerati Muslims and Chinese. Indians occupied the lowest rung in the economic and political structure. During the last two decades, however, considerable changes have taken place on account of constitutional reforms and the democratization of franchise laws. Although Mauritian society is an ethnically differentiated society, "there is no congruence between ethnic group, linguistic group, religious group and occupational group" (p. 51). The author points out that this "lack of congruence" among groups counteracts the forces tending to split the Mauritian society along rigid ethnic boundaries. and, as such, it represents an important unifying factor in this society. Since it is a report, the book contains rich demographic and ethnographic material. The third chapter, entitled "The Plural Society," and the twelfth chapter on "Political Structure" add much to the value of the book inasmuch as they bring into sharper focus the nature of this "plural society" by discussing how the various groups in Mauritius are getting articulated to each other, interacting and co-operating to produce a plural society.

This is a commendable effort and is a valuable addition to the growing literature on "Indian Communities Abroad," their internal organization, and their interaction with host societies.

RAM P. SRIVASTAVA

Head
Department of Anthropology
University of Saugar

RALPH H. RETZLAFF. *Village Government in India: A Case Study.* Pp. 140. New York: Asia Publishing House, 1962. $4.50.

This is a brief, but very significant study. It analyzes the traditional power and authority relations of an Indian village, and describes what effect ideas about democracy and centralized planning held by urban Indians, when implemented in the form of legislation, have had on a village. It illustrates the efficacy of the combination of the political scientists' drive for generalizability with the social anthropologists' concern for the detailed description of human behavior.

It has erroneously been believed that in premodern India most Indian villages were self-governing, and this self-government was carried out by *panchayats* (councils), which were thought to be village-wide representative bodies. Retzlaff begins his essay by pointing out that in the village—Kholapur, in Western Uttar Pradesh—

where he carried out a field study, traditionally there are at least four types of bodies and processes of decision-making and adjudication which can be subsumed under the term *panchayats:* The first are the caste *panchayats,* made up of members of one caste whose principal function "is to uphold the pattern of social behavior and the religious values of the members of that caste" (p. 18), and the second, the general meeting *panchayat,* made up of the important leaders of all the castes in the village, and which is concerned "with the broad range of problems which would now be described as civil and criminal in nature" (p. 20).

Retzlaff states that the membership of this *panchayat* varies with the problems presented. The third kind of *panchayat* the author terms the farmer-retainer *panchayat.* These *panchayats* are the direct expression of the role and power of Rajput and other landholders in the village, and are concerned with maintaining the economic status quo which binds together families exchanging various kinds of services. Fourthly, there are the single-purpose *panchayats* which are made up of parties interested in making decisions regarding a transitory situation. Cutting through the four types of *panchayats* is the process of consensus formation, through the utilization by the Rajput landholders of their power. Because of the intricate balance of alliances and antagonism found among the segments of the Rajput caste, this power is always exercised through the rhetoric of compromise.

On top of this existing system of utilization and distribution of power in the village, *panchayats* which were to be innovating political bodies, expressing in some measures the aspirations of the whole population, were introduced in 1949. Through a description of a *panchayat* election in 1949, the functioning of the elected *panchayat,* and a second *panchayat* election in 1955, we can see the conflict between the two systems of ideas about how villages should be governed, those of the villagers and those of the outsiders. But Retzlaff does note in this narrative that there are the beginnings of a process by which new local political alignments are emerging. And that in addition to old forms of consensus-building there are new ones as well beginning to emerge.

Retzlaff is far from being optimistic about the future of the statutory *panchayats* in relation to the role they are expected to play in village development. He does seem impressed though with the ability of some of the villagers to utilize a new institution, not always for the ends the planners conceived, but for ends some villagers think are good.

BERNARD S. COHN
University of Rochester

D. N. MAJUMDAR. *Himalayan Polyandry: Structure, Functioning and Culture Change: A Field-Study of Jaunsar-Bawar.* New York: Asia Publishing House, 1963. $10.00.

This book presents the results of some twenty-three years of intermittent research in a small mountain area of North India by the late Professor Majumdar, a well-known Indian anthropologist, and his students. The people described are the Indo-Aryan speaking, Hindu residents of Jaunsar-Bawar in the northwestern corner of the state of Uttar Pradesh. They are representatives of the western Pahari or "mountain" culture area—an area in which fraternal polyandry is or has been widespread. This accounts for the title of the book, which is somewhat misleading, since polyandry is only one of several themes in it. The Pahari culture area in its entirety extends throughout the lower Himalayas up to an altitude of about 8000 feet, from western Kashmir well into Nepal. It is sharply demarcated from cultures of the adjacent Indo-Gangetic plain, but they derive from a common source and have long been in contact. A conspicuous deficiency in Majumdar's book is his failure to indicate in any systematic way the place of the people he describes in relation to their mountain relatives and their plains neighbors. In fact, the book lacks any reference to other studies in village India or social anthropology, thereby leaving the reader without substantive or theoretical context.

Three villages which were used as "field centers" provide most of the data for the book. Description of the region and these villages is followed by generalized material on the way of life of the people of the entire area. This, the main part of the book, is very uneven in quality and detail. The most complete and valuable portions are detailed discussions of kinship structure in Chapter Four and of political organization in Chapter Five. These constitute an original contribution to the ethnology of India. The discussion of polyandry, included with that of kinship structure, is good but, as is characteristic of the book, important relevant facts and interpretations are unaccountably missing. There is, for example, only the barest mention that a "bride price" is asked, in marriage, although this may well be a crucial fact in accounting for the functioning of fraternal polyandry in the region. Nowhere is there a description of the marriage ceremony or the negotiations which precede it. The marriage and family systems are not compared to those of the plains, nor is mention made of polyandry in nearby Tibet, the nearby Punjab plains, or elsewhere in India. Since marriage and family and especially polyandry are major concerns of the author, these gaps are disconcerting.

The chapters on caste, economy, and religion are weak. There is no discussion of the system of exchange of goods for services which is widely known in North India as the *jajmani* system, although its existence is mentioned in passing. Little idea is conveyed of the nature of village religious belief and worship or of the social groups which are functional in religion although some festivals unique to the area are well described. Again, absence of comparative or contextual material is disturbing. One chapter is devoted to education and a final section analyzes the Community Development Program in Jaunsar-Bawar. These contain interesting material but little in the way of systematic interpretation. They would be valuable reading for officials planning to work in the area, but other authors have gone much farther in analyzing the general problems of planned change and specifically of community development in India. Unfortunately Majumdar makes no mention of their work.

In summary, this is an informative account of a little-known and interesting people. It is so written, however, that its appeal and usefulness will be restricted largely to those with a special interest in the region or in the social anthropology of India. Such people will find in it annoying gaps as well as illuminating facts.

GERALD D. BERREMAN
Associate Professor of Anthropology
University of California
Berkeley

WELLES HANGEN. *After Nehru, Who?* Pp. xvi, 303. New York: Harcourt, Brace and World, 1963. $6.95.

Nothing comes out more clearly in Welles Hangen's book than the fact of India's exciting and unequalled diversity. Its leaders, often regarded as members of a single English-educated elite, in fact are as different from one another as they all are from the country's illiterate peasantry. Portraits of seven men and one woman compose the body of this fascinating literary insight into contemporary India. Any of them might succeed Nehru, and one in particular, Y. B. Chavan, might succeed Nehru's successor—a development which Hangen believes will be the "supreme test for Indian democracy."

This is certainly one of the best single books for the general reader curious about the world's most perplexing free country, because Hangen combines an outsider's perspective with the sensitivity and warmth of one who has obviously enjoyed much of Indian living. The author, chief National Broadcasting Company correspondent for South Asia, has spent many days with the powerful figures whose prospects he gauges, and his personal reactions enrich the separate essays written on each one. Thankfully he abjures cynicism and the ridicule of popular figures that writers often resort to in order to prove intimate acquaintance with the facts—and the current rumors.

The "lotus with the steel stem," Finance Minister Morarji Desai, might succeed Nehru if, as is likely, the right wing of Congress becomes predominate. Desai would have to share power, however, with S. K. Patil, Food and Agriculture Minister, whose strength is rooted in Congress organizations and powerful business groups. Lal Bahadur Shastri, Home Minister and "the most authentically Indian" of the personalities described, might be a compromise candidate in case a factional struggle appeared imminent: Congress is unlikely to commit political suicide in a prolonged struggle for offices, and Shashtri might satisfy divergent groups. The left wing, even with Communist support, probably will not gain power immediately after Nehru. Krishna Menon and Indira Gandhi are its only national leaders, and both depend for their power on Nehru. Jayaprakash Narayan appears to be too far out in the wilderness to gain supreme power himself, but he might be "summoned to New Delhi to provide a respectable civilian facade for military rule." If the latter comes about, then General Brij Mohan Kaul, chief of the general staff, would be the likely leader.

This summary does no justice to the subtlety of the author's analysis, which is really not intended to set up betting odds on anything. After reading this book, few will deny Welles Hangen a firm place among current serious writers about India.

CHARLES H. HEIMSATH
Assistant Professor of
South Asian Studies
American University

GWENDOLYN M. CARTER (Ed.). *African One-Party States.* Pp. xii, 501. Ithaca, N. Y.: Cornell University Press, 1962. $7.25.

Recent events in one-party states in Africa, such as the showdown between President Senghor and Premier Dia in Senegal last December, the assassination of President Olympio in Togo in January, and in February the report of a plot against President Tubman of Liberia, underscore the need for and the timeliness of this book. The work of specialists with field experience in the countries of which they write, it consists of essays by Charles F. Gallagher on Tunisia; Ernest Milcent on Senegal; L. Gray Cowan on Guinea; Virginia Thompson on the Ivory Coast; J. Gus Liebenow on Liberia; and Margaret L. Bates on Tanganyika, with an introductory essay by Professor Carter.

As the editor indicates, the countries were chosen because of their differing political background and heritage, the essentially one-party form of their governments, and the absence in English of any comprehensive examination of each state's structure and characteristics. There is no absolute uniformity of treatment among these essays, except for perceptivity and readability, because of the circumstances peculiar to each country, but the adoption of a common outline comprising historical background, land and people, political process, and contemporary issues gives the volume coherence and makes cross reference easy.

The book is useful on several counts. The brief introductory essay is a cogent discussion of the phenomenon of the one-party state in Africa and its significance for the study of comparative government in its theoretical and practical aspects. In the other essays, ranging from sixty to eighty pages, the authors manage to assemble and interpret, without being elliptical or cryptic, a considerable amount of information both new or not conveniently found elsewhere. Each author also provides a valuable annotated bibliography. It would be at once invidious and meaningless to single out any one treatment for special commendation since each one is done well and has particular merit in its own right.

Taken as a whole the book provides a sound guide for the avoidance of the oversimplifications and easy generalizations that lurk in so innocent a phrase as "the one-party state," and, in addition, it furnishes a solid base for further study. As a contribution of "comparative theoretical analysis to the practical conduct of affairs," it can be said to have fulfilled admirably its stated purposes: "to broaden our knowledge of political practice and the motives underlying such practice and to aid in developing a more general comprehension of the meaning and significance of the new or redesigned forms and the ideas that characterize them." For these achievements all students of African affairs must indeed be grateful.

WILLIAM E. DIEZ
Professor of Political Science
University of Rochester

ANOUAR ABDEL-MALEK. *Égypte: Société militaire.* Pp. 380. Paris: Éditions du Seuil, 1962. No price.

Cairo-born Anouar Abel-Malek, professor of philosophy, and author in Arabic and in French of works on African subjects and, particularly, on Egypt, has undertaken in the present volume an analytical examination of the United Arab Republic. For about a score of years, up to 1959, he was active in the political and cultural movements of Egypt. Then he had to leave his native land. The army is the pivot of the political, ideological, and economic forces of today's Egypt, he writes, and it is one of the world's most regimented nations. It is a *nationalitaire* country, bent on reconquering a deeper consciousness of its national identity, as distinguished from "nationalism" which the author considers a basically negative dynamism.

It is in the sense of Egypt's millennial syncretism, says the author, that the army links together politics, economics, and ideology. Capitalism alone appears to have been impotent to meet the nation's urgent needs, groping as it is for a fuller understanding of its *mystique.* Abdel-Nasser, whose regime is moving toward socialism, has uprooted the country's deeply entrenched landed aristocracy and *compradore* bourgeoisie. Conditions for socialism are maturing in the wake of a greater appreciation of manual labor within a new set of values held by an increasing number of industrial workers, with technical experts in the van. In order to distribute the nation's meager resources more profitably, economic planning and priorities have been established, monopolies dismantled, and foreign capital dethroned.

Yet, living standards have, as yet, failed to improve, while farm labor is more redundant than ever, even in the face of all these efforts. Only 10 per cent of farm land has been affected by agrarian reform, simply because there is no more fertile soil along the Nile. It will be the higher industrial potential due to the added hydroelectric power that will be the major contribution of the Aswan High Dam, and not the two million additional acres it will produce. While the author concedes that Egypt's military society has made its contribution to the increased strength of the nation, he holds that it would have moved faster if it had enlisted the aid of the Marxist Socialists in its progress toward Nasser's type of socialism.

The book contains a good deal of factual information about industrialization, agrarian co-operation, and many other subjects. When it comes to interpretation, the author's bias cannot be overlooked. Also, Mr. Abdel-Malek produces no proof when he makes a statement that, in an allegedly collusive policy, President Truman and Winston Churchill early in 1952 sought to stem the forces of revolutionary nationalism in Iran and Egypt. The memoirs of Mr. Truman, which are unusually specific on matters of basic policy in international affairs, make no mention of any understanding, let alone collusion, with the British on such a matter of importance.

EMIL LENGYEL
Professor of History
Fairleigh Dickinson University

ECONOMICS AND LABOR

WILFRED MALENBAUM. *Prospects for Indian Development.* Pp. 325. New York: Free Press of Glencoe, 1962. $5.75.

The past year has been an especially fertile one with respect to the publication of books on Indian economic development and policy in the United States and England. It has been difficult for a peripatetic reader to keep up with the flow: W. B. Reddaway, John P. Lewis, Myron Wiener, Mrs. S. Epstein, and W. C. Neale have all come out with what one would expect to be major contributions to further foreign—and possibly Indian—understanding of both the general process and the problems of economic development in India, as well as understanding of details in specific geographic or problem areas. Dr. Malenbaum's long-awaited book on the problems of general planning in India, based on his accumulated knowledge of India and his work as the former director of the India project of the Massachusetts Institute of Technology, Center for International Studies, is to be welcomed as a worthy addition to this list.

In this book, Dr. Malenbaum has sought to go behind the formal plan and plan documents to the actual structural relationships in the Indian economy. He discusses both the plans and the achievements, and explains the gap between past plans and results in terms of the failure of the planning to be sufficiently geared to the realities of the Indian economy. "For this kind of disparity between plan and performance, closing the gap in the course of the next decade or two is not simply a matter of waiting for performance to catch up. Plans need to be formulated which are realistic with respect to the specific relationships of the economy. . . . [Plan] alternatives which will not be effective are those which neglect these behavior patterns, which simply assume, for example, that more of such familiar devices as taxing modern sectors and domestic borrowing of private savings will suffice. Closing the gap requires principally new actions, or at least new emphasis on the part of the Government."

He feels especially that the government in its planning has unduly stressed the expansion of public investment in the modern sectors, relative to total investment. The private sector is extremely important in India, not only in large-scale modern industry, but in small-scale industrial activities—which are almost entirely private—and in the agricultural sector especially, large parts of the economic activities of which are still outside the influence of the market. In the fields of both agriculture and small-scale industry, the government must play a much larger

220b

role than previously in stimulating economic development. This will have much greater consequences for employment than the government's past policy; it will also stimulate the development of the modern sector on a healthier basis than heretofore. This requires not only exhortation and money—which are quite plentiful; it requires more of the even scarcer resources of administrative skill and leadership being devoted to the rural and small-scale industry sectors. The author concludes by boldly presenting a program to achieve the results he feels to be necessary.

It is possible to criticize details of the book. However, both the aim of exploring the realities behind the plan and performance and the results of the book are to be strongly welcomed. It is to be hoped that Dr. Malenbaum's spadework will be followed by work with similar goals both on the general policy level and on the level of detailed exploration of specific sectors. Much of this further work, of course, will have to be done by appropriate Indian government offices—such as the Planning Commission—and by Indian scholars.

GEORGE ROSEN

The Rand Corporation
Santa Monica
California

V. K. R. V. RAO, A. K. GHOSH, M. V. DIVATIA, and UMA DATTA (Eds.). *Papers on National Income and Allied Topics,* Vol. II. Pp. xviii, 115. New York: Asia Publishing House, 1962. $8.00.

This is the second volume in a series of studies made up of papers on the national income of India and related topics. The first volume in the series appeared two years ago, and others in the series are planned for the future. This volume is better than its predecessor, for the papers contained in it are more carefully selected, so that their quality is, on the whole, superior, but also because only essays on a limited set of related topics are included. But the book is likely to be of value mainly to persons interested in the quantitative study of Indian national income and the conditions of its growth. For anyone

working on these questions, however, this book is obligatory reading.

The volume contains essays by different authors on two main sets of topics, namely, national income and its major components, especially consumption expenditure and interstate balance of trade. Both of these problems are of great importance. In fact, several of the papers in the first part, one on long-term growth of national income from 1900 to the 1950's, by K. Mukerji, and one on the breakdown of Indian national income by distributive shares, by M. Mukherjee, raise some of the most important questions in the national income study of a developing country. For in these countries empirical data on many essential variables are lacking, or where available quite defective, and both chapters show how some rather useful and potentially valuable indirect estimates of the changing magnitudes of these variables can be made. In this sense these chapters, though exclusively concerned with India, would be of value to persons studying national income problems in other developing countries.

Next to these two chapters, the three essays on interstate trade balance, one by B. Koti, one by S. Sivasubramonian, and a summarizing chapter by B. N. Ganguli, are of the greatest interest. In a large country like India in which there are sizable differences in per capita income and economic welfare in different regions, the problem of interregional or interstate distribution of income is of great interest. When this reviewer worked on the national income of the Union Territory of Delhi, estimates of interstate trade balances would have been of great value, for on their basis the economic role of Delhi as India's capital could have been estimated much more accurately than was possible with the facts available. The authors of these three papers cannot provide ultimate data on trade balances of the Indian states, but the three papers, especially the chapter by Ganguli, point to further research which needs to be done and contain suggestions of series of factual data which should be collected or the collection of which could be imposed by the relevant government offices, which would greatly contribute to fairly accurate estimations of trade balances between Indian states. The value of more accurate estimates of interstate trade balances would not be merely academic, but might provide an important tool for economic planning in India and might affect the location of new industries. It might, moreover, provide some indication of likely migratory patterns across state boundaries and other issues affecting the location of productive factors and their shift between different parts of India. Hence these initial and, in view of the shortage of adequate data, quite preliminary findings suggest further necessary research, the practical consequences of which might be of considerable importance.

The volume is introduced by an interesting and eloquent paper of V. K. R. V. Rao, the originator of national income studies in India and the main supporter of ongoing work in this field, which produces increasingly useful and valuable quantitative data on the economic performance of India. If the quality of the third volume to appear in this series maintains or even rises above the quality of the present volume, we will have an increasing amount of useful and genuinely valuable data for the study of India's economy.

BERT F. HOSELITZ
Professor of Economics and
    Social Science
University of Chicago

LEON V. HIRSCH. *Marketing in an Underdeveloped Economy: The North Indian Sugar Industry.* Pp. xix, 392. Englewood Cliffs, N. J.: Prentice-Hall, 1961. $4.50.

If other dissertations lived up to the standard set by this 1960 Ford Foundation Doctoral Award Winner the social sciences would have no cause to worry. Dr. Hirsch's book presents the results of a year of field work clearly, and—considering the possibilities of such a subject one might even say surprisingly—it is interesting to entertaining throughout. The substance of the study is an answer to the question of how sugar moves from the fields of the cane growers through the mills, the selling agents, and the wholesalers to the retailers, commercial consumers, and householders. The method was largely one of intensive interview with businessmen engaged in each stage of the marketing process, and much of the interest of the book stems from the detailed recounting of the interviews and the business histories of those interviewed. It is not a statistical study, for the "sample" is much too small, and Hirsch quite rightly avoided the alienation of his respondents which would have followed probing questions about the specific details of their transactions.

Two criticisms might be made. One, of style, is that another thorough reworking might have reduced the size without damaging the contents, for at times the reader is too easily able to anticipate from what he has already learned, and some of the appendices to chapters are unnecessary; but Hirsch was quite right to keep full reports of each business firm.

Second, Hirsch seems to feel that the sensitivity of the Indian businessmen he studied to prices and to new profit opportunities refutes the view that Indians are not yet market-oriented. But, as this reviewer understands the issue, it is not whether Indians already engaged in commerce are commercially rational—they would not survive if they were not—but whether those still in the villages, universities, schools, and bureaucracy regard profitability in the same way we do, and how they feel about the activities of Hirsch's businessmen.

Hirsch finds that Indian businessmen are not much interested in marketing, partly because consumers are not much interested in brands and packaging and so on, and that businesses do not restrict themselves to one level of operations. Large wholesalers "integrate backwards" into the functions of selling agencies, small ones "integrate forward" into retailing, but the sugar refineries stick strictly to manufacturing. When manufacturing businessmen wish to expand they add other kinds of factory operations, often quite different lines, to their family businesses. Variation of lines also marks the operations of marketing firms, and

Hirsch explains well the importance of the extended family to the organization of Indian business.

Marketing in an Underdeveloped Economy: The North Indian Sugar Industry is fun to read, and one does not have to be an economist or an Indianist to enjoy it.

WALTER C. NEALE
Associate Professor of Economics
University of Texas

WALTER GALENSON (Ed.). *Labor in Developing Economies.* Pp. x, 299. Berkeley and Los Angeles: University of California Press, 1962. $6.00.

This collection of essays is another product of the Inter-University Study of Labor Problems in Economic Development. It is a companion to the previously published book, *Labor and Economic Development* (1959). Like its predecessor, this volume consists of a series of studies of the labor movement and the problems of industrial relations in various newly developing countries. The five essays in this book discuss the situation in Argentina, Brazil, and Chile, written by R. J. Alexander; Indonesia, by E. D. Hawkins; Israel, by Irvin Sobel; Pakistan, by W. D. Weatherford, Jr.; and Turkey, by S. M. Rosen. There is no fundamental principle that underlies the inclusion of these particular countries except the fact that all are at various stages of economic development and illustrate the variety of possible industrial relations patterns.

A more or less standard format is followed in each essay. There is a brief introduction to the recent economic history and sociocultural factors which bear on the economic process. There is a consideration of the emergence of a wage labor force. We are then given a discussion of the growth of trade unions and the labor movement and the factors which have influenced these, the nature of employer policy, the character of employer-union relations, and the role of the state in the industrial relations process. The collection is introduced by a useful analytic summary by the editor.

It is impossible to summarize the implications to be drawn from these essays. The individual national experiences have been too diverse. However, two features seem to stand out in all of these essays. The first is that some form of working-class organization seems to emerge as an "inevitable" complement of the development of modern economic life. Such organization is not a derivative solely of the imposition of Western ideologies; it follows from the wage-labor relationship. The second feature is that the directive role of the state in the internal affairs of unions and in the whole industrial relations process will be much greater in newly developing countries than was historically the case in North Atlantic nations. Israel, by virtue of its peculiar career, may well be an exception to this generalization. If this judgment is correct, we can expect to see a considerable difference between the pattern of industrial relations in newly developing countries and that with which we are familiar in the United States.

This situation bothers most of the writers. They tend to see the experience of the countries they are describing through eyes focused on American institutions and with values shaped by this. Walter Galenson expresses this most clearly (p. 10). While such an approach can sharpen one's view of another society, its ahistorical implications can yield unfortunate implications. There is a tendency to imply that societies where labor developments are different from those in the United States are necessarily destined to be antidemocratic. The alternative possibility is that newly developing countries may well shape different institutional arrangements to achieve effective representation of group interests.

Not one of the essays is exciting. This reviewer found Alexander's too brief essay on Brazil, Argentina, and Chile and Sobel's essay on Israel analytically most satisfying. All of the essays provide a large amount of useful information.

MORRIS DAVID MORRIS
Professor of Economics
University of Washington

ROBERT W. CAMPBELL. *Accounting in Soviet Planning and Management.* Pp. 315. Cambridge, Mass.: Harvard University Press, 1963. $5.50.

The Soviet economy may be viewed as a giant corporation in which economic decisions are taken by administrators at the Head Office without the help of an automatic, price-generating market mechanism, but rather on the basis of quantitative information supplied by a vast army of accountants and statisticians. In an economy of this type, therefore, the quality and smooth flow of such information—and consequently, the validity and finesse of the accounting, and more specifically, of the costing tools—are of the utmost importance for efficient planning and management. More than in a market-oriented economy, where cost accounting is related only indirectly to the national allocation of resources, defective accounting parts in a Soviet-type economy, in which the whole system of prices and costs is determined by accounting alone, will bear directly on the functioning of the economic engine. Accounting, therefore, lies at the very center of the problem of economic planning in the Soviet Union, and the better the accounting tools, and the more adequate the accounting procedures in providing cost information to the planners, the less will be the waste motion in the economy, and the more efficient the performance. Given the wide implications and the pervasiveness of accounting in the Soviet setting, the proper point of view for a study of the problem is that of the economist knowledgeable in the tools and methods of accountancy. Professor Campbell fills both qualifications, and his thorough, microscopic study of Soviet accounting procedures sheds new light on a hitherto much neglected subject.

The study reports that in the accounting tools and methods as these are currently used in the Soviet Union, Soviet planners and managers have at best a clumsy, unreliable, rigid, and largely arbitrary instrument for the perceiving of alternatives, the framing of policies, and the making of decisions. Part of the trouble, no doubt, stems from Marxist dogma. Whatever its metaphysical merits, the dogma does not provide any theory of value that would be relevant to the problem of resource allocation, and by the same token deprives Marxist planners of guides in the formulation of cost accounting objectives. Some of the difficulty, for instance, in depreciation accounting, must be attributed to simple carelessness.

A more important reason for the failure of Soviet accounting to transmit the kind of information that would be useful in economic planning and in management at the enterprise level is the tailoring of accounting rules and procedures by the Head Office to the objective of plan fulfillment control. This implies centralization, uniformity, and ease of definition at the expense of subtlety, flexibility, and accuracy. It follows that the degree of conflict between the information required to check on plan performance and that needed for executing the plan is inversely proportionate to the extent to which centralization is, in fact, achieved. As it happens, the Soviet system is neither fully decentralized nor fully centralized, and thus the conflict persists.

Professor Campbell is to be complimented on his careful, clear, and competent presentation of this difficult, important, and as far as Western economists are concerned, little-known problem.

JAN S. PRYBYLA
Associate Professor of Economics
Pennsylvania State University

JOHN SHEAHAN. *Promotion and Control of Industry in Postwar France.* Pp. xiii, 301. Cambridge, Mass.: Harvard University Press, 1963. $5.95.

For those students of economic growth who find profit in models of actual experience and are critically skeptical of purely theoretical constructs, no matter how erudite, this study of French economic recovery and expansion since World War II will be welcomed with enthusiasm. Here is no simplistic monocausal explanation of the French economic miracle which mars a companion book on France—*In Search of France*—issued by Harvard University Press, but a multiple-factor analysis of great intelligence and imagination, written with a minimum of professional jargon.

In order to show how the French have

managed to score their remarkable success, Professor Sheahan has made case studies of five major industries—aluminum, steel, industrial equipment, automobiles, and cotton textiles—on the ground that growth has come from great advances in selective industries and not from moderate gains across the board or in agriculture. In the instances cited, all of the prewar clichés, so tirelessly uttered by students of the French economy, were found no longer to be applicable. A new generation of entrepreneurs and managers are bent upon modernizing plant and otherwise doing what is necessary to produce at prices which are competitive in the international market. The French people are willing to save out of current production in order to invest in capital goods for their future benefit. And the French state has shown leadership in encouraging growth, through "indicative planning," in enlarging the market through the European Economic Community, in aiding in the reconstruction of international multilateral trade, and in pursuing fiscal policies in harmony with economic expansion. Clearly the French economy in its most advanced sectors has gone through a transformation which has largely freed it of those retardative forces which were the despair of those who thought that the French should become economically modern, not only for their own material benefit, but also for their own military protection.

SHEPARD B. CLOUGH
Professor of European and
Economic History
Columbia University

JOSEPH A. RAFFAELE. *Labor Leadership in Italy and Denmark.* Pp. xviii, 436. Madison: University of Wisconsin Press, 1962. $10.00.

This is a perplexing volume. The diligent reader can derive from its pages some interesting comparative information on the Italian and Danish labor movements. For example, it is apparent that, by comparison to their Italian counterparts, Danish trade union leaders are more conservative, more intimately in-

volved in the formulation and management of public policy, and more pragmatically oriented to collective bargaining and the solution of "bread-and-butter" problems. Similarly, Italian employers are much less sanguine than the Danes about the role of the union in society, and particularly about the goals and aspirations of those who lead organized labor.

Even though the author's samples are small, he is successful in outlining a number of important dimensions along which Italian and Danish labor leaders differ. These include, for example, educational background, orientation to union leadership roles, attitudes toward industrial management, and views concerning the participation of organized labor in the political process. But, what emerges from Raffaele's data is confirmation for something that is already widely known, namely, that Italy is a badly fragmented culture, torn by extreme ideological conflict and not basically inclined in a bargaining or co-operative direction. It is this fragmentation in Italy, and the cultural fusion in Denmark, that are apparently both reflected in and reinforced by behavioral patterns in their respective labor movements.

However, the volume also has several serious defects. For example, the author could have paid more attention to prose style, particularly to syntax, and thus avoided a basic weakness in the book's structure. Equally distressing for the reader is the proliferation of exceedingly long quotations from interviews which tend to become boring, rather than illuminating, through repetition. The poor organization of the volume also serves to obscure whatever basic theses and propositions the author is attempting to expound.

The book's most serious weakness is its methodological confusion, the source of which can be gleaned from reading the chapter on methodology. The author is aware of the need for more systematic, empirical, and nonimpressionistic studies in the field of comparative labor movements. Indeed, he suggests that the execution of such a study would offer the key to understanding almost everything about a society, including its "national character." Yet, the author's own work is an imperfect implementation of this desirable goal. He, himself, for example, seems only approximately to comprehend salient aspects of the societies he analyzes. In this regard, it is doubtful that Italians are gifted by an almost unique capacity for close rapport in human relations. The author's findings themselves clearly demonstrate that it is exactly this rapport that is missing in Italy.

One has the impression that the author has experienced a basic introduction to empirical science and that he is committed to this type of endeavor. However, the management of this particular study is so inexpertly handled as to discredit the behavioral sciences. To be sure, the author does not intend this result. Nevertheless, it is a pity that data that seem to have such a rich flavor are not more imaginatively and rigorously treated.

JOSEPH LAPALOMBARA
Professor of Political Science
Michigan State University
East Lansing

WILLIAM H. MIERNYK. *Trade Unions in the Age of Affluence.* Pp. 180. New York: Random House, 1962. $1.95.

Another author has joined the ranks of the lamenters on the present state of trade unions in the United States. William H. Miernyk also recognizes that the position of American unionism has deteriorated since the mid-fifties. The number of union members has been stabilized or actually reduced; the share of union membership of the total work population has been cut; the bargaining power of some unions has been curtailed; the size of the annual improvements in wages and benefits has become more modest; problems of job security have gained precedence over direct economic gains; and the prestige and acceptance of unions have been diminished. Unlike other writers who have faced up to these conditions, the present writer is satisfied with description and engages in no prescription.

His recitation of recent trade union developments is jointed with extensive digressions on the views of academicians and journalists about trade unions and economic issues involving them, such as inflation. Unfortunately, most of these excursions do not contain the author's conclusions on the merits of the underlying theses. As a result, one is left with the over-all impression that this paperback is more a review of the literature of interpretations and polemics than a serious independent appraisal of trade unions. It would have been useful, since the author believed it important to present these writings at such length, for him to have appraised their competence and quality and provided the readers with some information on the reliance one can place upon American scholarship for adequately interpreting the national trade union scene. The present reviewer would not score it very highly.

Several of the theses discussed in this book are highly questionable. Just to indicate the general nature of the contrary positions, the following might be useful. The so-called maturity of unions is essentially another name for preoccupation with union administration. The question therefore is whether the present American Federation of Labor-Congress of Industrial Organizations and Industrial Union Department organizational efforts are an adequate answer to the demand for militancy. Are unions monopolies in some markets? Or is this question irrelevant and improperly presented, since they are bargaining agencies and not unilateral price setters? Is the question of whether union wage pressure contributes to inflation also immaterial since union wage demands are derived from managerial abuse of market power? Instead of asking whether unions restrict innovation, should not union policies be interpreted as pressures upon management and government to develop methods of aiding workers to adapt to economic and technical change? Is the judgment of the unions' political influence properly founded? Are not the author's standards unrelated to the unions' own concepts of goals, structure, and methods of operation? Is not the present impasse in collective bargaining due largely to management's unwillingness to join with unions in finding mutually acceptable answers to the economic problems of the new era?

The general point of view in this book is retrospective. Professor Miernyk turns to past events to provide a backdrop for explaining and contrasting the present state of affairs of unions. As a result there is a tendency to oversimplify the past. The battles of the New Deal period appear very tame, which makes the summary inadequate for understanding the present state of unions and the contrast between "militancy" and "maturity." This book, like others by academic writers, misses the main issue in the debate on the crisis within the trade union movement. The obvious facts can and have been well recited by the author, but he has not defined the dilemma confronting trade unions. It is essentially whether the principle of national union autonomy shall survive or whether more and more power shall be concentrated in the national trade union center. The leaders of the building trades unions and other strong units, as well as many academic writers, are unable to recognize any particular "crisis" in the present situation. The power of these organizations and the gains of their members remain unchallenged and in some instances there is active co-operation between them and management in maintaining this steady advance.

The issues are whether the "trade union movement," which is a tag which unites all unions in a coherent and identifiable institution, is becoming weaker and less effective, and if so, whether it is the obligation of the individual national units to surrender more power to a federation to enable it more actively to pursue their common purposes. The question of national union autonomy which dominated the scenes in the 1880's is rearing its head again, and is the central one for those concerned with the future of American unionism.

SOLOMON BARKIN

Deputy Director
Manpower and Social Affairs Division
Organisation for Economic
  Co-operation and Development
Paris

JOSEPH W. GARBARINO. *Wage Policy and Long-Term Contracts.* Pp. xi, 145. Washington, D. C.: Brookings Institution, 1962. $3.00.

Professor Garbarino's volume deals with a subject that is likely to attract continuous attention. The problems of wage policy, though somewhat overshadowed now by the more immediate issue of unemployment, will continue to remain in the forefront of public policy concerns. A great deal of statistical analysis has already thrown light on many questions related to the problems of the possible inflationary impact of wage changes and the "feasible" rate of wage increases. Most of the work has dealt with highly aggregated data—statistical series pertaining to productivity changes, movement of price indexes, and behavior of average hourly earnings in broad sectors of the economy. Further work on more detailed wage series —particularly outside of manufacturing—is desirable. But what is also badly needed is more detailed analysis of the course of decisions, contracts, and results of collective bargaining in particular industries— especially those in which the parties appear to exercise some degree of market power in their price and wage policies. It is in this latter area that Garbarino's study makes its particular contribution.

The evaluation of long-term contracts inevitably involves an appraisal of prescriptions for a "feasible rate of wage increase," that is, a rate of increase in wage rates compatible with a stable price level and, presumably, also with the existing— functional—distribution of income. Garbarino's study devotes two chapters to this problem. In the first of these, the author discusses the various complexities involved in the concept of "feasible rate" and gives some estimates of what this rate is likely to be. In the second of the two chapters, Garbarino deals specifically with the General Motors formula—annual wage increases to match over-all productivity gains and cost-of-living adjustments—and with the problem of whether the general application of such a formula could result in holding wage changes to the level of a "feasible rate." Garbarino's basic conclusion is that the General Motors formula is unsuitable as a standard of general wage policy; however, the formula is considered as workable in the cases of prosperous companies, characterized both by higher than average productivity gains and expanding work force.

The two chapters outlined above constitute probably the weakest part of Garbarino's study. Within the confines of the slim volume, the analysis is somewhat sketchy; the statistical evidence, derived from the studies of others, is not examined very thoroughly; and some judgments are offered without much support. Nevertheless, the discussion provides a useful summary of the basic problem and focuses attention on some of the most critical issues.

The most valuable contribution of the monograph—and it is valuable indeed—lies in the three chapters that deal with the development of the General Motors long-term contract formula, with the analysis of the development and the course of long-term contracts in some major industries, and with an appraisal of the "performance" of the actual long-term contracts as compared with some feasible alternative forms of wage agreements. These chapters provide not only a stimulating analysis of the actual experiences under the long-term contracts, but also a much needed perspective on the wage developments during the post-World War II years.

Garbarino's basic conclusion is that the various wage formulas incorporated in long-term contracts tended in actuality to produce wage costs rises in excess of the feasible rate of wage increase. The long-term contracts were particularly expensive in steel—an industry in which both the timing of the agreements and the characteristics of wage payments and structure increased the cost of settlement. But the author also indicates that the form of settlement *per se* should not be viewed as a major factor affecting the results of collective bargaining. The basic factors lie in the economic and power relationship of particular bargaining situations. The probable results of alternative forms of settlements would not differ greatly from the actual wage record.

This limited summary cannot do full justice to the contents of Garbarino's study. The monograph is a valuable contribution to the growing literature that is concerned specifically with the problems of public policy suggested by wage results of collective bargaining.

MARTIN SEGAL
Associate Professor of Economics
Dartmouth College

DUNCAN M. MACINTYRE. *Voluntary Health Insurance and Rate Making.* Pp. ix, 301. Ithaca, N. Y.: Cornell University Press, 1962. $6.50.

Professor MacIntyre's book *Voluntary Health Insurance and Rate Making* is primarily descriptive. It traces the evolution of health insurance and gives the current status of various health plans. Unfortunately, there is hardly any discussion of the objectives of health insurance. Little is said of the significant proportion of the population not insured and not likely to be insured under current conditions. Professor MacIntyre fails to discuss the public welfare problem, which current practices accentuate rather than ameliorate. It is not until the end of the volume is reached that we find the author's conclusion: "In this writer's opinion the health interests of American society will be served best by pluralism, choice, continued competition, and an enlarged reliance on government."

This reviewer feels that the spread of experience rating by private insurance companies, whose sole objective is profit, has curtailed the growth of Blue Cross plans and even forced Blue Cross into experience rating. The more widely experience rating is practiced the more surely do we deprive large segments of the population from becoming insured because the premium for the remaining population will take a disproportionate part of their incomes. These excluded persons will have to seek aid from public welfare agencies. Perhap this is what Professor MacIntyre meant by "an enlarged reliance on government."

The continued growth of experience

rating may offer choice to the higher income groups of our society, but to those with low incomes there is only one choice, and that is to remain uninsured. The commodity markets are able to supply nourishing foods, clothing suitable to the climate, and house furnishings at a wide range of prices so that even the lowest income groups have some choice. Although low-rent housing is difficult to obtain, there is still some available. Elementary education is free to all. Adequate health care, as important as any other consumer expenditure, is becoming increasingly less available to low-income groups.

Some significant remarks on experience rating were made by Frank Van Dyke and Ray E. Trussell in an article in THE ANNALS for September 1961. Say the authors: "Experience rating discriminates against high-risk groups. But another and more subtle effect of experience rating of health insurance is an increased premium for almost everyone when they become older. A young person whose group has a low premium today must pay a high premium when he is old, simply because his current premium does not include a factor for his increased use of medical services when he becomes old. This can be avoided through a lifetime, level premium for everyone. Except for a few special groups such as the New York State employees, almost all health insurance premiums, including Blue Cross, cost more for retired persons than for the working population."

This reviewer regrets the failure on the part of Professor MacIntyre to speculate on the possible effects on trends in experience rating of covering the hospital bills of the aged under Old-age, Survivors, and Disability Insurance. By removing this important risk group from the private sector, Blue Cross plans would be in a better position to compete with private insurance even though Blue Cross adhered to a community rating system.

DAVID M. SCHNEIDER
Director
Bureau of Research and Statistics
New York State Department of
Social Welfare

WARREN B. CATLIN. *The Process of Economics: A History of Economic Thought.* Pp. 788. New York: Bookman Associates, 1962. No price.

This treatise follows topical rather than chronological lines, and its level is appropriate to professional or preprofessional social scientists. It provides running commentaries on the literature on such subjects as theories of society, self-interest, altruism, welfare, population, production, rent, money, and business cycles, with discussions on points ranging from religious and family influences on writers to the editing of encyclopedia contributions. There is not much that is new in the way of material or interpretation, but a wealth of scholarship is displayed; probably few readers will lay the book down without seeing something which helps their understanding of the course of economic thought.

Recent developments get attention, including arguments for the expansion of government functions. Here, the author might have broadened his approach with advantage. As Adam Smith pointed out, what is called the public interest really may be the private interest of a pressure group. This aspect seems to be neglected here, when public ownership of utilities receives support despite the condition that at the present time it is being promoted, both in the United States and Canada, with the evident purpose of transferring part of the over-all cost of government from electricity users in affected areas— often prosperous—to taxpayers elsewhere.

Views sometimes are expressed which are unacceptable as presented. Thus, the author says that "philosophers, like Hobbes, Machiavelli, Schopenhauer, and Nietzsche," have "preached a gospel of hate and conflict." For Schopenhauer, particularly, this seems untrue. Either Schopenhauer's philosophy appears to be misrepresented or the word "hate" misused. Again, speaking of Soviet Russia, it is said that "such delicate flowers as health and welfare cannot be expected to thrive in a police state or one seemingly actuated by such imperialistic designs." This ignores the advances made by Soviet medicine, not only in research but in bringing reasonably good treatment to ordinary citizens. Occasionally, there are points which can be questioned in the main subject matter—the interpretation of economic theories and attitudes. One is the author's opinion that Malthus failed to reconcile the idea of diminishing returns with that of a surplus from agricultural labor. Did not Malthus do this sufficiently in his *Inquiry into the Nature and Progress of Rent?* In general, however, this aspect of the book merits high praise. The frequent incorporation of satirical asides seems to mar the presentation.

Edmund Whittaker
Professor of Economics
Hampden-Sydney College

T. W. Freeman. *A Hundred Years of Geography.* Pp. 334. Chicago: Aldine, 1962. $6.95.

This volume is a studiously written and quite readable compilation of facts and ideas about geography and geographers, published as one of a series of books on academic disciplines, each one "A Hundred Years of" its subject. In this case, the subject is divided systematically into chapters on conventional branches of geography—physical, regional, and political, for example—and many authors are quoted on each branch. The author of the book himself contributes substantive geographical data with justifiable confidence, particularly in two areas: the geography of Ireland and urbanization in England. In other areas he expresses his opinions less frequently and with some diffidence.

Probably the author is not primarily to blame for the fact that the book does not live up to its title or to the publisher's notices. Apparently he was persuaded to undertake the assignment of writing the book in order to fill a gap in the series, and this he has tried conscientiously to do, even though previously not particularly concerned with geographical theory and history. Consequently, it is not "an incisive survey of the development of the discipline as a science," though advertised as such, and it does not show "how the field has been differentiated from associated disciplines." Geography has developed as a discipline and has been differentiated from associated disciplines, but these facts are not made evident by this book. The title suggests a sequence of development in theory and method leading to the geographic discipline of the present, and such a developmental sequence has in fact occurred, but sequence and discipline are not revealed to readers of *A Hundred Years of Geography.*

If the book had been entitled "A British Geographer's Impressions of Geography and Geographers at Home and Abroad," it might have satisfied not only geographers at home, in Britain, but even those abroad, in America, Germany, and France. The author is clearly at home in Britain, but America and the European continent are viewed from a distance. Well-known American works have been consulted and are carefully quoted, but a background of knowledge and fullness and intimacy of understanding are lacking. German geography is even farther away and seen through the medium of American interpretation.

If the reader is willing to forgive the title and press notices and to accept the book as a sincere and good-natured British commentary, there remain at least two serious faults. (1) Geography is presented nationalistically in the book, as if American geographers all thought alike, and differently from British geographers, and as if German geographers were all alike. Actually, geography has become an international discipline in which geographers may differ among themselves individually or in groups, but not in unanimous national groups. (2) Geography is not brought up to date in the book. The most important steps toward making geography a scientific discipline have occurred within the last 35 years, and of this there is no hint in the book. There are quotations from recent literature, but they are selected in such a way as to reflect only older points of view. For one thing, environmentalism survives in the book, even though superseded in geographic thought by concepts of culture origin and dispersal as major explanatory processes. For another thing, ideas of static regional uniformity prevail in the book, whereas ideas of dynamic regional organization have become much more important in recent advances of geographic research. Accordingly, readers of the book, particularly nongeographers, should be on their guard against expecting to learn from it what modern geography is in progressive centers of learning. They may well expect to learn something of what geography was in a previous generation.

ROBERT S. PLATT
Professor Emeritus of Geography
University of Chicago

CHARLES ISSAWI and MOHAMMED YEGANEH. *The Economics of Middle Eastern Oil.* Pp. xiv, 230. New York: Frederick A. Praeger, 1963. $8.00.

J. E. HARTSHORN. *Politics and World Oil Economics: An Account of the International Oil Industry in its Political Environment.* Pp. 364. New York: Frederick A. Praeger, 1962. $8.50.

Historians, economists, politicians, and just general readers will find these two books on the vital international oil industry thoroughly engrossing. These are books for understanding, and not intended for entertainment. In both books the evidence points toward thoroughly sound scholarship.

In *The Economics of Middle Eastern Oil* there is a veritable mine of operating and investment information, as there should be since this is fundamentally a study of the investments and returns from the oil industry in the Persian Gulf countries. Although all the years since 1913 are touched on, the dozen years between 1948 and 1960 are given close and detailed treatment and study. The authors consider numerous aspects and influences, including geography, gas, refining, investments, prices, receipts, costs, returns, governmental receipts, recent changes and trends. They conclude that the future profits will continue to decline and that the exceedingly high returns of the early postwar period are a thing of the past.

Far less specialized and therefore having a wider appeal for the reader is *Politics and World Oil Economics,* which also shows consummate scholarship. Mr. Hartshorn, an editor of *The Economist,* also considers several aspects of the industry—but different aspects and those around the world. He discusses geography, economics, taxation, integration, marketing, consumers, common interests, self-sufficiency and pressures. Bigness and vertical integration, explains Mr. Hartshorn, are only the natural result of the economic factors playing on the complex oil industry. For example, the pattern of land ownership outside the United States has brought a strong tendency toward bigness—and large size often has meant vertical integration.

One interesting aspect of the oil industry is that it always must be on the move since the resources it develops it also exhausts. The sales policies of the major companies must not differ from the published prices—which is to say that the textbook definition of competition has little in common with the oil industry in practice. The charts and maps in Mr. Hartshorn's work are excellent, and a great aid to the reader. Another interesting aspect that this author brings out is the fact that abroad the oil industry pretends that at home it has no controls. Actually, the oil industry in the United States is carefully regulated—and much of that regulating comes from three members of the Railroad Commission of Texas, which decides on prorating and other matters.

Both these books will be of great value to the economic and the social historian, as well as to those interested in the political and diplomatic aspects of international affairs.

GERALD FORBES
Chairman
Department of History
Ouachita Baptist College
Arkadelphia
Arkansas

SOCIOLOGY AND ANTHROPOLOGY

ROBERT REDFIELD. *Human Nature and the Study of Society: The Papers of Robert Redfield,* Vol. I. Edited by Margaret Park Redfield. Pp. xvi, 507. Chicago: University of Chicago Press, 1962. $10.00.

Robert Redfield was of that generation of students, in the then Department of Sociology and Anthropology at the University of Chicago, who studied with Robert E. Park, a newspaper man, cum philosopher, cum sociologist, passionate believer in the possibility of a science of sociology, but indifferent to conventional boundaries between "disciplines"; Edward Sapir, anthropologist, linguist, social psychologist, poet, who likewise scorned the boundaries; and Fay Cooper Cole, an ethnologist and American archaeologist, faithful to the anthropological tradition of studying primitive peoples and prehistory, but outgoing, humanistic, a devoted teacher, and a witness for the defense at the Scopes evolution trial in Tennessee. Whether Redfield actually studied with George Herbert Mead, I do not know; at any rate, Mead was there in person and in the minds and words of Ellsworth Faris, Edward Scribner Ames, Park, *et al.* It is no wonder that Redfield—sharp in detailed observation from study of botany, keen in argument from study of law, a poet and philosopher from childhood— should have become the link that joined sociology with anthropology, the science of man with the intellectual and moral arts.

His first work, *Tepoztlan,* broke from anthropological tradition, in that it described a peasant village, not a primitive people. In it he distinguished *folk* from the urban *demos*—and concerned himself not with a *status quo ante,* but with a present condition and with processes of change. The rest of his career is contained, in germ, in that study. But the great tree is formed not by the seed alone, but by the exigencies of life and environment. Redfield's concept of "folk culture" was criticized. He took account of the criticism, broadened his studies, and ingested the work of his many students, and of other scholars.

The broadening and deepening of his concepts are recorded in this volume—the first of two—of his papers. They are presented under three headings: (1) "Anthropology as a Social Science: Methods and Principles," (2) "The Folk Society and Civilization," and (3) "Human Nature." While the papers are not put in the order in which Redfield wrote them, there is a certain progression in term. The last three papers of the middle section were written as chapters of a projected book on the nature of civilizations, by definition, city-centered. The last section, "Human Nature," dates from the last few years of his life, years of intense intellectual activity.

Some would make of Redfield the author and defender of a cliché. They could have learned better by reading his already published books. To any who still cling to such a stereotype of Redfield, I recommend that they give themselves the great pleasure of reading this volume. The editor has done a thoughtfully excellent job of arranging and introducing the selections. Raymond Firth has written an introduction putting Redfield's work into perspective.

EVERETT C. HUGHES
Professor of Sociology
Brandeis University

GABRIEL KOLKO. *Wealth and Power in America: An Analysis of Social Class and Income Distribution.* Pp. xii, 178. New York: Frederick A. Praeger, 1962. $4.85.

Wealth and Power in America is a briefly written, easily read, but profound book in its breadth and depth of statistical deduction. The wealth of which Professor Kolko speaks is, as all know, extremely unequally divided. How wretchedly divided it is, is the message of the work. In the so-called affluent years since World War II, Kolko has this to say: "Since 1947, one-half of the nation's families and unattached individuals have had an income too small to provide them with a maintenance standard of living, and

COLLEGIAN

He's a student at General Motors Institute. Today, he's absorbed in higher mathematics. Tomorrow, perhaps Plato and Aristotle ... political theory and psychology ... humanities and economics— in short, whatever makes for a well-rounded education. Next week, he may be on the job in an automobile plant. Twenty-four hundred other students like him are studying to be electrical, mechanical or industrial engineers, in one of the world's most unusual institutions of higher learning.

During their first four college years at GMI, students alternate between six weeks of intensive study at GMI and six weeks of paid work at one of 133 General Motors operations across the nation and in Canada. Their fifth year is entirely in the field ... preparing bachelor theses based on actual engineering projects of their sponsoring GM divisions.

Since its small beginning, 37 years ago, GMI has graduated 6,000 engineers. The great majority chose to remain with General Motors and today are employed in a wide range of technical and managerial positions in GM plants throughout the world. The educational investment in these people has been a beneficial one— not only for them and for General Motors—but for the many communities where they now work and live.

GENERAL MOTORS IS PEOPLE ...

Making Better Things For You

232b

The October 1963 issue of

Crime and Delinquency

is devoted to the new

Model Sentencing Act

drafted by the

ADVISORY COUNCIL OF JUDGES

and articles on it by

JUDGE GERALD F. FLOOD
Superior Court of Pennsylvania

DR. MANFRED S. GUTTMACHER
Chief Medical Officer
Supreme Bench of Baltimore

GEORGE EDWARDS
Commissioner of Police, Detroit

SANGER B. POWERS
Director of Corrections, Wisconsin

Single copy, $1.25

Annual sub. (with *NCCD News*), $5

National

Council on

Crime and

Delinquency

44 E. 23 St., New York 10, N. Y.

Kindly mention THE ANNALS *when writing to advertisers*

one-third have had an income too small to provide even an emergency standard of living."

This theme is never dropped, but is looked at in various facets, intensively, indisputably. The sociological disfunction of all this is easily seen in viewing the "income tenths" into which Kolko divides the population, and which are, in turn, his idea of class differentiation. The method makes for easy comparison. The top 10 per cent, who live in the sharpest contrast to at least seven or eight other segments of the population, live "in the prosperous and frequently sumptuous manner that most social commentators ascribe to the large majority of Americans."

Kolko's view of power is the corporate one. He asks: "Do a small group of very wealthy men have the power to guide industry, and thereby much of the total economy, toward ends they decide upon as compatible with their own interests? Do they own and control the major corporations?" He replies: "The answers must inevitably be affirmative." If the book falters at all, it is on the side of the academic hope that by the revelation of its truth it will bring many to the light, and somehow in that process the corporation will become democratized. There is no real political message in this, of course.

But the author does not claim to be a political strategist. He has merely given some very sharp tools to those who may prod America's policy-makers, the managers of its economic segment, the upper tenth.

FLOYD HUNTER

Berkeley
California

VANCE PACKARD. *The Pyramid Climbers: A Penetrating Look at the New Breed of Hustling, Well-Packaged Executives Scaling Corporate Heights.* Pp. x, 339. New York: McGraw-Hill, 1962. $5.00.

After many years of professional contact with socioeconomic-technological problems in the United States, the present reviewer comes away from perusing the author's fourth volume of criticism and satire with mixed reactions. He continues to feel

that Packard's books are well worth reading. They offer provocative insights into aspects of American life that are often overlooked by the professionals. What the author sets out to do is well enough expressed in the subtitle given above. The volume, however, lacks any mention of some of the most important developments in American corporate management over the last few decades; certain measures well-known to professionals and aimed at solving long-standing difficulties are largely overlooked in those last chapters which purport to offer remedies, "bold experiments," and "happier courses." And the broader socioeconomic matrix in which the "well-packaged" scalers of "corporate heights" are set is conspicuously absent.

To follow Packard's own schematic model, the current American socioeconomic scene might be viewed as an extended plane. On this, many individual enterprisers and executives and small related groups are seen—on the farms; in small offices occupied by lawyers, doctors, and engineers; as self-employed entrepreneurs; and in stores and shops. In this plane are also seen many structurally stratified pyramids, varying in height; among these are profit-seeking corporations, nonprofit corporations, educational institutions, church organizations, government hierarchies and bureaus, trade unions, and other complexly organized structures typical of a modern advanced society, which without them could never have attained affluence and other cultural satisfactions.

It is not contended here that Packard should have differentiated in detail among these numerous types of pyramidal structures essential to any highly organized economy. The main point is that many of the trends and characteristics—good as well as questionable—which he highlights apply not only to the hustling, money-grabbing executives on the profit-seeking pyramids, but to the executives on nearly all other pyramids as well—not to mention some of the self-employed on the plane below. Here are a few examples: (1) being expected to talk, dress, and work within a set pattern; (2) finding barriers against Negroes, Jews, women, noncollegians; (3) being screened and tested to locate candidates with cool heads, sound bodies, acceptable personalities, sense of propriety, and helpful wives; (4) running into age and salary timetables and cut-off dates; (5) having difficulties with mavericks or rebels and with bland, apathetic, or choleric overlords; (6) developing ulcers and psychoneuroses. All these abound throughout tension-ridden organized society, and not in profit-seeking corporations alone. "Manipulations, loss of dignity, stifled initiative, passiveness, invasion of home life" are experienced not only by corporate managers, "who often feel that within themselves something has been destroyed," but by many other Americans who have little if any direct contact with high living and are not particularly interested in scaling pyramids, of whatever variety. A broader view of American stratified pyramids and their climbers does not necessarily imply that the socioeconomic problems of an affluent society are less critical or disturbing than Packard suggests. However, being more diversified, they may be more insidious and thus harder to get at.

From Packard's account, one gets the impression that nothing of consequence has happened in the management field and in the selection and training of executives until the last few years, and that he himself has dug up the real answers, mention of which he reserves for the last few chapters. To these one looks with whetted expectation, only to end with disappointment. How do executives gain breadth? For some "it comes naturally." Others should work outside the business field for a while; they might be given sabbaticals; "immerse them in sensitivity training for two weeks"—which seems to be a combination of the "kill or cure"; or subject them to a reincarnated "Oxford Movement" of frank tell-all experience meetings. In addition, he mentions plans for achieving greater executive responsibility by "flattening" high pyramids or breaking them up into several smaller ones. This General Motors accomplished with marked success years ago, but the author apparently knows nothing of this. Nor does he men-

tion the hundreds of incentive plans that have been in operation for large-scale American industry for over a century, profit-sharing and management-sharing plans conspicuous among them. Significant management innovations of the present day, such as those by the Kaiser and United States Steel industries, to assure job security in the midst of fast-expanding automation, are also overlooked.

In general, it appears that Packard in his *Pyramid Climbers* has gotten into waters beyond his depth. However, he offers many interesting side lights on management mores. With these the aspiring young executive should be familiar, provided that in reading this book, he does not take it too seriously.

JOSEPH MAYER
Visiting Professor in Science and
  Technology
Southern Illinois University

SIDNEY GOLDSTEIN. *The Norristown Study.* Pp. xxi, 366. Philadelphia: University of Pennsylvania Press, 1961. $7.50.

This is a report on a multidisciplinary study of technological change and social adjustment, during the first half of the present century, in Norristown, situated in the metropolitan area of Philadelphia. The substance of the book is presented in a series of vignettes of some sixteen independent studies dealing with demographic changes, the growth of the economic structure, the effects of changes on the individual workers, and the acculturation of ethnic and religious groups. Since the several studies were prosecuted concurrently, they do not build on one another. Hence, apart from the string of certain funds of data, the virtues of a multidisciplinary research effort are left to the reader's imagination.

"Technological change" is inclusively defined to embrace changes "in plants, machinery, means of transportation and communication, and concomitant changes in methods of doing business and ways of living." That there should have been parallel changes in "social adjustment," that is, "behavioral reactions to technological changes, including both overt reactions and subjective reactions in terms of attitudes and values," hardly seems problematical. Could it have been the desire to preserve interdisciplinary congeniality that dictated so obtuse and, in fact, so redundant a problem statement?

The principal discovery is that technological change in Norristown came about mainly through industrial relocations rather than through technical innovations within local plants. The impact of such changes on employment rates and on intergenerational occupational mobility are understandable enough. But their effects on birth rates, the decline of orthodoxy among Jews, and the coverage in the press of the activities of minority groups are obscure, nor are they elucidated. A second finding of interest is that occupational mobility has tended to supplant migration as the means of meeting the labor force needs of industry. In this connection, the author notes the existence of "lower levels of worker attachments to specific occupational careers and jobs." That is an allusion, I take it, to the spread of task specialization in industry. Further, while the widening of the labor market area and the consequent increase in worker commuting distances are noted, there is only a belated awareness that the lengthening journey to work is also a substitute for migration. A closer look might have revealed that it is the more significant substitute.

These points of dissatisfaction aside, the various studies appear to have been well designed and carefully executed. The author's account of the total enterprise is workmanlike and unpretentious. The book should prove useful, among other ways, as a reference source for other groups contemplating multidisciplinary undertakings.

AMOS H. HAWLEY
Professor of Sociology
University of Michigan

EUGENE B. BLOCK. *And May God Have Mercy . . . : The Case Against Capital Punishment*. Pp. viii, 197. San Francisco: Fearon, 1962. $4.50.

The content of this excellent book is revealed by its chapter headings: "A Cause Symbolized"; "The Dark History"; "Is Death a Deterrent?"; "How Many Innocents?"; "Time Brings Vindication"; "Victims of Vengeance, Poverty, and Prejudice"; "What Is Insanity?"; "Abolition—the English Front"; "Abolition—the French Front"; "Abolition—the World Front"; "Abolition—the Home Front"; "Abolition—in California"; "The Voices of Protest"; "Looking Backward, Looking Ahead."

There are various criteria according to which one may judge such a work. Does it discuss which side has the burden of proving the relative effectiveness of death penalties and long prison sentences? Yes. Does it use statistics a bit too argumentatively? Yes. Does it mention the brutalizing effect of capital punishment? Yes. Does it emphasize that mostly we execute indigents, and quite indiscriminately at that? Yes. Does it concede that many murderers kill for profit and not just because of emotion? No. Does it discuss budgets eased by lifers assisting the staffs of prisons? No. Does it place in perspective the argument that we should kill men to save money? Yes. Does it query whether murderers should be saved and studied in order that we may learn to handle others in a way which will prevent crime? Yes. Does it overemphasize the occasional executions of persons for crimes they did not commit? Yes. Does it consider the problem of those tempted to murder in order to become central characters in capital trials? Yes. Does the author assume that executions would be justified if they were the most effective deterrent? No. Judged by these criteria, Mr. Block's book scores well. In passing, he even states the case for capital punishment; unpersuasively, but no more so than its proponents.

Two things more: we all are born under sentence of death. The question is not whether it is wrong for a murderer in our midst to die; the question is whether it is right for us to kill him. Seldom is the problem posed more poignantly than when the criminal is insane. *May God*

Have Mercy . . . should be read with realization that we permit execution of persons who killed while insane, excluding from jeopardy of the death penalty only those insane who were not aware of what they did, or unaware that it was wrong. This "right and wrong" test is not new. St. Luke tells us that from the Cross it was pronounced as a defense; a defense of the sane. Much earlier, our ancestors are supposed to have eaten from the tree of the knowledge of good and evil and thereby incurred the penalty of death. Must we judge lunatics by the same standard today?

MICHAEL VON MOSCHZISKER
Member of the
Philadelphia Bar

STUART KING JAFFARY. *Sentencing of Adults in Canada.* Pp. xii, 122. Toronto: University of Toronto Press, 1963. $4.95.

This is a slender study of the practices and consequences of sentencing under the Federal Criminal Code of Canada, the nucleus of which are summary statistical data on sentences imposed in the ten provinces. These are drawn from *Statistics of Criminal and Other Offences* for 1955, a volume published annually by the Dominion Bureau of Statistics. In view of the fact that the Parole Act of 1959, described as a "most important provision for the modification of court sentences," has now succeeded the Ticket-of-Leave Act, it is unfortunate that more recent data were not provided to reflect changes that must have occurred before the book was published. The significance of the parole legislation is described quite briefly in the Introduction.

Sentencing of Adults in Canada contains ten chapters, divided among four major parts, dealing broadly and briefly with the Classical foundations of Anglo-American sentencing, the sentences imposed in 1955 by Canadian courts, the transition in England and the United States to "a social rationale" in sentencing, and the significance of the work of the magistrates' courts in Canada. An index is included and a four-page appendix containing a chapter from the 1938 report of the Royal Commission to Investigate the Penal System of Canada, dealing with "general principles of criminology and penology." Materials in several chapters are drawn from the Archambault Report of 1938 dealing with the penal system of Canada, the Fauteux Report of 1956 on the remission service, and certain British governmental reports. Significant recent materials on sentencing published in the United States are not cited.

It may be apparent from what has been said that this study offers relatively little to serious students of sentencing beyond what has been available in more detail in other sources. However, it is apparently the first study that has been published on sentencing in Canada. It presents interesting, though limited, materials on the prevalence and length of prison sentences in Canada as compared to England and Wales, the Netherlands, and Sweden. Aside from the noncomparability of the data, it is difficult to draw meaningful inferences from these figures, since they derive from differing sociocultural contexts. It is clear, however, that in Canada, as elsewhere, there is considerable variation in sentencing generally and in the use of imprisonment, both as between different judges and in different parts of the country. This suggests the need to develop greater uniformity of practice through the use of standardized criteria for sentencing and to expand and diversify treatment resources.

It appears that Professor Jaffary sought in this volume chiefly to promulgate a "social rationale" of sentencing, somewhat loosely defined in terms of an individualized and rehabilitative justice. The reviewer is not convinced from the materials presented that, in fact, either in England or the United States, "the pendulum has made a complete swing in a century, from the rigorous logic of a Bentham to the practical social science of the twentieth century." Whatever has been the impact of the behavioral sciences on sentencing and corrections, it has patently done little to reduce crime rates, disparities in sentences, and criminal recidivism. It remains to be demonstrated that Freud contributed more than Bentham to the efficacy of social and legal control. Some latter-day skeptics have come to question where a largely permissive and clinical criminology may lead us during an era of normative deterioration.

PAUL W. TAPPAN
Walter E. Meyer Visiting Research
   Professor
Law School
Harvard University

PHILOSOPHY AND RELIGION

CARL J. FRIEDRICH (Ed.). *Nomos IV: Liberty.* Pp. xii, 333. New York: Atherton Press, 1962. $6.00.

For those interested in the niceties of definition and concept the fourth yearbook of the Society for Political and Legal Philosophy offers a wide range of critical thought, centered mainly on John Stuart Mill's "On Liberty." Celebrating the hundredth anniversary of its appearance in 1859, twelve of the sixteen articles deal directly with Mill and the four others with the problems of liberty in related terms. All of the sixteen authors are college professors, nine in political science, three in philosophy, two in law, one in history, and one in economics. Some wrote their papers for the 1959 meeting held at Columbia University; the rest grew out of it under the skilled editorship of Professor Friedrich.

The critiques of Mill's great essay are as varied as the authors. They range all over the field of law, authority, and social responsibility in relation to individual liberty, and the well-worn ideas of freedom from what and to do what. As intended, this is all criticism in the higher atmosphere of theory. But even so, it seems remarkable that hardly a reference is made to Marxism, which assuredly deals with a theory not now to be ignored in any discussion of liberty. To one who has lived like this reviewer in the midst of conflict over claims to liberty, the discussion presents a largely unreal world, not even

encompassing the world of legal theory with which the United States Supreme Court wrestles in defining and applying the limits of individual freedom and State intervention. The main sources of criticism are books by other philosophers than Mill and arguments unrelated to the realities of the great historic struggles for liberty.

As intellectual exercise the collection is stimulating reading; as a contribution to the great debates of our time it offers little guidance.

ROGER N. BALDWIN
Chairman
International League for the
   Rights of Man
New York City

JORDAN M. SCHER (Ed.). *Theories of the Mind.* Pp. xix, 748. New York: Free Press of Glencoe, 1962. $12.50.

This volume constitutes a sort of paean to the abiding tradition of mind, and at the same time it serves as a testimonial to the atomization of the intellectual as well as every other phase of culture. We may well regard this book, then, as a study in sociointellectual institutions. From it we learn that a belief in mind persists despite the fact that scientific psychologists have long sought to lay this ghost. The actual contents of the book consists of thirty-five essays by mathematicians, philosophers, psychiatrists, neurologists, anthropologists, and psychologists who write under the heading of mind, while some of them actively attempt to defend the historically instituted mind-body doctrine.

Since the existence of cultural institutions depends upon the reactions performed with respect to them, and since the writers have different societal backgrounds, we expect serious divergences in the views of the contributors. Accordingly the editor classifies the essays into (1) Mind as Brain, (2) Mind as Participation, and (3) Mind as Method. There are, of course, cleavages within these classes, and some of the essays of one heading might just as well be placed in another. Perhaps the strongest indication of the viability of the mind institution is that a number of writers simply use the word *mind* as the basis of a discussion of problems claiming their interest, such as probability processes in psychoanalytic psychiatry, social structure, growth of culture, material aspects of mental disease, conditioned reflexes, neural organization, and so on. One contributor writing on the actions of drugs on emotional phenomena says, "After I had accepted the responsibility for writing an article toward an understanding of the mind . . . I referred to the dictionary for a precise definition."

Both the tenacity of institutions and divergent attitudes toward them are excellently demonstrated by the writers for whom *mind* is not merely a name. Here are some samples of mind theories. Mind is (1) an entity, (2) integration, (3) idealism, (4) creative love, (5) something more than brain, (6) something more than a mechanical model, (7) a creating, evolving, emergent process. It is something else than simple perversity to be reminded of a lecture by a popular poet who offered as one definition of poetry, "a sliver of the moon in the belly of a frog."

The editor concludes that, after all the viewpoints are displayed, mind remains largely an enigmatic elephant of unknown dimensions and unco-ordinated aspects. In other words, anything but a verbal construction created as a successor to the Patristic soul and now persisting by institutional inertia.

J. R. KANTOR
Visiting Professor of Psychology
New York University

ERNEST BECKER. *The Birth and Death of Meaning: A Perspective in Psychiatry and Anthropology.* Pp. xiv, 210. New York: Free Press of Glencoe, 1962. $5.00.

Dr. Becker begins his introduction to this book by stating, "This is a rather ambitious book." It is indeed, the ambition being nothing less than to write "a readable book for newcomers to the study of human behavior," and "to offer an abstract scheme to even seasoned students of man, which may integrate into

a theory of human behavior." That Dr. Becker achieved his first ambition more successfully than he did his second is in no way to denigrate what is in every way a most commendable effort to compress such a worthy wish into only 174 pages.

This is an excellent book, well worth reading and pondering over, well worth recommending to anyone concerned about a "science of man." As such, it should make excellent reading for any student of psychiatry, psychology, sociology, or anthropology who has advanced beyond the initial stages of his contacts with any of these disciplines. The book is challenging enough to force any such student into the wider frame of reference necessary if he is truly to understand the ramifications and implications of his study of man and man's behavior.

Dr. Becker received his Ph.D. in anthropology from Syracuse University and is presently engaged in teaching and research in the Department of Psychiatry at the Upstate Medical Center of the State University of New York in Syracuse. The book grew out of a series of lectures he presented to the residents in psychiatry at that school and so is slanted primarily for their purposes. But it is clear that the author's intent is far beyond that limited purpose and involves far more than the disciplines of psychiatry and anthropology. Sociology, communication, psychoanalysis, and psychology are also included in the disciplines Dr. Becker attempts to integrate into a whole unified theory, being convinced that we should be able to "skip around between disciplines without having to be concerned about property rights."

Having said all of these glowing things about the book, it hardly seems right to carp about what seems to me to be Dr. Becker's misundersandings about some of psychoanalysis. But since this reviewer is a psychoanalyst and since the material of the book was originally directed to psychiatric residents, it seems necessary.

Dr. Becker takes Freud to task for his misinterpretation of the conflicts surrounding the time of the child's life which has come to be known as "oedipal." On the one hand he complains about Freud's early interpretations of the conflicts—especially their sexual nature—around this time, but he also gives full credit to the subsequent work of Erikson, Rappaport, and others in re-interpreting these same observed phenomena. Obviously psychoanalysis is a growing body of knowledge, in no way dedicated to the proposition that its founder had the last word on everything. As Robert Waelder makes clear in a recent review of "Psychoanalysis, Philosophy and Scientific Method" in the Fall 1962 issue of the *Journal of the American Psychoanalytic Association,* Freud's philosophy and even his metapsychology are constantly open to attack and revision as more and better data are supplied. This is what is happening under the leadership of Waelder, Rappaport, Gill, Menninger, Erikson, and others, but it is these later developments that Dr. Becker, like many other nonclinicians, seems to ignore, or not to be fully aware of.

But this, as I said, is carping. *The Birth and Death of Meaning* is an excellent book; it is well written, well thought out, provocative, and interesting. I do not hesitate to recommend it.

RICHARD G. LONSDORF
Departments of Psychiatry and Law
University of Pennsylvania

RONALD L. MEEK. *The Economics of Physiocracy: Essays and Translations.* Pp. 432. Cambridge, Mass.: Harvard University Press, 1963. $9.00.

The adoption of various physiocratic notions by modern economists has prompted a revaluation of physiocracy, leading in a few cases to a correction of time-honored prejudices. In the course of those studies, many writings of the school have been republished. Already the fragmentary *Collection des économistes et réformateurs sociaux de la France (1910)* gave precedence to the physiocrats. Two years ago, The French Institut National d'Études Démographiques republished a set of Quesnay's works, partly superseding the famous Oncken edition. With the present volume, another gap has been closed.

Since the full texts of Quesnay's writings, except those on "Natural Right" and on "Despotism in China," could not be obtained in English, Ronald L. Meek has translated some of his masterpieces: not only *Le tableau économique,* but several of his articles published in the *Grande encylopédie:* the "Dialogue on the Work of Artisans," the "General Maxims of the Economic Government of an Agricultural Kingdom," "Natural Right," extracts from Quesnay's and Mirabeau's common brain child "Rural Philosophy," and a few supplementary papers. While both the accuracy of the translations and the carefulness of the annotations deserve high praise, contemporary economists may regard five essays relegated to the rear of the book as the gist of the author's accomplishment. Though only loosely connected, these essays are shedding new light on the meaning and the historical setting of physiocracy.

Most revealing are some discussions on the origins of the system. Were the three "first" editions of the Economic Table, as generally believed, mutually inconsistent or did they supplement each other and convey the same message in different terms? Did Quesnay accept Cantillon's view that, since the farmer normally made three rents, each of them being roughly equal to one third of the produce of the farm, the "third rent" represented net profit? In this case, it was obvious that the farmer earned some sort of entrepreneurial income which, like the rent received by the landlord, maintained all other social classes and occupations and participated in the general process of reproduction (pp. 267–268). Equally significant are other perspectives. If, as the author suggests, Turgot's concept of profit already embraced disposable income in the original physiocratic sense of this term, was physiocracy at this time bound "to burst its seams" (p. 312)? Furthermore, should the physiocrats be regarded as the initiators and scapegoats of underconsumption theory? Should not, on the other hand, Smith's violent refutation of his great rival be taken less seriously since he, in fact, endorsed basic physiocratic concepts? Yet I cannot refrain from raising, at least, one objection. I do not see any way to separate physiocratic economics from their philosophical moorings by deriving their moral principles, as postulated by the author (p. 373), from the physical. Their philosophical moorings were the divine and ideal natural order. Therefore Quesnay's metaphysical approach cannot be questioned. He followed, throughout, Malebranche's "occasionalism."

FRITZ KARL MANN
Professor Emeritus of Economics
The American University
Washington, D. C.

CARL J. FRIEDRICH (Ed.). *Nomos V: The Public Interest.* Pp. xiii, 256. New York: Atherton Press, 1962. $6.00.

This is a difficult volume to review. There are nineteen contributors—a threat to consistency of design and clarity of exposition, even when all of them have been subjected to the severest editorial discipline. Moreover, Professor Friedrich's preface acknowledges, "the viewpoints expressed vary widely in outlook and methodology." So much so, he goes on to say, that no "obvious or self-evident sequence, either in terms of the several fields' approaches or the positions taken" is indicated. Under these circumstances, an average of twelve to thirteen pages affords an inadequate opportunity for each of the contributors to establish rapport with the reader. A sustained development of a single theme by affirmation and critical comment over the space here devoted to three or four of these essays should have been contrived, and any one of several of those included might have served as a nucleus. For example, Gerhart Niemeyer neatly sets the stage for one type of inquiry. He is concerned with the validity of the economist's traditional view of the public interest as an aggregate of private utilities in the perspective of Western political theory. He has time to adumbrate certain distinctions which might well have been developed into a most sensitive philosophical appraisal of the welfare state versus scientific socialism. But the impact is largely lost because no one else demonstrates any interest in precisely the same problem. It is manifestly impossible to document all of the frustrations engendered by comparable lacunae throughout the volume except for a few instances in which several contributors have selected a common target. W. Friedmann and George Nakhnikian, for example, manage to enliven a segment of thirty pages with some telling comments on Harold Lasswell's essay; and David Braybrooke, besides affording a focus for comment by several colleagues, uses twenty-five pages himself to set forth a genuinely provocative thesis.

Perhaps the moral is that some preliminary agreement on the problem posed by the use of the hackneyed tag "public interest" should precede a symposium of divergent views. Nothing very noteworthy is likely to be gained by disclosing the variety of views entertained by people who are not looking at the same thing. Those who are concerned with the use of public interest in an ethical context characteristically take the phrase as roughly synonymous with the general "welfare," "benefit," or "gain"—an ideal to be understood and, perhaps, professed. Given these terms of reference there is nothing ambiguous about the concept. On the other hand, those who are concerned with the use of public interest empirically as a datum for "explaining" rather than "understanding" conduct, have an entirely different problem of refining their terms. If one cannot isolate a public interest in terms of some identifiable configuration of the external environment, the term ought to be stricken from any scientific or quasi-scientific vocabulary.

I have a notion that if Professor Friedrich had himself contributed an essay by way of supplying a sense of direction to the whole enterprise, the results would have been vastly more impressive. And no one would have been better qualified to do so.

KENNETH C. COLE
Professor of Political Science
University of Washington

CHARLES FRANKEL. *The Democratic Prospect.* Pp. xii, 222. New York: Harper & Row, 1962. $4.00.

Some years ago, in *The Case for Modern Man*, Charles Frankel examined the continued viability of liberalism as a philosophy of history. His new book, a companion volume, examines the workability of democracy in the modern world. Mr. Frankel sees us bogged down in the "politics of malaise," haunted by the fear that modern mass society has made democracy obsolete. He examines in turn the "four ideals" of a democratic system: the consent of the governed, the open society, individual autonomy, and responsible government; his method is, first, to present in grim terms the reasons for our disillusionment, second, to show that the situation is actually not so bad as it has been painted, and finally to suggest concrete remedies for those problems which are real. The result is a soberly optimistic appraisal of democracy's opportunities in the twentieth century.

Space permits only the briefest indication of Mr. Frankel's diagnosis and proposals. Since men can usually influence government only through large groups, we must see to it that our voluntary organizations are democratically controlled and effectively operated if we are to have government by consent. If we are to enjoy an open society—by which Mr. Frankel means open to the exchange of ideas—professional organizations must do their job of educating a knowledgeable public; powerful noncommercial media of communication must somehow be established to provide an alternative to the existing commercial channels; and science education for the layman must be improved if he is to understand some of the key issues of our time. Personal autonomy is threatened by large-scale industrial organization and by the pressures of the welfare state; it can be preserved only by a reorganization of work and play which will give significance to both rather than, as so often at present, providing the insignificance of mass leisure as the chief anodyne for the insignificance of mass work. The welfare state, which came into being to help solve the residual problems of depression and war, must be refashioned to deal with the on-going institutional problems of automation, urbanization, and the like. Finally, to achieve responsible government, the legitimate roles of the expert and the bureaucrat must be understood both by themselves and by the public; real lines of communication must be kept open between government and citizen; and genuine public debate about social priorities must be engendered.

This summary statement does scant justice to Mr. Frankel's lucid argument. He has written a book of interest to all who cherish a democratic society.

RANSOM E. NOBLE
Professor of History
Pratt Institute

HARLAN CLEVELAND and HAROLD D. LASSWELL (Eds.). *Ethics and Bigness: Scientific, Academic, Religious, Political, and Military.* Pp. lxv, 542. New York: Conference on Science, Philosophy and Religion in Their Relation to the Democratic Way of Life (Distributed by Harper), 1962. $7.50.

This timely Jacob Ziskind Memorial publication is a companion to *The Ethic of Power*—reviewed in THE ANNALS, January 1963—and shares its stylistic strengths and weaknesses. The thirty papers—including the First Lyman Bryson Lecture in Appendix I, "Ethics and Politics" by Richard McKeon—were prepared for the sixteenth meeting of the Conference, held at the Jewish Theological Seminary of America, August 29 to September 1, 1960. The 38 contributors and discussants represent both academicians from the social sciences and leaders in political, military, academic, scientific, and religious institutions, so the symposium represents wholesome interaction between scholars who are "ivory tower" theorists and strategists and technicians who are involved in the practical problems of administration.

To the casual reader the title may seem a misnomer, for at first glance the emphasis appears to be less upon ethics than upon decision-making. Yet the essence of ethics lies in the relationships of values to decision-making. It is here that the social sciences, administrative policies, philosophies, and normative principles of the various religious systems meet. It is theoretically and practically sound to study the ethics of decison-making *in situ* where black and white intermingle in varying shades of gray and where choice often must be made between two sides motivated by equally high principles instead of in the moralist's chair where it seems simple to make clear distinctions between right and wrong. This symposium will be an enlightening revelation to anyone who believes that adopting codes of ethics which present incontestable moral standards for politicans and administrators is the solution to ethical problems. "Ethics cannot be legislated; they can only be taught" (p. 381).

Among the stimulating topics to which repeated references are made in many contexts are the dilemmas of practical action in a society of big-scale organizations, the extreme complexity of moral issues when both right and wrong are inextricably interwoven in every alternative of action, the necessity of compromise as a result, the self-deception which makes executives of all kinds believe that whatever promotes their own interests is in "the public interest," the inconsistences of Americans who set different standards of friendship—"influence peddling"—and goodwill—"bribery" or "unwarranted pressure" —for political bureaucrats from those applied to businessmen, the necessity and yet the concomitant dilemmas and temptations of bureaucracy, and the unrealistic ideoliges and myths pertinent to American political and economic institutions which are prevalent among our citizenry. An uneasy feeling which results from many of the contributions is that almost any action taken is "ethical;" that pragmatic considerations and existential rationalizations of individual office-holders are the final court of moral judgment.

The authors are not all agreed about the future of American society, the ideal organizational pattern for democratic government, and the merits of bureaucracy in this "era of blurred distinctions between 'public' and 'private,' between 'executive' and 'legislative' and indeed among the levels of government and between the political parties." Although numerous ethical issues could have been added to their discussion, it is an excellent resource for social scientists studying bureaucracy or decision-making, philosophers evaluating American society, and even prognosticators who wish to predict the future.

DAVID O. MOBERG
Professor of Sociology and Chairman
Department of Social Sciences
Bethel College
St. Paul
Minnesota

S. E. FINER. *The Man on Horseback: The Role of the Military in Politics.* Pp. 268. New York: Frederick A. Praeger, 1962. $6.50.

Politics and cognate terms—referring to issues over purposes and competition for place and authority and to settlement thereof—apply to all institutions but have special meaning with respect to a state, which consists of a body of people inhabiting a defined territory under a system of authority seated in that territory, pervading it, and exercising therein a monopoly of rightful coercion. As to the state, politics embraces determining who shall minister the monopoly of coercion— and for what purposes. One—the military —aspect of that monopoly relates primarily to securing the base. Another—the police —aspect relates to enforcing will within the base established. Civil supremacy denotes a political system with authority ascendant over both apparatuses. Those heading either apparatus may try to overturn civil supremacy by making their own apparatus arbiter, coercively pre-empting title to rule. Professor E. S. Finer's *Man on Horseback* is concerned with military instances—wide and frequent phenomena in much of the contemporary world. Characteristically, such assumptions occur in the name of supplanting politics. They usually result mainly in making the military's own sort of politics the prevailing sort.

Professor Finer, of the University of Keele, questions "a common assumption . . . that it is somehow 'natural' for the

armed forces to obey the civil power." To the contrary, "In practically every country . . . , except possibly in one or two of the proto-dynastic survivals . . . , the army is marked by the superior quality of its organization. Even the most poorly organized or maintained . . . is far more highly and tightly structured than any civilian group." Moreover, what he calls "the prestigious corporation of Order" is "more lethally and heavily armed than any other organization of the state." In Finer's view, "Instead of asking why the military engage in politics, we ought surely to ask why they ever do otherwise."

What "has prevented the military . . . from establishing its rule throughout the globe" is "technical inability to administer any but the most primitive community" and "lack of moral title to rule"—again not much of a factor in lands of low political culture but one of great import "in countries of mature or advanced political culture." Inevitable as they may be among politically weak states, such regimes are a symptom of rather than a cure for such weakness. Often their effect has been "the disorder if not the ruin of the economy," according to Finer. "By any world standards military regimes have shown less than average capacity for statesmanship or economics." He concludes: "If ever we are asked to endorse a military regime, we must surely ask ourselves whether any immediate gain in stability and prosperity it brings is not outweighed by the very great likelihood that, for an indefinite time to come, public life and all the personal expectations that hang upon it will continue to be upset, wilfully and unpredictably, by further military threats, blackmail, or revolt." This book sums up as an able rebuttal to the tendency to take military dictatorships among the emerging states at the face value of their own publicity.

CHARLES BURTON MARSHALL
Research Associate
Washington Center of Foreign
  Policy Research

ROBERT GORDIS. *The Root and the Branch: Judaism and the Free Society.*
Pp. xii, 254. Chicago: University of Chicago Press, 1962. $3.95.

The interfaith movement has in recent years given rise to a number of books in which adherents of one religious tradition try to explain themselves to the adherents of others. Jews, too, have indulged in this exercise of self-explanation. The philosophical background of Judaism, its symbolism, its observances, and its ideals have been the themes of some excellent volumes. *The Root and the Branch* is among the very best of this type of book.

The metaphor of the tree in the title is clarified in the subtitle: "Judaism and the Free Society." The author does not claim that Judaism is the root of the free society; its root is God, or God's word, or life rooted in the divine. What he does assert, with conviction and eloquence, is that Judaism has much to offer to those, of whatever faith, who are concerned with civilization and freedom, and their derivative social concepts. Intelligent, articulate, and immensely learned, Dr. Gordis wants to show how a Jew, thoroughly integrated into Western culture, views America and its problems and how he would like Christian America to view him and his problems. "It is my hope," he says in the Preface, "that our generation may thus be helped to discover how to cherish the ideals of liberty and diversity within the context of the human race." Judaism is very much relevant to life today.

After two brief chapters—some thirty pages—describing Judaism in modern times, Dr. Gordis devotes the remaining eleven chapters to a discussion of some general problems which the contemporary world must face. Among these are race relations, church and state, religion and education, ethics and politics, and nationalism and the world community. In each case, he presents a thoughtful and stimulating analysis of the problem and, alongside this analysis, the results of Jewish thought, teaching, and experience bearing upon it. The weakest chapter, in the sense of contributing little that might be considered new, is the one dealing with the world community. Perhaps this is due to the fact that, though ancient, Jewish universalism has been so widely accepted as to appear to offer little that is different. The other chapters are full of new ideas and interesting insights.

This is no ordinary book of apologetics. It never descends into the attitude of religious disputation so frequently to be found in many similar works. Even the chapter on the Jewish-Christian dialogue avoids the pitfall of recrimination and special pleading. Altogether, this is a refreshing book through which Christians might learn better to understand the faith of their Jewish neighbors, and Jews gain an appreciation of their own heritage as it applies to the problems of the present day.

SOLOMON GRAYZEL

Editor
Jewish Publication
Society of America

OTHER BOOKS

ADAMS, MILDRED (Ed.). *Latin America: Evolution or Explosion.* Pp. viii, 277. New York: Dodd, Mead, for the Council on World Tensions, 1963. No price.

ALDEN, JOHN RICHARD. *Rise of the American Republic.* Pp. xxi, 1030. New York: Harper & Row, 1963. $9.95.

ALEXANDER-FRUTSCHI, MARIAN CRITES (Ed.). *Human Resources and Economic Growth: An International Annotated Bibliography on the Role of Education and Training in Economic and Social Development.* Pp. xv, 398. Menlo Park, Calif.: Stanford Research Institute, 1963. $3.50.

ALPERT, PAUL. *Economic Development: Objectives and Methods.* Pp. x, 308. New York: Free Press of Glencoe, 1963. $6.95.

ARON, RAYMOND (Ed.). *World Technology and Human Destiny.* Pp. vi, 246. Ann Arbor: University of Michigan Press, 1963. $4.95.

AYROUT, HENRY HABIB. *The Egyptian Peasant.* Translated from the French by John Alden Williams. Pp. xxi, 167. Second (Revised) Edition. Boston: Beacon Press, 1963. $3.95.

BARBOUR, K. M. and R. M. PROTHERO (Eds.). *Essays on African Population.* Pp. x, 336. New York: Frederick A. Praeger, 1962. $7.50.

BARNA, TIBOR, in collaboration with WILLIAM I. ABRAHAM and ZOLTÁN KENESSEY (Eds.). *Structural Independence and Economic Development.* Proceedings of an International Conference on Input-Output Techniques, Geneva, Switzerland. Pp. x, 365. New York: St Martin's Press, 1963. $15.00.

BHARADWAJ, RANGANATH. *Structural Basis of India's Foreign Trade: A Study Suggested by the Input-Output Analysis.* Pp. vi, 121. Bombay: University of Bombay, 1962. Rs. 9.50.

BIRRENBACH, KURT. *The Future of the Atlantic Community: Toward European-American Partnership.* Pp. xii, 94. New York: Frederick A. Praeger, 1963. $3.50.

BLACK, EUGENE R. *The Diplomacy of Economic Development and Other Papers.* Pp. 176. Reprint. New York: Atheneum, 1963. $1.25.

BREDEMEIER, HARRY C., and JACKSON TOBY. *Social Problems in America: Costs and Casualties in an Acquisitive Society.* Pp. xv, 510. Fifth Printing. New York: John Wiley & Sons, 1963. $3.95.

BROGAN, D. W. *Abraham Lincoln.* Pp. xvii, 143. Reissue. New York: Schocken, 1963. $3.50 clothbound; $1.45 paper-bound.

BROWN, ROBERT ELDON. *Reinterpretation of the Formation of the American Constitution.* Pp. 63. Boston: Boston University Press, 1963. $3.50.

BUCHAN, ALASTAIR. *NATO in the 1960's.* Pp. 179. Second (Revised) Edition. New York: Frederick A. Praeger, 1963. $5.00.

BURNS, JAMES MACGREGOR, and JACK WALTER PELTASON. *Government by the People: The Dynamics of American National, State, and Local Government.* Pp. xiv, 914. Fifth Edition. Englewood Cliffs, N. J.: Prentice-Hall, 1963. No price.

BURSK, EDWARD, in association with JOHN F. CHAPMAN (Eds.). *New Decision-Making Tools for Managers: Mathematical Programing as an Aid in the Solving of Business Problems.* Pp. xv, 413. Cambridge, Mass.: Harvard University Press, 1963. $7.95.

CARR, ROBERT K., MARVER H. BERNSTEIN, and WALTER F. MURPHY. *American Democracy in Theory and Practice: National, State, and Local Government.* Pp. xxvi, 1052. Fourth Edition. New York: Holt, Rinehart and Winston, 1963. $8.75.

CAVAIOLI, FRANK J. *West Point and the Presidency.* Pp. iv, 154. New York: St. John's University Press, 1962. No price.

CHOISY, MARYSE. *Sigmund Freud: A New Appraisal.* Pp. 141. New York: Philosophical Library, 1963. $4.75.

CHU, VALENTIN. *"Ta Ta, Tan Tan" (Fight Fight, Talk Talk): The Inside Story of Communist China.* Pp. viii, 320. New York: W. W. Norton, 1963. $4.95.

COLE, DAVID L. *The Quest for Industrial Peace.* Pp. xi, 164. New York: McGraw-Hill, 1963. $4.95.

COLE, J. P. *Geography of World Affairs.* Pp. 319. Reissue. Baltimore: Penguin, 1963. $1.25.

CUNEO, ERNEST. *Science and History.* Pp. vii, 237. New York: Duell, Sloan, and Pearce, 1963. $3.95.

DAVAR, FIROZE COWASJI. *Iran and India through the Ages.* Pp. xv, 312. New York: Asia Publishing House, 1962. $8.00.

DE CONDE, ALEXANDER. *A History of American Foreign Policy.* Pp. xi, 914. New York: Charles Scribner's Sons, 1963. $12.00.

DELF, GEORGE. *Asians in East Africa.* Pp. ix, 73. New York: Oxford University Press, under the auspices of the Institute of Race Relations, London, 1963. $1.50.

DENTLER, ROBERT A., and PHILLIPS CUTRIGHT, assisted by ROBERT VAN DAM and PETER W. MORRISON. *Hostage America: Human Aspects of a Nuclear Attack and a Program of Prevention.* Pp. xiii, 167. Boston: Beacon Press, 1963. $3.95.

DODDS, GORDON B. *The Salmon King of Oregon: R. D. Hume and the Pacific Fisheries.* Pp. ix, 257. Chapel Hill: University of North Carolina Press, 1963. $6.00.

DOWUONA, M., and J. T. SAUNDERS (Eds.). *The West African Intellectual Community.* Papers and Discussions of an International Seminar on Inter-University Co-operation in West Africa, Held in Freetown, Sierra Leone, 11–16 December 1961. Nigeria: Ibadan University Press, for the Congress for Cultural Freedom, University College, Ibadan, 1962. No price.

DUTT, R. PALME. *Problems of Contemporary History.* Pp. 127. New York: International, 1963. $1.25.

ENKE, STEPHEN. *Economics for Development.* Pp. xxxii, 616. Englewood Cliffs, N. J.: Prentice-Hall, 1963. $11.65.

Evaluation of the Gram Sahayak Programme. Pp. vi, 144. New Delhi: Programme Evaluation, Planning Commission, Government of India, 1961. No price.

FAINSOD, MERLE. *How Russia Is Ruled.* Pp. ix, 684. Second (Revised) Edition. Cambridge, Mass.: Harvard University Press, 1963. $8.95.

FRANK, JEROME. *Courts on Trial: Myth and Reality in American Justice.* Pp. xiv, 441. Reprint. New York: Atheneum, 1963. $1.95.

FRANK, JEROME D. *Persuasion and Healings: A Comparative Study of Psychotherapy.*

Pp. xiv, 282. Reprint. New York: Schocken, 1963. $1.95.

GABRIELI, FRANCESCO. *The Arabs: A Compact History.* Translated by Salvator Attanasio. Pp. viii, 215. First English Edition. New York: Hawthorn, 1963. $4.95.

GENDLIN, EUGENE T. *Experiencing and the Creation of Meaning: A Philosophical and Psychological Approach to the Subjective.* Pp. xv, 302. New York: Free Press of Glencoe, 1962. $6.00.

GILPIN, ROBERT. *American Scientists and Nuclear Weapons Policy.* Pp. viii, 352. Princeton, N. J.: Princeton University Press, 1962. $6.95.

GOLDSCHMIDT, ROBERTO. *Nuevos estudios de derecho comparado.* Pp. 449. Caracas: Facultad de Derecho, 1962. No price.

GOMEZ, R. A. *Government and Politics in Latin America.* Pp. 128. Revised Edition. New York: Random House, 1963. 95 cents.

GORDON, GEORGE N., IRVING FALK, and WILLIAM HODAPP. *The Idea Invaders.* Pp. 256. New York: Hastings House, 1963. $4.95.

GORDON, LINCOLN. *A New Deal for Latin America: The Alliance for Progress.* Pp. vi, 146. Cambridge, Mass.: Harvard University Press, 1963. $3.25.

GROSS, RONALD (Ed.). *The Teacher and the Taught: Education in Theory and Practice from Plato to James B. Conant.* Pp. xii, 305. New York: Dell, 1963. $1.95.

HAPPOLD, F. C. *Mysticism: A Study and an Anthology.* Pp. 364. Baltimore: Penguin, 1963. 85 cents.

HENDERSON, EDITH G. *Foundations of English Administrative Law: Certiorari and Mandamus in the Seventeenth Century.* Pp. 204. Cambridge, Mass.: Harvard University Press, 1963. $5.00.

HIGHAM, JOHN. *Strangers in the Land: Patterns of American Nativism, 1860–1925.* Pp. xiv, 431. Reissue. New York: Atheneum, 1963. $1.95.

HILL, NORMAN L. *International Politics.* Pp x, 458. New York: Harper & Row, 1963. $7.00.

HOBSBAWM, E. J. *Primitive Rebels: Studies in Archaic Forms of Social Movements in the Nineteenth and Twentieth Centuries.* Pp. vii, 208. Second Edition. New York: Frederick A. Praeger, 1963. $5.00.

HONIGMANN, JOHN J. *Understanding Culture.* Pp. viii, 467. New York: Harper & Row, 1963. $6.75.

HOOK, SIDNEY. *Common Sense and the Fifth Amendment.* Pp. 160. Reprint. Chicago: Henry Regnery, 1963. $1.75.

HUSAIN, S. ABID. *Indian Culture.* Pp. xi, 67. New York: Asia Publishing House, 1963. $3.50.

JELAVICH, BARBARA (Ed.). *Russland, 1852–1871: Aus den berichten der Bayerischen gesandtschaft in St. Petersburg.* Pp. 156. Wiesbaden: Otto Harrassowitz, 1963. No price.

JEŚMAN, CZESŁAW. *The Ethiopian Paradox.* Pp. 82. New York: Oxford University Press, under the auspices of the Institute of Race Relations, London, 1963. $1.75.

JUNOD, VIOLAINE I., assisted by IDRIAN N. RESNICK. *The Handbook of Africa.* Pp. xiv, 472. New York: New York University Press, 1963. $10.00.

KAHN, ALFRED J. *Planning Community Services for Children in Trouble.* Pp. xi, 540. New York: Columbia University Press, 1963. $7.50.

KALDIS, WILLIAM P. *John Capodistrias and the Modern Greek State.* Pp. 126. Madison: State Historical Society of Wisconsin, for the Department of History, University of Wisconsin, 1963. $3.00.

KENT, COLONEL GLENN A. *On the Interaction of Opposing Forces under Possible Arms Agreements.* Pp. 36. Cambridge, Mass.: Center for International Affairs, Harvard University, 1963. No price.

KIRCHNER, WALTHER. *A History of Russia.* Pp. xi, 393. Third Edition. New York: Barnes & Noble, 1963. $4.95 clothbound; $1.95 paper-bound.

KLEINE-AHLBRANDT, WILLIAM LAIRD. *The Policy of Simmering: A Study of British Policy during the Spanish Civil War.* Pp. viii, 161. The Hague: Martinus Nijhoff, 1962. guilders 16.75.

LANCTOT, GUSTAVE. *A History of Canada,* Vol. I: *From Its Origins to the Royal Regime, 1663.* Translated by Josephine Hambleton. Pp. xv, 393. Cambridge, Mass.: Harvard University Press, 1963. $6.75.

LEE, HENRY. *How Dry We Were: Prohibition Revisited.* Pp. xii, 244. Englewood Cliffs, N. J.: Prentice-Hall, 1963. $4.95.

LEVETT, ADA ELIZABETH. *Studies in Manorial History.* Edited by H. M. Cam, M. Coate, and L. S. Sutherland. Pp. xviii, 399. Second Edition. New York: Barnes & Noble, 1963. $7.50.

LEVY, LEONARD W., and JOHN P. ROCHE (Eds.). *The American Political Process.* Pp. x, 246. New York: George Braziller, 1963. $5.00.

MCCONNELL, CAMPBELL R. *Economics: Principles, Problems, and Policies.* Pp. viii, 773. Second Edition. New York: McGraw-Hill, 1963. No price.

MCCOY, DONALD R., and RAYMOND G. O'CONNOR (Eds.). *Readings in Twentieth-Century History.* Pp. 631. New York: The Macmillan Company, 1963. $3.95.

MCCRACKEN, PAUL W., and EMILE BENOIT. *The Balance of Payments and Domestic Prosperity.* Pp. vii, 64. Ann Arbor: Bureau of Business Research, Graduate School of Business Administration, University of Michigan, 1963. No price.

MCENTIRE, DAVIS. *Residence and Race.* Pp. xxii, 409. Berkeley and Los Angeles: University of California Press, 1960. $6.00.

MAGRATH, C. PETER. *Morrison R. Waite: The Triumph of Character.* Pp. viii, 334. New York: The Macmillan Company, 1963. $10.00.

MALINOWSKI, B. *The Family among the Australian Aborigines: A Sociological Study.* Pp. xxx, 322. Reissue. New York: Schocken, 1963. $5.00 clothbound; $2.45 paper-bound.

MOORE, STANLEY. *Three Tactics: The Background in Marx.* Pp. 96. New York: Monthly Review Press, 1963. $2.25.

MUNSON, FRED C. *Labor Relations in the Lithographic Industry.* Pp. xvi, 272. Cambridge, Mass.: Harvard University Press, 1963. $6.50.

PATRICK, HUGH T. *Monetary Policy and Central Banking in Comtemporary Japan: A Case Study in the Effectiveness of Central Bank Techniques of Monetary Control.* Pp. xii, 219. Bombay: University of Bombay, 1962. Rs. 9.50.

PEATMAN, JOHN G. *Introduction to Applied Statistics.* Pp. xv, 458. New York: Harper & Row, 1963. $7.95.

PERETZ, DON. *The Middle East Today.* Pp. x, 483. New York: Holt, Rinehart & Winston, 1963. No price.

PETERSON, FLORENCE. *American Labor Unions: What They Are and How They Work.* Pp. x, 271. Second (Revised) Edition. New York: Harper & Row, 1963. $5.50.

PLISCHKE, ELMER. *Government and Politics of Contemporary Berlin.* Pp. xiv, 119. The Hague: Martinus Nijhoff, 1963. guilders 12.50.

Political Handbook and Atlas of the World: Parliaments, Parties, and Press as of January 1, 1963. Edited by Walter H. Mallory. Pp. x, 294. New York: Harper & Row, for the Council on Foreign Relations, 1963. $6.95.

RAPKIN, CHESTER, and WILLIAM C. GRIGSBY. *The Demand for Housing in Racially Mixed*

Areas: A Study of the Nature of Neighborhood Change. Pp. xx, 177. Berkeley and Los Angeles: University of California Press, 1960. $6.00.

RIVETT, KENNETH (Ed.). *Immigration: Control or Colour Bar: The Background to "White Australia" and a Proposal for Change.* Pp. xiv, 171. New York: Cambridge University Press, for the Immigration Reform Group, Melbourne, 1963. $2.50.

ROSSI, MARIO. *The Third World: The Unaligned Countries and the World Revolution.* Pp. xiv, 209. New York: Funk & Wagnalls, 1963. $4.00.

RUDOLPH, L. C. *Hoosier Zion: The Presbyterians in Early Indiana.* Pp. 218. New Haven: Yale University Press, 1963. $5.00.

SCOTT, M. F. G. *A Study of United Kingdom Imports.* Pp. xvi, 269. Cambridge, England: Cambridge University Press, 1963. $10.50.

SELSAM, HOWARD, and HARRY MARTEL (Eds.). *Reader in Marxist Philosophy: From the Writings of Marx, Engels, and Lenin.* Pp. 348. New York: International, 1963. $2.45.

SERVICE, ELMAN R. *Profiles in Ethnology.* (A Revision of *A Profile of Primitive Culture.*) Pp. xxix, 509. Revised Edition. New York: Harper & Row, 1963. $6.50.

SHIPTON, CLIFFORD K. *New England Life in the Eighteenth Century: Representative Biographies from Sibley's "Harvard Graduates."* Pp. xxvii, 626. Cambridge, Mass.: Belknap Press of Harvard University Press, 1963. $10.00.

SMITH, I. EVELYN. *Readings in Adoption.* Pp. 532. New York: Philosophical Library, 1963. $7.50.

SPRING, DAVID. *The English Landed Estate in the Nineteenth Century: Its Administration.* Pp. vi, 216. Baltimore: Johns Hopkins Press, 1963. $5.00.

SUMNER, WILLIAM GRAHAM. *Social Darwinism: Selected Essays.* Pp. x, 180. Englewood Cliffs, N. J.: Prentice-Hall, 1963. $1.95.

SUPPLE, BARRY E. (Ed.). *The Experience of Economic Growth: Case Studies in Economic History.* Pp. x, 458, xi. New York: Random House, 1963. $6.95.

SZENT-GYORGI, ALBERT. *Science, Ethics, and Politics.* Pp. 91. New York: Vantage Press, 1963. $2.50.

TILLETT, PAUL. *Doe Day: The Antlerless Deer Controversy in New Jersey.* Pp. xii, 126. New Brunswick, N. J.: Rutgers University Press, 1963. $5.00 clothbound; $1.95 paperbound.

TIRYAKIAN, EDWARD A. (Ed.). *Sociological Theory, Values, and Sociocultural Change: Essays in Honor of Pitirim A. Sorokin.* Pp. xv, 302. New York: Free Press of Glencoe, 1963. $5.95.

ULAM, ADAM B. *The New Face of Soviet Totalitarianism.* Pp. 233. Cambridge, Mass.: Harvard University Press, 1963. $4.95.

UNITED NATIONS TECHNICAL ASSISTANCE PROGRAMME. *Decentralization for National and Local Development.* Pp. iv, 246. New York: United Nations, 1962. No price.

UNITED NATIONS TECHNICAL ASSISTANCE PROGRAMME. *Public Administration Problems of New and Rapidly Growing Towns in Asia.* Report of the Regional Seminar on Public Administration Problems in New and Rapidly Growing Towns in Asia, New Delhi, India, 14–21 December 1960. Pp. iii, 90. New York: United Nations, 1962. No price.

VIDAL-NAQUET, PIERRE. *Torture: Cancer of Democracy: France and Algeria, 1954–62.* Translated by Barry Richard. Pp. 182. Baltimore: Penguin, 1963. 85 cents.

WAGNER, JEAN. *Les poètes nègres des États-Unis: Le sentiment racial et religieux dans la poésie de P. L. Dunbar à L. Hughes (1890–1940).* Pp. xvi, 637. Paris: Librairie Istra, 1963. No price.

WELTY, THOMAS. *The Asians: Their Heritage and Their Destiny.* Pp. viii, 344. Philadelphia: J. B. Lippincott, 1963. $4.95.

WHEARE, K. C. *Legislatures.* Pp. 247. New York: Oxford University Press, 1963. $1.70.

WILLIAMS, ALAN. *Public Finance and Budgetary Policy.* Pp. 283. New York: Frederick A. Praeger, 1963. $8.50.

WOOD, ROBERT C. *Suburbia: Its People and Their Politics.* Pp. xi, 340. Reprint. Boston: Houghton Mifflin, 1963. $2.50.

ZOLL, DONALD ATWELL. *Reason and Rebellion: An Informal History of Political Ideas.* Pp. ix, 373. Englewood Cliffs, N. J.: Prentice-Hall, 1963. $9.25.

INDEX

0534